Meaning, Frames, and Conceptual Representation

Thomas Gamerschlag, Doris Gerland,
Rainer Osswald & Wiebke Petersen (eds.)

d|u|p

Hana Filip, Peter Indefrey, Laura Kallmeyer,
Sebastian Löbner, Gerhard Schurz & Robert D. Van Valin, Jr. (eds.)

Studies in Language and Cognition

2

Thomas Gamerschlag, Doris Gerland,
Rainer Osswald & Wiebke Petersen (eds.)

2015

Meaning, Frames, and Conceptual Representation

d|u|p

**Bibliografische Information
der Deutschen Nationalbibliothek**
Die Deutsche Nationalbibliothek verzeichnet diese
Publikation in der Deutschen Nationalbibliografie;
detaillierte bibliografische Daten sind im Internet
über http://dnb.dnb.de abrufbar.

© düsseldorf university press, Düsseldorf 2015
http://www.dupress.de
Einbandgestaltung: Doris Gerland, Christian Horn, Albert Ortmann
Satz: Friedhelm Sowa, LaTeX
Herstellung: docupoint GmbH, Barleben

Gesetzt aus der Linux Libertine und der Linux Biolinum
ISBN 978-3-943460-87-2

Table of Contents

INTRODUCTION TO CONCEPT TYPES AND FRAMES

Functional Concepts and Frames
Sebastian Löbner 15

Representation of Concepts as Frames
Wiebke Petersen 43

NOMINAL CONCEPT TYPES AND DETERMINATION

Uniqueness of the Definite Article with Respect to Cognitive Frames
Ryo Oda 71

FrameNet, Barsalou Frames and the Case of Associative Anaphora
Alexander Ziem 93

The Definiteness Effect and a New Classification of Possessive Constructions
Yuko Kobukata & Yoshiki Mori 113

Referential Properties of Nouns across Languages
Doris Gerland & Christian Horn 133

THE MEANING OF ADJECTIVES, NOUNS, AND VERBS

Non-Intersectivity in Manner Adjectives
Sascha Alexeyenko 153

Converging Evidences on the Eventivity of Italian Nouns
Irene Russo & Tommaso Caselli 179

Diachrony of Stative Dimensional Verbs in French
Brigitte Schwarze & Hans Geisler 201

Semantic Fields

Linguistic Realizations of the Concept of FEAR
Liane Ströbel 219

Metonymic Euphemisms from a Cognitive Linguistic Point of View
Alexander Tokar 237

Concepts in Philosophy and Psychiatry

Philosophical Conceptual Analysis as an Experimental Method
Michael T. Stuart 267

Analyzing Concepts in Action-Frames
Gottfried Vosgerau, Tim Seuchter & Wiebke Petersen 293

Applying Frame Theory to Psychiatric Classification
Jürgen Zielasek, Gottfried Vosgerau, Wolfgang Gaebel, Karin Fauerbach, Irem Girgin, Sarah Jungbluth, Julia Weiland & Sebastian Löbner 311

Preface

The main topic of this volume is the central role of attributes and frames in the representation of meaning in linguistics and the cognitive sciences. Many of the articles are inspired by the influential work of Barsalou (1992) on the fundamental role of frames in human cognition. Barsalou's approach builds on two important insights: (i) features or attributes are essential for the structuring of conceptual representations and (ii) the values of attributes can themselves have attributes. The second point leads to recursively structured attribute value structures, i. e., to frames. As shown by Barsalou, frames provide a more adequate format for conceptual representations than simple feature lists. The first point, on the other hand, emphasizes the importance of functionality *per se*: not arbitrary many-to-many relations but functional, i. e., many-to-one relations constitute the backbone of conceptual organization.

The articles in this volume are organized into five sections according to the particular topics they address:

I. Introduction to Concept Types and Frames

The first section consists of two contributions which elaborate on the ideas outlined above and thereby serve as preparatory reading for the following articles, which deal with more specific topics. In his paper 'Functional Concepts and Frames,' **Sebastian Löbner** argues for the crucial role of functionality in the construction and organization of meaning. Starting out from Partee's rising temperature puzzle, he discusses the significance of individual and functional nouns in the analysis of intensional constructions. Both noun types are characterized by unique reference and together with sortal and relational nouns they form a system of four basic types of nouns. This system results from the two binary features 'inherent uniqueness' and 'inherent relationality' already assumed in Löbner (1985, 2011). In the second part of the paper, Löbner relates functional concepts to Barsalou's frame model by pointing out that frames are recursive attribute-value structures in which the attributes are functional concepts. Hence, if frames can be assumed as the general format of concepts in human cognition, this means, on the one hand, that categorization is handled in terms of functional concepts and, on the other, that functional nouns represent the type of concepts human cognition is based on.

Wiebke Petersen's contribution 'Representation of Concepts as Frames' is a reprint of a paper which was originally published in 2007. Petersen presents a first approach to the formalization of Barsalou's key ideas on frames as the general format of mental concepts. Her proposal also integrates the four-way system of nominal concept types proposed by Löbner. She defines frames as directed graphs with labeled nodes and arcs and demonstrates how the concept type distinction is reflected in the structure of the frame graphs of lexical concepts. Furthermore, Petersen provides a formal account of attributes and the connection between functional concepts and frame attributes which abandons the artificial distinction between types and attributes in type signatures.

II. Nominal Concept Types and Determination

The four papers in the second section of the volume are concerned with the concepts referred to by nominal expressions and the different ways the particular kind of reference is established. In her contribution 'Uniqueness of the Definite Article,' **Ryo Oda** discusses the so-called 'configurational use' of definite descriptions such as *the hospital* in a sentence like *In Paris, I caught the measles and I went to the hospital to receive treatment*. Oda argues that although this use at first sight seems to be problematic for the uniqueness theory of definiteness, it indeed can be regarded as expressing a unique role in a cognitive frame evoked by the context and the situation of utterance. More precisely, the hospital plays a unique role in a 'medical care' frame activated by the context of 'catching the measles.' In addition, Oda compares the configurational use of definites with definite associative anaphora pointing out both parallels and differences.

Alexander Ziem also investigates the reference of a particular type of nominal expression in his paper 'Barsalou Frames and the Case of Associative Anaphora.' He argues that traditional accounts of associative anaphora suffer from a number of shortcomings whereas a frame approach has the potential to overcome these deficits. In this regard, Ziem compares Barsalou's cognitive frame theory and the FrameNet enterprise as the currently most prominent approaches to frames and discusses the shortcomings and advantages of both. He then shows how the insights of both approaches can be combined in a proper analysis of associative anaphora.

In their paper 'The Definiteness Effect and a New Classification of Possessive Constructions,' **Yuko Kobukata** and **Yoshiki Mori** take a close look at the way in which possessive verbs such as English *have* and the noun referring to the possessum interact in determining the definiteness of the possessum NP. The authors argue that the definiteness of the object NP is dependent on the possessive interpretation of the construction, contrary to the established view that it results from the (in)alienability of the possessum. By comparing different readings of the possessive construction in English and Japanese, Kobukata and Mori propose a new classification of interpretations from which the definiteness of the possessum NP in both English and Japanese can be predicted.

Doris Gerland and **Christian Horn**'s article 'Referential Properties of Nouns across Languages' is a reprint of a paper that appeared first in 2010. Building on Löbner's theory of conceptual noun types, the authors present a study which tests the assumption that different noun types have a predisposition for particular determination types due to their respective referential properties. On the basis of typologically different languages Gerland and Horn show that a noun undergoes a systematic referential modification (or: type shift) if it is used with a different determination type. They furthermore introduce the notion of PEICs (permanently established individual concepts) which explains unexpected determination patterns of certain kinds of noun types.

III. The Meaning of Adjectives, Nouns, and Verbs

The three contributions in the third section of the volume deal with the conceptual properties of adjectives, nouns, and verbs. The particular questions the authors focus on highlight characteristics of the respective lexical category, such as the function of an adjective to serve as a modifier or the ability of nouns to refer to events. In his paper 'Manner Modification in Adjectives,' **Sascha Alexejenko** examines adjectives such as *skillful* in *skillful surgeon* which have traditionally been considered as non-intersective intensional modifiers. Alexejenko argues against the intensionality of these adjectives and proposes an alternative account in which they are analyzed as manner modifiers of event arguments introduced by the modified nouns. Alexejenko furthermore assumes that the event argument is bound by a generic quantifier in order to account for the fact that adjective noun combinations of the type under discussion are usually interpreted habitually and do not allow for nouns related to singular events as in *#a skillful inventor of an artificial language*.

Irene Russo and **Tommaso Caselli** deal with the meaning of event nouns in their contribution 'Converging Evidences on the Eventivity of Italian Nouns.' They propose a measure for the eventivity of deverbal and non-deverbal nouns that relies on syntagmatic cues in corpus data such as the co-occurrence of a noun with event-related verbs like *continuare* 'to continue' and *cominciare* 'begin' but also takes speakers' judgments into consideration. Russo and Caselli argue that a measure for eventivity is useful for practical implementations as well as for theoretical improvements and for the detection of coerced non-eventive nouns.

Brigitte Schwarze and **Hans Geisler** present an account of the evolution of a particular subclass of stative verbs in their article 'Diachrony of Stative Dimensional Verbs in French.' Verbs of this type encode a single dimension and allow for the specification of a value along this dimension. For instance, the verbs *peser* 'weigh' and *coûter* 'cost' encode the dimensions WEIGHT and PRICE, respectively, and permit the external realization of a value for this dimension as in *peser 2 kilos* 'weigh 2 kilos' and *coûter 5 euros* 'cost 5 euros.' The authors put a particular focus on stative dimensional verbs which evolve from verbs originally encoding sensorimotor concepts like main body postures (e. g. standing) or elementary hand actions (e. g. grasping). They investigate the historical processes which lead to the development of these verbs paying special attention to the relation between source concepts and the emergence of specific dimensional readings.

IV. Semantic Fields

The two articles in the fourth section investigate the meaning of expressions that belong to particular lexico-semantic fields. In her paper 'Linguistic Realizations of the Concept of FEAR,' **Liane Ströbel** investigates the semantic field of fear expressions in French. Based on a definition of the different stages and parameters involved in the experience of fear, Ströbel analyzes a variety of different aspects of the linguistic realization of the concept of 'fear.' Her investigation covers the semantic range of nominal fear expressions such as French *peur* and *anxiété*, the conceptual sources of prototypical fear metaphors and metonymies as well as verbal strategies and the reanalysis of fear lexemes as intensity markers.

Alexander Tokar presents a classification of mechanisms for the formation of metonymy-based euphemisms such as the use of *boyfriend* to refer to the taboo-marked concept 'male sexual partner in a non-marital sexual relationship.' In his contribution 'Metonymic Euphemisms from a Cognitive Linguistic Point of View,' metonymies of this type are analyzed as the product of a limited number of major strategies which all involve the violation of at least one of the three cognitive principles IMPORTANT OVER LESS IMPORTANT, SPECIFIC OVER GENERIC and MORE TRUE OVER LESS TRUE. Tokar also discusses the relation of metonymy-based euphemisms to euphemisms derived by different types of metaphors (conceptual vs. one-shot metaphors).

V. Concepts in Philosophy and Psychiatry

The last section contains philosophical and psychiatric papers which discuss conceptual analysis as an experimental method, analyze action-related concepts, and explore the structure of standard classificatory texts in psychiatry. In his paper 'Philosophical Conceptual Analysis,' **Michael T. Stuart** examines the role of intuitions in conceptual analysis. In particular, he argues for the significance of experimental interpretation as a foundation of philosophical conceptual analysis. The author develops the idea that Davidson's theory of radical interpretation, which involves the principle of charity, can serve as a basis for philosophical conceptual analysis. The central argument is that conceptual analysis functions analogously to linguistic understanding in general and therefore makes use of the same mechanisms: the use of the concept in question is interpreted on the basis of self-interpretation to maximize the truth of the underlying beliefs while rationality is presupposed.

The central thesis of grounded cognition is that concepts are grounded in sensorimotor processes. In their contribution 'Analyzing Concepts in Action-Frames,' **Gottfried Vosgerau**, **Tim Seuchter** and **Wiebke Petersen** argue for a frame-based analysis of action-related concepts as a means for understanding the theory of grounded cognition. They introduce frames for action-related concepts and discuss the advantages of a frame-based analysis over other methods of analysis. It turns out that frames are flexible enough to allow for a specification of the sensorimotor parts of a concept and to highlight abstraction mechanisms within concepts at the same time. The analysis also offers a way to represent modal attributes without introducing modal operators.

In their paper 'Applying Frame Theory to Psychiatric Classification,' **Jürgen Zielasek** and his coauthors explore the potential of frames for the description of the three disorders schizophrenia, specific phobias and Parkinson's disease. They apply Barsalou's frames to analyze the structure of operationalized classificatory texts which offer a rule-based method of diagnosis. Their results show that Barsalou's frame theory allows for a novel standardized approach to analyzing concepts of psychiatric classification which gives access to the internal structure of classification systems. The authors also discuss problems for the frame analysis that are yet to be solved, such as the representation of temporal and causal aspects of mental disorders.

References

Barsalou, L. W. 1992. Frames, concepts, and conceptual fields. In A. Lehrer & E. F. Kittay (eds.), *Frames, fields, and contrasts: New essays in semantic and lexical organization*, 21–74. Hillsdale, NJ: Lawrence Erlbaum Associates.

Löbner, S. 1985. Definites. *Journal of Semantics* 4. 279–326.

Löbner, S. 2011. Concept types and determination. *Journal of Semantics* 28. 279–333.

Introduction to Concept Types and Frames

Functional Concepts and Frames

Sebastian Löbner

Abstract
The central point of this paper is the observation that attributes in Barsalou frames are functional concepts. If Barsalou is correct in assuming that frames in his sense constitute the universal format of human cognitive representations, the observation means that human conceptualization is entirely in terms of functional concepts. This raises interest in this particular type of concept. Functional concepts appear in natural language mainly in the form of functional nouns. This type of noun did not get much attention in semantics. The paper therefore first reviews the notion of individual and functional nouns in formal semantics, departing from Barbara Partee's *rising temperature* puzzle. The second part turns to a general definition of Barsalou frames as recursive attribute-value structures with functional attribute and identifies functional concepts as their basic components. It is argued that the functional concept vocabulary is a recent development in natural language lexica which is closely related to scientific evolution.

1 Introduction

It is the aim of this paper to argue that functional concepts are of fundamental importance for semantic analysis and for cognitive theory. They are important for semantics because they constitute a logical and grammatical type of nouns of its own. They are important to cognitive theory because of the fundamental role they play in categorization. Following Barsalou (1992a, 1992b), I hypothesize that frames in Barsalou's sense constitute the universal format of concepts in human cognition; i.e. the universal format for the representation of arbitrary objects and categories. Frames in the sense of Barsalou's are recursive attribute-value structures, similar to those used e.g. in HPSG[1] and other formalisms. What

---
[1] Head-Driven Phrase Structure Grammar, initiated by Pollard & Sag (1994).

constitutes the connection between frames and functional concepts is the fact that the attributes in Barsalou frames are functional concepts which assign values to their arguments. If the hypothesis is correct, it follows that all representations of objects and categories in human cognition are exclusively in terms of functional concepts.

When I refer to "functional concepts", I do not mean words, but cognitive structures of representation, ultimately implemented in neuronal structures of the brain. Languages may have lexical expressions for some of these functional concepts, e. g. words such as English *name, size, shape, color, meaning, head, bottom, root, mother,* or *cholesterol level*. But languages differ widely in this respect. In those languages that exhibit a rich vocabulary of terms for functional concepts, many of these expressions are relatively young. It will be argued below that functional concepts play a key role in scientific theory. The repertory of functional concept terms in a language to a good deal reflects the stage of development of scientific reasoning. This holds in particular for abstract functional concepts. Nouns that carry the meaning of a functional concept will be referred to as "functional nouns". Functional concepts are not necessarily expressed by nouns. There are also verbs that immediately express functional concepts, e. g. *cost* or *weigh*, corresponding to the functional nouns *price* and *weight*, respectively (for a survey article see Gamerschlag 2014).

In the following, I will introduce the notion of functional concepts from a semantic point of view, by recalling and analyzing Partee's famous *rising temperature* paradox (§ 2). The discussion of functional nouns will then be embedded into the distinction of a system of four basic types of nouns, including in addition sortal, individual, and relational nouns (§ 3). In § 4, I will introduce Barsalou frames, showing that they essentially are networks of functional assignments in terms of attributes. This provides the crucial link between functional concepts and frames. § 5 will briefly discuss the role of frames, functional concepts, and functional nouns in science. § 6 will formulate the conclusions of the discussion.

2 Partee's paradox recalled

2.1 The temperature is rising

Montague (1973) cites an example of Barbara Partee's that constitutes an apparent paradox: The sentences in (1a) and (1b) do not entitle the inference of (1c).

(1) (a) The temperature is rising.
(b) The temperature is ninety.
(c) Ninety is rising.

The example appears to contradict a fundamental law of predicate logic, ascribed to Leibniz: If a predication P is true of an individual a, and a is identical with b, then P is also true of b.

(2) **Leibniz' Law**
P(a)   a predication about some individual a
<u>a = b</u>   identity of individuals a and b
P(b)   the same predication about b

Partee's example is not free of problems. It has been objected (cf. Jackendoff 1979) that (1b) does not constitute an identity statement but rather is used to express the location of the temperature value on a scale. According to Thomason (1979), the predication in (1c) constitutes a category mistake.[2] Also it may be objected that the expression *ninety* does not refer to the same object in (1b) and (1c). While these objections are justified from a linguistic point of view, they can be avoided in several ways (cf. Löbner 1981, Löbner 1979:23f, Lasersohn 2005). One way to save the argument intended by Partee is to consider examples such as the following:

(3) (a) The US president will change.
(b) The US president is Barack Obama.
(c) Barack Obama will change.

Assume we relate these sentences to some time when Barack Obama is in office as US president. Assume further that *change* in (3a) means 'be replaced'[3]. Obviously, (3a) and (3b) do not entail (3c) if *change* is taken in that meaning, which of course is necessary if (3) is taken to represent an instance of Leibniz' Law. In fact, it can be argued that (3c), with that reading of *change*, not only does not follow from the two premises, but in fact is semantically abnormal. A remaining problem with

---

[2] This fact does not really show that the argument is wrong. Whether (1c) is logically possible and does not follow from the two premises or whether the conclusion is necessarily false, or altogether senseless – the fact remains that the entailment is invalid.

[3] Single quotes are used for representing meanings and the contents of concepts.

(3) is the fact that sentences (3a) and (3c) both have another reading with *change* construed as 'become different'. With this reading of *change*, (3) does constitute a valid instance of Leibniz' Law. This problem does not arise in the German equivalents of the three statements if *change* is translated as *wechseln* which has the reading 'be replaced' but not 'become different':

(4)   (a)   Der US-Präsident wird wechseln.
        (b)   Der US-Präsident ist Barack Obama.
        (c)   Barack Obama wird wechseln.

What is expressed in (4), and was intended in (1), is the following. The referent of the subject NP varies with the time of reference: there is a temporal sequence of US presidents as there are temperatures varying in time. For the nouns *US-Präsident* and *temperature*, there are functions from times to persons and temperature values, respectively, which yield for every time the current referent of the noun. Note that for these nouns there is necessarily at most one referent at every time and in a given context.[4] In sentences like (5a,b), the NPs refer just to the actual values at the given time of reference, and the predications expressed by the respective VPs take these as their arguments.

(5)   (a)   The temperature is low.
        (b)   The US president is married.

Consequently, no paradox like that in (4) will arise with the sentences in (5); consider the valid inference in (6).

(6)   (a)   The US president is married.
        (b)   The US president is Barack Obama.
        (c)   Barack Obama is married.

Crucially, the predications in (4a) and (1a) express a change in time of what the subject refers to: the referent of *der US-Präsident* is replaced, as is the referent of the subject NP *the temperature* if the temperature rises. The first premise, therefore, is a statement of the type $p(f, t_e)$ where p represents the predication

---

[4] Uniqueness of reference here is not due to the definite article, but a fact inherent to the meanings of the nouns *US-Präsident* and *temperature*. The definite article is redundant. See Löbner (1985) and Löbner (2011) for the role of definiteness marking with functional nouns.

'change/wechseln' or 'be rising' and f represents the function from times to entities which assigns a US president, or a temperature, respectively, to every time; t_e is the implicit time of reference, or evaluation time, which the statement relates to. Roughly, (4a) says that there is a time $t > t_e$ where $f(t) \neq f(t_e)$; (1a) states that $f'(t_e) > 0$, where f' is the first derivative of f with respect to t, i.e. $df(t)/dt$. Thus, the content of (1a) and (4a) is a predication of the type:

(7)   (a) $p(f, t_e)$ where f: TIME $\longrightarrow$ E (E some appropriate set of entities)

The second premise in (4) and (1) states that the value of f for the time of reference t_e is a particular one. In (4), the second premise constitutes an identity statement, in (1) it can at least be taken as an equivalent of an identity statement.

(7)   (b) $f(t_e)$ = Barack Obama
               $f(t_e) = 90°$

In Leibniz' Law, the second premise states that the argument of the predication in the first premise is identical with some object b. The two statements in (7b) are identity statements about $f(t_e)$, i.e. about the individual that constitutes the value of the function f for the time of reference. This, however, is not the argument of the predication in (7a). p in (7a) has two arguments, the function f and the time t_e, and the two-place predication cannot be reduced to a one-place predication about $f(t_e)$: *der US-Präsident wird wechseln* is not a predication that just concerns the president of the US at time t_e; the analogue holds for the rising temperature statement.

Consequently, the apparent paradox can be resolved by observing that the second premise does not constitute a relevant identity statement for the Leibniz entailment.

2.2   The nature of the example

Partee's paradox is cited by Montague as an instance of an intensional subject construction in the first premise, something originally assumed not to exist (Lewis 1970). To see what an intensional construction is, let us first define the notion of an extensional construction. In the framework of Montague's[5], the extension

---

[5] Montague (1973)

of a noun is the set of its potential referents in a given context of utterance. (Montague would talk of a possible world index instead of a context of utterance.) For example, the extension of *cow* in a particular context of utterance would be the set of all cows given in that context of utterance. The extension of *US president* would be the (one and only) US president, the person in office, in that context. A sentence construction is extensional with respect to a certain NP position, if the NP can be replaced by any other NP with the same extension without changing the truth-value of the sentence. For example, the valid entailment in (6) shows that the sentence in (6a) (*the US president is married*) is extensional with respect to the subject position: Let (6b) (*the US president is Barack Obama*) be true; it then follows that the NPs *the US president* and *Barack Obama* have the same extension. Consequently, (6c) is true because the construction NP *is married* is a predication about the extension of the subject NP.

A construction is intensional, if it is not extensional. In Montague's terminology, the intension of an expression is a function that returns for every possible context of utterance the extension of the expression. In the case of *US president* and *temperature*, the intension returns the current US president and the temperature, respectively, for a given context of utterance. The sentences in (1a) and (4a) are intensional since the VP predicates about the extensions of the subject NP at more than one time, i.e. in different possible contexts of utterance. In intensional constructions, the truth value may change, if the NP is replaced by another NP with just the same extension. For example, if in a given context of utterance the US president is Michelle's husband, and the US president changes, it does not follow that Michelle's husband changes. Intensional constructions represent a predication about the intension of the NP which cannot be logically reduced to a predication about its extension (otherwise, the construction would be extensional).

Although (1a) is clearly not extensional, Partee's example met some opposition as an instance of a construction with intensional subject position. Examples of intensional (or 'opaque') constructions known in the historical context of the early 1970s were sentences such as the following, with an intensional object NP:

(8)   (a)   Hank is seeking a unicorn.

There are two readings to the sentence, one in which it entails (8b), and the crucial, opaque one, in which it does not.

(8)   (b)   There is a unicorn that Hank is seeking.

The source of intensionality here is different from the 'rising temperature' cases. The verb *seek* in its relevant reading does not express a predication about the extension of the object NP at all. The actual extension of the object NP does not matter. Hank may seek a unicorn even if no unicorns exist, in fact, even if Hank does not believe in the existence of unicorns himself. The object NP renders a description related to the intention of the seeker rather than to some object in the world. Because of the different nature of intensionality in the classical examples of the type in (8a), the rising-temperature examples were considered not intensional proper (e. g. Dowty, Wall & Peters 1981:279-286), although the non-extensional character manifest in the apparent failure of Leibniz' Law was mostly acknowledged.[6]

A further fundamental difference between the two types of intensionality concerns the logical type of noun involved. The construction in (8a) is possible with special verbs such as *seek, design, imagine, expect* and almost all types of nouns, including sortal nouns, relational nouns, proper names and functional nouns (see the next section for the distinction). The Partee example, by contrast, requires a special type of noun for its intensional NP argument, as we will see now.

3   Types of nouns

3.1   Individual nouns and concepts

The rising-temperature, or changing-president, construction represents a predication about the changing referent of the subject NP. The meaning of the noun must be such that it yields for every appropriate context of utterance a particular object as the unique referent. If the predication of the construction concerns variation in time, the subject noun has to define a function from times to an appropriate type of entities, e. g. persons or temperature values. Such nouns are of a particular logical type. They are inherently unique. The concept they express

---

[6] Jackendoff (1979) argues for an extensional analysis of *the temperature is rising*; see Löbner (1981) for a reply.

defines a function that returns a unique referent to every appropriate context of utterance.[7] In former publications I therefore referred to this type of nouns as "functional nouns", and the corresponding type of concepts as "functional concepts" ("FC1" in Löbner 1985, 1998) or "Funktionalbegriffe" in German ("FB1" in Löbner 1979). To avoid confusion, and join established terminology, e.g. in Janssen (1984), I will use the terms *individual concept* and *individual noun* here, as I did in Löbner (2011). Thus *temperature* and *US-Präsident* are **individual nouns**, and their meanings are individual concepts.

The subject terms of the rising-temperature or changing-president construction need not only express an individual concept that assigns referents to times. In addition, the underlying functions must be able to return different values at different times. Otherwise the predication about the temporal variation of the value of the function would be inapplicable for logical reasons. The latter requirement for the nouns in subject position is responsible for the awkwardness of the sentences in (1c) and (4c): NPs such as *ninety* or *Barack Obama* do not have different referents at different times.

The type of intensionality observed with (1a) and (4a) is also possible with transitive verb constructions such as:

(9) (a) The coach replaced the goalkeeper.
    (b) The government raised the exchange rate.

To see the difference between these intensional constructions and ordinary extensional ones, consider the verb *grow*. If I say, for example, the sentence in (10), I refer to a particular child now and the same child some time ago, when her height was measured the last time.

(10) The child has grown 2 centimeters.

Contrary to predications such as *wechseln* in (4a), *grow* here requires that the referent of the subject NP remains identical over time. It would be a joke playing with this logical requirement if I would use (10) for a situation where the child has been replaced by some other child which happens to be 2 cm taller than the

---

[7] Quite generally, there will be contexts where a given inherently unique noun fails to refer; every functional noun presupposes certain general conditions, or "appropriate context", for successful reference. For example, *US president* fails to refer if the time of reference is in the 16th century, or *husband of Amy* lacks reference if Amy is not married.

former one. The required constancy of the argument over time is what makes the verb *grow* in (10) an extensional predicate term.

Not incidentally, the verb *grow* can also be used in the intensional construction, similarly to *rise* in (1a), if the subject noun is an abstract individual noun:

(11)   The gross national product grew 0.3 per cent.

The GNP is an abstract figure; the noun refers to whatever is the current GNP value. If the GNP grows, the noun changes its referent. This is not true of persons, or trees. If they grow, it is only one attribute, among many, that changes; the growing organism remains the same organism.

The particular logical character of the constructions in (1a), (4a) and (9a,b) is veiled by the fact that the constructions not only use the same syntax as their extensional counterparts, but they also use the same vocabulary. First, the individual nouns occurring here can also be used as the heads of argument terms for extensional constructions (cf. (5a,b)); in fact they mostly are. Second, the predicate terms, mostly verbs, usually have extensional uses as well, which are more frequent, more basic and older. For example, *rise* can also be used extensionally as in (12a), and *wechseln* as in (12b):

(12)   (a)   The mercury is rising.
        (b)   Hans wechselt auf die andere Straßenseite.
               'lit. Hans changes to the other side of the street.'

In English or German, there do not seem to be many verbs that occur exclusively in the VP position of the rising-temperature construction. English *vary* and its German equivalent *variieren* are among the rare examples. The existence of pairs such as extensional *the mercury is rising* vs. intensional *the temperature is rising*, or the extensional vs. the intensional reading of *the president has changed* is rather typical.

Partee's paradox did not have too much impact on the intensionality debate in early formal semantics. Its importance lies in the fact that Partee came across a linguistic construction specific for individual nouns. The discovery of inherently unique nouns, and its significance, was not immediately recognized. In fact, intensional constructions of this type were widely ignored[8] and the relevance of the subcategory of individual nouns for other constructions was not realized[9].

3.2 Functional nouns and concepts

The noun *temperature* is used in (1) without a possessor specification and given that the example is to be interpreted out of any special context, no implicit possessor specification is presupposed to be provided. In this use, *temperature* means 'temperature of the air'. In general, however, the notion of temperature is a relational concept: temperature of some physical entity, be it a gas, a liquid or solid, or light.[10] Relational nouns like *temperature* – e. g. *size, weight, speed, color, shape* – denote a certain conceptual dimension of some object. The object is usually specified by means of a possessive construction. The whole denotes the unique value in that dimension of the 'possessor' object.

Similarly, the component *president* of the term *US president* is a relational noun, since a president, due to the underlying concept, is always the president of something, a country, some institution, society etc. In the compound *US president*, the modifier *US* specifies the possessor institution. A specification of a (non-relational) possessor for some relational noun combines with the originally relational concept to form a non-relational concept – such as *US_president* or *temperature_of_the_air* – which integrates the possessor concept into the relational concept.

Nouns which are both inherently unique and relational are **functional nouns**. English grammar allows for the omission of a possessor specification, but if unspecified the possessor has to be determined otherwise.[11] There are three major classes of functional nouns.

- **Role terms** for unique roles related to the possessor, where the possessor may be a person (*father*), an institution (*king*), an event (*speaker*), an ob-

---

[8] For exceptions see Janssen (1984) and Löbner (1979).

[9] These other constructions include "concealed questions" (see § 1.6 below).

[10] The special absolute use of the relational noun *temperature* is probably due to the fact that the modern notion of temperature derived from the historical meaning 'mixture'. The word *temperature* acquired its present meaning first in its application to the air (the temperature of the air was apparently considered resulting from a mixed composition of the air).

[11] There are many languages which require either an explicit possessor specification or some derelativizing morpheme for relational nouns. See Ortmann (to appear) for a general discussion and examples.

ject (*inventor*) etc. Examples are kinship terms for unique relatives such as mother, father, husband, or wife (in monogamous social systems), but also role terms for all sorts of other persons that stand in a unique relationship to somebody (*boss, best friend, landlord*). Many role terms relate their referent to an institution: terms for presidents, monarchs, and all the countless offices in public life.

- **Terms for unique parts** of the possessor play a central role in mereologies. They include body part terms for unique body parts such as *head, mouth, stomach,* or terms for parts of artefacts: *handle, keyboard, mouthpiece,* etc. or physical objects in general: *surface, top, tip, core* etc.
- **Terms for attributes (aspects, dimensions)** of the possessor: terms for scalar attributes such as *size, weight, temperature, price, value,* but also for nonscalar dimensions: *color, shape, meaning, name, function* etc.

There are, of course, also terms for nonunique roles such as *neighbor, friend, colleague,* or nonunique kinship terms: *son, sister, aunt* etc. Also many part-terms denote parts that may occur more than once, for example *eye, leg, bone, tooth*. These terms are all relational nouns in the narrower sense to be introduced in the next subsection.

NPs are primarily used referentially, i. e. as argument terms of a predication, for instance as subject or object NP. In referential use, functional and relational nouns are in need of saturation of their open possessor argument. This constitutes what I have called the "absoluteness constraint" on referential NPs.[12] Otherwise NPs with relational head nouns could not be interpreted in context because their reference cannot be resolved. One option of saturating the possessor argument is by explicit specification, e. g. in *temperature of the air* or *president of the US*. Alternatively, the specification of the possessor can, in many languages, be omitted and left to inference from the given context.[13] For example, *price* in (13) would be construed as referring to the price of something which is uniquely determined in the context:

(13)   The price is rising.

---

[12] Löbner (2011:299).

[13] For further ways of dealing with an open possessor argument of functional and relational nouns see Löbner (2011, § 5.3, § 6.2).

If a functional noun is combined with a possessor specification of the individual concept type, the result is an individual concept.[14] This follows from the fact that functional nouns determine their referent uniquely relative to a possessor. If the possessor itself is uniquely determined, so is the value of a functional concept for this possessor. Thus, functional nouns may yield NPs that constitute individual concepts. This is the case if the possessor is specified by means of a definite NP or if an implicit unique possessor is retrieved from the context.

For this reason, it is not only individual nouns[15] that enter the subject and object positions of intensional verbs, but very often functional nouns with an explicit or implicit unique possessor specification. In fact, I assume, functional nouns are even more frequent than individual nouns in these constructions. In this sense, the rising-temperature construction and its transitive counterpart are characteristic of inherently unique nouns in general, individual or functional.

(14) (a) *individual noun* — The temperature is rising.
(b) *functional noun, implicit unique possessor* The price is rising.
(c) *functional noun, explicit unique possessor* The price of the ticket is rising.
(d) *individual noun* — The US president will change.
(e) *functional noun, implicit unique possessor* The president will change.
(f) *functional noun, explicit unique possessor* The president of the US will change.

3.3 Sortal and relational nouns and concepts

Functional nouns are distinguished by two properties which set them apart from ordinary common nouns: inherent uniqueness and inherent relationality. Individual nouns are inherently unique, but not relational. Naturally, there are two more basic types of nouns.

Relational nouns in the narrower sense are relational, but not inherently unique. Nouns of this type include terms for potentially multiple roles such as

---

[14] See Löbner (2011, §4) for the compositional semantics of relational and functional nouns with possessor specifications, and in particular for the "transparency property" of functional nouns which makes them inherit the conceptual type from their possessor argument. The transparency property is first mentioned in Löbner (1998).

[15] Talking of nouns rather than NPs (or DPs) here is rather sloppy, although harmless. Of course, it is NPs (or DPs) rather than nouns that fill the subject and object positions of the constructions discussed. The difference can be neglected here, because in the examples we need to discuss, the NPs consist of just the noun, or the noun with a possessor specification, plus a definite article. In the cases discussed, the nouns are inherently unique. The definite article is redundant under these conditions. The whole NP then expresses the same concept as does the bare noun. (See Löbner 2011 for this account in the framework developed there.)

Functional Concepts and Frames

brother, neighbor, friend, colleague, contemporary etc. or multiple parts of objects. There are also a large number of relational nouns derived from verbs, such as *predication, use, statement, expression* and so on. Depending on the underlying verb, deverbal relational nouns may have more than one additional argument. For example, nominalizations from transitive verbs like *discovery* in *discovery of X by Y* have two additional arguments.

Sortal nouns constitute the great majority of "common nouns"; they are neither inherently unique nor relational. They specify their potential referents by means of characteristic properties. Thus they describe a sort (or category, or kind) of objects. Since the number of objects that meet the description may happen to apply in zero, or one, or more cases, sortal nouns are not inherently unique. Sortal nouns are very numerous; they include terms for natural kinds as well as for classes of artefacts or any other concrete or abstract objects.

			inherently unique	
	sortal nouns		**individual nouns**	
	dog table noun water		Paula pope weather	
	relation: –		relation: –	
	logical type: $\langle e,t \rangle$ unary pred. term		logical type: e individual term	
relational	**relational nouns**		**functional nouns**	
	part brother property		mother death age meaning	
	relation: to possessor		relation: to possessor	
	logical type: $\langle e,e,t \rangle$ binary pred. term		logical type: $\langle e,e \rangle$ unary function term	

Table 1: Types of nouns

The distinction in terms of inherent uniqueness and relationality gives rise to a system of four logical noun types (Table 1). The system is not complete as there are types of relational and functional nouns with more than one relational argument. The type distinction corresponds to basic types distinguished in first-order predicate logic: individual nouns are of type e (individual terms), sortal nouns of type $\langle e,t \rangle$ (one-place predicate terms), relational nouns of type $\langle e,\langle e,t \rangle \rangle$ (two-place predicate terms), and functional nouns of type $\langle e,e \rangle$ (one-place function terms). As I argued in Löbner (2011:283-286), the type distinctions for nouns (in a given lexical reading) are lexical, i.e. really inherent.

3.4 Two characteristic constructions for individual and functional nouns

Abstract functional nouns can be considered to correspond to attributes (or conceptual dimensions) of their "possessors", in the widest sense. For a given possessor, in a given context of utterance, the functional noun denotes the actual value that this attribute adopts. Like the "temperature of the air", the "price of a barrel oil", the "size of the pupil", the "meaning of *temperature*", "your cell-phone number" or the "speed of the rocket", the value of such an attribute is, or may be, variable over time and dependent on circumstances. Consequently, languages may provide intensional constructions such as in (1a) and (9) for the description of the variation of the attribute values.

Abstract individual and functional nouns, with a few exceptions such as terms meaning 'name', 'shape' or 'color', are comparatively young in English, German, and other European languages. Most of them are lexical innovations of the last three centuries. The verb vocabulary for predications about such abstract things as temperature, weight, price, stock exchange rate, voltage etc. was recruited from extensional-verb vocabulary. This development in lexicon and grammar is responsible for the co-existence of extensional and intensional uses of the same verbs.[16] Intensional verbs of the relevant type mostly denote movements and similar changes in their extensional uses, while their application to things like prices and temperature is metaphorical and/or metonymical. Not before the 18th century, the German verb *steigen* 'rise' for upward motion could be used to form a sentence that literally expressed 'the temperature rises'.[17] Apparently the modern construction in (15c) is built on the predecessors (15a) and (15b). (15a) is metonymical for the change of temperature indicated. Note that the mercury columns of traditional thermometers were vertical; it was not the whole column of mercury that rose, rather its tip. Thus, even (15a) involves a pars pro toto metonymy. The derived way of expression in (15b) metonymically abstracts from the mercury column, but still the subject is not the abstract notion of temperature. The thermometer itself, however, did not move anymore. Thus, this construction abandons the literal meaning of *steigen* 'rise'.

---

[16] For a collection of about three hundred relevant verbs see Löbner (1979:114-124).

[17] Evidence is provided by the entries in Grimm's dictionary, Grimm (1854/1984).

(15) (a) Das Quecksilber steigt.   'The mercury is rising.'
      (b) Das Thermometer steigt.   'The thermometer is rising.'
      (c) Die Temperatur steigt.   'The temperature is rising.'

Variability is accompanied by uncertainty. Thus a second type of construction deals with the possibility of different alternative values for a given functional concept. The corresponding verbs include epistemic predications like *know, estimate, guess, determine, be interested in, remember, tell* along with other verbs that presuppose alternatives, such as *choose, influence, control, delimit,* or *constrain,* predications of evaluation: *appreciate, discuss, fear,* or of co-variation *depend on, follow* etc.

(16) (a) Do you know the price of the download?
      (b) The number of victims cannot be determined yet.
      (c) The price depends on the exchange rate of the British pound.

In this type of constructions, the functional NP can be replaced by an interrogative clause, e.g. *Do you know what the price of the download is?* For this reason, these constructions were called "concealed questions". Concealed question constructions are not restricted to abstract functional nouns.

(17) (a) Bill does not know the capital of Belgium.
      (b) His mother could not be determined.

Similar to the rising-temperature construction, concealed questions borrow their syntax from ordinary predication formats, but exploit the concept type of individual and functional concepts for a different type of predication. Löbner (1979:129-141) contains a collection of about 1000 German verbs that can enter the concealed question or similar constructions.[18]

I mention these two types of constructions – the rising-temperature type and concealed questions – because they play a crucial role in scientific discourse. There are more constructions that require functional or individual concepts. One such construction in Russian is investigated in Partee & Borschev (2012).

---

[18] The notion of concealed question was introduced in Baker (1968); for a survey see Nathan (2006).

4 Frames in cognition

4.1 Barsalou's notion of frames

Among the various notions of frames and schemata defined and used in cognitive psychology, artificial intelligence, social interaction theory, and linguistics, the frame definition of Barsalou (1992a, b) is the most explicit, precise, and elaborate definition of this type of structure. According to Barsalou, a frame is a concept representation that is recursively composed out of attributes of the object to be represented, and the values of these attributes. In addition to the specification of attributes and their values, a frame may contain various kinds of constraints that restrict the values an attribute may adopt or define relations between the values of different attributes.

Barsalou represents frames with directed labeled graphs. A central node represents the object, or category of objects, which the frame represents; arcs connect nodes to further nodes. In Barsalou (1992a,b), the complex consisting of the possessor of an attribute, the attribute, and the value it adopts is graphically represented as in Figure 1:

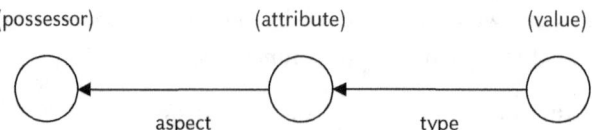

Figure 1: Possessor-attribute-value complex in Barsalou (1992a, 1992b)

The arc labeled "aspect" stands for "is an aspect of". The arc labeled "type" means "is of type". For example, if the three nodes in Figure 1 were taken to represent (from left to right) a tomato, the attribute COLOR[19], and its value red, the right arc would mean that red is of the type color. The label "type" is the same for all value-attribute connections.

Barsalou "define[s] an attribute as a concept that describes an aspect of at least some category members" (Barsalou 1992b:30). Values of attributes are defined as "subordinate concepts of an attribute" (Barsalou 1992b:31). This view of the relation between value and attribute focuses on a certain aspect of the relation between an attribute and the values it adopts. For every attribute there is the range of values which it can possibly adopt; it constitutes a space of alternatives.

---

[19] In this article, small caps are used for attribute terms.

Functional Concepts and Frames

Thus, an attribute-as-function essentially corresponds to the set of values it can adopt. In the sense of Carpenter (1992), the set of all possible values forms an ordered hierarchy of types.

The general correspondence between attributes and sets of values has been observed, among others, by Guarino (1992). The correspondence is reflected in a systematic ambiguity of linguistic expressions for attributes. A noun like *color* can be used both as a functional noun and as a sortal noun. This ambivalence is systematic[20]. An example of the functional, attribute use of the noun would be (18a). (18b) illustrates the sortal use; the statement is of the type represented by the central and the right nodes in Figure 1 and the "type" link between them.

(18) (a) The color of the potato is red.
      (b) Red is a color.

In (18b), the subject NP *red* refers just to a color as such, not to a color as a color of something. In (18a), however, *color* is an inherently relational noun. I consider the functional meaning as basic, because the sortal meaning can be easily derived from it, but not vice versa. In his definition of an attribute, Barsalou relates to the functional concept variant. But when he defines values as subordinate concepts of attribute, he conceives of attributes as sortal concepts for the possible values.

Complex frame elements such as in Figure 1 can be recursively connected by unifying a value node with another possessor node (an example is given in Figure 3 below), resulting in a subordinate specification of the value by another attribute and its value. Barsalou (1992b:33) discusses recursive attribute specification in terms of direct connections from attribute nodes to attribute nodes. For example, he remarks that the frame for 'vacation' may exhibit an attribute COMPANION which in turn has its own attributes such as AGE, FREE TIME, and PREFERRED ACTIVITIES. The chain VACATION – COMPANION – AGE is graphically represented as in Figure 2.

This representation, however, is a simplification of the relations involved. Regarding the example in Figure 2, COMPANION is an aspect, or attribute of a vacation. However, AGE is not an attribute of the attribute (for example, the attribute COMPANION is not an old or young attribute), but an attribute of the *value* of the attribute COMPANION, i.e. an attribute of the companion: the companion is of a

---

[20] In Löbner (2011:310) I called the shift from the functional reading to the sortal reading "Guarino shift", relating to the observation of the underlying ambivalence in Guarino (1992).

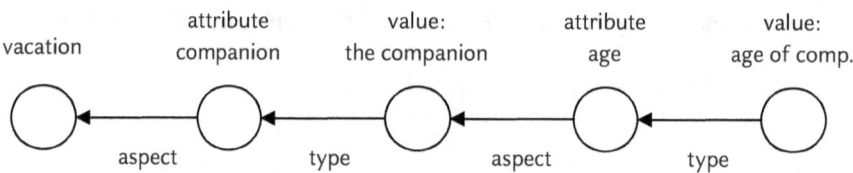

Figure 3: Attribute chain of Figure 2 revised

Barsalou does not explicitly state what kind of relation between possessor and value is established by an attribute. Obviously, different possessors can have the same value for a given attribute. The crucial question is, if an attribute may relate more than one value to a possessor at the same time. If not, the attribute constitutes a function. Implicitly, Barsalou appears to presuppose that attributes are functions. This is evident from the choice of examples for attributes he cites as well as from the fact that he talks of attributes "adopting values". The very use of the term *value* with respect to attributes would be inappropriate for nonfunctional relations. Still, the possibility would remain that some node might have the same attribute assigned to it more than once, e. g. two color attributes, representing an assignment of more than one color value.[21] Such a constellation, however, never occurs in Barsalou's frame examples.

It is therefore assumed (cf. Löbner 1998, Petersen 2007/2015) that the attributes in Barsalou frames constitute functions (to be precise, partial functions) that return one value for every possessor of the relevant type. This basic assumption allows a less complex way of graph representation, than the one depicted in Fig-

---

[21] There are, of course, multicolored objects, such as the Union Jack. But the Union Jack does not simply have the color red and at the same time the color blue and the color white. Rather, it consists of parts of homogeneous color, and it is these parts to which their respective color attribute assigns a value.

Functional Concej

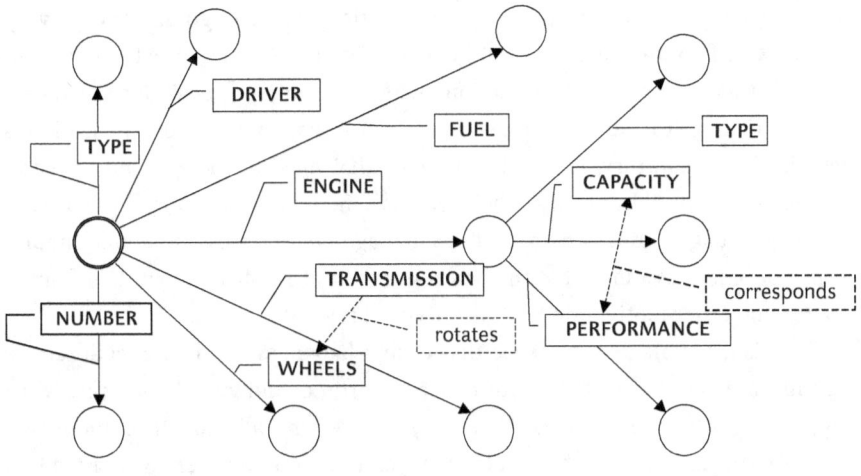

Figure 5: A frame for a car

The frame represents the values of the attributes by nodes not further specified. The broken-line elements represent two types of constraints. "Structural

---
[22] For a deeper and more formal treatment of the issues of Barsalou frames discussed here, see Petersen (2007/2015).

[23] See (Frege 1891).

invariants" represent constitutive relations between (the values of) attributes: the transmission rotates the wheels; similarly, the engine rotates the transmission, the driver operates the engine, the engine consumes the fuel. "Attribute constraints" capture global dependencies between the values of attributes: the greater the capacity of the engine, the higher its performance (as well as the consumption of fuel and the production of CO_2).[24]

Barsalou (1992a:§ 7) assumes that frames constitute the general format of concept representation, and hence of categorization, in human cognition. Frames can be used for modeling the structure of concepts as well as what Barsalou calls "conceptualizations", i. e. ad-hoc modifications of concepts in actual contexts.

4.2 Frames and functional concepts

The fact that attributes in Barsalou frames can be considered functions that assign a value to objects of appropriate type has a very important consequence: Attributes in Barsalou frames are functional concepts. This is of utmost importance for Barsalou's conception of categorization: **We categorize exclusively in terms of functional concepts**. Functional concepts constitute the representational "vocabulary" of categorization—where the notion "vocabulary" is meant metaphorically. It is not to be taken in the sense that cognitive categorization is verbal. To the contrary, it is to be expected that most of the attributes used in human cognition did not make their way as functional nouns into the lexica of human languages. But conversel, if a language does possess functional nouns, it may be safely assumed that they correspond to attributes in cognitive frames. There is no other motivation for this untypical type of nouns.

There is psychological evidence that in first language acquisition children assign meanings to nouns that favor concrete sortal or individual concepts, while suppressing attribute concepts: "One way children initially constrain the meanings of terms is to honor the whole object assumption and thereby assume that a novel label is likely to refer to the whole object and not to its parts, substance or other properties." (Markman 1990:58f). In addition to the "whole object assumption", the "taxonomic assumption" causes children to establish labels that "refer to objects of the same kind rather than to objects that are thematically related."

---

[24] There are further types of constraints (cf. Barsalou 1992a:37-40); for the present purpose it is not necessary to go deeper into the matter here.

(Markman 1990:59) Thus relational meanings for nouns are dispreferred. This does not mean, of course, that children are completely unable to learn relational or functional nouns, but the two strategies mentioned clearly establish sortal and individual nouns and the corresponding types of categorizations as the paradigm cases. The bias against relational and functional nouns corresponds to the fact that the referents of relational and functional nouns, for example roles, properties, and parts of objects do not exist independently; the cognitive isolation of such aspects requires abstraction.

4.3 General properties of frames

The first thing to observe about Barsalou frames is the fact that they represent sortal concepts. The attributes they employ are functional concepts but the whole frame is sortal: a concept that describes what it refers to in terms of certain properties, leaving open how many, if any, objects might satisfy this kind of characterization. A frame might contain specifications that narrow down the possible number of objects that meet them to one, but there is nothing in the structure of a frame telling that it is meant to represent exactly one object. For example, passports contain a perfect frame description of their respective bearers; the attributes they make use of are chosen in order to uniquely identify the bearer, but in principle they are still sortal frames: they might happen to describe no person at all, or exactly one person, or more than one if there happen to be two or more persons that meet the same description.

Given this observation, it is obvious that in addition to the frames Barsalou describes, one needs frames for types of concepts other than sortal. For relational and functional nouns, one needs frames with empty slots for the relational arguments. For individual and functional concepts, the structure of the frame must provide for unique reference. Still, these frames too will provide a mental description in terms of attributes, their values and constraints and relations correlating the values of attributes. Petersen (2007/2015) introduces frames of slightly different structures for the representation of relational, individual, and functional concepts.

One of the fundamental properties of frames is their flexibility. Frames can be reduced or enriched, by removing or adding attributes, or by changing the specification of attribute values. Attributes can be bundled into complex attributes; for example, the attributes LENGTH and WIDTH in a rectangle frame can be combined into SIZE. Conversely, attributes with complex values such as COLOR can be split into components. A further way of combining attributes is functional composition: the attribute EYE COLOR of a person is the composition of the attribute EYE and its subattribute COLOR.

Frames for concrete real objects are principally incomplete. A real object, such as a person, or a tree, can never be completely described. The human mind chooses frames of a composition, complexity, and specificity that are adapted to the needs of particular situations.

4.4 Restrictions on attributes and the embodiment of frames

If frames constitute the general format of knowledge representation in the human cognitive system, the question arises as to how this format is grounded, or embodied.[25] One general aspect is the question: What does constitute a possible attribute in human cognition? Obviously, the set of all values which an attribute may adopt must form a natural space: the cognitive system will not employ attributes which may adopt values out of an arbitrary set of entities including, say, colors, shapes, prices, fingers and ancestors. Rather the set of values which a given attribute may adopt must be composed of mutually exclusive alternatives; colors and shapes are not mutually exclusive (they can be freely combined), but different colors are. Also, it appears reasonable to maximize those spaces, making them encompass all alternatives rather than a subclass. The completeness requirement can be subjected to constraints in particular frames; for example the frame of a mouse will restrict the values of the attributes SIZE, WEIGHT, or LIFESPAN to ranges of values possible for mice. In addition, further constraints have been proposed. In his work on conceptual spaces, Gärdenfors (2000) argues for a general constraint that restricts the space of possible values of an attribute in a concept to be convex: if two values are within the attribute space, then the values between them are, too. Gärdenfors & Wargien (2012) extend the conceptual-spaces approach to concepts for actions and events. Jäger (2012) addresses a similar question. He applies statistical methods to the data of the World Color Survey[26] in order to investigate constraints on the composition of the extension

---

[25] For an extensive discussion of the psychological aspects of this issue, see Barsalou (1999).

[26] The WCS collects data on the use of basic color terms for a sample of 110 unwritten languages from an average of 24 speakers each. See Cook, Kay & Regier (2005) for details.

of color categories. The result is largely in accordance with Gärdenfors' convexity conditions; there are, however, exceptions: some speakers seem to have nonconvex color term extensions, for example one term covering black and white, but not the shades of grey between.

5 Frames and functional concepts in science

Frames and functional concepts play a central role in scientific thinking. Sciences in general deal with particular classes of objects, e. g. physical objects, living organisms, chemical substances, languages, human subjects, works of art etc. The objects of science are investigated in terms of their relevant attributes, where sciences differ in which attributes they address. For example, psychology, medicine, sociology, and economics are concerned with human individuals under various perspectives, dealing with different sets of attributes of the individual.

Together, the attributes constitute the, more or less, abstract objects of a science. For example, merely two attributes, MASS and LOCATION, constitute the mass point in physics. A chemical element is constituted by a small set of attributes, including its atomic number. Scientific theorizing investigates possible values of the attributes, possible combinations of the values of different attributes, correlations of values etc. These aspects are captured by different types of constraint in Barsalou's frame theory. To give an example from linguistics, a lexeme is defined by a frame such as in Figure 6; general constraints would capture the correspondence between phonological form and spelling of lexemes, or the dependence of word inflection on the part of speech that a lexeme constitutes.

Attribute terms play a central role not only in scientific terminology, but also in the very evolution of science. The notion of atomic number in chemistry evolved with the theory of atomic structure, and with it today's notion of a chemical element. Frames can be shown to underlie the conception of scientific classifications, as well as of types of processes such as chemical reactions; these underlying frames can, in turn, be used to analyze paradigm shifts in scientific evolution (see Chen & Barker 2000, Schurz & Votsis 2014).

The two typical constructions for functional nouns mentioned in § 3,4 directly correspond to needs of scientific discourse. The rising-temperature construction meets the need of being able to verbally describe changes of the values of attributes and correlations between them. Concealed questions are involved in

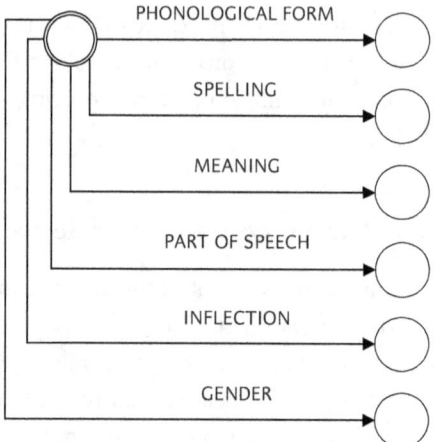

Figure 6: Frame for a lexeme

talk about possible values of attributes. Thus it appears plausible that abstract functional nouns and the characteristic constructions they figure in emerged in co-evolution with scientific theory and practice.

6 Conclusion

The discussion aimed to show that the distinction of conceptual types of nouns is of fundamental importance for understanding not only the semantics of nouns, but human cognition in general. Among conceptual types of nouns, functional nouns are of particular interest. From a linguistic point of view, functional nouns constitute a rather marginal class in grammar, as witnessed by their late emergence in natural language vocabularies and, concomitantly, by the parasitic character of the constructions they are used in. In linguistic theory, too, they have been enjoying little attention, sharing their fate of disregard with individual concepts. The distinction between inherently relational and non-relational nouns (see Table 1) is generally acknowledged. However, the fact that there are types of nouns that are inherently unique, namely individual and functional nouns, is rarely recognized, except for the inherent uniqueness of proper names and personal pronouns.[27]

---

[27] Matushansky (2008) even denies inherent uniqueness of proper names, arguing for a sortal concept, type $\langle e,t \rangle$, analysis.

When Janssen titled his 1984 paper "Individual concepts are useful", this was a reaction to the disregard of inherently unique concepts in the development of Formal Semantics following Montague (1973). From the perspective of this article, Janssen's statement is actually an understatement. The immediate connection between functional concepts and frames shows that functional concepts figure most fundamentally in human concept formation. If Barsalou is correct in assuming that the basic structure of all concepts in human cognition is frames, then functional nouns represent the type of concepts which our entire cognition is based on. Attribute concepts, i.e. instances of functional concepts, form the structure of the mental representations in our cognitive system: we categorize whatever we categorize in terms of functional concepts. The relatively complex logical type $\langle e,e \rangle$ of functional concepts is the elementary unit of concept formation, while the logically elementary type e of individuals corresponds to concepts of unlimited complexity.

One has to assume that the mental representations of the meanings of linguistic expressions are of the same structure as concepts in general. Consequently, propositions and lexical meanings basically have the structure of frames, if Barsalou is right. This observation might pave the way for a unified theory of decomposition and composition that conceives of meanings as represented by frames. Such a perspective would offer a basis for integrating the results of formal semantic research with those of cognitive psychology and neuroscience.

Acknowledgments

The research for this paper was supported by the German Science Foundation (DFG) grant FOR 600, Research Unit "Functional Concepts and Frames".

References

Baker, C. L. 1968. *Indirect questions in English*. Doctoral dissertation, University of Illinois, Urbana, Ill.

Barsalou, L. W. 1992a. *Cognitive psychology. An overview for cognitive scientists*. Hillsdale, NJ: Lawrence Erlbaum Associates Publishers.

Barsalou, L. W. 1992b. Frames, concepts, and conceptual fields. In A. Lehrer & E. F. Kittay (eds.), *Frames, fields, and contrasts: New essays in semantic and lexical organization*, 21–74. Hillsdale, NJ: Lawrence Erlbaum Associates Publishers.

Barsalou, L. W. 1999. Perceptual symbol systems. *Behavioral and Brain Sciences* 22. 577–660.

Carpenter, B. 1992. *The Logic of Typed Feature Structures*. Cambridge: Cambridge University Press.

Chen, X. & P. Barker 2000. Continuity through revolutions: A frame-based account of conceptual change during scientific revolutions. *Philosophy of Science* 67. 208–223.

Cook, R., P. Kay & T. Regier 2005. The world color survey database: History and use. In H. Cohen & C. Lefebvre (eds.), *Handbook of Categorisation in the Cognitive Sciences*, 223–242. Amsterdam: Elsevier.

Dowty, D. R., R. E. Wall & S. Peters 1981. *Introduction to Montague Semantics*. Dordrecht: Reidel.

Frege, G. 1891/1969. *Funktion und Begriff*. Jena. Quoted from the reprint in G. Patzig (ed.), *Funktion, Begriff, Bedeutung*. Vandenhoeck & Rupprecht. Göttingen. 1969. English translation *Function and Concept,* in T. Geach & M. Black (eds.), *Translations from the Philosophical Writings of Gottlob Frege*, 22–41. Oxford, New York: Blackwell.

Gamerschlag, T. 2014. Stative dimensional verbs in German. *Studies in Language* 38. 275–334.

Gärdenfors, P. 2000. *Conceptual Spaces: The Geometry of Thought*. Cambridge, MA: MIT Press.

Gärdenfors, P. & M. Warglien 2012. Using conceptual spaces to model actions and events. *Journal of Semantics* 29. 487–519.

Grimm, J. & W. Grimm 1854/1984. *Deutsches Wörterbuch*. Reprint. München: Deutscher Taschenbuch Verlag.

References

Guarino, N. 1992. Concepts, attributes, and arbitrary relations. Some linguistic and ontological criteria for structuring knowledge bases. *Data & Knowledge Engineering* 8. 249–261.

Jackendoff, R. 1979. How to keep ninety from rising. *Linguistic Inquiry* 10. 172–176.

Jäger, G. 2012. Using statistics for cross-linguistic semantics: a quantitative investigation of the typology of color naming systems. *Journal of Semantics* 29. 521–544.

Janssen, T. M. V. 1984. Individual concepts are useful. In F. Landman, F. Veltman (eds.), *Varieties of Formal Semantics*, 171–192. Dordrecht: Foris.

Lasersohn, P. 2005. The temperature paradox as evidence for a presuppositional analysis of definite descriptions. *Linguistic Inquiry* 36. 127–134.

Lewis, D. 1970. General semantics. *Synthese* 22. 18–67. Reprinted in Davidson & Harman (eds.), *Semantics of Natural Language*, 1972, 169–218. Dordrecht: Reidel.

Löbner, S. 1979. *Intensionale Verben und Funktionalbegriffe. Untersuchung zur Syntax und Semantik von wechseln und den vergleichbaren Verben des Deutschen.* Tübingen: Narr.

Löbner, S. 1981. Intensional verbs and functional concepts: more on the "rising temperature" problem. *Linguistic Inquiry* 12. 471–477.

Löbner, S. 1998. Definite associative anaphora. In S. Botley (ed.), *Approaches to discourse anaphora: proceedings of DAARC96 – Discourse Anaphora and Resolution Colloquium, Lancaster University July 17th–18th 1996*. Lancaster: Lancaster University. Available also at http://semanticsarchive.net/Archive/mU3YzU1N/Loebner_Definite_Associative_Anaphora.pdf.

Löbner, S. 2011. Concept types and determination. *Journal of Semantics* 28. 279–333.

Markman, E. M. 1990. Constraints children place on word meanings. *Cognitive Science* 14. 57–77.

Matushansky, O. 2008. On the linguistic complexity of proper names. *Linguistic and Philosophy* 31. 573–627.

Montague, R. 1973. The proper treatment of quantification in ordinary English. In J. Hintikka, J. Moravcsik & P. Suppes (eds.), *Approaches to Natural Language. Proceedings of the 1970 Stanford Workshop on Grammar and Semantics*, 221–242. Reidel. Dordrecht.

Nathan, L. E. 2006. *On the Interpretation of Concealed Questions*. Ph.D. Diss., M.I.T, Dept. of Linguistics and Philosophy. Cambridge, Mass.

Ortmann, A. (to appear). Uniqueness and possession: typological evidence for type shifts in nominal determination. In M. Aher, D. Hole, E. Jerabek & C. Kupke (eds.), *Logic, language, and computation. 10th International Tbilisi Symposium on Logic, Language, and Computation, TbiLLC 2013*. Berlin, New York: Springer.

Partee, B. H. & V. Borschev 2012. Sortal, relational, and functional interpretations of nouns and Russian container constructions. *Journal of Semantics* 29. 445–486.

Petersen, W. 2015. Representation of Concepts as Frames. In Gamerschlag T., D. Gerland, R. Osswald & W. Petersen (eds.), *Meaning, Frames, and Conceptual Representation*, 39–63. Studies in Language and Cognition 2. Düsseldorf: Düsseldorf University Press. (Reprinted from J. Skilters, F. Toccafondi & G. Stemberger (eds.), Complex Cognition and Qualitative Science. Volume 2 of *The Baltic International Yearbook of Cognition, Logic and Communication*, 151–170, University of Latvia, Riga, 2007.)

Pollard, C. & I. A. Sag 1994. *Head-Driven Phrase Structure Grammar*. Chicago, London: The University of Chicago Press.

Schurz, G. & I. Votsis 2014. Reconstructing scientific theory change by means of frames. In T. Gamerschlag et al. (eds.), *Frames and Concept Types: Applications in Language and Philosophy*, 93–109. Dordrecht: Springer.

Thomason, R. H. 1979. Home is where the heart is. In P. A. French, T. E. Uehling, & H. K. Wettstein (eds.), *Contemporary Perspectives in the Philosophy of Language*, 209–219. Minneapolis: University of Minnesota Press.

Author

Prof. Sebastian Löbner
Departement of Linguistics and Information Science
Heinrich-Heine-University Düsseldorf
Düsseldorf, Germany
loebner@phil.hhu.de

Representation of Concepts as Frames

Wiebke Petersen

Abstract

Concepts can be represented as frames, i.e., recursive attribute-value structures. Frames assign unique values to attributes. Concepts can be classified into four groups with respect to both relationality and referential uniqueness: sortal, individual, proper relational, and functional concepts. The paper defines frames as directed graphs with labeled nodes and arcs and it discusses the graph structures of frames for sortal and relational concepts. It aims at a classification of frame graphs that reflects the given concept classification. By giving a new definition of type signatures, the status of attributes in frames is clarified and the connection between functional concepts, their sortal uses, and their associated attributes is explained.

1 Introduction

According to Barsalou (1992), frames, understood as recursive attribute-value structures, are used as a general format in accounting for the content of mental concepts. The attributes in a concept frame are the general properties or dimensions by which the respective concept is described (e.g., COLOR, SPOKESPERSON, HABITAT...)[1]. Their values are concrete or underspecified specifications (e.g., [COLOR: red], [SPOKESPERSON: **Ellen Smith**], [HABITAT: **jungle**] ...). For example, *ball* can be characterized by [SHAPE: **round**], specifying its concrete shape, and [COLOR: **color**], specifying that it has a color which is not further specified. The attribute values can themselves be complex frames and thus described by additional attributes. E.g., the value **jungle** of the attribute HABITAT can be further

---

[1] Throughout the paper we will mark types by using small, bold letters, while attributes are written in small capitals.

specified by attributes like AVERAGE TEMPERATURE or RAIN SEASON. Frames are thus recursive, and it is this feature that renders them flexible enough to represent information of any desired grade of detail.

Barsalou & Hale (1993) argue that frame theory is independent with respect to various theories of categorization such as checklist theory (cf. Katz 1972; Lyons 1977), exemplar theory (cf. Rosch & Mervis 1975; Brooks 1978), prototype theory (cf. Rosch 1973, 1975; Smith & Medin 1981) or connectionist networks (cf. McClelland & Rumelhart 1981; Shanks 1991). Frames are rather a model for the representation of concepts and therefore establish an alternative to pure feature-list representations. The advantage of frames over predicates of First Order Logic is that they do not force one to stipulate a fixed arity and that substructures can be addressed via labeled symbols instead of ordered argument positions.

Being motivated primarily by empirical research, Barsalou's focus in developing his frame theory was not on giving a formal theory. However, a formal theory of frames is necessary if they are to be employed in knowledge management or language-processing systems and it is the project of developing such a formal theory that concerns us here. For our account of concept decomposition we will use Barsalou's (1992) cognitive frame theory as a starting point. We will show how frames can be represented by labeled graphs and will establish a type system based on them. Our aim is to develop a formal theory of frames that enables us to describe all kinds of concepts and that is plausible as an adequate basis for a frame-based cognitive semantics explaining both decompositional and compositional phenomena in a unified way.

In aiming at the decomposition of *concepts* that are expressible by nouns, our approach aligns with well-established graph-based knowledge representation formalisms that focus on *situations* such as frame semantics (Fillmore 1982) and on *propositions* as in conceptual graph theory (Sowa 1984).

1.1 Frame-based knowledge representation

Frame structures appeared in several disciplines in the 1970s. In Cognitive Science, their introduction led to a paradigm change (cf. Fahlmann 1977; Minsky 1975): Instead of being taken as atomic units, concepts came to be understood as classes of highly structured entities describable in terms of recursive attribute-value structures. Feature lists and binary features represented a preliminary stage in this process (cf. Chomsky & Halle 1968). The frame perspective also became prominent in Artificial Intelligence (AI) and Linguistics. One of the best-known frame-based knowledge representation languages of AI is KL-ONE (Brachman & Schmolze 1985), which is the predecessor of a whole family of knowledge representation languages, the socalled description logics (cf. Donini et al. 1996; Baader et al. 2004).

In Linguistics, frames were first introduced in Fillmore's case grammar in order to represent verbs and the relational roles of their arguments (Fillmore 1968). This early work laid the foundations for the development of frame semantics (Fillmore 1982). Kay (1979) introduced the idea of describing language signs with complex frame structures and proposed frame unification for their manipulation. These frame structures are now known in Computational Linguistics (CL) as feature structures and are heavily used in unification-based grammars (cf. Shieber et al. 1983; Shieber 1986). Inspired by the work of Aït-Kaci on Ψ-terms (Aït-Kaci 1984), type hierarchies with appropriateness conditions were introduced in CL in order to restrict the set of admissible typed feature structures (Carpenter 1992).

Further knowledge representation structures that are related to frames are Semantic Networks (cf. Quilian 1968; Helbig 2006) and Conceptual Graphs (cf. Sowa 1984, 2000).

1.2 A classification of concepts

Concepts can be distinguished with respect to both their relationality and their referential uniqueness (Löbner 1985). Sortal and individual concepts are non-relational and thus typically have no possessor argument. Sortal concepts (e. g., *apple*) denote classical categories and have no unique referents. Individual concepts (e. g., *Mary*), in contrast, have unique referents. Proper relational and functional concepts are both relational in that their referents are given by a relation to a possessor (e. g., *brother of Tom, mother of Tom*). It is characteristic of functional concepts (e. g., *mother*) that they establish a right-unique mapping from possessors to referents and thus are uniquely referring.[2] In contrast, unique reference is not generally implied for proper relational concepts (e. g., *brother*). Figure 1 shows the resulting concept classification.

---

[2] Note that throughout this paper the term *functional concept* is always used in the sense of describing a concept that establishes a *functional mapping*. Hence, *functional* in this paper does not mean that the concept denotes objects which have a special function.

The meaning of a given concept may be shifted: E.g., the concept *mother* which, in its normal use, is uniquely referring and relational (*the mother of Tom*) and thus functional can be also used in contexts like *Mothers like gambling* or *The mothers of the constitution were wise*, where it is used as a sortal or proper relational concept, respectively. Such meaning shifts are always context triggered.

	non-unique reference	unique reference
non-relational	SC, sortal concept: person, house, verb, wood	IC, individual concept: Mary, pope, sun
relational	RC, proper relational concept: brother, argument, entrance	FC, functional concept: mother, meaning, distance, spouse

Figure 1: classification of concepts

Most languages reflect the classification of concepts. E.g., in English, nouns expressing concepts without unique reference (SCs and RCs) are usually used without a definite article. Nouns expressing relational concepts (RCs and FCs) are usually used in possessive constructions, where the possessor is specified synthetically (*the cat's paw*) or analytically (*the paw of the cat*). However, there is a considerable variation in the expression of definiteness and possession across languages.[3]

2 Frame graphs

Our concept-decomposition framework should be formally explicit and cognitively adequate. Therefore, we aim at keeping our frame model as simple and rigid as possible. We do not want to introduce any elements into our model language for merely technical or computational reasons. In Petersen & Werning (2007) we explain how our frame model can be extended to account for cognitive typicality effects. By using oscillatory neural networks as a biologically motivated model, we show how frames might be implemented in the cortex.

Since frames for concepts are recursive attribute-value-structures, each attribute of a frame establishes a relation between the objects denoted by the concept and

---

[3] The four concept classes (sortal, individual, proper relational, and functional) are mutually exclusive and jointly exhaustive. For more details on our concept classification, on its linguistic reflections, and on context-triggered meaning-shifts have a look at the webpages of the research group FOR600 *Functional Concepts and Frames* (http://www.phil-fak.uni-duesseldorf.de/fff).

Representation of Concepts as Frames

the value of the attribute; e. g., the attribute SEX in the frame for *woman* assigns the value **female** to each denoted object. In accordance with the examples in Barsalou (1992), we assume that attributes in frames assign unique values to objects and thus describe functional relations. The values themselves can be complex frames. Section 3 discusses attributes in frames in greater detail.

We model frames as connected directed graphs with labeled nodes (types) and arcs (attributes). Our definitions follow the notational conventions in Carpenter (1992).

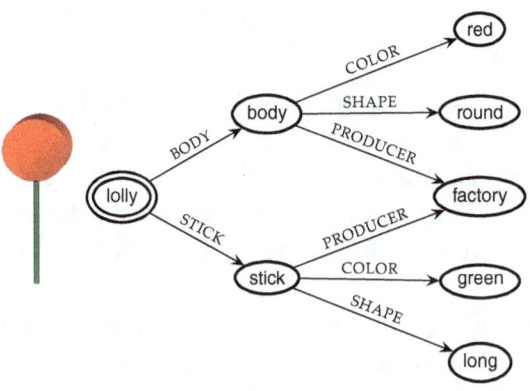

Figure 2: lolly frame

Figure 2 shows the graph of an example frame representing knowledge about lollies with long green sticks and round red bodies produced in factories. The double-encircled node **lolly** is the central node of the frame; it shows that the graph represents a frame about lollies. The outgoing arcs of the **lolly**-node stand for the attributes of the represented lollies and point to their values. Hence, each denoted lolly has a stick and a body. The values of the attributes BODY and STICK are themselves complex frames, both having three attributes, namely COLOR, SHAPE and PRODUCER. The fact that the stick and the body of each denoted lolly are produced in the same factory is indicated by the single **factory**-node to which the two PRODUCER-arcs from **stick** and **body** point. The single **factory**-node excludes the possibility that the body is produced in a candy factory in Belgium while the stick is produced in a paper mill in Canada.

1

Definition 1 *Given a set* TYPE *of types and a finite set* ATTR *of attributes. A frame is a tuple* $F = (Q, \bar{q}, \delta, \theta, \nleftrightarrow)$ *where:*

- *Q is a finite set of nodes,*
- *$\bar{q} \in Q$ is the central node,*
- *$\delta :$ ATTR $\times Q \to Q$ is the partial transition function,*
- *$\theta : Q \to$ TYPE is the total node typing function,*
- *$\nleftrightarrow \subseteq Q \times Q$ is a symmetric and anti-reflexive inequation relation.*

Furthermore, the underlying undirected graph (Q, E) with edge set $E = \{\{q_1, q_2\} \mid \exists a \in$ attr$: \delta(a, q_1) = q_2\}$ is connected.

The underlying directed graph of a frame is the graph $(Q, \vec{E})$ with edge set $\vec{E} = \{(q_1, q_2) \mid \exists a \in$ attr$: \delta(a, q_1) = q_2\}$

If $\theta(\bar{q}) = t$, we say that the frame is of type t; and if $\theta(q) = t$ is true for a node q, we call the node q a *t-node*. Furthermore, if $\delta(a, q_1) = q_2$ is true for a frame, we say that the frame has an *a-arc* from q_1 to q_2; this *a*-arc is an *outgoing arc* for node q_1 and an *incoming arc* for q_2. Contrary to other frame definitions, we do not demand that all nodes of a frame can be reached via directed arcs from its central node.[4]

The types are ordered in a type hierarchy, which induces a subsumption order on frames: "We think of our types as organizing feature structures into natural classes.[...] Thus it is natural to think of the types as being organized in an inheritance hierarchy based on their generality", (Carpenter 1992:11).

Definition 2 *A type hierarchy* (type,$\sqsupseteq$) *is a finite partial ordered set which forms a join semilattice, i. e., for any two types there exists a least upper bound. A type t_1 is a* subtype *of a type t_2 if $t_1 \sqsupseteq t_2$.*

Definition 3 *Given a type hierarchy* (TYPE,$\sqsupseteq$) *and a finite set* ATTR *of attributes. A frame $F = (Q, \bar{q}, \delta, \theta, \nleftrightarrow)$* subsumes *a frame $F' = (Q', \bar{q}', \delta', \theta', \nleftrightarrow')$, notated as $F \sqsubseteq F'$, if and only if there exists a total function $h : Q \to Q'$ such that:*

- $h(\bar{q}) = \bar{q}'$,
- *if $q \in Q$, $a \in$ ATTR, and if $\delta(a, q)$ is defined, then $h(\delta(a, q)) = \delta'(a, h(q))$,*
- *for each $q \in Q$: $\theta(q) \sqsubseteq \theta'(h(q))$,*
- *if $q_1 \nleftrightarrow q_2$, then $h(q_1) \nleftrightarrow' h(q_2)$.*

---

[4] The claim that all nodes of a frame can be reached from its central node is common in most frame theories (cf. Carpenter 1992; Barsalou 1992) because they usually consider only frames for sortal concepts.

Representation of Concepts as Frames

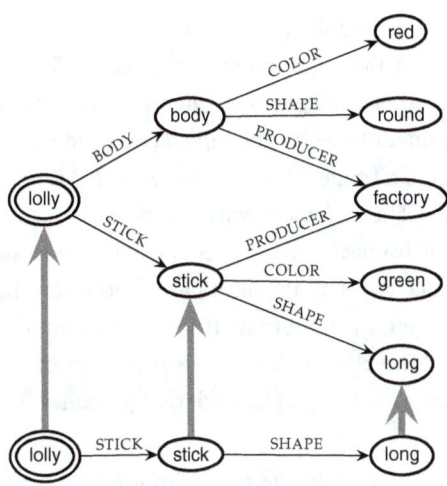

Figure 3: subsumption example

An example of the subsumption relation is given in Figure 3: It shows a rather unspecific *lolly*-frame subsuming the more specific *lolly*-frame from Figure 2. Bold arrows mark the function h from Definition 3. The example shows that Definition 3 captures our general understanding of subsumption: When a concept A subsumes a concept B then A is more general than B, i. e., A imposes less restrictions on the objects it denotes than B.

The definition of frames as labeled graphs yields the problem that two frames with different node sets are always different, even if all the labels match. E. g., the two frames $F = (Q, \bar{q}, \delta, \theta, \leftrightarrow)$ and $F' = (Q', \bar{q}', \delta', \theta', \leftrightarrow')$ with $Q = \{a,b\}, \bar{q} = a, \delta(G,a) = b, \theta(a) = s, \theta(b) = t$ and $Q' = \{c,d\}, \bar{q}' = c, \delta'(G,c) = d, \theta'(c) = s, \theta'(d) = t$ are unequal due to the different node sets ($Q \neq Q'$) although they can both be drawn as ⓢ→⓽. Since the two frames F and F' subsume each other, i. e. $F \sqsubseteq F'$ and $F' \sqsubseteq F$, the subsumption relation defines no partial order on frames, but merely a preorder.

Looking at the lolly example in Figure 2 it is obvious that the information represented in a frame does not depend on the concrete set of nodes. It depends rather on how the nodes are connected by directed arcs and how the nodes and arcs are labeled. However, it is not possible to simply replace the nodes in the frame definition by their labels, since two distinct nodes of a graph can be labeled with the same type. E. g., we could modify the *lolly*-frame in Figure 2 so that the

49

stick and the body of the described lollies were produced in two distinct factories, where one is located in Belgium and one in Canada. The frame in the middle of Figure 4 shows another example of a frame with several equally typed nodes. Therefore, it is convenient to define the *alphabetic variance* relation: A frame F is an *alphabetic variant* of a frame F' (written as $F \sim F'$) if and only if $F \sqsubseteq F'$ and $F' \sqsubseteq F$ are both true. The alphabetic variance relation is an equivalence relation over the collection of frames. It follows immediately that subsumption modulo the alphabetic variance relation defines a partial order on the equivalent classes of frames. From now on, to simplify matters, we will not distinguish between a frame and its equivalence class under alphabetic variance.

In order to characterize the graphs underlying frames, we use the following terminology:

Definition 4 *A node $q_0 \in Q$ is said to be a* root *of a frame $F = (Q, \bar{q}, \delta, \theta, \leftrightarrow)$ if for each $q \in Q$ there is a finite sequence of attributes $a_1 \ldots a_n \in$ ATTR * with $\delta(a_n, \ldots, \delta(a_2, \delta(a_1, q_0)) \ldots) = q$, i.e., q_0 and q are connected by a finite directed path.*

Definition 5 *A node $q \in Q$ is said to be a* source *of a frame $F = (Q, \bar{q}, \delta, \theta, \leftrightarrow)$ if q has no incoming arc (i.e., q has indegree 0). Analogously, q is a* sink *of a frame if q has no outgoing arc (i.e., q has outdegree 0).*

The frame in Figure 2 has exactly one source, namely the node labeled **lolly**, and five sinks, i.e., the nodes labeled **red**, **round**, **factory**, and **green**, **long**. The source of this frame is simultaneously a root of the frame.

A frame is said to be *acyclic* if the underlying directed graph is acyclic, i.e., if it is not possible to find a way along directed arcs leading from a node back to itself. It is obvious that an acyclic frame has at most one root. Our experience in decomposing concepts into frames indicates that frames for lexical concepts are generally acyclic. Through our involvement in the research group FOR600 *Functional Concepts and Frames*, we have access to more than a hundred frame graphs of different lexical concepts that were drawn by approximately twenty (test) persons; none of the frames are cyclic. However, there are some rare self-referential concepts like *egoist* or *narcissist* whose frame graphs have to be cyclic.[5] In spite of these exceptions, we consider only concepts with acyclic frames in this paper.

---

[5] Thanks to Magdalena Schwager for pointing out the problem of self-referential concepts to us.

Representation of Concepts as Frames

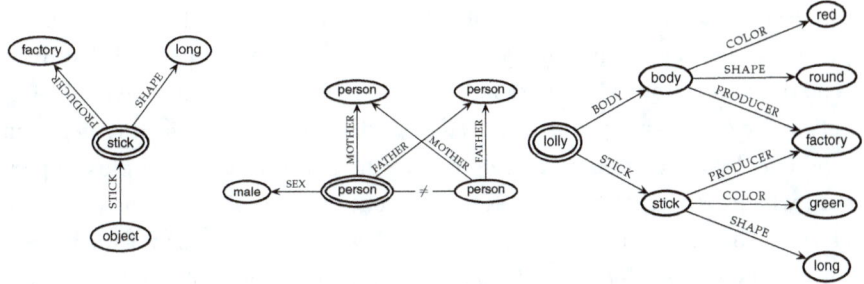

Figure 4: frames for different concepts (left: *stick*; middle: *brother*; right: *lolly*)

Figure 4 shows three frames belonging to concepts of three different concept classes (again the central nodes are double-encircled).[6] The right frame for the sortal concept *lolly* has already been discussed above. The left frame represents the functional concept *stick* and the frame in the middle corresponds to the proper relational concept *brother*. The *stick*-frame characterizes a stick by *being the stick of an object* (i. e., by a functional relation) and by additional sortal features like *being long* and *being produced in a factory*. Functional concepts differ fundamentally from sortal concepts, since their potential referents are the values of an attribute which is identical with the functional concept. Although the *stick*-frame seems to be a substructure of the frame for the sortal concept *lolly*, the fundamental difference is encoded inherently in the graph structure of the frames: The central node of the functional frame, i. e., the frame for the functional concept *stick*, has an incoming arc while that of the sortal frame for *lolly* has solely outgoing arcs. Both frames characteristically have a root. It is the incoming arc (labeled by an attribute corresponding to a functional concept) which establishes the functional relation from potential possessors to the referents of the functional concept.

The frame for the proper relational concept *brother* is more complex. It describes a brother as a male person for which a second person exists with whom it shares mother and father. The undirected arc between the two **person**-nodes labeled with ≠ indicates the inequality relation and ensures that the two nodes

---

[6] Throughout this paper we do not deal with individual concepts since they require a rather different treatment: The graphs underlying their frames do not differ but their central nodes are not labeled by arbitrary types but by particular entity types. Petersen & Werning (2007) give some examples of frames for individual concepts.

51

can never be unified.⁷ The peculiarity of this frame is that the two nodes labeled **person** cannot be reached along directed paths from each other and that there is no third node from which both nodes can be reached. Thus, the potential referents of the central **person**-node are characterized by the sortal feature *male* and especially by the existence of a referent for the non-central source of type **person**, which represents the possessor argument of the proper relational concept *brother*. The connection between the central node and the node for the possessor argument is established indirectly via the shared values of the FATHER- and MOTHER-attributes. Since the relation between a person and his or her mother (or father) is a many-to-one relation, the *brother*-frame does not set up a functional relation between the possessor argument and the referents of the central node. It is characteristic for a *proper relational frame*, i.e., a frame for a proper relational concept, that it has a node which is a source but from which the central node is not reachable along directed arcs.

The example frames show that what type of concept is represented by an acyclic frame is determined by the properties of the central node and the question whether or not the frame has a root or a source. In the remainder of this section we therefore use the binary features "± has source" (±ES), "± has root" (±ER), "± central node is a source" (±CS), and "± central node is a root" (±CR) to classify directed acyclic graphs with central nodes. In order to gain a complete list of possible classes we apply the attribute exploration technique known from Formal Concept Analysis (FCA) (Ganter & Wille 1999), which is implemented in the software *Concept Explorer*.⁸ During an attribute exploration, *Concept Explorer* successively presents implications of properties (in the terminology of FCA: attribute implications) which the user must either accept or reject (by offering a counter example). The process ends when the canonical universe of the properties is completed (Osswald & Petersen 2003), i.e., the closure of sets of compatible properties is determined. The procedure guarantees that the number of implications presented is minimal. Figure 5 shows the result of the exploration: The implicational statements on the left are those which we affirmed during the exploration process. The resulting concept lattice is given on the right side of the figure.

---

⁷ The inequality relation becomes important as soon as information combining procedures like unification are applied to frames, as these procedures have to preserve explicitly stated inequalities.

⁸ http://conexp.sourceforge.net/

Representation of Concepts as Frames

(1) necessarily $+ES$;
(2) if $-ER$, then $-CR$;
(3) if $-CS$, then $-CR$;
(4) if $+ER$ and $-CR$, then $-CS$;
(5) if $+CS$ and $-CR$ then $-ER$;
(6) if $+CS$ and $+ER$ then $+CR$;
(7) if $+CR$ then $+CS$ and $+ER$.

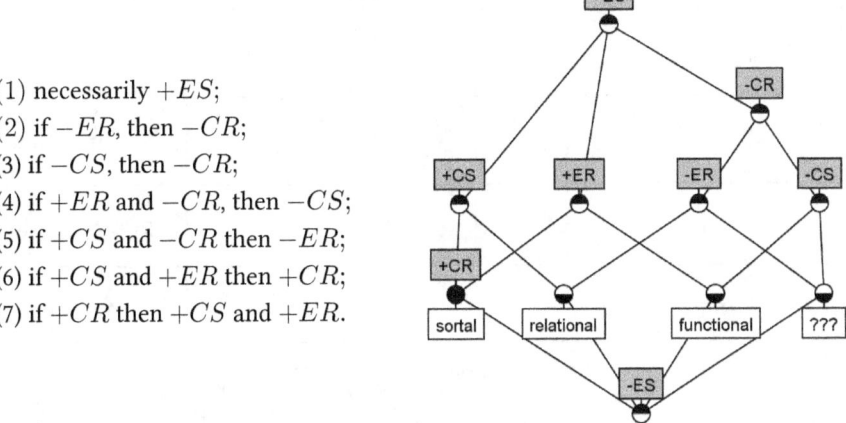

Figure 5: basis of implications and concept lattice

The seven implicational statements are true for the following reasons: The second and the third statement follow immediately from the meaning of the existential quantifier and the definition of roots and sources. Since an acyclic directed graph can be physically modeled by a system of tubes where each tube has a slope, the remaining statements can be easily verified: Roots in such a tube system can be easily recognized by the fact that water flows through all tubes if it is poured in at a root. A source in such a tube system is a tube junction that is not reached by water poured into the system at any other point. Since water cannot run upwards, it cannot flow in circles. Hence, there is never more than one root in a tube system; and if there is a root, it is necessarily the only source of the system as well. The statements (1) and (4)-(7) follow immediately from these considerations.

Taking into account the implicational statements in Figure 5, there are four property distributions remaining that are consistent. Hence, the chosen properties classify acyclic frames into four classes. Figure 6 lists them and shows a typical graph with the required properties for each distribution.

Definition 6 *A* sortal frame *is an acyclic frame whose central node is a root. A* relational frame *is an acyclic frame with a source which is not the central node. A* proper relational frame *is an acyclic frame with at least two sources of which one is the central node. A* functional frame *is an acyclic frame with a root which is not the central node.*

CR	CS	ER	ES	typical graph	frame class
+	+	+	+		sortal
−	−	+	+		functional
−	+	−	+		proper relational
−	−	−	+		???

Figure 6: classification of acyclic frames

From our experience in modeling concepts with frames, we expect that, at least in typical unmarked cases, the first three frame classes in Figure 6 correspond to the concept classes discussed in section 1.2.

Conjecture 1 *In general, sortal concepts are represented by sortal frames, functional concepts are represented by functional frames, and (proper) relational concepts are represented by (proper) relational frames. However, not every arbitrary acyclic frame models a cognitively relevant or even lexicalized concept.*

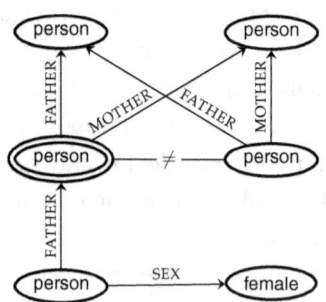

Figure 7: frame for *father of a niece*

The fourth frame class does not correspond as nicely to a concept class as the others do. We assume that frames for this class model non-lexicalized concepts like *father of a niece* whose frame is given in Figure 7.

We only found one frame belonging to the fourth class that seems to be lexicalized, namely the one for *brother-in-law* (and analogically for *sister-in-law*). The

Representation of Concepts as Frames

corresponding frame is shown on the left in Figure 8.[9] Nevertheless, *brother-in-law* only *appears* to be a concept whose frame belongs to the fourth frame class as the right frame of Figure 8 illustrates. Since the *spouse*-relation is a symmetric one-to-one relation, the direction of the SPOUSE-arc of the frame can be reversed. The content of the left frame can be paraphrased as *male person who is the spouse of someone who has a sibling* and the right one as *male person whose spouse has a sibling*. Since *brother-in-law* is a proper relational concept that takes one possessor argument (*my brother-in-law*), the paraphrases of the two frames show that the left one analyzes *brother-in-law* incorrectly as a relational concept with an extra argument.

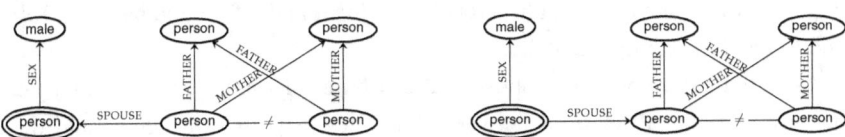

Figure 8: two frames for *brother-in-law*

From the frames in this section we can draw two main conclusions: First, the arguments of relational concepts are modeled in frames as sources that are not identical to the central node. Second, the functionality of functional concepts is modeled by an incoming arc at the central node.

3 Attributes and type signatures

As Guarino (1992) points out, frame-based knowledge engineering systems[5] as well as feature-structure-based linguistic formalisms normally force a radical choice between attributes and types. Therefore, frames like the one in Figure 2 are common, where the rather unspecific value *stick* is assigned to the attribute STICK. The parallel naming of the attribute STICK and the type **stick** suggests a systematic relationship between the attribute and the type that is not captured by the formalism. 5

A second problem addressed in Guarino (1992) concerns the question which binary relations should be expressed by attributes. If one allows attributes to be

---

[9] Strictly speaking, *brother-in-law* is polysemous; it means either *brother of spouse* or *husband of sibling*. We only consider the latter meaning here.

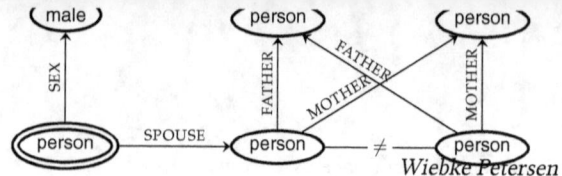

unrestricted arbitrary binary relations, this leads to frames like the following one, which was first discussed in Woods (1975):

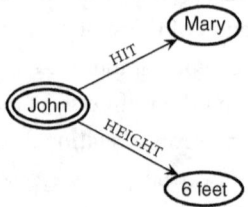

Although HEIGHT and HIT can be represented by binary predicates, the ontological status of the link established between **John** and **6 feet** and between **John** and **Mary** differs fundamentally.

As stated before, we presuppose that attributes of frames establish many-to-one, i. e., functional relations between the nodes they are attached to and their values. The question arises how attributes and functional concepts are connected. All sample attributes we have used so far (STICK, COLOR, ...) correspond to functional concepts. Guarino (1992) distinguishes between the *denotational* and the *relational* interpretation of a relational concept. This distinction can be used to explain how functional concepts can act as concepts and as attributes: Let there be a universe $\mathcal{U}$ and a set of functional concepts $\mathcal{F}$. A functional concept (like any concept) denotes a set of entities:

$$\Delta : \mathcal{F} \to 2^{\mathcal{U}}$$

(e. g., $\Delta(\text{mother}) = \{m | m \text{ is the mother of someone}\}$).

A functional concept also has a relational interpretation:

$$\varrho : \mathcal{F} \to 2^{\mathcal{U} \times \mathcal{U}}$$

(e. g., $\varrho(\text{mother}) = \{(p, m) | m \text{ is the mother of } p\}$).

Additionally, the denotational and the relational interpretation of a functional attribute have to respect the following *consistency postulate* (Guarino 1992): Any value of a relationally interpreted functional concept is also an instance of the denotation of that concept. E. g., if $(p, m) \in \varrho(mother)$, then $m \in \Delta(mother)$.

Furthermore, the relational interpretation of a functional concept f is a function, i.e., if $(a,b), (a,c) \in \varrho(f)$, then $b = c$.

These considerations allow us to clarify the ontological status of attributes in frames: Attributes in frames are relationally interpreted functional concepts. Hence, attributes are not frames themselves and therefore are unstructured. Frames decompose concepts into relationally interpreted functional concepts. Thus, functional concepts embody the concept type on which categorization is based. The differentiation between the denotational and the relational interpretation of functional concepts is consistent with Barsalou's view on attributes: "I define an attribute as a concept that describes an aspect of at least some category members. For example, *color* describes an aspect of *birds*, and *location* describes an aspect of *vacations*. A concept is an attribute only when it describes an aspect of a larger whole. When people consider *color* in isolation (e.g., thinking about their favorite color), it is not an attribute but is simply a concept", Barsalou (1992:30).

In the theory of typed feature structures, it is common to enrich the plain type hierarchy by an appropriateness specification. It regulates which attributes are appropriate for feature structures of a special type and restricts the values of the appropriate attributes (Carpenter 1992).[10] We adapt this technique in order to restrict the class of admissible frames. However, we consequently dismiss the artificial distinction between attributes and types in our definition of type signatures: In contrast to the standard definition (Carpenter 1992:86) the attribute set is merely a subset of the type set. Hence, attributes occur in two different roles: as names of binary functional relations between types and as types themselves.

Definition 7 *Given a type hierarchy* (type, $\sqsupseteq$) *and a set of attributes* attr $\subseteq$ type. *An appropriateness specification on* (type, $\sqsupseteq$) *is a partial function* Approp : attr $\times$ type $\to$ type *such that for each $a \in$ attr the following holds:*

• attribute introduction: *There is a type* Intro$(a) \in$ type *with:*
  – Approp$(a, \text{Intro}(a)) = a$ *and*
  – *for every* $t \in$ type: *if* Approp(a, t) *is defined, then* Intro$(a) \sqsubseteq t$.
• specification closure: *If* Approp(a, s) *is defined and* $s \sqsubseteq t$, *then* Approp(a, t) *is defined and* Approp$(a, s) \sqsubseteq$ Approp(a, t).

---

[10] Type signatures can be automatically induced from sets of untyped feature structures, i.e., frames where the central node is a root and in which only the maximal paths are typed. With FCAType, an implemented system for such inductions is available (Kilbury et al. 2006; Petersen 2006).

- attribute consistency: If $\text{Approp}(a, s) = t$, then $a \sqsubseteq t$.

A type signature *is a tuple* (type, $\sqsupseteq$, attr, Approp), *where* (type, $\sqsupseteq$) *is a type hierarchy,* attr $\subseteq$ type *is a set of attributes, and* Approp : attr × type → type *is an appropriateness specification.*

The first two conditions on an appropriateness specification are standard in the theory of type signatures (Carpenter 1992), except that we tighten up the attribute introduction condition. We claim that the introductory type of an attribute 'a' carries the appropriateness condition '$a : a$'. With the attribute-consistency condition we ensure that Guarino's consistency postulate holds and that Barsalou's view on frames, attributes, and values is modeled appropriately: "At their core, frames contain attribute-value sets. Attributes are concepts that represent aspects of a category's members, and values are subordinate concepts of attributes", (Barsalou 1992:43). Hence, the possible values of an attribute are subconcepts of the denotationally interpreted functional concept. This is reflected in the type signature by the condition that the possible values of an attribute are restricted to subtypes of the type corresponding to the attribute.

We call a frame *well-typed* with respect to a type signature if all attributes of the frame are licensed by the type signature and if additionally the attribute values are consistent with the appropriateness specification.

Definition 8 *Given a type signature* (type, $\sqsupseteq$, attr, Approp), *a frame* $F = (Q, \bar{q}, \delta, \theta, \leftrightarrow)$ is well-typed *with respect to the type signature, if and only if for each $q \in Q$ the following holds:*

If $\delta(a, q)$ is defined, then $\text{Approp}(a, \theta(q))$ *is also defined and* $\text{Approp}(a, \theta(q)) \sqsubseteq \theta(\delta(a, q))$.

The definition of the appropriateness specification guarantees that every arc in a well-typed frame points to a node that is typed by a subtype of the type corresponding to the attribute labeling the arc. The decomposition of concepts into frames requires that the frame in question be well-typed.

A small example type signature is given in Figure 9. The appropriateness specification is split up into single appropriateness conditions: The expression 'TASTE: **taste**' at type **objects** means that the attribute TASTE is appropriate for frames of type **objects** and its value is restricted to frames of type **taste** or subtypes of **taste**. The attribute conditions are passed on downwards. Hence, the type **apple** inherits the appropriateness condition 'TASTE: **taste**' from its upper neighbor **ob-**

Representation of Concepts as Frames

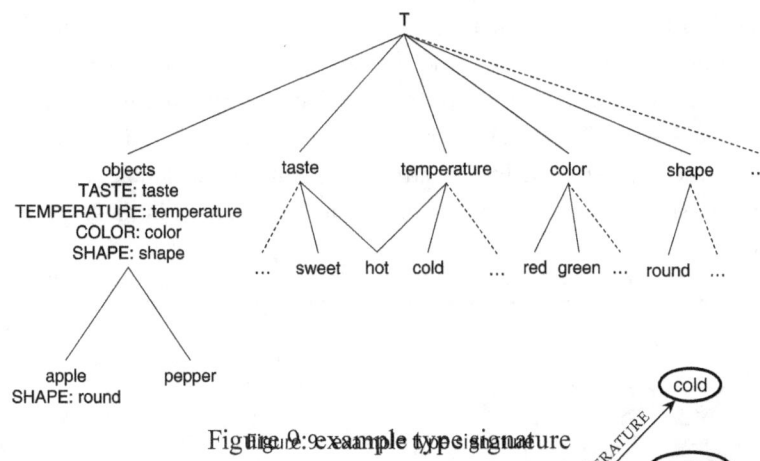

Figure 9: example type signature

A small example type signature is given in Figure 9. The appropriateness specification is split up into single appropriateness conditions. The expression TASTE: **taste** at type **objects** means that the attribute TASTE is appropriate for frames of type **objects**, and its value is restricted to frames of the type **taste** or subtypes of **taste**. The attribute conditions are passed on downwards. Hence, the type **apple** inherits the attribute types where the fattness is well-typed while the second from its upper neighbor **objects**. It also inherits the appropriateness condition SHAPE: **shape**, but tightens it up to SHAPE: **round**, which is permissible by the specification closure condition. The definition of the type signature makes sure that the permissible values of an attribute are subtypes of the attribute type. Hence, the possible values of TASTE, i.e., **sweet, hot, sour,** and so forth, are subtypes of the type **taste**. Notice that the subtypes of an attribute type are not generally attribute types themselves. Figure 10 shows two frames, where the first one is well-typed, while the second one violates the appropriateness condition SHAPE: **round** at type **apple**.

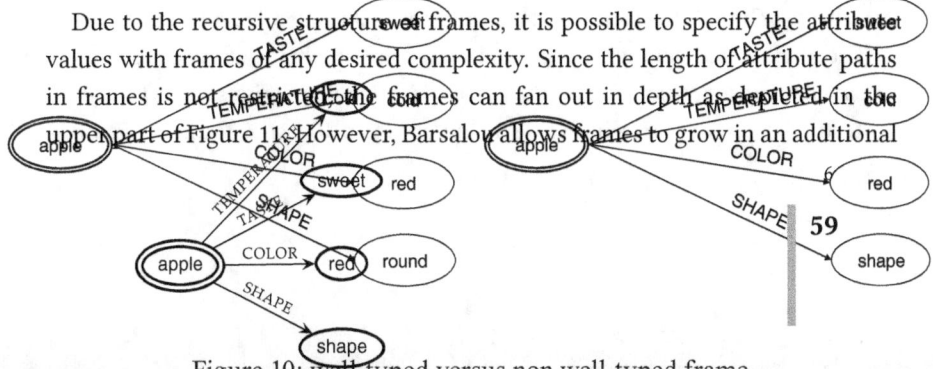

Figure 10: well-typed versus non well-typed frame

Due to the recursive structure of frames, it is possible to specify the attribute values with frames of any desired complexity. Since the length of attribute paths in frames is not restricted, the frames can fan out in depth as depicted in the upper part of Figure 11. However, Barsalou allows frames to grow in an additional respect: "Within a frame, each attribute may be associated with its own frame of more specific attributes. [...] These secondary attributes often have frames as well. [...] Even these attributes [of frames of secondary attributes] continue to have frames", Barsalou (1992:33). The possibility of further specifying attributes as well as their values by additional attributes results in the double recursive and self-similar structure of Barsalou's frames, which is depicted in the lower part of Figure 11.

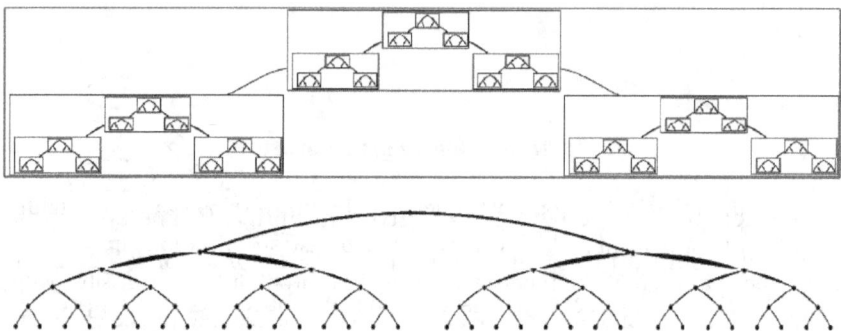

Figure 11: Fanning out of classical frames (top) and Barsalou's self-similar frames (bottom)

Our approach to frames, which reflects the parallelism of the denotational and the relational interpretation of functional concepts in the definition of type signatures, captures Barsalou's idea about frames, but avoids the double recursive structure. Since attributes are types at the same time, further attribute-value pairs can specify them; this is in accordance with Barsalou's claim that "frames represent all types of concepts, whether they are free-standing concepts, such as *bird* and *vacation*, or whether they are attributes such as *color* for *bird* and *location* for *vacation*", (Barsalou 1992:31). However, this further specification will only take place if the attribute is used as a type, i.e., if it labels a frame node, and never when it is used as a functional attribute and labels a frame arc. Our *lolly*-frame in Figure 2 exemplifies this perspective: The attribute *stick* labels an arc as well as a node, but it is the value of the attribute to which further attribute arcs are attached, such that it constitutes the sortal *stick*-subframe in Figure 12.

The attributes PRODUCER, COLOR and SHAPE are attributes of sticks and not of the attribute STICK, since STICK is the partial function that assigns sticks to objects. Note that the *stick*-frame in Figure 12 differs from the *stick*-frame in Figure 4

Representation of Concepts as Frames

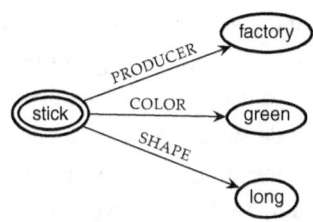

Figure 12: Frame for the sortal reading of *stick*

(left) in that it does not relate the stick to an object to which it is attached. If it is not embedded into a larger object frame (e. g., a *lolly*-frame) it models the sortal reading of *stick* as in the sentence *these days sticks are mostly produced in big factories*. Such context-triggered meaning-shifts from relational concepts to non-relational readings are very common; the frame structures of the concepts help to explain and visualize them. However, we would like to emphasize that the *stick*-frame of Figure 4 (left) must not be confused with the attribute STICK itself: *Stick* is a functional concept whose functional frame is given in Figure 4 (left); although it is functional, it denotes – like the sortal *stick*-frame in Figure 12 – sticks. However, in contrast to the sortal frame its denotation is determined by a functional relation from a possessor argument (here the potential referents of the **object**-node). The attribute STICK is the relationally interpreted functional concept *stick* and therefore a function; it is not a frame.

The ability to give explicit frames for functional concepts that differ fundamentally from frames for the sortal readings of those concepts is a novelty. It is made possible by our novel definition of frames, which no longer demands that the central node be a root of the frame graph. We know of no other explicit approach to frames for functional concepts.

Having motivated our approach to type signatures[7] we will now sketch how it offers an elegant solution to problems in grammar engineering that occur when frames are employed as semantic representations. To model how adjectives modify the meaning of a noun it has to be explained that in a phrase like *red body* the value **red** is assigned to the attribute COLOR, while *round body* modifies the value of the attribute SHAPE. An unsatisfactory solution would be to have a single rule for each adjective dimension, i. e., for each attribute. Instead, we propose to introduce the notion of a *minimal upper attribute* of a type. An upper attribute of a type is an attribute which is a supertype of the type with respect to the type

61

hierarchy. Hence, a minimal upper attribute of a type is a minimal element of the set of upper attributes of the type. According to the type signature in Figure 9, the minimal upper type of **red** is **color** and the one for **round** is **shape**. Hence, we can formulate a single rule for all those cases: Simplified, it states that in a frame which represents the meaning of a phrase consisting of an adjective and a noun, the type corresponding to the adjective is assigned as a value to the minimal upper attribute of the adjective type. Such a rule would even capture some interesting cases of ambiguity. Consider the polysemous adjective *hot*, which means either *being very warm* or *being very spicy*. In a type hierarchy the type **hot** could be placed such that it is a subtype of the attribute type **temperature** as well as of the attribute type **taste** (cf. Figure 9). Then **hot** has two minimal upper attributes and the above mentioned rule applied to the phrase *hot pepper* would result in two frames: one representing a very spicy pepper [TASTE: **hot**] and one representing a very warm pepper [TEMPERATURE: **hot**], which could be part of a dish. Due to space limits, we cannot go into more detail here, but a publication focusing on this issue is in preparation.

4 Conclusion

We have presented a new approach to frames which discards the claim that the central node of a frame is its root, which is a common claim in standard frame theories. In addition, we have dismissed the artificial distinction between types and attributes in type signatures. Those two adaptations enable us to give a classification of acyclic frame graphs that mirrors the classification of concepts into sortal, proper relational and functional concepts. In particular, the promising fact that in our frame theory the structure of a functional (but also of a proper relational) concept differs fundamentally from that of the corresponding sortal concept assures us that our modifications to standard frame theory can open up new insights into concept decomposition.

However, a lot of work still has to be done. We need to develop a unification operation in order to account for frame composition. Individual concepts also have to be accommodated in our frame theory. Furthermore, we expect the discovery of new ways to explain phenomena from fields such as composition, metonymy, metaphors, and meronymy. Finally, powerful software devices have to be developed in order to test our frame model in real knowledge engineering or language processing tasks.

Acknowledgements

I would like to thank my colleagues in the research group *Functional Concepts and Frames* for invaluable discussion and input. Special thanks go to Peter Bücker and Rafael Cieslik for their help editing this text and to an anonymous reviewer for helpful hints concerning its readability. Research for this paper was made possible by the grant FOR600 of the German Research Foundation.

References

Aït-Kaci, H. 1984. *A Lattice Theoretic Approach to Computation Based on a Calculus of Partially Ordered Type Structures*: University of Pennsylvania dissertation.

Baader, F., D. Calvanese, D. L. McGuinness, D. Nardi & P. F. Patel-Schneider (eds.). 2004. *The Description Logic Handbook: Theory, Implementation, and Applications*. New York: Cambridge University Press.

Barsalou, L. W. 1992. Frames, Concepts, and Conceptual Fields. In A. Lehrer & E. F. Kittay (eds.), *Frames, Fields, and Contrasts*, 21–74. Hillsdale NJ: Lawrence Erlbaum Associates Publishers.

Barsalou, L. W. & C. R. Hale. 1993. Components of conceptual representation: From feature lists to recursive frames. In I. Van Mechelen, J. Hampton, R. Michalski & P. Theuns (eds.), *Categories and Concepts: Theoretical Views and Inductive Data Analysis*, 97–144. San Diego CA: Academic Press.

Brachman, R. & J. G. Schmolze. 1985. An overview of the KL-ONE knowledge representation system. *Cognitive Science* 9 (2). 171–216.

Brooks, L. R. 1978. Nonanalytic concept formation and memory for instances. In E. Rosch & B. B. Lloyd (eds.), *Cognition and Categorization*, 169–211. Hillsdale, NJ: Erlbaum.

Carpenter, B. 1992. *The Logic of Typed Feature Structures*. Cambridge: Cambridge University Press.

Chomsky, N. & M. Halle. 1968. *The Sound Pattern of English*. New York, NY: Harper & Row.

Donini, F. M., M. Lenzerini, D. Nardi & A. Schaerf. 1996. Reasoning in Description Logics. In G. Brewka (ed.), *Principles of Knowledge Representation*, 193–238. Stanford, CA: CSLI Publications.

Fahlmann, S. E. 1977. *A System for Representing and Using Real-world Knowledge*: MIT dissertation.

Fillmore, C. J. 1968. The Case for Case. In E. Bach & R. T. Harms (eds.), *Universals in Linguistic Theory*, 1–88. New York: Holt, Rinehart and Winston.

Fillmore, C. J. 1982. Frame semantics. In *Linguistics in the Morning Calm*, 111–137. Seoul: Hanshin Publishing Co.

Ganter, B. & R. Wille. 1999. *Formal Concept Analysis: Mathematical Foundations*. Berlin: Springer.

Guarino, N. 1992. Concepts, Attributes, and Arbitrary Relations – Some Linguistic and Ontological Criteria for Structuring Knowledge Bases. *Data & Knowledge Engineering* 8 (3). 249–261.

Helbig, H. 2006. *Knowledge Representation and the Semantics of Natural Language*. Berlin: Springer.

Katz, J. 1972. *Semantic Theory*. New York: Harper & Row.

Kay, M. 1979. Functional Grammar. In *Proceedings of the Fifth Annual Meeting of the Berkeley Linguistic Society*, 142–158. Berkeley, CA: Berkeley Linguistic Society.

Kilbury, J., W. Petersen & C. Rumpf. 2006. Inheritance-based models of the lexicon. In D. Wunderlich (ed.), *Advances in the Theory of the Lexicon*, 429–477. Berlin: Mouton de Gruyter.

Löbner, S. 1985. Definites. *Journal of Semantics* 4 (4). 279–326.

Lyons, J. 1977. *Semantics* (2 Volumes). Cambridge University Press.

McClelland, J. L. & D. E. Rumelhart. 1981. An interactive activation model of context effects in letter perception: Part 1. An account of basic findings. *Psychological Review* 86. 287–330.

Minsky, M. 1975. *The Psychology of Computer Vision* chap. A Framework for Representing Knowledge, 211–277. New-York: McGraw-Hill.

Osswald, R. & W. Petersen. 2003. A Logical Approach to Data-Driven Classification. In A. Günter, R. Kruse & B. Neumann (eds.), *Advances in Artificial Intelligence, Proceedings of the 26th Annual German Conference on AI (KI 2003)*, vol. 2821 Lecture Notes in Computer Science, 267–281. Springer.

References

Petersen, W. 2006. FCAType – a System for Type Signature Induction. In S. B. Yahia & E. M. Nguifo (eds.), *Proceedings of the 4th International Conference on Concept Lattices and their Applications (CLA 2006)*, Faculté des Sciences de Tunis, Université Centrale.

Petersen, W. & M. Werning. 2007. Conceptual Fingerprints: Lexical Decomposition by Means of Frames – a Neuro-cognitive Model. In *Conceptual Structures: Knowledge Architectures for Smart Applications, Proceedings of ICCS 2007*, vol. 4604 Lecture Notes of Computer Science, 415–428. Springer.

Quillian, R. 1968. Semantic Memory. In M. Minsky (ed.), *Semantic Information Processing*, 216–270. Cambridge, MA: MIT Press.

Rosch, E. & C. Mervis. 1975. Family resemblances: Studies in the internal structure of categories. *Cognitive Psychology* 7(4). 573–605.

Rosch, E. 1973. Natural categories. *Cognitive Psychology* 4. 328–350.

Rosch, E. 1975. Cognitive reference points. *Cognitive Psychology* 7 (4). 532–547.

Shanks, D. R. 1991. Categorization by a connectionist network. *Journal of Experimental Psychology: Learning, Memory, and Cognition* 17. 433–443.

Shieber, S., H. Uszkoreit, F. Pereira, J. Robinson & M. Tyson. 1983. The formalism and implementation of PATR-II. In B. J. Grosz & M. Stickel (eds.), *Research on Interactive Acquisition and Use of Knowledge*, 39–79. Menlo Park, CA: SRI International.

Shieber, S. M. 1986. *An Introduction to Unification-Based Approaches to Grammar*. Stanford, CA: CSLI.

Smith, E. E. & D. Medin. 1981. *Categories and Concepts*. Cambridge, MA: Harvard University Press.

Sowa, J. 2000. *Knowledge Representation: Logical, Philosophical and Computational Foundations*. Pacific Grove, CA: Brooks Cole Publishing Company.

Sowa, J. F. 1984. *Conceptual Structures*. Reading, MA: Addison-Wesley.

Woods, W. A. 1975. What's in a Link: Foundations for Semantic Networks. In D. Bobrow & A. Collins (eds.), *Representation and Understanding: Studies in Cognitive Science*, 35–82. Academic Press.

Notes on the reprint

This text was originally printed in 2007. It is one of the first articles introducing a formalization of Barsalou's frame account and connecting it to Löbner's classification of concept types (this volume). It has to be emphasized that the claim that a frame reflects the type of the represented concept by pure graph properties (see Figure 6) only holds for acyclic frame graphs of simple *lexical* concepts in their basic reading. As soon as the argument of a relational concept is saturated, it is not relational anymore. For example, while *brother* is a proper relational concept, *brother of Anne* is a sortal concept denoting the set of all brothers of Anne. The frame graphs for both concepts do not differ with respect to the graph properties discussed in the present article, but only with respect to node labels.

A similar problem occurs when concepts are shifted from one concept type to another. For instance, take the functional concept *flat*. A tenant can usually only live in one flat while a landlord can own more than one flat. Hence, *flat* is a functional concept if it is read as the flat of someone who is living there. It is a proper relational concept if it is read as the flat of someone who is renting it out. Furthermore, *flat* is shifted to a sortal concept when one abstracts away from its function of living in or being rented out such that *flat* solely refers to the physical 3-dimensional object of a constellation of rooms. In order to account for both argument saturation and concept type shifting, the argument nodes have to be explicitly distinguished (see Petersen & Osswald 2014 for details).

At the end of Section 3, I discuss the idea of modeling adjectival modification in terms of minimal upper attributes. This idea has been worked out in Petersen et al. (2008). However, note that this analysis is restricted to intersective adjectives and captures adjectival modification by means of modification operations on frames. An alternative solution with a broader coverage of different adjective types would consist of modeling adjectives as frames in their own right which are composed with the noun frames via frame unification.

Petersen, W. & T. Osswald (2014). Concept composition in frames: Focusing on genitive constructions. In Gamerschlag et al. (eds.), *Frames and Concept Types. Applications in Language, Cognition, and Philosophy*, vol. 94 of Studies in Linguistics and Philosophy, 243–266. Springer: Heidelberg.

Petersen, W., J. Fleischhauer, H. Beseoglu & P. Bücker. A frame-based analysis of synaesthetic metaphors. *The Baltic International Yearbook of Cognition, Logic and Communication*, New Prairie Press, 3, 1–22, 2008.

References

Acknowledgements

I would like to thank Marie-Luise Fischer for her help in editing this reprint. My current research on frames is made possible by the Collaborative Research Center 991, funded by the German Research Foundation.

Author

Wiebke Petersen
Departement of Linguistics and Information Science
Heinrich-Heine-University Düsseldorf
Düsseldorf, Germany
petersew@phil.hhu.de

Nominal Concept Types and Determination

Uniqueness of the Definite Article with Respect to Cognitive Frames

Ryo Oda

Abstract

It has often been argued in the relevant literature that the use of the singular definite article can be explained with the uniqueness theory, which postulates that the singular definite requires the existence of only one entity that meets the description. However, there are many instances of singular definites, which seem contrary to the uniqueness requirement, as illustrated by *the hospital* in the example "In Paris, I caught the measles and I went to the hospital to receive treatment." Some researchers have claimed that the use of such a singular definite cannot be adequately explained with the uniqueness theory. Others have argued that *the hospital* in this example refers not to a particular hospital in reality but to the unique role "hospital" within a "city" frame. This paper argues that the cognitive frame that supports the felicitous use of the definite *the hospital* in this example is not an inflexible "city" frame but a flexible "medical care" frame, which is evoked by the linguistic context and the situation of the utterance. The paper aims to explain the enigmatic use of singular definite descriptions in English, with special reference to cognitive frames, and to illustrate the affinity between the definites in configurational use and the definite associative anaphora.

1 Previous research and problems encountered

1.1 Uniqueness

This paper examines the use of the singular definite article in English[1]. The previous related literature has often argued that the use of the singular definite

---

[1] At the outset of this study, we began with the analysis of articles in French and then extended our study to the use of articles in English. The uses of definite descriptions in English and in French are not entirely parallel. However, with regard to the use of a definite description without any unique referent explicitly introduced in the context that we will deal with in this paper, the definite descriptions in English and in French behave in an almost similar manner. Thus, the problems and

article can be explained with the uniqueness theory[2]. According to this theory, the speaker uses the definite article when he/she supposes that his/her hearer can apply a unique referent to the definite description or can uniquely identify the referent (Russell 1905, Lambrecht 1994, Gundel, Hedberg & Zacharski 1993, 2001). The comparison of examples (1) and (2) as well as the examination of example (3) will provide us a general view of this fundamental principle.

(1) Could you pass me *the pen*?

(2) Could you pass me *a pen*?

(3) It is not *a solution*, but *the solution*.

In example (1), the use of the singular definite article in *the pen* implies that there exists only one pen in the immediate situation and the hearer can identify this unique pen. In example (2), on the other hand, the use of the singular indefinite article implies that there can be more than one pen in the immediate situation. Similarly, in example (3), the singular indefinite in *a solution* presupposes that there can be more than one solution, whereas the singular definite in *the solution* indicates that this is the only solution. However, there are many instances where the use of the singular definite is contrary to the uniqueness requirement.

(4) Emma had a bad headache yesterday, and she went to buy some medicine at *the pharmacy*.

In example (4), suppose that there is more than one pharmacy in the city where Emma lives. The employment of the singular definite article in *the pharmacy* is quite appropriate, even though the interlocutor does not know exactly which pharmacy Emma went to. The uniqueness condition, thus, does not seem to be fulfilled here. In this paper, the pertinence of the uniqueness condition in instances such as those exemplified above will be addressed.

---

our analysis of these problems to be proposed herein with regard to definite descriptions in English will apply mostly to French definite descriptions. Because of space limitations, the discussion and data in this paper will be concerned exclusively with the use of articles in English.

[2] Aside from the uniqueness theory, the following familiarity condition has been proposed in some previous literature: the referent of the definite description is familiar within the discourse (Christophersen 1939, Heim 1983). However, we will start off by assuming that the use of the singular definite description is predominantly governed by the uniqueness condition, and will not discuss here the validity of the familiarity theory.

1.2 Birner & Ward (1994)

Birner and Ward cite examples (5) and (6) to illustrate the validity of the uniqueness theory.

(5) Your 10:00 appointment – a Mr. Johnson – said he'd be late because he had to stop at *the bank* first. (Birner & Ward 1994)

(6) As soon as my cousin arrived in Santiago, she broke her foot and had to spend a week in *the hospital*. (*Ibid.*)

(7) *While in Santiago, Bill broke his foot and was rushed to *the big hospital*. (*Ibid.*)[3]

In example (5), it is obvious that there is more than one bank in the city, but the use of the singular definite article in *the bank* is appropriate even if the hearer does not know exactly which bank is being spoken about. Similarly, there must be several hospitals in Santiago in example (6), but the use of the singular definite in *the hospital* is adequate even if the hearer cannot identify the hospital in question. Singular definites of this nature do not have any obvious referent in the preceding context, either in the hearer's memory or in the immediate situation. Birner and Ward notice two points from these examples. First, such singular definites are used to refer to "locations" in general, the point which we do not agree with, as will be shown later. Second, this use of the singular definite is acceptable only if the intended referent is not relevantly differentiated from other referents denoted by the same noun phrase in the context. Thus, the modifier *big* attached to *the hospital* distinguishes the referent from the other hospitals in example (7), and this differentiation makes the expression *the big hospital* infelicitous, unless the hearer can identify this particular hospital. Because there is much evidence in support of their second viewpoint, we agree with it. However, Birner and Ward[4] conclude that the uniqueness condition is not a necessary condition for the felicitous use of the definite article, because as examples (5) and (6) show, the intended referent is not always uniquely identifiable.

At this point, we would like to raise two questions: Does the use of such a singular definite really deny the validity of the uniqueness theory? Furthermore,

---

[3] In this paper, the asterisk (*) indicates ungrammaticality or infelicity in the context.

[4] Birner & Ward (1994) maintain that familiarity is neither a necessary nor a sufficient condition for the felicitous use of the definite article.

why is it that some singular definite descriptions, when being introduced in the context without a uniquely identifiable referent, can often refer to a location?

1.3 Epstein (1999)

Epstein (1999) adopts cognitive frames to analyze the definite article. According to him, when a noun phrase designates a role, it refers to a fixed property, but not to a particular individual.

(8)   *The President* is elected every four years. (Epstein 1999)

(9)   *The President* is giving a speech tonight. (*Ibid.*)

In example (8)[5], the noun phrase *the President* is most likely to be interpreted as the role that designates the property of "being President." Meanwhile, in example (9), the same noun phrase, *the President*, is most likely to be interpreted as the value that denotes the particular individual fulfilling the role of the President at the time of utterance; in the context of 1962, the value that satisfies the role of the President of the United States of America is John F. Kennedy; in 2013, it is Barack Obama. Following this idea, Epstein developed the theory that "definite descriptions frequently refer to roles representing stereotypical elements within cognitive frames." (Epstein 1999:126)

Birner and Ward also examined the concept of the cognitive frame while analyzing the singular definite; they arrived at the conclusion that the definite without an obvious antecedent (or a uniquely identifiable referent) cannot be explained with cognitive frames.

(10)   The first thing we did upon arriving in Santiago was to go to *the park* and have a relaxing picnic lunch. (Birner & Ward 1994)

(11)   When I was six years old, I had to spend a night in *the hospital*, and I was terrified. (*Ibid.*)

Birner and Ward rejected the analysis of the definite article in terms of cognitive frames because "there is typically more than a single park within a given city" (Birner & Ward 1994:99). However, in example (10), the use of the singular defi-

---

[5] In this example, the definite *the President* can also be considered as an instance of a functional concept definite (Löbner 1985, 1998).

nite in *the park* is felicitous, and in example (11), "there is no mention of a city that can give rise to a frame that might plausibly contain a hospital" (*Ibid.*:99). Epstein disagrees with Birner and Ward, explaining that the definite *the park* in examples such as (10) does represent a stereotypical element within the "city" frame; it is not important to identify the exact park where the speaker went. Epstein points out that "the availability of frame-knowledge is not dependent on explicit mention of the frame itself in the surrounding discourse"(Epstein 1999:128).

We agree with Epstein that a cognitive frame, regardless of whether it is explicitly mentioned, can be activated and used in a discourse. However, we will argue that his analysis of examples (10) and (11) utilizing the "city frame" needs to be modified.

1.4 Abbott (2001)

Abbott (2001) categorizes "configurational uses of nouns" (i. e., "non-unique definites" according to her terminology[6]) into six subcategories: "proprietary items," "traditionally unique items," "predicate nominals," "products of writing," "locations," and "types." In this paper, we will not examine each of the six subcategories individually for configurational uses of nouns. Abbott cites examples (12)–(15) as those of definites of "traditionally unique items."

(12) [Hotel concierge to guest, in a lobby with four elevators]
You're in Room 611. Take *the elevator* to the sixth floor and turn left. (Birner & Ward 1994)

(13) Switch *the light* on. (Löbner 1985)

(14) Your 10:00 appointment – a Mr. Johnson – said he'd be late because he had to stop at *the bank* first. (Birner & Ward 1994) = (5)

(15) Kim spent the night in *the hospital*. (Abbott 2001)

Talking about example (12), Abbott argues, "for a long time after the invention of elevators, it must have been customary for buildings to have only one" elevator.

---

[6] Some previous studies, including Abbott (2001), have often adopted the term "non-unique definites" to refer to definite descriptions whose referents cannot be uniquely identified by the interlocutor. However, we prefer the term "configurational uses of nouns," as used by Löbner (1985), or "definites in configurational use," because, as we will see later, the referent of a singular definite of this type will in fact be considered to be a unique element (or a unique role) within a cognitive frame.

The same holds true for electric lights in example (13): it should be the case that there has always been only one electric light in a room. This explanation also holds true for *the bank* in example (14) and for *the hospital* in example (15). Abbott identifies such definites as "traditionally unique items." She confirms that her approach does not essentially contradict Epstein's frame analysis. The reason why Birner and Ward reject the frame analysis is that, nowadays, a city generally has many parks, many hospitals, etc. According to Abbott, however, the frame analysis is effective in the explanation of this phenomenon because "if we go back to when these usages were first being established, it may have been true that there was typically only one of these things per town, or at least one salient thing for any group of people."

1.5 Löbner (1985, 1998)

Löbner (1985) distinguishes three types of nouns: sortal, relational, and functional nouns. "Sortal nouns classify objects, whereas relational nouns describe objects as standing in a certain relation to others." "Functional nouns relate objects unambiguously (or one-to-one) to others," while "the referent (or value) of a functional noun depends, in general, on the situation referred to." This logical-semantic distinction of nouns is significant for the analysis of definites. According to Löbner (1985), "the meaning of the definite article consists in the indication that the noun is to be taken as a functional concept." Löbner (1998) also argues that "the head noun of an associative anaphora NP is taken as an FC2" (i. e., a functional concept that has both a situational and a possessor argument) and the FC2 interpretation of the head noun yields a one-to-one relation between the referent of the definite associative anaphora and the possessor (or the trigger), hence warranting the "uniqueness" of the referent. The relation between the referent of a definite associative anaphora and the possessor is based on general knowledge, or more specifically, the discourse referent network, which constitutes a "frame." Löbner's (1998) frame concept is inspired by Barsalou's frame, which we will examine later.

1.6 Perspective

Our fundamental claim concerning the singular definite is as follows: all singular definites are explained with the uniqueness theory, and even singular definites, which do not seem to have any uniquely identifiable referent (i. e., "non-unique definites" according to the terminology developed in some previous research), satisfy the uniqueness condition within a cognitive frame. However, we will argue that the cognitive frame involved in several examples such as *the hospital* or *the bank* in examples (5), (6), (11), and (15) above is not a fixed idea such as a "city" frame, as Epstein or Abbott claim. Birner and Ward observe that the singular definites in configurational use are generally used to refer to locations. We shall presently illustrate why singular definites of this type often – but not always – refer to locations.

The zero article plays a part in some varieties of English. We notice the frequent appearance of the word "hospital" without an article in British English, for instance, in expressions such as "*in hospital, go to hospital, leave hospital, be taken to hospital,* and *be airlifted to hospital*," whereas the definite article in American English is often retained in the same expressions, as in "*in the hospital, go to the hospital, leave the hospital, be taken to the hospital,* and *be airlifted to the hospital.*" Our analysis of this point is founded on reflection about data derived from the American English style. Furthermore, as it has already been pointed out in some previous research, even in American English, bare nouns are used in several idioms such as "*go to school*" or "*go to church.*" This paper, however, will not deal with the problem of bare nouns, but focus on the opposition of singular definites with singular indefinites.

2 The unique role within a cognitive frame

2.1 Cognitive frame

A cognitive frame is a network of knowledge that connects various events, situations, persons, objects, or their characters and the entire spectrum of relations among these elements. Cognitive frames were first conceived of by Minsky (1974, 1977) and Schank & Abelson (1977) within the domain of artificial intelligence, and then applied to the domain of cognitive science. Our notion of cognitive frame is inspired by Fauconnier's (1984, 1994) mental space theory and Barsalou's (1992) frame theory. Barsalou's frames are based on an attribute-value structure, within which attributes are figuring in the scheme. Barsalou's "attribute" is equivalent to "dimension," "variable," "slot," or "role" under other theories. In this paper, we adopt the term "role." Barsalou also assumes that "frames are dynamic relational structures whose form is flexible and context dependent" (Barsalou 1992:21) and "frames can represent exemplars and propositions, prototypes and membership, subordinates and taxonomies" (*Ibid.*:21) as well as "conceptual combinations, event sequences, rules, and plans" (*Ibid.*:21). We illustrate a simplified version of a cognitive frame for "wedding" in Figure 1.

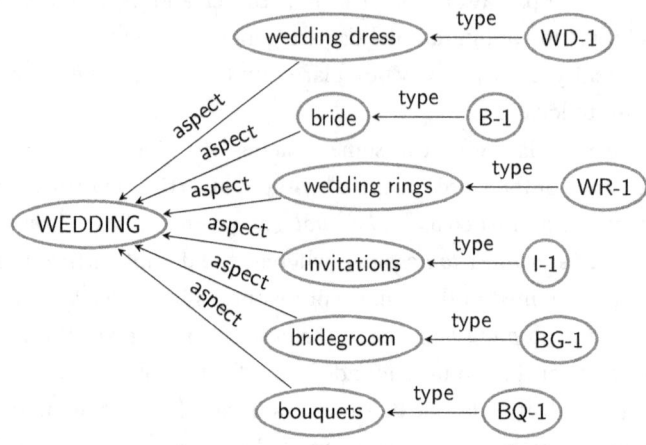

Figure 1: Wedding frame

As shown in Figure 1, the "wedding" frame has a central node labeled with "wedding," and nodes for each "role" (i. e., "attribute" according to Barsalou's terminology), more specifically, "bride" and "bridegroom," "wedding dress," "wedding rings," "bouquets," "invitations," and so forth, and nodes for its "value." The links between the central node and the nodes for roles are assigned general labels such as "aspect," and the links between the nodes for roles and those for values are assigned general labels such as "type." As Löbner (1998) notices, the roles figuring in cognitive frames are functional concepts. Thus, a cognitive frame, in the case of definite associative anaphoras, guarantees the connection between an anchor (which is represented by a central node) and its roles, hence warranting the use of a definite article for each role. Example (16) shows how the cognitive frame for "wedding" works in discourse.

(16) A : How are you?
       B : I'm fine. And you? Have you already written *the invitations*? And have you thought about *the bouquets*?
       A : Yes, but I haven't chosen *the dress* yet…

B : Really? And *the wedding rings*? You've got them already?
A : Yes, Benjamin, he does everything very quickly.

Example (16) is a conversation between two friends, who met on the street, and one of whom would soon get married. Even if none of them referred to the context of a wedding, they could use definite descriptions such as *the invitations, the bouquets, the dress,* and *the wedding rings* at first mention. The use of these definites is possible because speaker B knew well about her friend's wedding and they had in common the cognitive frame for a wedding. When a wedding is presented explicitly or implicitly, the wedding frame is brought forth, and the roles that are a part of this frame are activated and ready to be mentioned with a definite article. Each role within a cognitive frame can correspond to various values, namely various individuals in the real world.

As Barsalou (1992) asserts, we share with each other both cognitive frames founded on an event or a situation, such as a "wedding" frame or an "anniversary" frame, and cognitive frames characterized by an individual or an object, such as the "house" frame, as illustrated in example (17).

(17) [An invited guest, to whom a couple is showing their new house, asks] Where is the kitchen?

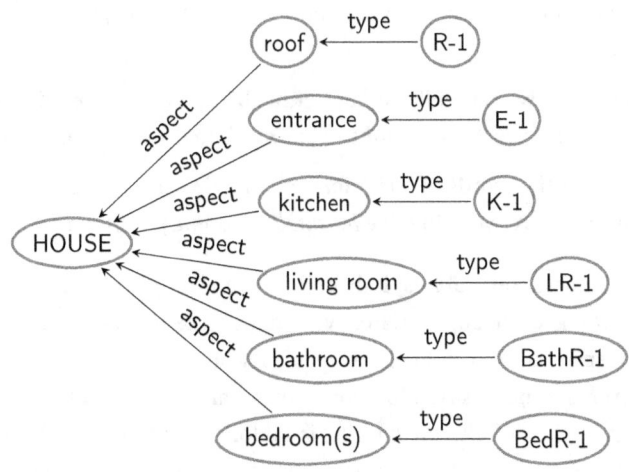

Figure 2: House frame

In example (17), the guest can justly say *the kitchen*, using a definite article, at first mention, because as shown in Figure 2, the "house" frame contains as "roles" a roof, an entrance, a kitchen, a living room, a bathroom, (a) bedroom(s), and so forth. Hence, in a situation where the "house" frame is evoked or activated, we can employ a definite article without an explicit antecedent to mention the roles with an existential presupposition in the "house" frame.

It must also be mentioned that cognitive frames are culturally and socially defined, and the elements contained in a cognitive frame may vary across different cultures and languages and are subject to personal variations.

2.2 Flexibility of cognitive frames: which of the cognitive frames is inferred?

Singular definite descriptions without a unique referent explicitly introduced in the context (i.e., singular definites in configurational use) are considered to perform a unique role within a cognitive frame. The approach in terms of cognitive frames concerning this issue has already been adopted by Epstein and other researchers; however, we will propose another interpretation of cognitive frames for several instances that Epstein (1999) and Abbott (2001) have analyzed.

Compare examples (18), (19), and (20) to ascertain the cognitive frames that permit the use of the definite *the hospital*.

(18) In Paris, I caught the measles and I went to the hospital to receive treatment.

(19) [In Paris, a woman talks about her husband who is an engineer.]
He is going {*to *the hospital*/to *a hospital*} to do some wiring.

(20) [In Paris: the words of a member of a movie camera crew]
Last week, we went to {**the hospital*/*a hospital*} to film a scene.

There are, of course, several hospitals in Paris. In example (18), the singular definite *the hospital* is quite appropriate, even though the hearer cannot identify the particular hospital in Paris where the speaker visited. In examples (19) and (20), too, the hearer is in no position to know which particular hospital is being talked about; however, the definite *the hospital* is no longer adequate, and the indefinite *a hospital* is obligatory instead. Where does this difference in the acceptability of the definite *the hospital* stem from? The answer lies in the different cognitive frames evoked in each example.

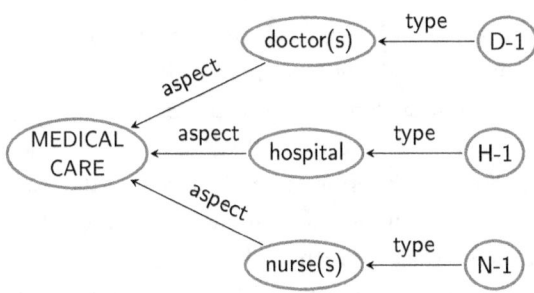

Figure 3: Medical care frame

In example (18), the context of "catching the measles" brings about a "medical care" frame, which includes "doctor(s)," "nurse(s)," "hospital," etc. In the context of this "medical care" frame, the hospital plays a unique role. On the other hand, in example (19), it is a "wiring" frame that is evoked, which comprises "wiring diagram," "screwdriver(s)," "plier(s)," etc., as stereotypical constituents; "hospital" does not figure in this frame. Similarly, in example (20), it is a "movie filming" frame that is called up, which has "director," "cameraperson(s)," "projector(s)," "scenario," "actor(s)," etc., as stereotypical roles, but not "hospital." In other words, there is no intrinsic relation between a hospital and a wiring repair job or the filming of a movie. That is why we cannot use the definite expression *the hospital* in examples (19) and (20). Hence, we may conclude that the cognitive frame supporting the felicitous use of the definite *the hospital* in example (18) is not a "city" frame but a "medical care" frame or a "surgery" frame, which involves "doctor(s)," "nurse(s)," "hospital," etc., as roles.

Now, let us compare example (21) with (22) and example (23) with (24). Suppose that, in the context of all these examples, there are several banks and swimming pools in the city where the speakers live.

(21)   I'll stop at *the bank* to withdraw some money.

(22)   I'll go {*to *the bank*/to *a bank*} for a job interview.

(23)   It's so hot out today! I'll go to *the swimming pool* this afternoon.

(24)　[on cell phone] Listen, my darling, I'm at work. I must go to deliver a pizza {to *the swimming pool/to a swimming pool} and I don't really have time to talk to you now…

In example (21), the speaker can use the definite description *the bank* without having a particular bank in mind, and it will not matter whether the hearer cannot identify the bank in question. Since the cognitive frame for "withdrawing money" typically includes "bank," "cash card," "ATM," etc., as constituent elements, the definite description *the bank* performs a unique role in this cognitive frame. In example (22), however, the use of the definite *the bank* is not appropriate if the hearer does not know exactly which bank the speaker is talking about; this is because the cognitive frame in question is that of "a job interview," and a job interview frame does not presume a "bank." That is why we use the indefinite *a bank* and not *the bank*. The same argument can be applied to examples (23) and (24). In example (23), the use of the definite *the swimming pool* is quite natural since the speaker is going to the pool to swim, and it is a perfectly acceptable usage even if the hearer does not know which particular swimming pool is being referred to, and even if the speaker himself/herself does not know which swimming pool he/she is going to. Since the cognitive frame for "swimming" typically contains a "swimming pool," the definite *the swimming pool* performs a unique role within this frame. On the other hand, if the speaker in example (24) is working in a pizzeria and if he/she is going to a swimming pool to deliver a pizza, he/she does not use the definite *the swimming pool*; instead, he/she uses the indefinite *a swimming pool*. A swimming pool is a place for people to swim, and it has nothing to do with the delivery of pizza. The context in example (24) calls up a cognitive frame for "delivery of pizza," and this frame does not have "swimming pool" as one of its typical elements; thus, the use of "swimming pool" with the definite article is unacceptable because "swimming pool" does not play a unique role.

Through comparing the given examples, we may reasonably conclude that the acceptability of configurational uses of nouns such as *the hospital* or *the bank* is not due to the "city" frame, as Epstein or Abbott claim, but owing to frames such as a "medical care" frame, which contains "hospital" as a unique role, or a "withdrawing money" frame, which contains "bank" as a unique element.

2.3 Location nouns

Birner & Ward (1994) observe that definite descriptions in configurational use with singular countable head nouns are generally used in references to locations[7], and Abbott (2001) agrees. Nevertheless, Epstein (1999) disagrees, and so do we. Indeed, most of the definites in configurational use in the examples that we have examined thus far are location nouns such as "hospital," "bank," and "swimming pool." This is because locations such as hospitals, banks, swimming pools, post offices, cinemas, and pharmacies are part of the services we seek in everyday life, and consequently, these locations are quite naturally connected to the cognitive frames that are recalled when these services are mentioned or suggested. For instance, in banks, we deposit or withdraw money; we go to the swimming pool for a swim, not for the delivery of a pizza. In hospitals, we undergo medical treatment or an operation or we may visit someone there. People, in general, do not go to a hospital to repair wires or to film movie scenes. Similarly, our usual activity in post offices is to buy stamps and send letters or parcels. In other words, information about the relation between these locations and their utilities is constructed and crystallized in the form of knowledge networks, otherwise known as cognitive frames. That is why locations are quite likely to figure as stereotypical elements and function in unique ways within cognitive frames.[8] Another reason why definites in configurational use frequently represent locations is that information concerning a location appears, in many cases, in the background of a discourse, but rarely as its theme. That is, the identification of the location is not necessarily essential in the discourse concerned. The configurational use of nouns is acceptable only when there is no necessity to identify the referent of this definite in the discourse in question (cf. Birner & Ward[9]). This is because

---

[7] Birner & Ward (1994) maintain that non-unique definite descriptions ("definite descriptions in configurational use" or "configurational uses of nouns" in our terms) generally occur with one of the following three types of nouns: mass nouns (*the milk*), plural nouns (e.g., Pass *the rolls*), and location nouns.

[8] It is plausible to assume that a location noun by itself can evoke some cognitive frame. However, it is not the simple use of a location noun that permits the employment of a definite article with this location noun. For example, in example (20), we may suppose that the noun "hospital" evokes a "hospital" frame, but this is not the frame where the referent of *the hospital* is to be anchored to; the entire context in example (20) triggers off a "movie filming" frame, and therefore, the definite *the hospital* is irrelevant. The use of the definite *the hospital* inevitably needs to be anchored in a cognitive frame that is related to the functions of a hospital.

[9] We do not agree with Birner & Ward (1994) that the uniqueness condition cannot account for all uses of the singular definite article. Nevertheless, Birner and Ward appropriately claim that

a role within a cognitive frame must be an element that is neither differentiated nor individualized in context: a "role" should be able to take different values in the real world; therefrom, its name "role" originated.

Now, consider another set of examples involving location nouns. Examples (25) and (26) describe a scene wherein one person calls up his friend's cell phone. The caller asks his/her friend about his/her whereabouts, and the friend answers him/her. We may suppose that there are many hospitals in the city where these two people live.

(25) a. I'm in *the hospital*. / I'm at *the hospital*.
      b. I'm in *a hospital*. / I'm at *a hospital*.

(26) a. *I'm <u>in front of</u> *the hospital*.
      b. I'm <u>in front of</u> *a hospital*.

It is possible to use a definite article in "I'm in the hospital," as shown in example (25)[10], even if the hearer cannot identify the particular hospital in question. In example (26), however, if the hearer is not in a position to identify the hospital in question, it is unacceptable to employ a definite article, as in "I'm in front of the hospital"; instead, we use an indefinite article and say "I'm in front of a hospital." What, then, is the basis for such a usage?

Note that there are certain nuanced differences in example (25) between the usage of the definite article, as in (25a) "I'm in the hospital," and the usage of an indefinite article, as in (25b) "I'm in a hospital." The use of the definite *the hospital* implies that the speaker is in a hospital to receive medical treatment or consult a doctor (in "I'm *in* the hospital") or to visit someone who has been hospitalized (in "I'm *at* the hospital"). There are no such implications in the use of the indefinite *a hospital*. The utterance "I'm in a hospital" simply means that the speaker is in a hospital for a reason that has no relation to the function of a hospital—to deliver flowers, perhaps, or to repair elevators. We are fairly certain that the use of the definite *the hospital* triggers a cognitive frame that inevitably implies elements

---

"whenever the referent is not uniquely identifiable on the basis of the definite NP, it must be both undifferentiated and not relevantly differentiable in context." (Birner & Ward 1994)

[10] The interpretation of example (25a) varies depending on whether "in" or "at" is used. The utterance "I'm *in* the hospital" implies that the speaker is in the hospital as a patient to receive medical treatment, while the utterance "I'm *at* the hospital" means that the speaker is at the hospital as a visitor: he/she is visiting someone who has been hospitalized.

such as "consultation," "medical treatment," "operation," or "visit to a sick person." On the other hand, the act of being in front of a hospital in example (26) hardly evokes the functions that are attributable to a hospital. If someone is *inside* a hospital, we are more liable to imagine that the person is there to receive medical care or to visit a sick friend. But if someone is *in front of* a hospital, we do not necessarily infer that this person is on his/her way to consult a doctor. That is why no cognitive frame that contains "hospital" is activated to permit the use of the definite *the hospital* in example (26). These pieces of data demonstrate that the appropriateness of the definite *the hospital* in configurational use depends not on whether the definite designates a location, but on whether the definite is used in a context in which an appropriate cognitive frame with "hospital" is evoked.

We will now present obvious examples to demonstrate that singular definites in configurational use are not limited to location nouns.

(27)　　No problem, I'll get *the maid* to do it. (Epstein 1999)

(28)　　Waiter, I demand to see *the menu*! (*Ibid.*)

(29)　　A : I'd like a cappuccino, but I don't know if they have it…
　　　　B : You have only to ask *the waiter*.

(30)　　A : I'd like a cappuccino, but I don't know if they have it…
　　　　B : *You have only to ask *the waiter with blue eyes*.

As Epstein (1999) explains, the sentence in example (27) with the singular definite *the maid* may be used either in a hotel or in a home where there are several maids; he argues, "(28) would be felicitous in a situation where both the speaker and the waiter can see an entire stack of menus on the counter." Similarly, the use of the singular definite *the waiter* in example (29) is quite natural even if there are several waiters working in this café at the moment of utterance. However, none of these definites in configurational use refers to a location. The acceptability of the definites *the menu* and *the waiter* is explained both by attributing it to the presence of some cognitive frames such as an "order in a café" frame, which includes "menu" and "waiter" as a unique role, and by attributing it to the fact that these definites are elements that are neither relevantly differentiated nor individualized in context. Therefore, the use of the definite "the waiter *with blue eyes*" in example (30) is not adequate as a configurational use of nouns.

There is another well-known type of definite in configurational use that does not designate a location.

(31)   He tripped on *the leg of the chair*.

(32)   After landing, I got on *the wing of the plane* and looked up to the sky.

In general, a chair has four legs and a plane has two wings, and yet, the use of the singular definite article for the head noun in *the leg of the chair* or *the wing of the plane* is not paradoxical in the examples above. As Löbner (1998) and Barker (2005) notice, possessive definite descriptions can be quite often used "in contexts in which more than one object satisfies the content of the description" (Barker 2005). Barker refers to this type of possessive definite description as a "possessive weak definite." Namely, possessive weak definites belong among the definites in configurational use that we have discussed thus far. Since the problem of possessive weak definites has been fully discussed in previous research like by Löbner (1985, 1998) and Barker (2005), we will not go too far into this matter here, but we would simply point out that as shown in examples (31) and (32), there are many instances of possessive weak definites, that is, possessive definite descriptions in configurational use, that do not refer to locations.

2.4   Definite associative anaphora

It is quite evident that there is a certain affinity between the definite in configurational use and the definite associative anaphora, because both definites have relevance to some cognitive frame. In this section, we will illustrate their resemblance in addition to a slight difference between them.

The configurational use of definite descriptions is felicitous when the noun functions as a unique role within a certain cognitive frame, which is activated by the linguistic context or the immediate situation. There are occasions when an anterior context explicitly introduces some cognitive frame or others with a linguistic expression, but it is not always the case. Even without any obvious expression that triggers a cognitive frame, we employ a singular definite description when the hearer is supposed to (re)construct the cognitive frame in question that has a particular noun with a unique role. Examples (33) and (34) report the utterances of a man who has arrived late for his appointment and is offering an excuse after a brief greeting.

(33) I'm sorry, but {the bus/the taxi} had engine trouble.

(34) I'm sorry, my car sideswiped {*the bus/*the taxi/a bus/a taxi}.

While offering an excuse for being late, the speaker in example (33) may use the definite *the bus* or *the taxi*, whereas the speaker in example (34) uses the indefinite *a bus* or *a taxi*. Where does this difference in acceptability of the definite description come from? Our explanation is as follows: if someone arrives behind schedule, out of breath, and mentions "the bus" or "the taxi," the situation forces us to interpret this bus or this taxi as the bus or the taxi that the speaker took. It means that the hearer in example (33) reconstructs a cognitive frame of "traffic" or "transportation" containing "a bus" or "a taxi" as a unique role. The bus or the taxi that the speaker had employed in reality corresponds to the bus or the taxi that exists within this cognitive frame. On the other hand, there is nothing in example (34) that activates a cognitive frame of "traffic" or "transportation" involving a bus or a taxi as a unique role, which would surely bring about a minor collision. In other words, when we drive a car, we do not necessarily have an accident with a car or a taxi. Therefore, there is no existential presupposition of a unique bus or taxi playing a role within a cognitive frame; the speaker thus inevitably uses an indefinite description, "a bus" or "a taxi." Reconsider examples (33) and (34) from a different viewpoint. In example (34), if the speaker uses a definite description such as *the bus* or *the taxi*, saying "I'm sorry, my car sideswiped the bus" or "I'm sorry, my car sideswiped the taxi," the hearer will ask him "Which bus?" or "Which taxi?" On the other hand, even though the speaker uses the definite *the bus* or *the taxi*, the hearer in example (33) will not pose this question because the definite *the bus* or *the taxi* indeed functions as a unique role within the cognitive frame. This fact shows, again, that the singular definite description as a unique role within a frame is employed in a context where the identity of the referent does not come into question.

As Du Bois (1980), Löbner (1985), Epstein (1999), and others have noted, the mechanism of the uniqueness of an element in a frame resembles the mechanism of associative anaphora. Consider examples (35), (36), and (37).

(35) I caught *a taxi* in front of the library. *The driver* was very friendly.

(36) I am terribly afraid of going to *the dentist*. *The drill* terrifies me...

(37) I tried to *hang myself*... but *the chair* didn't want to fall.

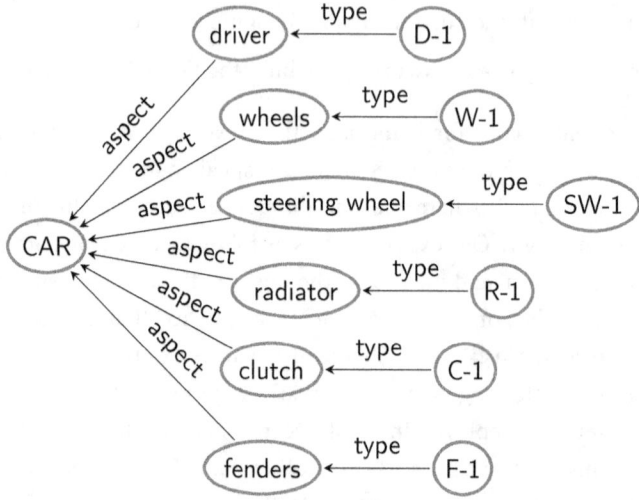

Figure 4: Car frame

In associative anaphora, the anaphoric relation between the antecedent and the anaphoric expression is frequently established by some cognitive frame. In the cognitive frame of "taxi" or "car," shown in Figure 4, we can evoke elements such as "driver," "steering wheel," "radiator," and "clutch," and this "car" frame in example (35) permits the associative anaphora between "a taxi" and "the driver." The anaphoric relation in example (36) between "the dentist" and "the drill" is founded in a "dentist" frame, which includes elements such as "assistant(s)," "chair," and "drill." The anaphoric relation in example (37) between the contextual antecedent *hang oneself* and its anaphoric expression "the chair" is also guaranteed by the cognitive frame of "suicide by hanging oneself," which contains "rope" and "chair" as stereotypical components. In these three examples concerning definite associative anaphora, it is a cognitive frame that appeared in the previous context that connects the antecedent with its anaphoric expression. In the case of the configurational uses of definite descriptions, there is no antecedent or no cognitive frame introduced explicitly in the discourse, but the definite in configurational use performs a unique role in some cognitive frames that are supported by the situation of utterance. Even if there is no explicit antecedent or no expression introducing a cognitive frame, the configurational use of nouns is validated through the same mechanism as in the case of associative anaphora.

3 Conclusion

In this paper, we have demonstrated that the use of definite descriptions, which has been considered by some researchers to be highly resistant to any explanation with the uniqueness theory, stems from certain unique roles within cognitive frames evoked by linguistic contexts, circumstances of utterances, or the immediate situation. Epstein (1999) has already adopted the frame approach in his analysis of the definite, but it seems to us that there is a misunderstanding about the nature of a cognitive frame for the configurational use of some definites such as *the hospital* or *the bank*. We have argued that the cognitive frame supporting the acceptable use of the definite *the hospital* is not the "city" frame but a "medical care" frame, or a "visit to a sick person" frame, and so forth. The definites in configurational use often – but not always – refers to a location, as previous researchers have noticed, and we have explained the reason for this high frequency of location nouns in definites of this type: locations such as hospitals, banks, and post offices are related with the services we seek in our daily life; the general use of common services creates certain cognitive frames and typical roles associated with these frames, which supports the configurational uses of nouns.

One of the most essential characteristics of the definite description is that it represents a referent that can be uniquely determined either on the basis of a cognitive frame, on the basis of a discourse domain, or by shared knowledge. Some previous studies on this subject have devoted too much attention to the identification of the referent in reality. However, what is important in the study of the definite description is not to identify the referent in reality, but to discover the cognitive frame, the discourse domain, or the shared knowledge on which the interpretation of the definite description is founded. In the configurational uses of definite descriptions, it is a cognitive frame or knowledge network that serves as the primary domain for possible interpretations of the definite description.

References

Abbott, B. 1999. Support for a unique theory of definite descriptions. In T. Matthews & D. Strolovitch (eds.), *Proceedings from Semantics and Linguistic Theory IX*, 1–15. Ithaca: Cornell University.

Abbott, B. 2001. Definiteness and identification in English. In N. T. Enikö (ed.), *Pragmatics in 2000: Selected Papers from the 7th International Pragmatics Conference*, Vol. 2, 1–15. Antwerp: International Pragmatics Association.

Abbott, B. 2006. Definite and indefinite. In K. Brown (ed.), *The Encyclopedia of Language and Linguistics*, 2nd ed., Vol. 3, 392–399. Oxford: Elsevier.

Barker, C. 2005. Possessive weak definites. In J.-Y. Kim, Y. Lander & B. H. Partee (eds.), *Possessives and Beyond: Semantics and Syntax*, 89–113. Amherst, MA: GLSA Publications.

Barsalou, L. 1992. Frames, concepts, and conceptual fields. In A. Lehrer & E. F. Kittay (eds.), *Frames, Fields, and Contrasts: New Essays in Semantic and Lexical Organization*, 21–74. Hillsdale, NJ: Lawrence Erlbaum Associates.

Birner, B. & G. Ward, 1994. Uniqueness, familiarity, and the definite article in English. *BLS 20*, 93–102.

Christophersen, P. 1939. *The Articles: A Study of their Theory and Use in English*. Copenhagen: Munksgaard.

Du Bois, J. W. 1980. Beyond definiteness: the trace of identity in discourse. In W. L. Chafe (ed.), *The Pear Stories. Cognitive, Cultural, and Linguistic Aspects of Narrative Production*, 203–74. Norwood: Ablex.

Ducrot, O. 1972. *Dire et ne pas dire*. Paris: Hermann.

Epstein, R. 1998. Reference and definite referring expressions. *Pragmatics and Cognition* 6 (1/2), 189–207.

Epstein, R. 1999. Roles and non-unique definites. *BLS 25*. 122–133.

Fauconnier, G. 1984. *Espaces mentaux*. Paris: Les éditions du Minuit.

Fauconnier, G. 1994. *Mental Spaces: Aspects of Meaning Construction in Natural Language*. Cambridge: Cambridge University Press.

Gundel, J. K., N. Hedberg & R. Zacharski 1993. Cognitive status and the form of referring expressions in discourse. *Language* 69. 274–307.

Gundel, J. K., N. Hedberg & R. Zacharski 2001. Definite descriptions and cognitive status in English: why accommodation is unnecessary. *English Language and Linguistics* 5-2. 273–295.

References

Hawkins, J. A. 1978. *Definiteness and Indefiniteness: A Study in Reference and Grammaticality Prediction*. London: Croom Helm.

Heim, I. 1983. File change semantics and the familiarity theory of definiteness. In R. Bäuerle, Ch. Schwarze & A. von Stechow (eds.), *Meaning, Use, and Interpretation of Language*, 164–189. New York: Walter de Gruyter.

Kadmon, N. 1990. Uniqueness. *Linguistics and Philosophy* 13. 273–324.

Karttunen, L. 1976. Discourse referents. In J. D. McCawley (ed.), *Syntax and Semantics 7: Notes from the Linguistic Underground*, 363–386. New York: Academic Press.

Lambrecht, K. 1994. *Information Structure and Sentence Form: Topic, Focus, and the Mental Representations of Discourse Referents*. Cambridge: Cambridge University Press.

Löbner, S. 1985. Definites. *Journal of Semantics* 4, 279–326.

Löbner, S. 1998. Definite associative anaphora. In S. Botley (ed.), *Approaches to discourse anaphora: proceedings of DAARC96 – Discourse anaphora and Resolution Colloquium*. UCREL Technical Papers Series, Vol. 8. Lancaster University.

Minsky, M. 1977. Frame-system theory. In P. N. Johnson-Laird & P. C. Wason (eds.), *Thinking. Reading in Cognitive Science*, 355–376. Cambridge: Cambridge University Press.

Récanati, F. 1996. Domains of discourse. *Linguistics and Philosophy* 19, 445–475.

Russell, B. 1905. On denoting. *Mind* 14, 479–493.

Schank, R. C. & R. P. Abelson 1977. Scripts, plans and knowledge. In P. N. Johnson-Laird & P. C. Wason (eds.), *Thinking. Reading in Cognitive Science*, 421–432. Cambridge: Cambridge University Press.

Author

Ryo ODA
Kwansei Gakuin University
ryocat@hotmail.com

FrameNet, Barsalou Frames and the Case of Associative Anaphora

Alexander Ziem

Abstract
This paper introduces and compares the currently most important approaches to frames: the FrameNet project pursued at the 'International Computer Science Institute' in Berkeley and Barsalou's cognitive frame theory supplemented by Löbner's concept type theory. On the basis of empirical findings of a case study on associative anaphora, it is argued that both approaches complement each other in several respects. While, for example, Barsalou's theory concentrates on sortal concepts, disregarding semantic and syntactic valences of each word in each of its senses, FrameNet focuses on relational concepts, particularly verbs and deverbal nouns. In contrast to frames as described in terms of valency patterns within FrameNet, linguistic approaches drawing on Barsalou's theory emphasize that frames are embedded structures having a rich internal structure. By comparison, serious shortcomings and drawbacks of each approach become apparent.

1 Introduction

The notion *frame* goes back to Minsky's influential paper on knowledge representation (Minsky, 1975), and since then it has been a central, but also ambiguous and controversial, concept in many disciplines (for an overview cf. Ziem, 2008, pp. 13-35), including cognitive semantics (e.g., Fillmore, 1976, 1977, 1985, 2006), computational linguistics (Petersen, 2007/2015, among others), artificial intelligence (e.g., Charniak, 1976; Hayes, 1980), cognitive psychology (e.g., Schank & Abelson, 1977; Barsalou, 1992), and Media Sciences (Scheufele, 2003; Matthes, 2007). In spite of the vivid discussions in the 1980s, in current research the frame concept seems to have become less attractive. However, there are two exceptions. On the one hand, Fillmore's early account of semantic frames has been put into practice within FrameNet, a large-scale computational lexicography project hosted at the University of Berkeley, California (for an overview cf. Boas, 2005; Fillmore, Johnson & Petruck, 2003). Similarly, also Barsalou's frame theory has recently been readdressed and further developed, namely in the research projects "Frames and functional concepts" (FOR 600) and "The Structure of Representations in Language, Cognition, and Science" (SFB 991), both hosted at the University of Düsseldorf.

The starting point of the present paper is the fact that both approaches seem to be based on a mutually shared definition of frames. While FrameNet sees frames as a "script-like conceptual structure that describes a particular type of situation, object or event, along with its participants and props" (Ruppenhofer et al., 2010, p. 5), Barsalou (1992, p. 21) proposes that "frames are dynamic structures whose form is flexible and context-dependent". However, significant differences relate to the theoretical prerequisites of each approach. Barsalou's frame model is cognitive in nature; it addresses frames as *mental* entities. FrameNet, on the other hand, is first and foremost a *linguistic* approach to lexical meaning grounded in the concept of semantic and syntactic valency. As a result, both approaches differ substantially in the way their methodology is put into practice.

Taking so-called associative anaphora (henceforth: AA) as a 'test case', this paper aims at providing a theoretical and methodological comparison of the two currently most sophisticated approaches to frames. An associative anaphor establishes indirect reference to a previously introduced discourse referent (e.g., *key* → *car*, cf. Ex. 1). Focusing on the resolution of indirect text reference, the present paper addresses the following kinds of issues, among others: How does FrameNet and a Barsalou-inspired approach to frames account for reference resolution in the case of AA? Do both approaches adequately describe and explain the phenomenon addressed? And most importantly: Given the results of the case study, what are the assets and drawbacks of each approach? Is it possible to (partly) integrate both approaches in one another, yielding a more comprehensive frame theory?

The paper is structured as follows. In Section 2, I will briefly introduce the most important properties of associative anaphora. This section also provides a preliminary typology of AAs, including definite associative anaphors with either verbal or nominal antecedents as its most important subclasses. Section 3 sketches out Barsalou's approach to frames and its extensions yielded in the research project FOR 600 insofar as it is relevant for applications to DAAs. Likewise, Section 4 introduces the methodology offered by FrameNet in order to investigate DAAs. Finally, Section 5 summarizes and compares the results. Based on these findings, it draws some conclusions pointing to promising perspectives for future frame-semantic research.

2   The case of associative anaphora

Following the standard definition, an AA, sometimes also called "bridging anaphor" (Clark, 1975) or subsumed under "indirect anaphor" (Schwarz, 2000) is a first-mentioned use of a definite or indefinite expression that establishes indirect reference to a previously introduced discourse referent in a text (Löbner, 1998). In (1), for example, the reader mentally creates a concept for the anaphoric NP *the key* that includes information about the previously introduced discourse referent *car*, yielding the more complex concept "Peter's car key". The possessor argument of *key* is saturated with conceptual information that the antecedent *his car* provides.

(1)   Peter walked to his car [antecedent]. He had forgotten **the key** [associative anaphor].

When a referential use of an NP prompts the reader to construe a concept for this entity, the lexical frame is subsequently enriched by idiosyncratic information either provided by the context or inferred from background knowledge. In the context of (1), for example, the concept associated with *key* indirectly relates to the NP *his car*. More specifically, *the key* is interpreted as the key of Peter's car. Note that associative anaphors have no deictic quality; in order to determine the reference of the noun *key*, for example, a conceptual representation of the respective referent is construed solely by means of information provided by the discourse referent *car* and the AA. It is thus the linguistic and not the situational context of the anaphorically used definite NP *the key* that helps to identify the referent of the NP.

To gain a deeper understanding of forms and functions of AAs in texts, it is useful to distinguish between different types of AAs (for a typology based on so-called "activation types" cf. Schwarz, 2000). First, a frequently found distinguishing criterion relates to definiteness/indefiniteness of AAs.

(2)   They passed an old monastery. **A window** was smashed.

Indefinite associative anaphors, such as exemplified in (2), are exceptional; the majority of AAs belong to the class of definite associative anaphors (henceforth: DAAs). This class comprises four important subclasses, exemplified in (3)-(6). As the examples (3) and (4) indicate, antecedents of DAAs may be verbal or nominal. Note that the class of DAAs with nominal antecedents comprise not only deverbal nouns, like *search* in (4), which are inherently relational, but also sortal nouns, like *house* in (5), which lack this feature (for the distinction of noun types cf. Horn & Kimm, 2014, also: Löbner, 1998).

(3)   Peter bought a new Mercedes. **The price** was lower than expected.
(4)   The search lingers on, but **the key** remains lost.
(5)   They reached Peter's house. **The window pane in the door** had been smashed.

Another distinguishing criterion concerns the kind of reference to be established between AAs and their antecedents (Greber, 1993; Kleiber, 2001). Associative-anaphoric reference may be direct or indirect. Indirect DAAs are characterized by nominal DAAs whose referents are not indirectly anchored in the concept associated with the antecedent but in a sub- or superordinate concept. In the case of (6), for example, the associative anaphor *the menu* is not interpreted as the waiter's but as that of the restaurant in which the waiter is serving.

(6)   The waiter came to our table. He had forgotten **the menu**.

In this view, DAAs with verbal antecedents also belong to the class of indirect DAAs since they are indirectly anchored in a concept associated with the antecedent's concept. In (3), for example, the DAA *the price* is not the price of buying but the purchase price of the product. Table 1 summarizes the subclasses of AAs mentioned so far. In the following I will concentrate on DAAs as the prototype of AAs.

In the case of DAA, it is the definiteness of the NP that triggers a referential interpretation of the NP. Discussing different theories of definiteness, Lyons (1999) distinguishes between (a) the familiarity approach (exemplified in Heim, 1982) which assumes that the definite article exhibits familiarity to both speaker and

Table 1: Types of associative anaphora (AA)

Type of AA	Example	Referential properties of AA
Direct definite associative anaphora	Peter walked to his car. He had forgotten **the key**.	Relational, unique reference of nominal antecedent
Direct indefinite associative anaphora	Peter passed the house. **A window** was smashed.	Relational, non-unique reference of nominal antecedent
Indirect definite associative anaphora 1. with a nominal antecedent 2. with a verbal antecedent	The waiter came to our table. He had forgotten **the menu**. Marie left Berlin yesterday. **The train** was late again.	Relational, unique 'indirect' reference(transitive verb)

hearer, and (b) the identifiability approach which hypothesizes that the definite article indicates that the addressee is able to identify the referent on the basis of given information. In either approach, the definite article in (1) gives rise to a referential reading of *key* in such a way that it is interpreted as Peter's car key. Analogously, in (2) the DAA unambiguously denotes one particular concept that serves as a semantic role of the verbal antecedent. This brief description of DAAs suffices to test and compare in Section 2 FrameNet and Barsalou frames regarding their descriptive adequacy.

Traditional approaches to AA suffer from three shortcomings. However, as I will argue later, a frame theory that incorporates insights from both Barsalou's and FrameNet's approach might be capable of overcoming these deficits. First, traditional approaches fail to explain the 'felicity conditions' required for anaphoric-reference resolution. In his still influential approach, Hawkins (1978, p. 107), for example, hypothesizes that frequent co-occurrences of the anaphoric and antecedent expression license anaphoric reference. The frequency condition, however, is not met in many attested examples of associative anaphors (Löbner, 1998, p. 10). Second, it is not clear how contextually 'enriched' anaphoric meanings emerge. While Heim's formal approach assumes an additional mechanism, namely "accommodation" (Heim, 1982, p. 370), Schwarz (1996) postulates very abstract semantic constraints. Still, it is anything but obvious how these semantic constraints or accommodations may account for instances such as (1)-(6). Finally, a principal problem lies in explicating the relations holding between anaphors and their antecedents. The relations holding between DAAs and their antecedents seem to be less restricted than commonly assumed in literature. Within traditional frameworks (e. g., Greber, 1993, pp. 379-387; Kleiber, 2001, pp. 263-296), it seems to be problematic to delimit the number of relations, and it is hard to provide a precise and maximally exhaustive classification without creating a potentially unlimited number of relations. In the next sections, the application of FrameNet and Barsalou frames aims at elucidating both the analytic assets and drawbacks of each approach.

3 Investigating associative anaphora with Barsalou frames

3.1 Frames as recursive attribute-value-structures: Barsalou's approach and its extensions in FOR 600

In several papers the cognitive psychologist Lawrence W. Barsalou has outlined a cognitive frame theory that tries to take account of empirical findings in the field of cognitive and experimental psychology (Barsalou, 1992, 1993; Barsalou & Hale, 1993). In contrast to FrameNet, Barsalou's approach is designed as a genuinely cognitive theory aiming at a comprehensive account of human knowledge representation. Thus, Barsalou's primary objective is *not* to develop a semantic theory but a psychologically realistic theory of knowledge representation, including semantic representations as one component. Accordingly, Barsalou (1992, p. 21) postulates that frames, defined as recursive attribute value-structures, provide "the fundamental representation of knowledge in human cognition". He presents arguments why his frame theory is explanatorily more adequate than traditional feature list representations of categories. In terms of the application scope of frames, however, it is striking that the great majority of instances discussed in Barsalou (1992) (e. g., *car, vacation, bird, mare, animal*) are limited to nominal sortal concepts.

Barsalou's frame theory has been adapted, extended, and slightly modified within a linguistic framework. Based on ideas developed in Löbner (1998) and other papers addressing a theory of concept types (cf. Löbner 2011 for an overview), the research unit "Frames and Functional Concepts" (FOR 600) as well as the research project "The Structure of Representations in Language, Cognition, and Science" (SFB 991) aim at developing a semantic theory allowing for deep lexical-semantic decomposition within a formal-logical framework. As a first step, a formal theory of frames based on Barsalou frames was developed (Petersen, 2007/2015). Major advances concern the integration of nominal concept types, including their interaction with determination. More specifically, Löbner's concept theory and Barsalou frame approach were integrated into one another in such a way that frame attributes (in Barsalou's sense) are essentially equated with functional concepts. Hence, it is assumed that attributes are characterized by two constitutive features: relationality and uniqueness of reference. Assuming that each attribute denotes precisely one entity of the respective frame allows for mathematical modeling and formalizations of frames. As we will see in the following paragraph, this assumption is also highly relevant for explaining the resolution of AAs.

3.2 Putting Barsalou frames into practice: DAAs with nominal antecedents

In Section 2, it has become evident that a distinguishing feature of DAAs is uniqueness of reference. That is, a DAA is always interpreted in such a way that it unambiguously refers to precisely one entity which has indirectly been introduced into the discourse. To come straight to the point: It is one of the major merits of Barsalou's approach to DAAs (extended by Löbner's concept type theory) to provide a comprehensive explanation of this property of DAAs.

It is argued that a DAA refers to the (value of an) attribute in the frame of the antecedent in such a way that the DAA is construed as a functional concept. More specifically, Löbner (1998) argues that definite associative anaphors equate with functional concepts for which a possessor and a situational argument are specified in context. And since functional concepts are equated with frame attributes, a DAA is interpreted as an attribute of the frame evoked by its antecedent. To illustrate, consider again (1) where the definite article gives rise to a referential reading of *key* in such a way that it is interpreted as the key for Peter's car.

(1) Peter walked to his car [antecedent]. He had forgotten **the key** [associative anaphor].

For instances such as (1) it is characteristic that the built-up concept is functional because it meets the conditions of relationality and uniqueness of reference (for an overview of concept types and their properties see Löbner 2011; cf. also Horn & Kimm, 2014). Its indirect reference is unique in that the number of possible referents is restricted to only one indirect referent, namely Peter's car. The observation that DAAs correspond to attributes in the frame of the antecedent's referent provides an opportunity to gain insights in the composition of these frames. To the extent that the respective attribute can be considered a necessary component of the antecedent frame, one obtains information about meaning components of the antecedent nouns.

According to this theory, the head noun of a definite associative-anaphoric NP undergoes a type shift if its underlying lexical concept is not functional (for critical discussions of type shifts cf. Horn & Kimm, 2014). In example (1) a type shift is not necessary since the underlying lexical concept of *key* is already functional: there is prototypically one and only one key that belongs to a car. Compare, however, example (7), where *window* – the head noun of the associative-anaphoric NP – is not functional but relational on the lexical level.

(7)   They reached Peter's house. **The window pane in the door** had been smashed.

The underlying lexical concept of window is relational (and not functional) because a house usually has more than one window. The possible referents of *window* is thus not restricted to only one referent. In order to facilitate uniqueness of reference, *window* is the object of a shift from a relational to a functional concept with a possessor argument specified by the antecedent. Such conceptual shifts are always necessary if the head noun of an NP surfacing as a DAA is non-functional on the lexical level; only functional concepts allow for unique reference.

Moreover, a frame-theoretical account of DAAs based on Barsalou's frame conception and Löbner's concept type theory correctly predicts the type of relation holding between anaphors and antecedents, and it also provides substantial suggestions how discourse referents in a text may be represented as Barsalou frames. Since it is assumed that the DAA has a functional head by default, every possible type of attribute in a frame representing the referent of the antecedent NP is also a possible type of DAA. The types usually enumerated in literature, such as parts, roles, contiguity relations, etc. (cf. Greber, 1993; Kleiber, 2001; Schwarz, 2000, among others), are all subsumed under this methodology. This approach thus abandons any thematic restrictions on DAAs and their underlying relation, without having to rely on empirical corpus evidence, since the argument presented here is theoretical in nature. On the other hand, the approach is more restrictive than traditional approaches in observing that the relation between the referent of the antecedent and the DAA referent must in fact be a functional one (cf. Löbner, 1998, 2011).

According to Barsalou (1992), recursivity constitutes an essential property of frames. The principle of recursivity also holds for a DAA in that it may be the possessor of another DAA, thereby forming a chain that represents relations between discourse referents in a network structure (for details cf. Ziem, 2012). Hypothesizing that DAA referents themselves are also represented in frames, the theory models DAAs as direct conjunctions of antecedent frames and DAA frames. If a DAA is the possessor of another DAA, frames are recursively linked to each other, constituting a complex frame network of newly introduced discourse referents. This is the case in (8).

(8) It was late when John arrived at his brother's house. **The door** was closed. Last week, John had lost **the key**, but fortunately he had received a substitute straight away.

In (8), *door* is interpreted as the door of the house mentioned before, while *key* is conceptualized as the key for this door. Once associative-anaphoric references are resolved, the construed concepts are 'enriched' by context information, yielding the complex concepts "the door of John's brother's house" respectively "the key for the door of John's brother's house". Modeling such chains of DAAs in frame networks could ultimately lead to a representation of correlated discourse referents in one single frame.

To conclude, Barsalou's frame theory supplemented with Löbner's concept type theory takes account of at least three basic properties of DAAs. By equating a DAA with a functional concept surfacing as an attribute of the frame evoked by the antecedent, the approach first successfully explains the difference between definite and indefinite associative anaphors: the reference of DAAs, but not the reference of IAAs, is unique in that it is directed to precisely one entity indirectly introduced into the discourse world before. Second, it correctly predicts the relations holding between a DAA and its antecedent(s). Instead of postulating an arbitrary number of relation types, it is hypothesized that the number of DAAs (attributes) associated with a frame is potentially unlimited. Finally, recursivity, as a constitutive property of Barsalou frames, allows explanation of chained associative-anaphoric references, that is, NPs serving as DAAs and antecedents (for other DAAs) at the same time. However, a major shortcoming concerns the limitation of the approach to DAAs with *nominal* antecedents. It is anything but clear whether the approach can be successfully applied to DAAs with verbal antecedents, simply because both Löbner's concept type theory and Barsalou's frame theory are restricted to nominal frames. Currently, however, Robert Van Valin and Rainer Osswald are developing a theory of verb meaning based on Barsalou frames. In the long run, this theory might help to extend the application scope of Barsalou frames in the realm of AAs.

4 Investigating associative anaphora within FrameNet

4.1 Frames as valency pattern: background to FrameNet

Frames, as defined in FrameNet and Fillmore's early seminal studies on semantic frames (e. g., Fillmore, 1976, 1977, 1985), are rich conceptual knowledge structures underlying and motivating the meaning(s) of lexical items and phrasal units. Building on this definition, the FrameNet project pursued at the International Institute of Computer Science in Berkeley tries to develop an online lexical database for English documenting the semantic and syntactic valences of a word in each of its senses (Ruppenhofer et al., 2010, p. 5). It has been, and still is, one of the major aims of FrameNet to put Fillmore's early theoretical ideas about semantic frames into practice by developing an annotation tool that allows for data-driven, rather than introspective, lexical-semantic investigations. At the end, the database is supposed to provide all semantic information required for adequately understanding lexical and phrasal units in context (Fillmore, Wooters & Baker, 2001).

In FrameNet, the target units are so-called lexical units, that is, word-meaning pairings. The starting point is the assumption that each word (in each of its senses) evokes a frame providing a set of "frame elements" (FEs); each sense of a polysemous word thus belongs to a different frame (Ruppenhofer et al., 2010, p. 5). FEs are equated with semantic and/or syntactic roles that a lexical unit takes. A distinction is made between peripheral and core FEs – a distinction that seems to be analogous to the argument-adjunct differentiation in valency grammar. Unlike valency grammar, however, FEs are not limited in number since they are identified – and subsequently defined – "bottom-up", that is, on the basis of annotated sentences. It is hypothesized that frames are not isolated entities in the language user's mind. Rather, they are linked by a system of frame-to-frame-relations with one another. Fillmore & Baker (2010, p. 330) list seven relations falling into three groups: (a) generalization relations ("inheritance", "perspective", "using"), (b) event structure relations ("subframes", "precedes"), and (c) systematic relations ("causative of", "inchoative of"). I will come back to them later when analyzing instances of DAAs.

Due to the valency-oriented view on word meaning, FrameNet primarily focuses on frames associated with verbs, relational nouns, and adjectives. Presently, about 7,700 lexical units have been annotated on the basis of approximately 173,000 sentences. About 3,260 verb senses, 2,940 noun senses, and 1,440 adjective senses have been identified. The exemplary investigations of associative anaphora in the next paragraph will build on these data, particularly on the (sub-)frames fully annotated so far. Note, as mentioned before, that the methodology offered by FrameNet only allows for detailed investigations of those associative anaphors whose antecedents surface as verbs or relational nouns; in contrast to Barsalou's approach to frames, FrameNet does not focus on sortal nouns as frame-evoking elements even though they are also addressed and covered in the database.

4.2 Putting FrameNet frames into practice: DAAs with verbs and deverbal nouns as antecedents

Although FrameNet's main focus is on frame-semantic investigations of lexical units within the limits of the sentences they are embedded in, in a couple of papers and books it has been argued persuasively that frames play also a crucial role in the domain of text semantics. Fillmore (1984), for example, takes the view that text semantics, on a par with lexical semantics, constitute the most prominent level of semantic investigations. In line with this view, Fillmore & Baker (2001) illustrate that 16 frames provide semantic prerequisites for the understanding of a small story about a criminal process. Thus, it is principally possible to apply the FrameNet methodology to textual phenomena such as AAs.

How does a FrameNet approach to AA proceed? To begin with, consider (9) where the referent of the definite noun phrase (NP) *the car* refers indirectly to the concept of driving introduced before.

(9)   We drove [antecedent] to Frankfurt yesterday. **The car** [associative anaphor], however, was a bit too small.

In FrameNet terms, *drive* evokes in (9) the Operate_vehicle frame providing VEHICLE as one of its core elements. By virtue of frame-to-frame relations, the Operate_vehicle frame imposes a particular perspective on the related Use_vehicle frame. Hence, the associative anaphor *the car* specifies one particular FE of the frame evoked by the antecedent. In (9) associative anaphoric reference succeeds because VEHICLE is not overtly realized in the first sentence. Given the local context provided in (9), the so-called "definite null instantiation" (cf. Ruppenhofer et al., 2010, p. 24) of the FE VEHICLE is instantly accessible.

More generally, one can conclude that a FrameNet approach to associative anaphora supports the assumption that an associative anaphor is anchored in the frame evoked by the antecedent in such a way that it conceptually specifies one of the FEs provided by the antecedent frame. This also holds for cases such as (4) mentioned above:

(4)   The search lingers on, but **the key** remains lost.

Unlike (9), the antecedent *the search* is a deverbal noun. However, both the deverbal noun *the search* as well as the verb *search* evoke the Scrutiny frame. Thus, the frame associated with the verb and the deverbal noun provides the same FEs, among them the core FE PHENOMENON (that is, in traditional case grammar terms, the semantic role "object"). In (4) it is precisely this FE that is further specified by the associative anaphor *the key*.

As mentioned above, beyond verbs and deverbal nouns also sortal nouns surface as AAs. For example, in (7) *pane* is interpreted as a specification of the FE DESCRIPTOR inherent in the Buildings frame evoked by *house*. Sortal nouns like *house* challenge the FrameNet approach in numerous respects, since such nouns are characterized as words that "typically serve as dependents rather than clearly evoking their own frame" (Ruppenhofer et al., 2010, p. 5). Although artifact and natural kind nouns have "a minimal frame structure on their own", it is nonetheless hard to see how analyses within a FrameNet approach can fully take account of this subclass of AAs.

Note that FrameNet does not systematically differentiate between different types of concepts. Unlike the approach to associative anaphora introduced in

Section 3, relational, functional, sortal, and individual concepts are distinguished from one another only in terms of their varying valency pattern. As a result, a FrameNet approach to associative anaphora is not able to support the strong hypothesis that definite associative anaphors and functional concepts share the constitutive properties of relationality and uniqueness of reference. I consider this a methodological drawback, since the property of functionality correctly predicts uniqueness of anaphoric reference in the case of definite associative anaphors. In (4), for instance, the referent of *the key* is identified with the entity being searched for.

As mentioned above, FrameNet cannot account for associative anaphors whose antecedents surface as sortal nouns since they lack valency. It is worthwhile noting, however, that this does not apply to all cases. Even though in (10), for example, *soup* is a sortal noun, FrameNet does provide an explanation for the associative-anaphoric reference triggered by *spoon*.

(10)   When the waiter served the soup, he noticed that he had forgotten **the spoon**.

In contrast to prototypical instances of DAAs with sortal nouns as antecedents, as evidenced in (1), (2), and (5), a distinguishing feature of (10) is that the anaphor and its antecedent are mediated by the inferred Ingestion frame, in which the soup concept specifies the FE INGESTIBLES while the spoon concept specifies the FE INSTRUMENT. In (10) it becomes apparent why it is useful to distinguish between frame invocation and evocation (Ruppenhofer et al., 2010, p. 15 f.) – a distinction that is missing in Barsalou's approach. The associative anaphor *spoon* is related to its antecedent *soup* by the invoked Ingestion frame. In the case of frame invocation, a FrameNet approach to associative anaphora correctly predicts that both anaphor and antecedent specify FEs (here: INGESTIBLES, INSTRUMENT) of the invoked frame.

While, however, instances such as (10) constitute a sub-class of definite DAAs with antecedents surfacing as sortal nouns, other DAAs with sortal nouns as antecendents cannot be explained within the framework provided by FrameNet. Yet, in turn, FrameNet allows for concise analyses of definite associative anaphors with verbs and deverbal nouns as antecedents. As shown above, these classes of DAAs cause serious problems for Barsalou's approach to frames.

Can a FrameNet approach to associative anaphora account for recursive anaphor-antecedent structures? Although neither Fillmore himself nor his collaborators seem to consider recursivity a property of semantic frames, there is no fundamental caveat to integrating recursivity into frame-semantic investigations of associative anaphors. Like in (11), an associative anaphor (*the car*) may be followed by a subsequent sub-associative anaphor (*the owner*) thereby forming a chain of indirect textual references that expresses relations between discourse referents in a network structure.

(11) Today, Peter <u>drove</u> back home. He borrowed **the car** from a friend. **The owner**, however, was Fred.

The NP *the car* is embedded in a recursive frame structure in such a way that it specifies the FE VEHICLE of the Operate_vehicle frame evoked by *drive*, and at the same time it evokes the Vehicle frame whose FE POSSESSOR is specified by the associative anaphor *owner*.

5 Conclusions

To sum up, Barsalou's approach to frames differs from FrameNet in a number of respects. Most importantly, Barsalou envisages a *cognitive* theory of knowledge representation in which frames are addressed as a universal mental representation format. Moreover, Barsalou's theory is based on empirical evidence in the field of cognitive psychology. On these grounds, Barsalou defines frames as recursive attribute-value structures. FrameNet, on the other hand, is a genuine linguistic project in that it is both grounded in an extended model of semantic as well as syntactic valency and realized as a large-scale corpus project. Accordingly, frames are not – at least not first and foremost – defined in cognitive terms but in accordance with the annotation categories: on the basis of annotated data FEs and frame-to-frame-relations are identified, and on the basis of these data core FEs are distinguished from peripheral FEs. Although in FrameNet recursivity is not supposed to be a defining feature of frames, each so-called "frame definition" made available for each annotated frame comprises a set of attested frame-to-frame relations (cf. also Fillmore et al., 2003, pp. 304-313). Hence, frames are interconnected with one another, albeit in a much more restrictive way than in Barsalou's approach which hypothesizes that each frame element (attribute, value) is recursive in nature. Table 2 summarizes the most important commonalities and differences of both approaches to cognitive frames.

Table 2: Commonalities and differences of Barsalou's and FrameNet's approach to frames

	Barsalou's approach to frames	FrameNet
Theory-oriented aspects	- cognitive theory of mental representation	- linguistic theory based on semantic and syntactic valency
	- focus on sortal nouns	- focus on verbs and deverbal nouns
	- compatible with concept type theory	[unspecified and not integrable]
Methodology	- partly data-driven, partly introspection	- data-driven, bottom-up investigations by rich semantic annotations
Frame structure	- distinction between attributes and values	- distinction of peripheral and core frame elements
	- recursivity	[unspecified but integrable]
	[unspecified and impossible]	- distinction between types of frame relations
Application of frames in the domain of AA	- focus on relational and functional nouns	- focus on deverbal nouns and verbs
	[unspecified but integrable]	- distinction between frame evocation and invocation
	- integration of relational/functional concepts and theory of determination	- integration of relational concepts
	- focus on nominal antecedents	- focus on verbal antecedents

What are the benefits of a FrameNet and a Barsalou-inspired approach to associative anaphora? In contrast to the latter, FrameNet allows for explaining anaphors with antecedents surfacing as verbs and deverbal nouns. Given the analysis above, investigations of associative anaphors provide insights into the composition of frames evoked by verbs and deverbal nouns on the text level, since associative anaphors specify FEs of the frame evoked by the anchor frame element. Subsequently, new FEs may be defined on the basis of annotated anaphors, and lexical entries provided by FrameNet may be supplemented accordingly. Note also that each associative anaphor establishes a specific semantic relation to its antecedent and thus offers linguistic evidence for frame-to-frame-relations. Composition and inheritance, as described by Fillmore & Baker (2001), are ubiquitous relation types but besides the frame-to-frame relations identified by FrameNet many more seem to be relevant to resolve associative anaphors (cf. Kleiber, 2001; Greber, 1993). To this end, an interesting issue for future research would be whether attested relations are item-specific or rather stable across exemplars within a domain.

A fundamental caveat of a FrameNet approach to associative anaphors concerns the exclusion of sortal nouns as frame-evoking lexical units (Ruppenhofer et al., 2010, p. 5). In turn, Barsalou has developed his frame theory on the basis of sortal concept. However, he does not seem to be aware of the limitations involved in this approach; at least the reader is left wanting some reflections on the linguistic nature of the analyzed concepts. In Löbner (1998) and within the research projects SFB 991 and FOR 600, Barsalou's frame theory is supplemented by Löbner's concept type theory, yielding a substantial theoretical extension in that attributes are equated with functional nouns. Nonetheless the extended Barsalou approach still focuses on nominal concepts. A full-fledged frame theory of verb frames based on Barsalou's approach has not yet been developed.

Apart from sortal concepts also individual and relational concepts are integrated in Barsalou's frame theory, namely in such way that sortal, relational, and individual concepts may constitute frame attributes if they are shifted, or coerced, to functional concepts due to linguistic cues such as definitness markers (cf. Löbner, 2011). At this point, however, the empirical issue arises whether it is useful to principally restrict frame attributes to the set of functional concepts. IAAs, as exemplified in (2), prototypically surface as relational nouns (e.g., *window*), and due to the property of indefiniteness, they are not object of a conceptual shift. But, then, are there *empirical* reasons for the assumption that they do not figure as attributes in the frame evoked by the antecedent? In the case of DAAs, on the other hand, equating attributes with functional concepts helps to explain the cognitive mechanism underlying anaphora resolution: Since DAAs are interpreted as functional concepts in context, their possible referents are restricted to only one referent. In this respect, a FrameNet approach to DAA does not provide a suitable account of DAA resolution; at the same time, no principal problems arise in the domain of IAAs. A more comprehensive theory of AA based on Barsalou frames has to address the following research issues: To what extent and under which conditions do head nouns of DAAs call for type shifts in order to motivate a functional interpretation of the nouns in question?

To conclude, FrameNet and Barsalou's approach complement each other in such a way that the latter concentrates on sortal concepts functioning as frame-evoking elements, while FrameNet focuses on relational concepts, particularly verbs and deverbal nouns. Barsalou disregards semantic and syntactic valences of each frame-evoking word, whereas valency provides the very basis for the FrameNet methodology. This finding gives rise to issues of the following kind: How can FrameNet account for sortal nouns serving as associative anaphors? And how can, in turn, Barsalou's approach account for verbs serving as associative anaphors? What's the theoretical status of sortal nouns within FrameNet, and in what respect do verb frames differ from noun frames in Barsalou's approach? More generally, which linguistic elements evoke frames in each approach? It is beyond the scope of this article to provide answers to these questions. However, as I hope to have shown, there are several complementary research aspects of FrameNet and Barsalou's approach to frames and its extensions within FOR 600 and SFB 991. The diverging viewpoints and starting assumptions stimulate each other, pointing to a more comprehensive frame theory.

6 Acknowledgment

Many ideas introduced and discussed in this paper were developed in close cooperation with collaborators of the research unit "Functional Concepts and Frames" (FOR 600) and the SFB 991 "The Structure of Representations in Language, Cognition, and Science", both funded by the German Research Foundation (DFG). In particular, I am indebted to the speaker of the research project, Sebastian Löbner, as well as Christian Horn and Nicolas Kimm.

References

Barsalou, L. W. 1992. Frames, concepts, and conceptual fields. In E. F. Kittay & A. Lehrer (eds.), *Frames, fields, and contrasts: New essays in semantic and lexical organization*, 21–74. Hillsdale, NJ: Lawrence Erlbaum Associates.

Barsalou, L. W. 1993. Flexibility, structure, and linguistic vagary in concepts: Manifestations of a compositional system of perceptual symbols. In A. C. Collins, S. E. Gathercole & M. A. Conway (eds.), *Theories of memory*, 29-101. London: Lawrence Erlbaum Associates.

Barsalou, L. W. & C. R. Hale 1993. Components of conceptual representation: From feature lists to recursive frames. In I. Van Mechelen, J. Hampton, R. Michalski & P. Theuns (eds.), *Categories and concepts: Theoretical views and inductive data analysis*, 97–144. San Diego, CA: Academic Press.

Boas, H. C. 2005. From Theory to Practice: Frame Semantics and the Design of FrameNet. In S. Langer & D. Schnorbusch (eds.), *Semantik im Lexikon*, 129–160. Tübingen: Narr.

Charniak, E. 1976. A framed painting: The representation of a common sense knowledge fragment. *Cognitive Science* 1. 355–394.

Clark, H. H. 1975. Bridging. In R.C. Schank & B.L. Nash-Webber (eds.), *Theoretical issues in natural language processing*, 169–174. New York: Association for Computing Machinery.

Fillmore, C. J. 1976. The need for a frame semantics within linguistics. In H. Karlgren (ed.), *Statistical Methods in Linguistics* 12, 5–29.

Fillmore, C. J. 1977. Scenes-and-frames semantics. In A. Zampolli (ed.), *Linguistic Structures Processing*, 55–81. Amsterdam/New York/Oxford: North Holland.

Fillmore, C. J. 1985). Frames and the semantics of understanding. *Quaderni di Semantica* 6 (2). 222–254.

Fillmore, C. J. 2006). Frames Semantics. In K. Brown (ed.), *Encyclopedia of Linguistics and Language*, Vol. 4, 613–620. Amsterdam: Elsevier.

Fillmore, C. J., C. R. Johnson & M. R. Petruck 2003. Background to FrameNet. *International Journal of Lexicography* 16 (3), 235–250.

Fillmore, C. J., M. R. Petruck, J. Ruppenhofer & A. Wright 2003. FrameNet in Action: The Case of Attaching. *International Journal of Lexicography* 16 (3), 297–332.

Fillmore, C. J. & C. F. Baker 2010. A Frames Approach to Semantic Analysis. In B. Heine & H. Narrog (eds.), *The Oxford Handbook of Linguistic Analysis*, 313–339. Oxford: Oxford University Press.

Fillmore, C. J. & C. F. Baker 2001. Frame Semantics for Text Understanding. *Proceedings of WordNet and Other Lexical Resources Workshop*. NAACL, Pittsburgh, June, 2001.

Fillmore, C. J., C. Wooters & C. F. Baker 2001. Building a Large Lexical Databank Which Provides Deep Semantics. *Proceedings of the Pacific Asian Conference on Language, Information and Computation*. Hong Kong.

References

Greber, E. 1993. Zur Neubestimmung von Kontiguitätsanaphern. *Sprachwissenschaft* 18 (4). 361–405.

Hawkins, J. A. 1978. *Definiteness and Indefiniteness. A Study in Reference and Grammaticality Prediction.* London: Croom Helm.

Hayes, P. J. 1980. The Logic of Frames. In D. Metzing (ed.), *Frame Conceptions and Text Understanding*, 451–458. Berlin/New York: de Gruyter.

Heim, I. 1982. *The semantics of definite and indefinite noun phrases.* Dissertation. Schriftenreihe des Sonderforschungsbereichs 99, Linguistik, Nr. 73. Konstanz: Universität Konstanz.

Horn, C. & N. Kimm 2014. Concept types in German fictional texts. In T. Gamerschlag, D. Gerland, R. Osswald & W. Petersen (eds.), *Concept Types and Frames. Applications in Language and Philosophy*, 343–362. Dordrecht, NL: Springer.

Kleiber, G. 2001. *L'anaphore associative.* Paris: Presses Universitaires de France.

Löbner, S. 1998. Definite associative anaphora. In S. Botley (ed.), *Approaches to discourse anaphora: proceedings of DAARC96.* Lancaster: Lancaster University. [Available at http://user.phil-fak.uni-duesseldorf.de/~loebner/publ/DAA-03.pdf]

Löbner, S. 2011. Concept types and determination. *Journal of Semantics* 28 (3), 279–333.

Lyons, C. 1999. *Definiteness.* Cambridge: Cambridge University Press.

Matthes, J. 2007. *Framing-Effekte. Zum Einfluss der Politikberichterstattung auf die Einstellungen der Rezipienten.* München: Verlag Reinhard Fischer.

Minsky, M. 1975. A framework for representing knowledge. In P. Winston (ed.), *The Psychology of Computer Vision*, 211–277. New York: McGraw-Hill.

Petersen, W. 2015. Representation of Concepts as Frames. In Gamerschlag T., D. Gerland, R. Osswald & W. Petersen (eds.), *Meaning, Frames, and Conceptual Representation*, 39–63. Studies in Language and Cognition 2. Düsseldorf: Düsseldorf University Press. (Reprinted from J. Skilters, F. Toccafondi & G. Stemberger (eds.), Complex Cognition and Qualitative Science. Volume 2 of *The Baltic International Yearbook of Cognition, Logic and Communication*, 151–170, University of Latvia, Riga, 2007.)

Ruppenhofer, J., M. Ellsworth, M. R. Petruck, R. C. Johnson & J. Scheffczyk 2010. *FrameNet II: Extended Theory and Practice.* September 14, 2010. [Available at: https://framenet2.icsi.berkeley.edu/docs/r1.5/book.pdf].

Schank, R. C. & R. P. Abelson 1977. *Scripts, Plans, Goals and Understanding. An Inquiry into Human Knowledge Systems.* Hillsdale: Erlbaum.

Scheufele, B. 2003. *Frames - Framing - Framing-Effekte. Theoretische und methodische Grundlegung sowie empirische Befunde zur Nachrichtenproduktion.* Wiesbaden: Westdeutscher Verlag.

Schwarz, M. 2000. *Indirekte Anaphern in Texten. Studien zur dömanengebundenen Referenz und Kohärenz im Deutschen.* Tübingen: Niemeyer.

Schwarz, M. 1996. Lexikalische und konzeptuelle Restriktionen beim Verstehen direkter und indirekter Anaphern. In F. Hundsnurscher & E. Weigand (eds.), *Lexical Structures and Language Use*, 399–407. Tübingen: Niemeyer.

Ziem, A. 2008. *Frames und sprachliches Wissen. Kognitive Aspekte der semantischen Kompetenz.* Berlin/New York: de Gruyter.

Ziem, A. 2012. Token-Konzepte, Type-Konzepte und das Prinzip der Rekursivität. In E. Fricke & M. Voss (eds.), *68 Zeichen für Roland Posner. Ein semiotisches Mosaik / 68 Signs for Roland Posner. A Semiotic Mosaic*, 69–79. Tübingen: Stauffenburg.

Author

Alexander Ziem
University of Düsseldorf
Faculty of Philosophy
ziem@phil.hhu.de

The Definiteness Effect and a New Classification of Possessive Constructions

Yuko Kobukata & Yoshiki Mori

Abstract

In this paper, we argue that the occurrence of the definiteness effect in possessive constructions is predictable once we know what type of interpretation is obtained in the construction. Previous studies concerned with this issue have generally assumed that there is a strong correlation between the effect and the notion of inalienability expressed by the object. We argue, however, that this is not true. Rather, what we need to take into consideration is the interpretation of the construction as a whole, and by doing so, we can provide a unified explanation of the distribution of the effect in possessive constructions both in English and Japanese. We propose that the readings of possessive constructions should be divided into "possessive" interpretation and "holding" interpretation. Secondly, we argue that English *have* is polysemous and has a control reading, while the Japanese verbs *iru* ('be') and *aru* ('be') cannot express the control relation. Thirdly, we argue that the definiteness effect in *there* constructions is different from that in possessive constructions in terms of information structure. Fourthly, we argue that there are two more possessive constructions in Japanese in addition to possessive constructions using *iru* ('be') and *aru* ('be'), and that they are all related to typological patterns of possessive constructions.

1 Introduction: The definiteness effect and inalienability

It has apparently been accepted that there is a strong correlation between the definiteness effect observed in English possessive constructions and inalienable possession expressed by the object of *have* (de Jong 1987, Keenan 1987, Partee 1999).

When inalienable possession is expressed by using a relational noun such as *sister*, which implies that the possessee is conceived of typically as being inseparable from the possessor, the definiteness effect arises, which can be found in (1).

(1)   John has a/*the sister.

By contrast, the effect does not seem to be relevant to alienable possession denoted by the object. In the following examples, in which a nonrelational noun is used as an object expressing alienable possession, the effect does not arise.

(2)   John has a/the book.

These kinds of facts lead many researchers to formulate that the definiteness effect in English possessive constructions is due to inalienability.

However, this issue would seem to require further consideration. The following example, for example, cannot be accounted for by the previous studies, since the effect does arise even when a nonrelational noun is used as the object.

(3)   Q.   What will you give to Eliza for her birthday?
       A.   Eliza has a/*the mirror, so I won't give one to her.

In this dialogue, where Eliza's ownership of a mirror is in question, the addressee must use an indefinite object rather than a definite one.

Also, there is another sense in which most previous works still come short of accounting for the definiteness effect in possessive constructions. For instance, in some cases the effect does not arise even when relational nouns are used as objects, as can be seen in (4).

(4)   John has his sister as a dance partner.

In (4), the object noun phrase includes a relational noun *sister*. According to the previous studies, a relational noun is supposed to be a crucial factor in determining the occurrence of the definiteness effect. However, contrary to their expectations, the effect does not arise here.

These facts given in (3A) and (4) should be problems for any previous approaches, where the definiteness effect in possessive constructions is assumed to be due to the notion of inalienable possession. In other words, this allows us to predict that the effect should not be relevant to the conceptual distinction between inalienable and alienable possession described by the object in the first place.

In order to identify the definiteness effect of the verb *have* (henceforth, we will abbreviate the effect as "DE"), a new classification will be proposed based on its readings. This new classification is very useful to account for the DE in possessive constructions both in English and Japanese.

This paper is organized as follows. In Section 2, we show that the occurrence of the DE in possessive constructions is NOT predictable from the inalienability of the object noun phrases only. Rather, we claim that it depends on the way in which the possessive construction is interpreted. In Section 3, we point out the differences between English *have* and Japanese verbs *iru* ('be') and *aru* ('be'). More precisely, the Japanese verbs cannot encode a specific possessive relation, which is available only in English possessive constructions. In Section 4, we argue that the DE in *there* constructions and possessive constructions cannot be accounted for from the same perspective. In Section 5, we point out that there are other possessive constructions in Japanese in addition to possessive constructions with *iru* ('be') and *aru* ('be'). We argue that they are all related to the main typological patterns of possessive constructions Stassen 2009 claims.

2 English and Japanese possessive constructions

As was suggested in section 1, the DE in English possessive constructions does not have a strong relation to the inalienability expressed by the object. Moreover, this is not a peculiar fact about English. Rather, it is at least a cross-linguistic fact. The same problem holds for Japanese possessive constructions. That is, the occurrence of the DE has nothing to do with inalienability described by the object.

2.1 Subjecthood

In Japanese possessive constructions, stative predicates *iru* ('be') and *aru* ('be') are used. These verbs take a subject with dative case and an object with nominative case, which is shown in (5a). Note that the same case pattern (-DAT + -NOM + *iru*/*aru* ('be')) is found when a locational or an existential meaning is encoded as in (5b).

(5) (a) *Kanojo-ni-wa otooto-ga   iru.*
she-DAT-TOP brother-NOM be
'She has a brother.'

(b) *Kooen-ni   kodomo-ga   iru.*
The park-DAT child/children-NOM be
'There is a child in the park./There are children in the park.'

Although both sentences in (5a) and (5b) take the same case pattern (-DAT -NOM), the grammatical relation that the nominative phrase assumes is different (Kishimoto 2000, 2005). As Kishimoto argues, there are four diagnostic methods for identifying grammatical subjects in Japanese possessive constructions.

One of the tests for identifying a grammatical subject is reflexivization. The Japanese reflexive *zibun* ('self') can only take a subject as its antecedent. The contrast between (6a) and (6b) shows that the antecedent of *zibun* ('self') is a dative phrase but not a nominative phrase:

(6) (a) *John$_i$-ni zibun$_i$-no kodomo-ga i-ru/a-ru (koto)*
John-DAT self-GEN child-NOM be   (thing)
'John has his own child.'

(b) **Zibun$_i$-no tomodati-ni kodomo$_i$-ga i-ru/a-ru (koto)*
self-GEN friend-DAT child-NOM be   (thing)
'A friend of his$_i$ has a child$_i$.'   (Kishimoto 2005:169)

There is another test for identifying which phrase in the construction is the grammatical subject. We can identify the subject by checking the distribution of controlled PRO.

(7) (a) *Watasi-wa John$_i$-ni [PRO$_i$ kodomo-ga atte] hosii to*
I-TOP   John$_i$-DAT   child-NOM be   want that
omotta.
thought
'I wanted John to have a child.'

(b) **Watasi-wa kodomo$_i$-ni [John-ni PRO$_i$ atte] hosii to*
I-TOP   child-DAT John-DAT   be   want that
omotta.
thought
'I wanted a child$_i$ for John to have PRO$_i$.'   (Kishimoto 2005:170)

The null element PRO in the acceptable example in (7a) is coindexed with the dative phrase *John*. When PRO is coindexed with the nominative phrase *kodomo-ga* in (7b), on the other hand, the example is unacceptable.

In addition to controlled PRO, there is another type of PRO which is not controlled and has arbitrary reference. This is so-called arbitrary PRO. Arbitrary PRO is also limited to subject position.

(8)   (a)   [PRO kodomo-ga aru/iru] koto-wa   ii   koto da.
                child-NOM be   that-TOP good thing COP
               'It is a good thing to have a child.'
       (b)   *[John-ni   PRO aru/iru] koto-wa   ii   koto da.
               John-DAT   be   that-TOP good thing COP
               'It is a good thing for John to have PRO.'   (Kishimoto 2005:171)

Irrespective of which verb, *aru* ('be') or *iru* ('be'), is used, the dative phrase can have an arbitrary PRO interpretation as shown in the example in (8a), while the example in (8b) shows that the nominative phrase cannot have such an arbitrary interpretation. There is a fourth diagnostic for identifying grammatical subjects in Japanese possessive constructions. Subject honorification is used to express the speaker's respect toward the grammatical subject with a particular marking on the verb. In (9), the speaker pays deference towards the referent of the dative phrase *Yamada-sensei* ('Prof. Yamada'), but not towards the referent of the nominative phrase *zaisan* ('fortune').

(9)   Yamada-sensei-ni   zaisan-ga   o-ari-ni-naru.
       Yamada-Prof.-DAT fortune-NOM be-HON
       'Prof. Yamada has a fortune.'   (Kishimoto 2000:57)

Therefore, these facts suggest that the subject of the verb *aru* ('be') and *iru* ('be') in possessive constructions is a dative phrase not a nominative phrase.

2.2   The DE and the interpretation of the possessive construction

When a relational noun is used as the object in Japanese possessive constructions, some cases display the DE. As is observed in (10), the object nominative phrase *otooto-ga* ('brother-NOM') is incompatible with strong determiners including the definite article.

(10) #Kanojo-ni-wa {sono/arayuru/hotondo-no/subete-no}
    she-DAT-TOP {the/every/most-GEN/all-GEN}
    otooto-ga iru.
    brother(s) be
    'She has the/every/most-GEN/all-GEN brother(s).'

By contrast, the following case does not exhibit the DE although a relational noun is used as the object.

(11) John-ni-wa   Mary-no   otooto-ga   iru.
    John-DAT-TOP Mary-GEN brother-NOM be
    'John has Mary's brother (in some role/for some purpose).'

The sentence in (11) does not describe John's sibling relationship. Rather, the relation between *John* and *otooto* is contextually dependent. For example, *otooto* could be just John's helper.

The same holds for nonrelational objects. The DE does not usually arise when a nonrelational noun *hon* ('book') is used as the object, as in (12).

(12) John-ni-wa   ano hon-ga   aru.
    John-DAT-TOP that book-NOM be
    'John has that book.'

However, the DE can arise even when a nonrelational noun is used as the object of *iru* ('be') and *aru* ('be'). The object phrase *okane* ('money'), which is a nonrelational noun, is compatible with the weak determiners *takusan-no* ('plenty of-GEN'), *ikuraka-no* ('some-GEN') as (13a) shows, but it is incompatible with strong determiners, which is observed in the examples in (13b).

(13) (a) Kanojo-ni-wa {takusan-no/ikuraka-no}   okane-ga   aru.
        she-DAT-TOP {plenty of-GEN/some-GEN} money-NOM be
        'She has {plenty of/some} money.'
    (b) #Kanojo-ni-wa {sono/arayuru/hotondo-no/subete-no/kanojo-no}
        she-DAT-TOP {the/every/most-GEN/all-GEN/she-GEN}
        okane-ga   aru.
        money-NOM be
        'She has {the/every/most/all/her} money.'

On the basis of these examples, we claim that the previous studies, in which the DE is dependent upon the inalienability of the object, are not entirely on the right track.

Now, we are arguing against the previous works, proposing that the DE must be accounted for in terms of the interpretation of the possessive constructions independent of the inalienability of the object. Specifically, we postulate that there are two different interpretations, the "possessive" interpretation and the "holding" interpretation. To make these interpretations clear, first consider the following case.

(14)   John has a wife of his own.

The sentence in (14) includes a relational noun. The example expresses an inherent property attributed to the subject. We call this kind of interpretation a "possessive" interpretation. It should be noted here that this interpretation can also be obtained by using a nonrelational noun expressing alienable possession as in (15):

(15)   Eliza has a car.

The utterance in (15) can typically mean that Eliza is the owner of a car. The car belonging to her can be treated as her property. That is, the example (15) can be assumed to have a "possessive" interpretation.

On the other hand, the following acceptable examples (16) and (17), where the second conjunct can negate the implication conveyed in the first conjunct, show what the "holding" interpretation is. They describe that the subject can avail herself of the object but cannot claim ownership to it, which Heine (1997) calls temporary possession. Again, this interpretation can be obtained using both a relational and a nonrelational noun expressing inalienable and alienable possession respectively.

(16)   Eliza has a <u>mirror</u>, but it doesn't belong to her.   (nonrelational noun)

(17)   Ann has a <u>sister</u> as her secretary, but she doesn't have a sister of her own.   (relational noun)

The occurrence of the DE can be well predicted if we take these interpretations into consideration. The DE arises when a "possessive" interpretation is obtained, while it does not when a "holding" one is obtained:

(18) *John has the sister (of his own).

(19) Q. What will you give to Eliza for her birthday?
      A. Eliza has a/*the mirror, so I won't give one to her.

The sentences in (18) and (19A) obtain a possessive interpretation. Note that in these examples, both relational and nonrelational nouns are used as the objects. The DE arises when the possessive interpretation is obtained, irrespective of the type of object noun phrases. By contrast, the acceptable sentences in (20A) and (21) obtain a holding interpretation. They display no definiteness effect.

(20) Q. What can I use to hold these papers down?
      A. Eliza has a/the/John's mirror. (But it's not hers.)

(21) Anne has Bill's sister as secretary.

Also, in these sentences, relational as well as nonrelational nouns are used as the objects. In the traditional view, it is an inalienability described by an object that causes the DE in possessive constructions. It is clear, then, that the distinction inalienable vs. alienable possession only is inadequate as a means of accounting for the distribution of the DE in possessive constructions. The DE must be accounted for in terms of the interpretation of the construction in question.

3 Subclassification of the "holding" interpretation in terms of information structure

When English possessive constructions do not display the DE, i.e., when they have a "holding" interpretation, the senses of *have* are assumed to be polysemous. Tham (2006) argues that the meaning of *have* can be distinguished based on the informational status of the object. In this section, we follow Tham's suggestion to set up a subclassification of the "holding" interpretation in a possessive construction.

When the object conveys new, focus information for the addressee, the English possessive construction is assumed to be focal and "presentational":

(22)   Q: Who can help John?
         A: He has <u>Sally</u>.

(23)   A: We need more trimmings for the tree.
         B: The tree has <u>all those lights we got last year</u>.   (Tham 2006:145)

When both sentences in (22A) and (23B) are uttered in response to the preceding questions (22Q) and (23A) respectively, the definite object *Sally* in (22A) and *all those lights we got last year* in (23B) convey the new focus information for the hearer. We will call the interpretation obtained here the focus (presentational) reading.

It should be noted that the sentences in (22A) and (23B) do not concretely specify a holding relation between the entities of the subject and the object; the relation between them is contextually dependent.

In contrast, when the object carries old, presuppositional information, the construction acquires a typical sense of holding meaning, which is attributable to the verbal interpretation of *have*. We will call this reading a nonfocal, "control" reading. Consider the following case in (24):

(24)   Q: Where is my umbrella?
         A: John has it.

In (24A), the pronoun *it* refers to an entity already familiar from the previous discourse. And the sentence maintains a typical holding interpretation.

It should be noted here that the subject of *have*, in the control sense, must be animate. On the one hand, the focus reading allows for an inanimate subject. As we have shown earlier, the context in (23) makes the object of *have* in (23B) new information. In this case, the object in (23B) is compatible with the inanimate subject *the tree*. On the other hand, the subject must be animate when the control reading is obtained. The utterance in (25a), for example, sets up the context so that the object in (25b) is old information for addressee. The reply (25b), therefore, is not felicitous.

(25) (a) Where are the mirrors?
 (b) #The bathroom has them.
  (^{ok} They are in the bathroom.)
  (^{ok} Mowgli has them.) (Tham 2006:144)

In this connection, we call attention to the fact that a cross-linguistic contrast can be observed with respect to the "holding" *have*: In Japanese possessive constructions, the definite object is felicitous only when it conveys new information, which is shown by the example (27A). Unlike English possessive constructions, the control reading is not available in Japanese possessive constructions, as in (29A) (cf. Tham (2006) about Chinese).

(26) Q: Who can help John?
 A: He has Sally/that man.

(27) Q: *Dare-ga   John-o   tetsudau koto-ga   dekiru no?*
  who-NOM John-ACC help   thing-NOM can   Q
  'Who can help John?'
 A: *John-ni-wa   {Mary/ano ojisan}-ga   i-ru.*
  John-DAT-TOP {Mary/that man}-NOM be
  'John has {Mary/that man}.' (cf. Kishimoto 2005)

(28) Q: Where is my umbrella?
 A: John has it.

(29) Q: *Watasi-no kasa   doko-ni a-ru no?*
  My   umbrella where be   Q
  'Where is my umbrella?'
 A: **John-ni   (sono kasa-ga)   a-ru.*
  John-DAT (the umbrella-NOM) be
  'John has it.'

There are languages in which the objects are not allowed to bear old information when the DE does not arise. According to Tham (2005, 2006), an example of such a language is Mandarin. To make this concrete, compare the question-answer pairs in (30) and (31).

(30) Q. *Sanmao ca   shenme dongxi?*
  Sanmao wipe what   thing

The Definiteness Effect and a New Classification of Possessive Constructions

    'What is Sanmao wiping/polishing?'
   A. *Sanmao you na xie jingzi.*
    Sanmao have that some mirror
    'Sanmao has those mirrors.'   (Tham 2006:146)

(31) Q. *Na xie jingzi zai nar ne?*
    That PL mirror be at where Q-PRT
    'Where are those mirrors?'
   A. *#Sanmao you (na xie jingzi).*
    Sanmao have that some mirror
    'Sanmao has those mirrors.'   (Tham 2006:146)

4 Differences between the DE in possessive constructions and the DE in *there* constructions

There constructions are known to be used for information structural purposes, i.e., the post-verbal noun phrase conveys new, focus information for the addressee. It is commonly agreed in the literature that *there* constructions can be used to introduce hearer new entities (cf. Abbott 1992, 1993). That is, it is generally anomalous to assert the existence of an entity presumed to be familiar for the addressee. Thus, naturally enough, noun phrases with determiners such as *the, every, both, most*, as well as proper names and pronouns, are excluded from the post-verbal positions in *there* constructions, hence an unacceptable sentence **There are the candidates for the job.* Even in *there* constructions with a list interpretation, where post-verbal noun phrases are definite, the definite phrases should not be used anaphorically. In this sense, *there* constructions with a list-reading as well as 'normal' *there* constructions (with a non list reading) are felicitous as long as post-verbal noun phrases convey new information for the hearer. In other words, the DE in the *there* construction is attributed to its presentational function.

  In possessive constructions both in English and Japanese, on the other hand, there is not such a restriction on the information structure of the objects, when the constructions show the DE. That is, the objects can convey old information as well as new. Observe the following examples:

123

(32)   Q: Is John married?
       A: He has a beautiful wife.
       (cf. It is a beautiful wife that John has.)

The utterance in (32A), where the object *a beautiful wife* conveys new information, is a felicitous response to the question in (32Q).

On the other hand, the objects in English possessive constructions can also express old information:

(33)   Q: Who has a wife/lover?
       A: John has a wife/lover.
       (cf. It is John who has a wife.)

The question in (33Q) sets up a context in which the subject *John* in the felicitous response (33A) is focused, while the object *a wife* or *a lover* is presupposed.

It should be noted that the same explanation can be applied to the objects in Japanese possessive constructions:

(34)   (a)   *John-ni-wa   otooto-ga   i-ru.*
             John-DAT-TOP brother-NOM be
             'John has a brother.'
       (b)   *John-ni   i-ru no wa   otooto   dake da.*
             John-DAT be   that-TOP brother only COP
             'It is only a brother that John has.'
       (c)   *Otooto-ga   i-ru no wa   John da.*
             brother-NOM be   that-TOP John COP
             'It is John who has a brother.'   (Kishimoto 2005:228-229)

As the sentences in (34b) and (34c) illustrate, not only *otooto* ('brother') in the object position in (34a) but also *John* in the dative subject position in (34a) can appear in the focus position of the pseudo-cleft constructions. Thus, the objects in Japanese possessive constructions also do not have to bear new information; they can also express old information for the addressee.

In sum, the DE in *there* constructions and in English and Japanese possessive constructions cannot be accounted for from the same perspective. The DE in *there* constructions is accounted for in terms of the presentational function. By contrast, the objects of possessive constructions both in English and Japanese do

The Definiteness Effect and a New Classification of Possessive Constructions

not have to convey new information; the information structure of the objects is underspecified.

5 Varieties of possessive constructions in Japanese

In what follows, we point out that there seem to be several competing possessive constructions besides possessive constructions with *iru* ('be') and *aru* ('be') in Japanese. We argue that they are all related to main typological patterns of possessive constructions Stassen (2009) claims.

5.1 'Eel' constructions in Japanese as a focus reading

In this section, we claim that so-called 'eel' constructions, which are allegedly peculiar to Japanese, are another sort of possessive constructions Japanese possesses, corresponding to the English possessive constructions with a focus reading.

To recapitulate a focus reading and a control (nonfocal) reading, which are subclasses of a holding interpretation, let us first look at the following contrast. The sentences in (35aA) and (35bA) obtain a focus reading, while the sentence in (36A) receives a control reading:

(35) (a) Q. Which group are you taking around?
 A. I have the old ladies. (But I can't seem to find them.)
 (b) Q. Who is taking which group around?
 A. I have the old ladies. (But I can't seem to find them.)

(36) Q. Where are the old ladies?
 A. I have them. (#But I can't seem to find them.)

As we have examined earlier, the Japanese verbs *iru* ('be') and *aru* ('be'), originally existential verbs BE, can be used when a focus reading is received (cf. (27A)). Even when a focus reading is obtained, however, the verbs *iru* ('be') and *aru* ('be') are not always available. As shown in (37aA) and (37bA), a special construction seems to be used in some cases:

(37) (a) Q. *Kimi-wa dono guruupu-wo tsurete iru no?*
 you-TOP which group-ACC take Q
 'Which group are you taking around?'

	A.	*Watashi-wa obaasantachi da.*
		I-TOP old ladies COP
		'I am taking around the old ladies.'
	A'	**Watashi-ni-wa obaasantachi-ga iru.*
		I-DAT-TOP old ladies-NOM be.pres
		'I am taking around the old ladies.'
(b)	Q.	*Dare-ga dono guruupu-wo tsurete iru no?*
		who-NOM which group-ACC take Q
		'Who is taking which group around?'
	A.	*Watashi-wa obaasantachi da.*
		I-TOP old ladies COP
		'I am taking around the old ladies.'
	A'	**Watashi-ni-wa obaasantachi-ga iru.*
		I-DAT-TOP old ladies-NOM be.pres
		'I am taking around the old ladies.'

The sentence (37aA) and the sentence (37bA) are so-called 'eel' constructions in Japanese, which are said to be fairly peculiar to Japanese (cf. Okutsu 1978). 'Eel' constructions contain the copular verb *-da*, which is different from *iru* ('be') and *aru* ('be'). The copular verb *-da* in this construction appears in place of other semantically specific verbs. Suppose that you are in a Japanese restaurant and call a waitress to order a delicious grilled eel and rice. You will give your order with the following words:

(38)   *Boku-wa unagi da.*
       I-TOP eel COP
       'What I want to eat is an eel./I'll have/take an eel.'

The copular verb *-da* in this construction is a shortened substitute for all possible specific verbs (*taberu* ('to eat/to have'), *chuumonsuru* ('to order'), etc.). For a felicitous use, some sort of "pair-list" reading with the contrastive topic is necessary.

5.2 Varieties of Japanese possessive constructions and their typological status

So far, we have suggested two varieties of the possessive constructions in Japanese: the one with the originally existential verbs *aru* ('be') and *iru* ('be') and the other

The Definiteness Effect and a New Classification of Possessive Constructions

with the copular verb -*da* (COP). In this section, we suggest another possessive construction in Japanese based on the continuative form of the verb *mot*- ('take,' 'hold': TAKE).

In the following possessive constructions with *mot*- ('take,' 'hold') (39)–(40), a possessive interpretation is intended, because each example expresses an inherent property attributed to the subject. As is illustrated in (39) and (40), under a possessive interpretation, nonrelational nouns, but not relational nouns can be used in the object position. It should be noted here that this construction is acceptable only if the subject is animate and the object is inanimate.

(39)   (a)   *Watasi-wa {ie/kaisha}-o   mot-teiru.*
             I-TOP   {house/company}-ACC take-CONT
             'I have a house/company.'   (nonrelational, inanimate)
   (b)   **Watasi-wa untenshu-o mot-teiru.*
             I-TOP   driver-ACC take-CONT.
             'I have a chauffeur.'   (nonrelational, animate)

(40)   (a)   **Watasi-wa 8-gatsu-ni   tanjoobi-o   mot-teiru.*
             I-TOP   August-DAT birthday-ACC take-CONT
             'My birthday is August.'   (relational, inanimate)
   (b)   *Watasi-wa {*imooto/??musuko}-o mot-teiru.*
             I-TOP   {sister/son}-ACC   take-CONT
             'I have a sister/son.'   (relational, animate)

Also, the animacy restriction of this kind holds for the object of possessive constructions with *mot*- ('take,' 'hold') when a focus reading is received:

(41)   Q: *Watashi-ni-wa nani-ga   aru no?*
            I-DAT-TOP   what-NOM be Q
            'What (on earth) do I have?'
   A: *Kimi-wa daiteitaku-o mot-teiru.*
            you-TOP villa-ACC   take-CONT
            'You have a villa.'

(42)   Q: *Dare-ga   John-o   tetsudau koto-ga   dekiru no?*
            who-NOM John-ACC help   thing-NOM can   Q
            'Who can help John?'

A: *John-wa {Mary/ano ojisan}-o   mot-teiru.
   John-TOP {Mary/that man}-ACC take-CONT
   'John has Mary/that man.'

(43) A. Sono ki-ni-wa   mou sukoshi kazari-ga   iru   ne.
        the tree-DAT-TOP a little more trimmings-NOM need PRT
        'We need more trimmings for this tree.'
     B. *Kono ki-wa   kyonen katta denkyu-o   mot-teiru   yo.
        this tree-TOP last year bought light-NOM take-CONT PRT
        'The tree has all those lights we got last year.'

Moreover, the same restriction can be found in a control reading, which is received when the object conveys old information:

(44) Q. Dare-ga   Chomsky-no hon-o   mot-teiru   no?
        who-NOM Chomsky's book-ACC take-CONT Q
        'Who is holding the Chomsky book?'
     A. John-ga   Chomsky-no hon-o   mot-teiru.
        John-NOM Chomsky's book-ACC take-CONT.pres
        'John is holding the Chomsky book.'

(45) Q. Dare-ga   obaasantachi-o tsure-teiru no?
        who-NOM old ladies-ACC take-CONT Q
        'Who's taking the old ladies?'
     A. *Jane-ga   obaasantachi-o mot-teiru.
        Jane-NOM old ladies-ACC take-CONT.pres
        'Jane has them.'

In sum, there are three kinds of possessive constructions in Japanese: possessive constructions with the verb BE, 'eel' constructions with the copular verb *-da*, and possessive construction with the verb *mot-teiru* ('take'). This indicates that a natural language may have plural strategies to express the notion of possession. In this connection, Stassen (2009) has newly proposed a typology of possessive constructions. His classification with four major classes is introduced in (46). Japanese possessive construction with BE roughly corresponds to (46a), whereas the construction with the transitive verb *mot-teiru* can be related to constructions with transitive *have* (46d). 'Eel' constructions with the copular verb *-da* are compared with (46b).

(46) (a) The locational possessive: Korean
(b) The topic (or double subject) possessive: Highland Chontal
(Tequistlatecan)
(c) The *with* possessive: Bari (Nilo-Saharan, Nilotic)
(d) The *have* possessive: Miskito (Chibchan in Nicaragua)
(e) minors (genitive, adjectival, conjunctional, ...)

6 Concluding remarks

In this paper, we firstly argued that every instance of contexts in which the DE is found in possessive constructions is attributed to the possessive interpretation of the construction, and not to the inalienability expressed by the object. The explanation in terms of a new classification of interpretations is adequate enough to account for the DE in possessive constructions both in English and Japanese.

Secondly, we argued that the approach in terms of information structure makes it clear that there is a difference between English and Japanese possessive constructions. Put differently, only English *have* allows possessive constructions to have a control reading. The Japanese verbs *iru* ('be') and *aru* ('be'), however, cannot license the old or presupposed object.

Thirdly, the DE in *there* constructions and in possessive constructions both in English and Japanese differ from one another in that the former comes from the presentational function of *there* constructions and the latter, by contrast, cannot be attributed to a restriction on the information structure of the object.

Finally, we have argued that there are at least three different possessive constructions in Japanese, namely, possessive constructions with *iru* ('be') and *aru* ('be'), 'eel' constructions with the copular verb *-da* and possessive constructions with the verb *mot-teiru* ('take'). We have argued that they are all related to typological patterns of possessive constructions.

In sum, we have proposed a "verbal solution" with respect to the DE phenomena in the object position of the verb *have*. This is contrasted to the traditional "nominal solutions," which are based on the distinction of the object head noun in its inalienability or relationality. However, the latter need not be rejected in our verbal solution. Whereas the strong theory in the verbal solution means that the verbal meaning alone ("possession" vs. "holding") decides on the existence of DE on the object irrespective of the argument structure of the object NP, the weak theory may well concede that its argument structure plays a part depending on the verbal meaning. We have argued that the meaning of the verb is settled first in the given context, which then determines the argument structure of the object NP. Therefore, the VP level is inevitably involved in this theory (on its grammatical part).

References

Abbott, B. 1992. *Definiteness, existentials, and the 'list' interpretation.* Proceedings of SALT II, 1–16. Columbus, Ohio: The Ohio State University.

Abbott, B. 1993. *A pragmatic account of the definiteness effect in existential sentences.* Journal of Pragmatics 19. 39–55.

de Jong, F. 1987. *The compositional nature of (in)definiteness.* In Reuland, E. & A. ter Meulen (eds.), The Representation of (In)definiteness, 270–285. Cambridge, Mass: MIT Press.

Heine, B. 1997. *Cognitive Foundations of Grammar.* Oxford: Oxford University Press.

Keenan, E. L. 1987. *A Semantic Definition of Indefinite NP.* In Reuland, E. & A. ter Meulen (eds.), The Representation of (In)definiteness, 286–317. Cambridge, Mass: MIT Press.

Kishimoto, H. 2000. *Locational Verbs, Agreement, and Object Shift in Japanese,* The Linguistic Review 17, 53–109.

Kishimoto, H. 2005. *Toogo Koozoo to Bunpoo Kankei (Syntactic Structure and Grammatical Relation).* Tokyo: Kurosio Publishers.

Okutsu, K. 1978. *Boku wa unagi da no bunpoo (The grammar of 'boku wa unagi da').* Tokyo: Kurosio Publishers.

Partee, B. H. 1999. *Weak NP's in HAVE Sentences.* In J. Gerbrandy, M. Marx, M. de Rijke, & Y. Venema, (eds.), JFAK, CD-Rom, Amsterdam: University of Amsterdam.

Stassen, L. 2009. *Possession: towards an explanatory model,* Handout from the Presentation at Verbal and Nominal Possession Workshop, held at the University of Düsseldorf.

Tham, S. W. 2005. *Representing Possessive Predication: Semantic Dimensions and Pragmatic Bases,* Ph.D. dissertation, Stanford University.

References

Tham, S. W. 2006. *The Definiteness Effect in Have Sentences*. In Pascal Denis et al. (eds.), Proceedings of the 2004 Texas Linguistics Society Conference, 137–149. Somerville, MA: Cascadilla Proceedings Project.

Authors

Yuko Kobukata
University of Tsukuba
Graduate School of Humanities and Social Sciences
ykobu@f2.dion.ne.jp

Yoshiki Mori
The University of Tokyo
Department of Language and Information Sciences
mori@boz.c.u-tokyo.ac.jp

Reprint: Originally published in Y.-S. Kang, J.-Y. Yoon, J. Hong, J.-S. Wu, S. Rhee, K.-A. Kim, D.-H. Choi, K.-H. Kim & H.-K. Kang (eds.), *Universal grammar and individual languages*. Proceedings of SICOL 2010. Seoul, University of Korea, 2010.

Referential Properties of Nouns across Languages[1]

Doris Gerland & Christian Horn

Abstract

In this paper, we argue that nouns in each of their lexicalized meanings have certain referential properties encoded in their lexical entries. Due to these referential properties, the meaning variants of nouns are predisposed for certain determination. However, in actual use nouns often occur in grammatical contexts that differ from these predisposed uses. On the basis of data from typologically different languages, we argue that such grammatical variations follow systematic referential modification patterns of the respective meaning variant of a noun. In accordance with Löbner (2010), we will refer to the underlying cognitive processes as type shifts and show that they provide a stimulating approach to widely discussed phenomena such as definite article splits and alienability splits.

1 Introduction: Types of nouns and types of determination

Over the past few decades, several noun-type distinctions have been discussed, including considerations about common nouns, proper nouns, count nouns, and mass nouns (e. g., Krifka 1989, Chierchia 1998, Payne & Huddleston 2002, Pelletier 2009). The distinction between sortal and relational nouns is generally taken as a distinction between one-place predicates and two- (or more-) place predicates (Partee 1983/1997, Barker 1995, Jensen & Vikner 2002, Asudeh 2005). Löbner

---

[1] The research reported in this paper was financed by the German Research Foundation, research unit FOR 600, "Functional Concepts and Frames". We would like to express our gratitude to Sebastian Löbner, Albert Ortmann, Nicolas Kimm, and James Kilbury. This paper is based on our considerations in 2009 and 2010 and on an earlier outline of Löbner's theory of concept types and determination in (2010), published (2011).

(1985, 2010) takes this distinction as a starting point for a classification of nouns into four logical types that differ with respect to their referential properties, i. e., UNIQUENESS (inherently unique vs. nonunique) and RELATIONALITY (inherently relational vs. nonrelational). Löbner distinguishes between sortal nouns ('SN' such as *flower, table*), relational nouns ('RN'; *sister, friend*), functional nouns ('FN'; *mother, president*), and individual nouns ('IN'; *sun, pope*, proper names). Within this classification, individual and functional nouns are inherently unique in the sense that the number of possible referents is restricted to one in a given context. In contrast, for sortal and relational nouns the number of possible referents is unrestricted. Relational and functional nouns are inherently relational and require the specification of an additional argument for reference. Löbner (2010) assumes that the lexical referential properties of nouns influence the way they are used grammatically. In accordance with their referential properties, functional and relational nouns can be seen as predisposed for possessive use. Due to their inherent uniqueness, individual and functional nouns exhibit a predisposition for definite use. However, the classification of nouns into four logical types faces some challenges, including the following: (1) Most nouns are polysemous (Pustejovsky 1995, 1996, Yael 2000). Lexicalized (Löbner 2010) meaning variants may have different logical types due to their different referential properties. If nouns can be classified with respect to their logical type it seems plausible to assume one logical type for each lexical entry of a noun. We refer to the logical type of a lexical entry as its **lexical type**. In this paper, we will use Löbner's terms SN, RN, FN, IN to refer to the lexical types of meaning variants. (2) One can observe that in actual use (e. g., within the NP) the logical type of a noun often differs from its lexical type. Sortal nouns, for example, often occur with definite marking (*the table, this flower*). However, if the lexical distinction holds, these uses can be explained by systematic type shifts. Löbner (2010) argues that nouns can be shifted between the four type classes. Hence, we need another term to refer to the logical type of a noun in actual use. In order to stay close to the established terms, we will speak of sortal concepts (SC), relational concepts (RC), individual concepts (IC), and functional concepts (FC) in such cases. For illustration, consider the following examples:

(1)   *The sun is rising.*

(2)   *The suns are rising.*

(3) A sun is rising.

(4) This sun is rising.

Sun can be regarded as an IN (i. e., as a unique, cf. Hawkins 1978, Lyons 1999). In everyday life, we experience only the one sun of our solar system rising. (2)–(4) contradict this perception and require the (mental) construction of a situation with more than one sun. This effect is reflected by the mismatch of number (as in (2)) and determination (as in (3), (4)) in contrast to the lexically unique reference of the noun. In these contexts, the IN *sun* is shifted to an SC.

(5) Maria is Peter's mother.

(6) Maria is the mother.

(7) Maria is a mother of Peter.

(8) Maria is a mother.

Conceptually, every person has only one mother and a mother is always the mother of someone. Hence, *mother* is a FN. The use in (5) is perfectly interpretable without further context and agrees with the lexical type of the noun. In (6) mother is used as an IC; it still occurs with the definite article but without a possessor argument. Hence, without further context, the utterance in (6) would naturally lead to the addressee asking the question "Whose mother?"[2] In both (7) and (8) *mother* occurs with the indefinite article. (7) sounds awkward since the uniqueness condition is given up and the mother is shifted to a relational concept. Still, (7) may be acceptable in certain contexts (e. g., if Maria is Peter's stepmother). However, the crucial point is that such contexts are – in contrast to (5) – required for interpretability. The expression in (8) differs from (7) in the nonpossessive use which leads to a focus on the sortal characteristics of being a mother; here *mother* is shifted to a SC.

The goal of our paper is to present typological evidence for the noun type classification and to have a closer look at type shifts. For these purposes, it seems obvious to look at languages that explicitly reflect the categories UNIQUENESS (inherently unique vs. nonunique) and RELATIONALITY (inherently relational vs. non-

---

[2] Horn (thesis, in prep.), takes this characteristic of [+R] nouns as a test criterion for distinguishing [+R] from [-R] concept types.

relational) grammatically, the more fine-grained the better. As for the uniqueness distinction, we will focus on several regional variants spoken in Germany which exhibit two different definite articles (Ebert 1971, Hartmann 1982, Himmelmann 1997, Studler 2004, Schwager 2007, Schwarz 2009). These articles are assumed to mark different kinds of uniqueness, i.e., inherent uniqueness and inherent nonuniqueness (section 2). We also highlight a phenomenon mostly neglected so far, i.e., the unpredicted use of inherently nonunique nouns with the weak definite article. For the relationality distinction, we investigate typologically different languages that show explicit marking for different kinds of relationality with a strong focus on alienable and inalienable possession (section 3).

2 Insights from definiteness marking

2.1 Approaches to uniqueness

Many approaches to unambiguous reference focus on the function of the definite article. Lyons (1999) and Abbott (2004) discuss the principle approaches: according to the familiarity account (Heim 1982), the definite article indicates that the referent of the particular NP is already familiar to both speaker and addressee. The identifiability approach assumes, as Lyons (1999) points out, that the definite article directs the addressee to the referent by signaling that she is able to identify the intended referent (Chafe 1976, Birner & Ward 1994). Löbner (1985) builds his theory on a third approach, the uniqueness theory (Russell 1905, Strawson 1950, Donnellan 1966). The main assumption of the uniqueness approach is that the definite article indicates that there is only one entity which satisfies the used definite description, i.e., an entity that is unique. Löbner (1985) proposes a distinction between semantic and pragmatic definiteness that also includes uniqueness coming from other parts of the expression. For semantic definiteness the referent is established independently of the immediate situation or context of utterance. Pragmatic definiteness depends on special situations and contexts for the nonambiguity (and existence) of a referent. In this paper, we will use the terms semantic and pragmatic uniqueness instead and reserve the term definiteness to refer to the grammatical marking of uniqueness. We will apply the distinction to the analysis of some regional variants in Germany that exhibit two definite articles, one often referred to as the strong, the other as the weak definite article. This article split has been analyzed as reflecting semantic versus pragmatic uniqueness (cf.

Löbner 1985 for Fering, Ripuarian, Himmelmann 1997 for Ripuarian, Studler 2004 for Alemannic, Schwager 2007 for Bavarian, Ortmann 2014 also for Dutch and Swedish): pragmatic uniqueness is signaled by the strong, semantic uniqueness by the weak definite article. If we consider INs and FNs as semantically unique and SNs and RNs as pragmatically unique, one might expect that SNs and RNs only occur with the strong definite article. However, we will provide a type shift-based explanation as to why the latter also occur with the weak definite article under certain conditions.

2.2 Definite article splits in language

A frequently mentioned example is Frisian, a West-Germanic language, as investigated by Ebert (1971). Table 1 shows the paradigm of the definite article split for Frisian Fering (spoken on the island of Föhr).

	masc.	fem.	neutr.
weak	a	at	at
strong	di	det	det

Table 1: Definite articles (singular) in Fering (forms according to Ebert 1971)

Ebert (1971) argues that the use of the weak definite article ('A-article') signals that the speaker presupposes the referent of the NP is either part of the universe of discourse (we prefer the term 'participants' shared reference set', henceforth 'SET') or is related to a familiar referent in a well-known relationship. The strong definite article ('D-article') contains an additional deictic element which points to the situation of utterance, to anaphoric or cataphoric specifying information, and helps to select the appropriate referent. Hence, INs and FNs which refer uniquely by definition should occur with the weak definite article, unless they undergo shifts that change their logical type.

Fering (Ebert 1971: 71,97)

(9) A   san skiinjt   (10)   Kreske fing een üüb anöös
     DEF$_{WEAK}$ sun shine   Kreske got one on DEF$_{WEAK}$ nose
     'The sun is shining.'   'Kreske got hit on her nose.'

San ('sun') as an individual noun has already been discussed. In (9) it is used with the weak definite article as predicted. Nöös ('nose') is a good example of an FN since every person has one and only one nose. In accordance with the predictions, it occurs with the weak definite article in (10). In contrast, the anaphoric use of the Fering SN *kü* ('cow') in (11) and the Bavarian SN *biachl* ('book') in (12) requires the strong definite article. It signals that the referent is only referred to in anaphoric use.

Fering (Ebert 1971: 107)

(11) Peetje hee an kü   slaachtet.   Jo   saai, det   kü   wiar äi sünj.
      Peetje has a cow slaughtered they say DEF$_{STRONG}$ cow was not healthy
      'Peter slaughtered a cow. They say the cow was not healthy.'

Bavarian (Schwager 2007)

(12) Da   Maxi hod a biachl kaft. Sei Mama hod des   biachl scho
      DEF$_{WEAK}$ Maxi has a book bought his mom has DEF$_{STRONG}$ book already
      glesn.
      read
      'Maxi bought a book. His mom has already read the book.'

Proper names in Bavarian, such as *Maxi* in (12), and in Ripuarian (*et Waltraud*) in general occur with the weak definite article. However, Hartmann (1982) reports that proper names may also be used with the strong definite article (*dat Waltraud*) in Ripuarian if the speaker is annoyed about the respective person which can hence be considered a marked use of the proper name.

2.3   Permanently established ICs

As we will see now, SNs and RNs may occur with the strong or with the weak definite article when shifted to ICs or FCs – something which is not predicted by Löbner's approach. With respect to the noun type classification, INs would naturally refer within the participants' shared reference set. One question that is widely discussed in the literature (also in different terms and different frameworks) is when an IC actually becomes part of the reference set (cf. Hawkins 1978, Prince 1992, Gundel, Hedberg & Zacharski 1993, Ariel 1998, for example). We cannot fully answer this question here but want to shed some light on it from the noun type perspective. An IC may be the result of an ad hoc shift for reference in the respective situation of utterance only. Also, ICs may become more permanent between participants and hence refer just like proper names. Consequently, we assume that in such cases type shifts are not required and the IC is established as what we will call a 'permanently established IC' (PEIC) within the participants' shared reference set. In this view, PEICs are semantically unique within the respective SET. This could, for example, be the case for ICs that have been used frequently enough or those that are seen as very prominent between participants so that a PEIC would reduce the cognitive effort of disambiguation and type shifting. For illustration, imagine a family that has a dog. Within the family, the SN *hünj* ('dog', Fering) refers as a PEIC to the dog (of the family) just like its given name. This analysis is reflected by the use of the weak definite article in (13) (cf. also Hawkins 1978: 117 'larger situation use with specific knowledge').

Fering (Ebert 1971: 83)

(13)   *A   hünj hee tuwwark.*
        DEF$_{WEAK}$ dog has toothache
        'The dog has toothache.'

Ebert (1971) calls such concepts 'situative Unika' ('situational uniques'). However, to refer to a dog on the street or in anaphoric use, the strong definite article is generally used (*Det hünj hee tuwwark*). The German dialects Ripuarian (spoken in the Rhineland) and Bavarian reflect the use of the weak definite article discussed so far. Consider the SN *kenk* ('child') in (14a) which is shifted to an IC with the strong definite article indicating that the child is not part of the SET. *Kenk* in (14b) and *kind* (15) are other examples of PEICs (e. g., in the sense of "our own child" or "the child that we take care of").

Ripuarian (Hartmann 1982: 196)

(14)   (a)   *Dat   kenk es am   jriene*
               DEF$_{STRONG}$ child is PROGR cry
               'The child is crying.'
        (b)   *Et   kenk es am   jriene*
               DEF$_{WEAK}$ child is PROGR cry
               'The child is crying.'

Bavarian (Schwager 2007)

(15)   *Ogott, mia ham vogessn,   das ma 's   Kind abhoin!*
        o.god we   have forgotten   that we DEF$_{weak}$ child pick.up
        'Oh god, we forgot to pick up the child!'

PEICs and INs can differ with respect to their lexical type. Whereas INs are lexically constructed as uniquely referring to one entity only, PEICs can be the result of shifts of any noun type. They are not necessarily lexically unique. With respect to their uses, however, INs and PEICs resemble each other. Proper names (belonging to INs in Löbner's classification), for example, may have only one referent within a certain SET but also multiple potential referents in a different SET. PEICs may refer semantically uniquely between very few participants only or (as an extreme) within a whole speech community. They can also be seen as one way of assigning a noun a unique referent which can be temporary or become lexicalized.

3 Insights from possession marking

3.1 Approaches to possession and alienability

Several notions of possession have been proposed (cf. Seiler 1983, Heine 1997, McGregor 2009). We follow Heine (1997) in interpreting possession as all kinds of constructions in language that express a conceptual relation between entities. Within these relations, the possessor is seen as the grammatical realization of the entity that owns the other entity or entities, has control over it, is it's producer or represents a whole entity with the other being part of it. In a possessive construction, we refer to the entity that is possessed, controlled, produced or part-of as the possessum. Some languages reflect different relations grammatically (cf. Seiler 1983). They distinguish, for example, between certain possessive constructions exclusively used for kinship relations and body-part relations on the one hand and other kinds of possessive constructions for all other kinds of relations on the other (cf. Chapell & McGregor 1996). According to McGregor (2009), the most widespread distinction with respect to possession is that between alienable and inalienable possession (Nichols 1988), often referred to as an alienability split. For alienable possession, the relation between possessor and possessum is separable and not inherently determined; moreover, the relation need not be permanent. In contrast, inalienable possession is considered inseparable under normal conditions, and the kind of relation is fixed (cf. McGregor 2009). The inalienability of a relation between possessor and possessum is determined by the semantics of the latter, i.e., the kind of relation is inherent (Seiler 1983). Heine (1997: 10) lists the following terms as primary candidates for inalienable relations: kinship terms

(*Peter's mother*), body parts (*The girl's nose*), relational spatial concepts (*The end of the semester*), part-whole relations (*The trees branch*), physical and mental states (*Lisa's strength*), nominalizations (*The planting of the bananas*), and what Heine calls individual concepts[3] (*name, voice*). Not all languages that exhibit an alienability split treat all mentioned candidates as inalienable. The language specific distribution heavily depends on cultural concepts (McGregor 2009).

The alienability split is often grammatically reflected in language, sometimes to a very fine-grained extent (cf. Classical Nahuatl in 3.2). According to Seiler (1983), inherently relational (including inalienable) nouns tend to occur unmarked or less marked across languages since the kind of relation between possessor and possessum is already determined by the latter and needs not to be made explicit. Contrastively, alienable nouns tend to occur with additional lexical material in possessive constructions, such as classifiers or predicative possession. Seiler calls this relation 'established' since the kind of relation has to be made explicit. Some possessive markers used in alienable possessive constructions provide further information about the kind of established relation (as shown in section 3.2 for Oceanic classifier languages or as can be stated for predicative possession). Ortmann & Handschuh (2004) link the analysis of alienability splits with Löbner's noun type classification, an approach we will follow in 3.2. We will also see that the different marking of alienable and inalienable nouns can provide clues for the identification of lexical and shifted types (see also Partee & Borschev 2000).

3.2 Alienability splits in language

Ortmann & Handschuh (2004) analyze three Mayan languages (Yucatec, Itzaaj, and Mam) with respect to the so-called derelationality marker. They consider this kind of marker a shift marker indicating the conceptual shift from an inalienable RN to a SC. Compare the examples in (16).

Yucatec (Mayan; Lehmann, 1998: 70 ff)

(16) (a) in tàatah
P'OR1SG father
'my father'

---

[3] Heine (1997) uses the term 'individual concept' to refer to individual characteristics of persons and entities.

(b) *le tàatah-tsil-o'*
 DF father-DEREL-ART
 'the father'

The FN *tàatah* ('father') receives no special marking when used in accordance with its lexical type (16a). The possessive pronoun only indicates whose father is referred to. When used in a nonrelational way, the derelativization morpheme *-tsil-* is added to the noun in order to signal that the inherent relationality has been given up as in (16b) (Ortmann & Handschuh 2004). This kind of shift marker occurs also in Paamese, Cahuilla, Koyukon and Q'eqchi indicating the process of 'derelativization' (Seiler 1983) or 'absolutivization' (Lehmann 1998).

Paamese (Oceanic; Crowley 1996: 417)

(17) vat-in a-vat
 head-3SG.POSS DEREL-head
 'his/her head' 'head'

Cahuilla (Uto-Aztecan; Seiler 1983: 25)

(18) hé-puš púč-il
 3SG.POSS-eye eye-DEREL
 'his eye' 'eye'

Koyukon (Athabaskan; Thompson 1996: 654-667)

(19) se-tlee' k'e-tlee'
 1SG-head DEREL-head
 'my head' 'head'

Q'eqchi (Mayan; Kockelman 2009: 346)

(20) in-ch'ool ch'ool-ej
 1SG-heart heart-DEREL
 'my heart' 'heart'

The use of inalienable body-part terms (such as 'head' in (17), (19), 'eye' in (18), and 'heart' in (20)) as SCs requires an additional marker for derelativization. Thus, they are explicitly marked when shifted from an inalienable FN ('head', 'heart') or RN ('eyes') to a SC. In Paamese, the suffix for derelativization is only realized when the inalienable noun is used absolute (Crowley 1996). When shifted to an alienable noun, a marker indicating alienability is required (*vat ona-k*, head POSS-1SG, 'my head' (in the sense of 'my leader') (Crowley 1996: 421)). In Koyukon, however, the morpheme indicating derelativization occurs also in the alienable relational construction: *se-k'e-k'e-tlee'*; 'my (animal's) head' (Thompson 1996: 667, Löbner 2010).

Classical Nahuatl not only exhibits a marker for derelativization (21a) for the absolute use of a relational noun but also one marker for alienable and one for inalienable constructions:

Classical Nahuatl (Amerindian, Launey 1981: 100 f)

(21)   (a)   *omi-tl*
    bone-DEREL
    'bone'
       (b)   *m-omi-yo*
    2SG-bone-INAL
    'your bone (part of your skeleton)'
       (c)   *m-omi-uh*
    2SG-bone-AL
    'your bone (on a plate)'

Bone is a RN and can be realized as an inalienable (21b) or alienable RC (21c) with the respective morphemes. According to Launey (1981: 89–105) the use of the alienability morpheme on an inalienable noun indicates that the possessum is external to the possessor, i. e., the part-whole relation is given up. Thus, the inherent relation is not the one expressed in the alienable possessive construction; instead a different kind of relation is established.

Oceanic classifier languages exhibit an alienability distinction which reflects Seiler's assumptions in that they mark inalienable relations only with a possessive suffix and alienable relations with additional classifiers. Depending on the richness of the possessive classifier system, the relation established can be made more explicit and indicate the kind of possession (e. g., a legal ownership possession or a possession for food purposes). Lichtenberk (1983: 148) states that the use of possessive ("relational" in his terms) classifiers is not determined by the properties of the possessum but by the nature of the relation between possessor and possessum. The possessive classifier categorizes the possessum with respect to the relation to its possessor (Lichtenberk 2009: 263). In Manam, kinship terms, body parts, and part-whole terms belong to the category of inalienable entities. When used in a possessive construction, they take a personal possessive suffix indicating person and number of the possessor. Alienable nouns are additionally marked with one of the two possessive classifiers depending on what kind of relationship they encode. *'ana-* indicates that the possessum is food or something associated with food (garden, bottle, basket), while *ne-* is used for all other kinds of possession.

Manam (Oceanic; Lichtenberk 2009: 249)

(22) (a) *paŋana-gu*
head-1.SG.POSS
'my head'
(b) *uma 'ana-gu*
garden POSS.CLF-1SG.POSS
'my garden'

The FN *paŋana* ('head') in (22a) takes only the possessive suffix representing its inherent kind of relationality. It is used with the inalienable possessive marker in accordance with its lexical type. For the SN *uma* ('garden') the 'food'-possessive classifier is used (22b). However, FN and RN can also take possessive classifiers. Consider the FN *paŋana* ('head') in the following examples:

Manam (Lichtenberk 1983: 302)

(23) (a) *paŋana 'ana-gu*
head POSS.CLF-1.SG.POSS
'my head (to eat)'
(b) *paŋanane-gu*
headPOSS.CLF-1.SG.POSS
'my head (I found, I cut off)'

In (23a) and (23b), a different kind of possession is established and the possessive relationship is indicated no longer by the possessive suffix only but by a possessive classifier which now specifies the relation between possessor and possessum. In (23a) *paŋana* occurs with the food-possessive classifier, while in (23b) the general possessive classifier is used to indicate that the established relation differs from the inherent one and does not concern food. In both (23a) and (23b), the inalienable FN is shifted to an alienable FC in a specified relation which does not take the preferred relation (which is determined by the possessum) into account. Toqabaqita, another Oceanic language, has no possessive classifiers but uses a separate marker for alienable possession.

Toqabaqita (Oceanic; Lichtenberk 2005: 343)

(24) (a) *gwau-ku*
head-1SG
'my head'

(b) *gwau nau*
   head 1SG.POSS
   'my (e. g., fish) head'

The inalienable FN *gwau* ('head') occurs with a suffix indicating person and number of the possessor and is used in accordance with its lexical type in (24a). In (24b), the relation is established with a separate possessive marker expressing an alienable kind of relation and the FN is shifted to an alienable FC. (25a) and (25b) show that different meaning variants of nouns can have different lexical types:

Toqabaqita (Oceanic; Lichtenberk 2005: 345)

(25) (a) *fote-ku*
   shoulder.blade-1SG
   'my shoulder blade'
 (b) *fote nau*
   paddle 1SG.POSS
   'my paddle'

The relational meaning variant of *fote* ('shoulder blade') is used in accordance with its lexical type in the inalienable construction (25a) and the sortal variant in (25b) in the alienable construction.

An alienability split can also be observed in Hungarian. In adnominal possessive constructions, the possessum always takes a possessive marker that agrees with the person and number of the possessor. Certain nouns, however, take an additional suffix when used with the third-person singular possessive marker (Moravcsik 2003) and differ with respect to their meaning (Elekfi 2000).

Hungarian (Finno-Ugric, own data)

(26) (a) *a cipő talp-a*
   DEF shoe sole-POSS3SG
   'The shoe sole'
 (b) *Péter talp-a*
   Peter sole-POSS3SG
   'Peter's sole (of foot) '
 (c) *Péter talp-j-a*
   Peter sole-AL.SHIFT-POSS3SG
   'Peter's sole (of a shoe)'

Examples (26a) and (26b) illustrate the use of the RN *talp* ('sole') in accordance with its lexical type. A sole is typically a part of a shoe or a foot. In (26c), an alienable ownership relation is established. This modification is marked by the j-suffix and applies systematically for certain nouns in Hungarian (Elekfi 2000). When the j-suffix is not realized, only the inherent interpretation is possible. The established relation always results in an alienable relation. Note that the j-suffix can only be realized in combination with the possessive suffix.

4 Conclusion

The purpose of this paper was to present typological evidence for the noun type classification with respect to uniqueness and relationality and to introduce the notion of permanently established ICs. With respect to uniqueness, Fering, Bavarian and Ripuarian have shown that FNs and INs generally occur with the weak definite article when used in accordance with their lexical types; proper names as INs in the unmarked case also take the weak definite article but also allow the strong definite article in pejorative uses. SNs and RNs, in contrast, may occur both with the strong as well as with the weak definite article when shifted to ICs or FCs. We have argued that the use of the weak definite article signals that the speaker considers the referent of the NP to be a permanently established IC in the shared reference set with the addressee. In contrast, the use of the strong definite article indicates that the referent is not part of the set at the time of utterance. Hence, we can summarize that the distribution of the two definite articles in principle matches the predictions made by the noun type classification. The data show that SNs, RNs and FNs can be shifted to ICs. These ICs may refer within the context of utterance only (and then occur with the strong definite article) or become referentially permanently established (and then occur with the weak definite article) within the respective shared reference set. We conclude that permanently established ICs refer semantically uniquely within the respective shared reference set. With respect to their uses, INs and PEICs resemble each other, which is reflected by the use of the weak definite article in the languages investigated.

For relationality, the investigation has also shown further support for the noun type distinction. First, Yucatec Mayan, Koyukon, Cahuilla, Paamese, Q'eqchi, and Classical Nahuatl exhibit a derelativization morpheme which clearly indicates a type shift from an inalienable RN/FN to an SC. Second, the analysis of alienability splits in the languages investigated has shown that in inalienable possessive constructions, we only find inalienable RNs and FNs used in accordance with their lexical type. Hence it seems that these constructions are good indicators for lexical RNs and FNs. In contrast, all noun types can be used in alienable possessive constructions which signal for nonrelational nouns and inalienable nouns a shift to an alienable RC or FC. In the languages investigated, such shifts are marked with a possessive marker for alienable possession. The investigated Oceanic classifier languages exhibit possessive classifiers for different kinds of alienable possession. These classifiers not only indicate a shift of the noun but also explicitly indicate the kind of established alienable possession.

References

Abbott, B. 2004. Definiteness and Indefiniteness. In L.R. Horn & G. Ward (eds.) *The Handbook of Pragmatics*, 122–149. Oxford: Blackwell.

Ariel, M. 1998. Referring and Accessibility. *Journal of Linguistics* 24. 65–87.

Asudeh, A. 2005. Relational nouns, pronouns, and resumptions. *Linguistics and Philosophy*. 28 (4). 375–446.

Barker, C. 1995. *Possessive descriptions*. Stanford: CSLI Publications

Birner, B. & G. Ward 1994. Uniqueness, Familiarity, and the Definite Article in English. In *Proceedings of the Twentieth Annual Meeting of the Berkeley Linguistics Society: General Session Dedicated to the Contributions of Charles J. Fillmore*. 93–102.

Chafe, W. 1976. Givenness, Contrastiveness, Definiteness, Subjects, Topics, and Point of View. In C. Li (ed.), *Subject and Topic*, 27–55. New York: Academic Press.

Chapell, H. & W. McGregor 1996. *The grammar of inalienability*. Berlin: Mouton de Gruyter.

Chierchia, G. 1998. Reference to Kinds across Languages. *Natural Language Semantics* 6 (4). 339–405.

Christophersen, P. 1939. *The articles. A study of their theory and use in English*. Copenhagen: Munksgaard.

Crowley, T. 1996. Inalienable possession in Paamese grammar. In Chappell, H. & W. McGregor (eds.), *The Grammar of Inalienability*, 385–434. Berlin, New York: Mouton de Gruyter.

Donnellan, K. 1966. Reference and Definite Descriptions. *Philosophical Review* 77. 281–304.

Ebert, K. 1971. *Referenz, Sprechsituation und die bestimmten Artikel in einem nordfriesischen Dialekt.* PhD thesis. University of Kiel.

Elekfi, L. 2000. Semantic differences of suffix alternates in Hungarian. *Acta Linguistica Hungarica* 47. 145–177.

Gundel, J., N. Hedberg & R. Zacharski 1993. Cognitive Status and the Form of Referring Expressions in Discourse. *Language* 69. 247–307.

Hartmann, D. 1982. Deixis and Anaphora in German Dialects. The Semantics and Pragmatics of two definite Articles in dialectical varieties. In Weissenborn, J. (ed.), *Here and there*, 187–207. Amsterdam: Benjamins.

Hawkins, J. 1978. *Definiteness and Indefiniteness.* London: Croom Helm.

Heim, I. 1982. *The semantics of definite and indefinite noun phrases.* PhD Thesis, University of Massachusetts Amherst.

Heine, B. 1997. *Possession. Cognitive source, forces, and grammaticalization.* Cambridge: CUP.

Himmelmann, N. 1997. *Deiktikon, Artikel und Nominalphrase: Zur Emergenz syntaktischer Struktur.* Tübingen: Niemeyer.

Horn, C. (in prep.). *Nominal concept types and determination in German* (PhD thesis). University of Düsseldorf, Düsseldorf.

Kockelmann, P. 2009. Inalienable possession as grammatical category and discourse patterns. *Studies in Language* 33 (1). 25–68.

Krifka, M. 1989. Nominal reference, temporal constitution and quantification in event semantics. In Renate Bartsch, Johan van Benthem and Peter van Emde Boas (eds.), *Semantics and Contextual Expressions*, 75–115. Dordrecht: Foris.

Launey, M. 1981. *Introduction à la langue et à la littérature aztèques. Tome 1: grammaire.* Paris: L'Harmattan.

Lehmann, C. 1998. *Possession in Yucatec Maya.* Munich: Lincom.

Lichtenberk, F. 1983. *A Grammar of Manam.* Honolulu: University of Hawaii Press.

Lichtenberk, F. 2009. Attributive possessive constructions in Oceanic. In W. McGregor (ed.), *The expression of possession*, 249–291. Berlin, New York: Mouton de Gruyter.

Löbner, S. 1985. Definites. *Journal of Semantics* 4. 279–326.

References

Löbner, S. 1998. Definite Associative Anaphora. Ms. Download: http://www.phil-fak.uni-duesseldorf.de/asw/personal/loebner/publikationen/

Löbner, S. 2010. Types of nouns, NPs, and determination. Ms, University of Düsseldorf.

Löbner, S. 2011. Concept Types and Determination. *Journal of Semantics* 28(3). 279–333.

Lyons, C. 1999. *Definiteness*. Cambridge: Cambridge University Press.

McGregor, W. 2009. *The expression of possession*. Berlin, New York: Mouton de Gruyter.

Moravcsik E. 2003. Inflectional morphology in the Hungarian noun phrase. In Plank, F. (ed.), *Noun Phrase Structure in the Languages of Europe*, 113–252. Berlin/New York: de Gruyter.

Nichols, J. 1988. On alienable and inalienable possession. In Shipley, W. (ed.). *In Honor of Mary Haas: From the Haas Festival Conference on Native American Linguistics*, 557–609. Berlin: Mouton de Gruyter.

Ortmann, A. & C. Handschuh 2004. Semantic factors of valence-changing processes with nouns: possession in the Mayan languages. DGfS Meeting. Handout, Mainz, 25.2.2004.

Ortmann, A. 2014. Definite article asymmetries and concept types: semantic and pragmatic uniqueness. In: T. Gamerschlag, D. Gerland, R. Osswald & W. Petersen (eds.) Frames and concept types: Applications in Language and Philosophy, 293–321. Dordrecht: Springer.

Partee, B. 1983/1997. Uniformity vs. versatility: the genitive, a case study. Appendix to Theo Janssen (1997): Compositionality. In van Benthem, J. & A. ter Meulen (eds.), *The Handbook of Logic and Language*, 464–470. Amsterdam: Elsevier.

Partee, B. & V. Borschev 2000. Possessives, favorite, and coercion. In A. Richl & R. Daly (eds.), *Proceedings of ESCOL99*, 173–190. Ithaca, NY: Cornell University.

Payne J. & R. Huddleston 2002. Nouns and noun phrases. In Huddleston, R. & G. Pullum (eds.), *The Cambridge Grammar of the English Language*, 227–271. New York: Cambridge University Press.

Pellertier, J. 2009. *Kinds, Things, and Stuff: Mass Terms and Generics*. Oxford: Oxford University Press.

Prince, E. 1992. The ZPG letter: Subjects, Definiteness and Information Status. In. S. Thompson & W. Mann (eds.), *Discourse Description: Diverse analyses of a fundraising text*, 295–325. Philadelphia: John Benjamins.

Pustejovsky, J. 1996 (ed.). *Lexical semantics. The problem of polysemy*. Oxford: Clarendon Press.

Pustejovsky, J. 1995. *The generative lexicon*. Massachusetts: MIT Press.

Russell, B. 1905. On Denoting. *Mind* 14. 479–493.

Schwager, M. 2007. (Non-)Functional Concepts: Definite Articles in Bavarian. Handout, 8th Szklarska Poręba Workshop, Feb 23–25, 2007. Download: http://zis.uni-goettingen.de/mschwager/research.html

Schwarz, F. 2009. *Two Types of Definites in Natural Language*, PhD Thesis, Univ. of Massachusetts Amherst.

Seiler, H. 1983. *Possession as an operational dimension of language*. Tübingen: Narr.

Strawson, P. 1950. On Referring. *Mind* 59. 320–344.

Studler, R. 2004. Voller und reduzierter Artikel in der schweizerdeutschen NP.

Bracic, S. et al. (eds.), *Linguistische Studien im Europäischen Jahr der Sprachen. Akten des 36. Linguistischen Kolloquiums in Ljubljana*, 625–635. Frankfurt a. M.: Lang.

Thompson, C. 1996. On the grammar of body parts in Koyukon Athabaskan. In Chapell, H. & W. McGregor (eds.), *The grammar of inalienability*, 651–676. Berlin: Mouton de Gruyter.

Yael, R. 2000 (ed.). *Polysemy: theoretical and computational approaches*. Oxford: Oxford University Press.

Authors

Doris Gerland & Christian Horn
Departement of Linguistics and Information Science
Heinrich-Heine-University Düsseldorf
Düsseldorf, Germany
gerland@phil.hhu.de,
chorn@phil.hhu.de

The Meaning of Adjectives, Nouns, and Verbs

Non-Intersectivity in Manner Adjectives*

Sascha Alexeyenko

Abstract
This paper examines a class of adjectival modifiers that includes such adjectives as *skillful, careful, good, active*, etc., which have been traditionally analyzed as non-intersective, intensional modifiers, based on the substitution failure test. The paper provides arguments against the intensional analysis of these adjectives and further develops an alternative account in terms of manner modification of events proposed by Larson (1998), according to which an event argument is present in the semantic structure of nouns modified by adjectives of this type. Furthermore, it suggests that the event variable is bound by a generic quantifier in this case, which accounts for the restrictions on the type of eventualities that these adjectives can take as arguments.

1 Introduction: Substitution Failure

It has long been recognized that the part of speech "Adjective" in English is semantically not uniform and not all English adjectives can be given an extensional analysis in terms of properties of individuals. This has usually been demonstrated using entailment patterns and the possibility of substitution with co-extensional terms. As to the former, not all adjectives license both the *NP is an N* and *NP is Adj* entailments from *NP is an Adj N*, as, e. g., *married* does:

---
* This text was written as far back as 2009/2010 and thus contains ideas that I no longer believe in or that have been developed further since. However, a revision of this paper would have meant to write a new paper, therefore I decided to leave it basically unchanged, except for some minor corrections.

(1)   Peter is a married engineer.
   (a) ⊨ Peter is an engineer.
   (b) ⊨ Peter is married.

An analogous pair of entailments cannot be drawn, for instance, for *electrical*, simply because (2b) is ungrammatical:

(2)   Peter is an electrical engineer.
   (a) ⊨ Peter is an engineer.
   (b) ⊭ *Peter is electrical.

If being electrical were a property of Peter ascribed independently of his property of being an engineer, as it is the case with being married, *electrical* should be able to occur predicatively.

Furthermore, an analysis of all adjectives in English as properties of individuals is not able to account for the following fact of substitution failure with co-extensional terms, observed at least as early as in Parsons (1968):

(3)   (a) Francis is a skillful surgeon.
      (b) Francis is a violinist.
      ―――――――――
      (c) ⊭ Francis is a skillful violinist.

The reason for the lack of implication in (3) is intuitively clear: Being skillful means quite different things for a surgeon, a violinist, a driver, etc. Thus, the meaning variability arises due to attribution of skillfulness to different activities, for skillful with respect to making a surgery implies something else than skillful with respect to playing the violin. Yet, postulating different meanings for *skillful* would be certainly an inelegant and inadequate solution that would vastly overcomplicate the lexicon. A more adequate solution may be found on the level of semantic composition.

Note that the entailment patterns alone would not attest *skillful* as a problematic case for the property of individuals analysis, since Francis' being a skillful surgeon seems to entail Francis' being skillful. However, the substitution failure in (3) suggests that this is not quite right; rather, the sentence in (3a) entails that Francis is skillful with respect to his being a surgeon, but not skillful *simpliciter*.

In fact, the substitution failure test played a central role in early semantic theories of adjectives as an argument for an intensional analysis. I will show, however, that the lack of substitutivity may have different reasons and thus cannot be used as an unequivocal indicator for a single semantic phenomenon, such as intensionality, for instance. In this paper, I will focus on one semantic phenomenon that gives rise to substitution failure and is associated with adjectives like *skillful, careful, good, active*, etc., which I refer to as *manner adjectives* throughout the paper. I will argue that substitution failure with manner adjectives is due to the presence of a hidden event argument in the logical form that they are predicated of.

The structure of the paper is as follows. Section 2 outlines Siegel's (1976) intensional analysis and discusses its drawbacks. Section 3 shows that substitution failure may have different reasons, all of which can be explained in terms of hidden relationality, including the case of manner adjectives. Section 4 provides a formal semantic analysis of manner adjectives as predicates of events and suggests that the event variable is bound by a generic quantifier in this case, which accounts for the restrictions on the type of eventualities that can be modified by manner adjectives. Finally, Section 5 contains some concluding remarks and considerations regarding future work.

2 Previous Analyses: Modification of Intensions

2.1 Siegel's (1976) Doublet Theory

In early formal semantic approaches, in particular, in the *Doublet Theory* developed by Siegel (1976), the entailment and substitution failure data have been interpreted as reflecting a semantic type ambiguity within the word class of adjectives. On the one hand, Siegel's classification distinguishes adjectives like *male, aged, nude, blond, tall, married*, etc. that are given an extensional analysis as properties of individuals (of type $\langle e, t \rangle$ extensionally), for which a conjunction account illustrated in (4) holds:

(4) $[\![\text{male nurse}]\!] = \lambda x.[\textbf{male}(x) \ \& \ \textbf{nurse}(x)]$

Siegel establishes the term "intersective" for this type of adjectives, since the semantic composition of such adjectives with nouns can be characterized in terms of an intersection of their extensions.

On the other hand, *electrical* in (2) and *skillful* in (3) are examples of "non-intersective" adjectives, along with *good, careful, medical, former, alleged, potential*, etc. The conjunction account cannot be true of them: The entailment and substitution failure data speak against it. In terms of sets, these adjectives are subsective, rather than intersective, since the extension of an NP containing an adjective of this type is a subset of the extension of its head noun.

Siegel analyzes adjectives like *electrical* and *skillful* as intensional modifiers, which operate on the intensions rather than the extensions of predicates (extensionally they are thus properties of properties, type $\langle\langle e, t\rangle,\langle e, t\rangle\rangle$):

(5) ⟦skillful surgeon⟧ = $\lambda x.[\textbf{skillful}(\hat{\ }\textbf{surgeon})](x)$

Thus, Siegel accounts for substitution failure with non-intersective adjectives by appealing to intensionality: Applied to different intensions, they do not necessarily give the same value.

2.2 Arguments Against the Intensional Analysis

Siegel's analysis of adjectives faces a number of problems, which suggest that it provides a too course-grained classification of adjectives and, at the same time, makes too strong predictions. In what follows, I will briefly discuss these problems.

2.2.1 Heterogeneity in Non-Intersective Adjectives

The distinction between intersective and non-intersective adjectives appears to be not differentiated enough, since it neglects obvious semantic and syntactic differences within the class of non-intersective adjectives. First, they reveal quite different entailment patterns, as summarized below:

(6) NP is a *musical* N   NP is a *skillful* N   NP is an *alleged* N
      ⊨ NP is an N   ⊨ NP is an N   ⊭ NP is an N
      ⊭ *NP is musical   ?⊨ NP is skillful   ⊭ *NP is alleged

In order to account for these differences, Siegel formulates meaning postulates which ensure correct entailments. For instance, the meaning postulate in (7) guarantees the subsectivity entailments that can be drawn from *electrical engineer* in (2). Similarly, another meaning postulate is needed for the so-called "privative"

Non-Intersectivity in Manner Adjectives

adjectives, like *alleged* and *former*, which license neither the entailment *NP is an Adj*, nor the entailment *NP is an N*. This introduces a diversity into the class of non-intersective adjectives, but the semantic motivation for it is missing.

(7) $\Box[[\alpha(\hat{\ }\beta)](u) \to \beta(u)]$

Relatedly, different non-intersective adjectives can have different syntactic distributions. For example, whereas *skillful* can be used both attributively and predicatively, *medical* and *alleged* allow only for the attributive use:

(8)   (a) Ruth is a skillful nurse.
      (b) This nurse is skillful.

(9)   (a) Robert is a medical assistant.
      (b) *This assistant is medical.

(10) (a) Oswald is the alleged murderer of Kennedy.
      (b) *This murderer is alleged.

Intuitively, these distributional and entailment facts hint at semantic differences among non-intersective adjectives that are not reflected in Siegel's classification. I assume that the semantic heterogeneity of non-intersective adjectives is a result of the fact that substitution failure, which is used as the main method to attest (non-)intersectivity in Siegel's analysis, may have different reasons. We will see in Section 3 that a number of semantic phenomena can trigger substitution failure.

More generally, the content of the notion of non-intersectivity is not very specific. It is used in the first instance to say what certain predicates *are not*, namely, that they are not properties of individuals, rather than to explain what they *are*. The idea that they modify intensions does not say much about their semantics, as the exact mechanism of this modification is not specified in detail. Furthermore, the diversity within the class of non-intersective adjectives suggests that there may be more than one mechanism of non-intersective modification.

Finally, the simple version of intersectivity, which is assumed by Siegel (and, in fact, many others), is not unproblematic either. According to it, an intersective adjective is just a one-place predicate which applies to an individual independently of the predicate denoted by the head noun. This view on adjectival modification implies that there may be no semantic influence of the modified noun on the adjective (or the other way around). However, this appears not to be quite the case. The meaning variation in the adjectives in such examples as *male dentist / male suit, nude person / nude rock, red tomato / red hair / red wine / red face* suggests that the simple version of the conjunctive account does not work as neatly as assumed even for what is usually taken as paramount examples of intersective adjectives. A critical discussion of the notion of intersectivity is, however, outside the scope of this paper; more on this issue can be found, e. g., in Lahav (1989) and Bosch (1995).

2.2.2 Modification Beyond Intensions

The idea of intensional modification arose from the consideration that certain adjectives cannot denote semantically independent properties of individuals and that the first candidate they most obviously depend on is the semantics of their head nouns. There is however some evidence that the semantic dependence of non-intersective adjectives goes beyond their dependence on the meaning of the modified nouns.

First, some non-intersective adjectives can modify what Bolinger (1967) called "semantically bare nouns", such as *woman, person,* or *guy*.[1]

(11)   (a) Benjamin is clearly an experienced guy.
         (b) Not always will the most skillful person win.

Obviously, *experienced* and *skillful* in (11) mean 'experienced / skillful with respect to some activity'; these activities are however not recoverable from the intensions of the nouns *guy* and *person*. In this connection, Siegel (1976) suggests that adjectives like *experienced* and *skillful* are ambiguous between an intersective and a non-intersective reading and that their occurrences with semantically bare nouns, as in (11), are intersective. Moreover, she assumes that, in fact, the majority of English adjectives are "doublets", i. e., have two distinct lexical entries for the intersective and the non-intersective variant. It is unclear, however, how *experienced* and *skillful* can be intersective in (11) if they mean 'experienced / skillful *with respect to* something'.

---

[1] Note, however, that not all non-intersective adjectives can modify such nouns; for instance, *medical* and *alleged* cannot. This is yet another manifestation of heterogeneity among non-intersective adjectives.

Some adjectives seem to be in fact good candidates for cases of ambiguity; see, for instance, the contrast between *criminal* in (12a) and (12b), where the meaning difference is quite obvious and the entailments are different. Yet, it is questionable that the majority of English adjectives are ambiguous in this sense. There just seems to be little difference in meaning between *skillful* when applied to *surgeon*, as in (3), and *skillful* when applied to *person*, as in (11), that would justify such a complication of the lexicon.

(12) (a) A criminal lawyer has studied the aspects of criminal law.
      (b) A criminal policeman engaged in a stitch-up cannot hide now so well as before.

Second, Hare (1957), Sampson (1970), and Beesley (1982), among others, showed that non-intersective modification cannot be tied to the meaning of the modified nouns, because context can always suggest a different interpretation. For instance, in the context of a chess school that specializes in teaching musicians, *skillful violinist* in (13) will be interpreted relative to playing chess, rather than relative to playing the violin (cf. Beesley 1982: 221):

(13) A: How are your new students?
      B: I've got some very skillful violinists.

Such examples clearly demonstrate that non-intersective modification cannot be reduced to the modification of noun intensions, although the *default* interpretation of adjectives like *skillful* may in fact be relative to the meaning of their head nouns.

3   Reasons for Substitution Failure

As discussed in Section 2.2.1 above, one of the problems with Siegel's account is the semantic diversity of adjectives falling under the label of non-intersective modifiers. It has been suggested that this diversity results from the fact that substitution failure, which is used by Siegel to attest adjectives as intersective or non-intersective, can be triggered by different factors. This section discusses some of such factors. Note that the classes of adjectives associated with these factors cut across the intersective/non-intersective distinction, since the adjectives discussed in Sections 3.1 and 3.2 are intersective according to Siegel, while those in Sections 3.3 and 3.4 are non-intersective.

3.1 Gradable Adjectives

The following example from Partee (1995) demonstrates that substitution failure can occur with gradable adjectives, such as *tall* and *expensive*:

(14)   (a)   Win is a tall 14-year-old.
       (b)   Win is a basketball player.

       (c) $\not\models$ Win is a tall basketball player.

However, the reason of substitution failure in this case is generally assumed not to be intensionality, but rather the fact that the semantics of gradable adjectives depends on a *standard of comparison*, which is calculated with respect to a relevant *comparison class* (cf., e. g., Cresswell 1976, Klein 1980, von Stechow 1984, Bierwisch 1989, Kennedy & McNally 2005, Kennedy 2007).[2] More specifically, it is a change in the standard of comparison for the set of individuals denoted by the head noun that can give rise to substitution failure with gradable adjectives.

For instance, in Partee's example above, the class of basketball players introduces a specific standard of comparison for tallness which is different (higher) from the standard of tallness for 14-year-olds. Being a tall 14-year-old thus does not imply being a tall basketball player because one has to be significantly taller than an average teenager and even an average adult in order to be attested as a tall basketball player. In other words, one's height can be above the standard of tallness for 14-year-olds, but still below the standard of tallness for basketball players, as shown formally in (15) on a degree-based approach to the semantics of gradable adjectives in the spirit of Kennedy (2007).

(15)   (a)   **14-year-old(win)** & $\exists d$ [**tall(win)** = d & $d \geq \mathbf{d}_s^{14}$]
       (b)   **basketball-player(win)**
       (c) $\mathbf{d}_s^{bp} > \mathbf{d}_s^{14}$

---

[2] This view is also adopted by Siegel (1976), who assumes that gradable adjectives are intersective and thus has to accept the fact that substitution failure cannot be used as an unequivocal test for non-intersectivity.

(d) $\not\models$ **basketball-player(win)** & $\exists d$ **[tall(win)** $= d$ & $d \geq \mathbf{d}_s^{bp}$**]**

This analysis of substitution failure with *tall* in (14) predicts that substitution failure will not occur in the inverse direction, that is, that the implication from a higher standard to a lower one should be valid. This prediction is, of course, borne out, as (16) demonstrates.

(16) (a) Win is a tall basketball player.
     (b) Win is a 14-year-old.
     ―――――――
     (c) $\models$ Win is a tall 14-year-old.

Note that the fact that substitution failure with gradable adjectives occurs only in one direction distinguishes them from manner adjectives such as *skillful*, with which implications in both directions do not hold; for instance, neither the substitution in (3) nor the inverse one are valid. This suggests that substitution failure with manner adjectives cannot be due merely to changes in the standards of comparison for different comparison classes.

3.2 Color and Material Adjectives

Adjectives that denote colors and materials, such as *red* or *wooden*, are often regarded as typical instances of intersective adjectives. Interestingly, they can nevertheless give rise to substitution failure, as, e. g., in the following example:

(17) (a) This object is a red grapefruit.
     (b) This object is a juggling ball.
     ―――――――
     (c) $\not\models$ This object is a red juggling ball.

Although the example in (17) is somewhat artificial (in general, it appears not to be easy to construct natural examples of this sort with color and material adjectives), the logic of substitution of co-extensional terms seems to be preserved in it. Intuitively, substitution failure has little to do with intensionality in this case; rather, it originates from the fact that a color or material property can be attributed to an object as a whole, while being true only of a relevant part of it. Thus, *red pen* is true of a pen even if only its external part or only its internal part (i.e., the ink) is red and *glass table* is true of a table even if its legs are made out of metal – important is that it has a glass plate. And since it usually remains implicit which part is relevant in such cases, reference to the object as a whole may imply a switch between different relevant parts of it and this, in turn, will lead to substitution failure, like in (17). The implicit ascription of redness only to certain relevant parts of the same object in this example, namely, to the internal part when it is conceptualized as a grapefruit and to the surface when it is conceptualized as a juggling ball, can thus be formalized as follows:[3]

(18) (a) **grapefruit(this-object)** & $\exists x$ **[inside-part(x)(this-object)** & **red(x)]**
      (b) **juggling-ball(this-object)**

      (c) $\not\models$ **juggling-ball(this-object)** & $\exists x$ **[outside-part(x)(this-object)** & **red(x)]**

If the semantic representation of (17) is as given in (18), the non-validity of this implication is explained without appeal to intensionality, namely, as being due to the presence of an implicit parameter, relative to which the adjectival property is predicated.

3.3 Relational Adjectives

Also relational adjectives, such as *electrical* and *medical*, are able to trigger substitution failure, as can be shown with the following example. Imagine that Carl is a young man produced during the early days of in vitro fertilization and, as such, is a medical miracle; besides, he is a student of architecture.[4] In this context we have:

(19) (a) Carl is a medical miracle.
      (b) Carl is a student.

      (c) $\not\models$ Carl is a medical student.

---

[3] Which part of an object is relevant is probably a matter of world knowledge in some cases and can be inferred from the context of utterance in some others.

[4] I am indebted to Muffy Siegel, who suggested me a slightly different version of this example.

Naturally, the fact that Carl is a medical miracle as well as a student does not imply that he is a medical student. According to Siegel, the reason for this lack of implication is that adjectives like *medical* are non-intersective intensional modifiers. But there is also an alternative analysis of such denominal relational adjectives, according to which the semantic structure of a relational adjective contains the predicate denoted by its base noun (i. e., the noun it is derived from) and a relational predicate that links the internal argument of the base noun and the internal argument of the noun modified by this adjective (cf., e. g., Mezhevich 2002, Fradin 2008). Hence, under this analysis, the non-validity of the implication in (19) is due to a change in the implicit relation; specifically, the fact that Carl is a miracle *produced* by medicine does not imply that he *studies* medicine:

(20)   (a)   **miracle(carl)** & $\exists x \, [\mathbf{R}^{prod}(\mathbf{carl})(x) \, \& \, \mathbf{medicine}(x)]$
        (b)   **student(carl)**
        _____
        (c) $\not\models$ **student(carl)** & $\exists x \, [\mathbf{R}^{stud}(x)(\mathbf{carl}) \, \& \, \mathbf{medicine}(x)]$

Thus, also in the case of relational adjectives, intensionality is not the only possible explanation of substitution failure; it can as well be explained by the presence of an implicit relation.

3.4   Manner Adjectives

What the analyses of substitution failure with gradable, color/material, and relational adjectives discussed in Sections 3.1–3.3 have in common is the assumption about the presence of a hidden parameter in the semantic structure: a standard of comparison, a relevant part, or an additional relation. Accordingly, substitution failure occurs if there is an implicit change in this parameter. Similarly, also substitution failure with manner adjectives like *skillful*, cf. (3), can be accounted for as a result of a change in a hidden parameter, rather than as a matter of intensionality, given that there are reasons to assume that there is some hidden parameter in this case as well. Section 4.1 below shows that there are indeed reasons to assume an additional parameter to be present in the semantic structure of nouns modified by manner adjectives, namely, a Davidsonian *event argument* (see also McConnell-Ginet 1982, Larson 1998, for arguments to this extent).

4 Event-Based Analysis of Manner Adjectives

4.1 Presence of Event Arguments

There are several pieces of data that speak in favor of an event-based analysis of manner adjectives.[5] First, NPs containing manner adjectives can be paraphrased in terms of verbal structures with manner adverbs, as is pointed out already in Vendler (1968), cf. the examples below.

(21) (a) Peter is a careful driver.
 (b) ~ Peter drives carefully.

(22) (a) David is a just king.
 (b) ~ David rules justly.

When the manner adjective is interpreted relative to the meaning of the noun it modifies, the verb in such paraphrases is related to the modified noun morphologically, like in (21), or at least semantically, like in (22). By contrast, in cases when the relevant interpretation is suggested by the context, as in the example in (13) from Section 2.2.2, repeated in (23) below, the head noun of the manner adjective and the verb in the paraphrase can be completely unrelated semantically.

(23) [*in a chess school for musicians*]
 A: How are your new students?
 B: I've got some very skillful violinists.
  ~ I've got some violinists who play chess very skillfully.

Crucially, the adverbs in such paraphrases are *manner adverbs*, which are standardly treated in event semantics as co-predicates of the event argument introduced by the verb (cf. Davidson 1967, Parsons 1990). Thus, in order to have a unified analysis of manner adverbs and manner adjectives, also the latter need to be analyzed as predicates of events. This would imply that an event argument is present in the semantic representation of phrases like *careful driver* and *just king*, being responsible for substitution failure with manner adjectives.

Note also that the possibility of manner adverbial paraphrases distinguishes manner adjectives both from intersective adjectives and from other types of non-

---
[5] These data were not considered by Siegel (1976) and cannot be easily incorporated into her intensional theory.

intersective adjectives, which either do not have adverbial counterparts at all (*tally*), or whose adverbial counterparts are not manner adverbs (*medically, allegedly*), as the unavailability of the corresponding adverbials of the form *in a(n)* ADJ *way* demonstrates (**in a medical way*, **in an alleged way*).[6]

(24) (a) Win is a tall basketball player.
     (b) ↛ *Win plays basketball in a tall way.

(25) (a) Robert is a medical assistant.
     (b) ↛ *Robert assists in a medical way.

(26) (a) Oswald is the alleged murderer of Kennedy.
     (b) ↛ *Oswald murdered Kennedy in an alleged way.

Second, manner adjectives can modify event nominalizations, as the examples below show, which provides further evidence for an analysis of them as predicates of events.

(27) (a) Peter's careful driving
     (b) David's just rule

Since manner adjectives can normally be predicated both of DPs that denote individuals, as in (28a), and of DPs that denote events, e. g., DPs containing event nominalizations, as in (28b), it is not immediately clear if they should be analyzed as predicates of individuals or predicates of events.

(28) David is a skillful violinist.
     (a) David is skillful (w.r.t. playing the violin).
     (b) David's violin playing is skillful.
     (c) David plays the violin skillfully.

It should be pointed out in this connection, though, that in fact not all manner adjectives can be predicated of individual-denoting DPs, while all of them can be predicated of DPs denoting events, as is shown in (29) and (30) for *deep* and *lawful*.

---

[6] For a discussion of different semantic classes of adverbs, see, e. g., Ernst (2002).

(29)   John is a deep sleeper.
   (a) *John is deep (w.r.t. sleeping).
   (b) John's sleep is deep.
   (c) John sleeps deeply.

(30)   John is a lawful owner of a Cadillac.
   (a) *John is lawful (w.r.t. owning a Cadillac).
   (b) John's ownership of a Cadillac is lawful.
   (c) John owns a Cadillac lawfully.

The contrast between (28), on the one hand, and (29)–(30), on the other hand, suggests that, while manner adjectives are event modifiers, the meaning of many of them "involves properties of an agent", as Mittwoch (2005, p. 77) put it discussing a related case of manner adverbs, which allows such manner adjectives to be predicated of individual-denoting DPs, as in (28a).

Thus, in what follows, I will analyze manner adjectives as predicates of events, as has been suggested also by Larson (1998). In particular, Larson argued, first, that some nouns contain in their semantic structure both an individual and an event argument and, second, that adjectives can be predicated of the individual or of the event argument of nouns. He furthermore assumed that some adjectives, such as, e.g., *beautiful*, can be predicated of either argument, giving rise to an ambiguity represented in (31) below. The manner interpretation of *beautiful* is thus captured by the semantic representation in (31b).[7]

(31)   Olga is a beautiful dancer.
   (a) Qe [**dancing**(e,olga) ... **beautiful**(olga,C)]   ("Olga is beautiful")
   (b) Qe [**dancing**(e,olga) ... **beautiful**(e,C)]   ("Dancing is beautiful")

Larson does not specify the event quantifier (and hence also the connective) in these semantic representations, but suggests that a natural candidate for it is a generic quantifier. Intuitively, this is right, as is evident from the fact that the verbs in the paraphrases in (21)–(23) above have a habitual interpretation. Indeed, sentences like that in (31) do not seem to allow a true episodic interpretation; if there is only one *actual* event of Olga's beautiful dancing, (31) can be true only

---

[7] C in (31) represents the comparison class relative to which *beautiful* applies.

in case this single event is interpreted as an indication for a series of *potential* future events of her beautiful dancing (i. e., a generic interpretation with only one actual instantiation). Further, such sentences also do not seem to require a plain extensional universal interpretation, tolerating exceptions; not every single event of Olga's dancing must be beautiful for (31) to be true. Being a *modalized* universal quantifier (Krifka et al. 1995), the generic quantifier adequately captures these features. Section 4.2 will present some additional data which provide further evidence for the presence of a generic quantifier in the semantic structure of sentences like (31).

Given this analysis of modification by manner adjectives, substitution failure with them can be accounted for without reference to intensionality, namely, as being due to an implicit change in the modified event, as shown formally in (32) for the substitution failure in (3).[8]

(32)   (a)   GENe [**make-surgery(francis)**(e)][**skillful**(e)]
       (b)   GENe [**C(francis)**(e)][**play-violin(francis)**(e)]
       —————
       (c) $\not\models$ GENe [**play-violin(francis)**(e)][**skillful**(e)]

Larson (1998) assumes that sentences like that in (31) have one non-eventive and one eventive reading, formalized in (31a) and (31b), respectively. In fact, however, sentences of this type seem to have at least two distinct eventive interpretations, which becomes particularly apparent when the noun modified by the manner adjective is an *-er* nominalization. One of them, which I will refer to as the 'non-occupational' interpretation, corresponds to Larson's reading in (31b); its semantic representation for *Peter is a skillful teacher* is given below.

(33)   Peter is a skillful teacher.   [non-occupational reading]
       GENe [**teach(peter)**(e)][**skillful**(e)]
       'In contextually appropriate situations in which Peter teaches, he teaches skillfully.'

Importantly, the non-occupational interpretation in (33) does not imply that Peter is a teacher professionally, nor that he teaches habitually; it merely states

---

[8] In this paper, I use the generic quantifier GEN, which is associated with a tripartite structure (cf., e. g., Krifka et al. 1995). However, see, e. g., Rimell (2004), Boneh & Doron (2008), who argue against GEN and propose instead the non-quantificational habitual operator HAB.

that, whenever he teaches, he does so skillfully, i. e., that he is skillful at teaching (e. g., when he helps someone with assignments).[9] Thus, on this reading, *Peter is a skillful teacher* is equivalent to *Peter teaches skillfully*:

(34) Peter teaches skillfully.
      GENe [**teach(peter)**(e)][**skillful**(e)]

Yet sentences like *Peter is a skillful teacher* also have an 'occupational' interpretation, which is not discussed in Larson (1998). This reading does imply that Peter is a (professional) teacher or, at least, that he teaches habitually; this entailment is secured by an additional conjunct, as in the semantic representation below.

(35) Peter is a skillful teacher.   [occupational reading]
      GENe [**C(peter)**(e)][**teach(peter)**(e)] & GENe' [**R(peter)**(e')][**skillful**(e')]

An important difference between the occupational and the non-occupational readings is the fact that, unlike the latter, the former does not require the event modified by the manner adjective to come from the semantics of the modified noun; rather, the relevant event may also be provided contextually. Accordingly, the event predicate in (35) is left underspecified (**R**), such that it can be understood as, e. g., **play-chess** in a context of a chess school for teachers (see the discussion of example (13) in Section 2.2.2), even if its default value in most contexts is probably **teach**. Furthermore, the possibility to supply the relevant event predicate **R** contextually also accounts for the interpretations available to such sentences as in (11), in which manner adjectives modify semantically bare nouns like *person*, whose semantics can hardly suggest an event.

Finally, let us briefly discuss the interaction between manner modification and the availability of the occupational and the non-occupational readings. In the case of predicative nouns, the non-occupational reading emerges only in the presence of manner adjectives; the occupational reading is, by contrast, always available:

(36) (a) Peter is a teacher.   [occupational]
      (b) Peter is a skillful teacher.   [occupational/non-occupational]

---

[9] In this sense, the non-occupational reading is a version of the "Port-Royal Puzzle" (Leslie 2008, 16–17), which is otherwise usually constructed with bare plural subjects (cf. Carlson 1977).

Given the analysis above, the lack of the non-occupational reading with non-modified predicative nouns can be explained as follows. Since the predicate denoted by the noun specifies the restrictor of GEN on the non-occupational reading, cf. (33), in the absence of a manner adjective there would be no material to fill its nuclear scope.

The situation in the case of habitual verbs is similar. In addition to the occupational reading, which is available to such non-modified habitual verbs as *teach* or *drive the bus* (Lawler 1973), they also acquire a non-occupational reading when a manner adverb (or some other modifier) is present:

(37) (a) Peter teaches. [occupational]
(b) Peter teaches skillfully. [occupational/non-occupational]

Like (36b), (37b) can be interpreted both occupationally and non-occupationally, even if its occupational reading might be less salient than in the non-modified version in (37a).

4.2 Restrictions on Event Types

According to the analysis presented in Section 4.1, manner adjectives are predicated of an event argument which is bound by a generic quantifier. Since GEN undergoes the Plurality Condition on quantification (cf., e. g., de Swart 1991), this analysis predicts that manner adjectives should be no good with nouns that contribute "once-only" predicates of events, i. e., predicates denoting singleton sets of events. This prediction is borne out, as we will see in what follows.

In most of the examples used so far, the underlying eventualities are activities, such as *drive*, *rule*, or *play the violin*, which do not prohibit a repetitive interpretation. Some of these examples are repeated below.

(38) (a) Peter is a careful driver.
(b) David is a just king.
(c) John is a skillful violinist.

By contrast, manner adjectives seem not to be easily compatible with nouns that are derived from achievement and accomplishment verbs, as the following examples demonstrate.

(39) (a) #John is a skillful inventor of an artificial language.
  (b) #John is a skillful discoverer of a continent.

(40) (a) #John is a skillful painter of a landscape.
  (b) #John is a skillful designer of a theatre.

Yet, what is responsible for the oddness of the sentences in (39) and (40) is not the aspectual class of the base verbs itself (achievements/accomplishments), but the fact that these particular achievements and accomplishments are once-only predicates. The examples in (41)–(43) show that manner adjectives easily combine with nouns formed from achievements/accomplishments which can be repetitive – due to the presence of a bare plural or mass noun complement.

(41) John is a skillful inventor of computer languages.

(42) John is a skillful finder of water.

(43) John is a skillful painter of landscapes.

If modification by manner adjectives is only possible when the modified event is repetitive, manner adjectives should be compatible with nouns derived from stage-level states (e. g., *sleep, hold, wait*, as well as Dowty's (1979) "interval statives" like *sit, stand, lie*), but not individual-level states, since the latter, unlike the former, are once-only predicates as well (de Swart 1991). This seems to be the case, as the examples below demonstrate:[10]

(44) (a) John is a loud/sensitive sleeper.
  (b) John is a patient waiter.

(45) (a) #John is a good owner of a Cadillac.
  (b) #John is a skillful lover of Mozart.

In fact, however, the infelicity of the sentences in (45) may have to do with agentivity, rather than with repetitivity. Individual-level states are not agentive (differently from stage-level states, cf. Katz 2008), while manner adjectives like

---

[10] The sentences in (45) possibly become slightly better if the states denoted by *own* and *love* are coerced to what Katz (2008) calls the "event-related" reading, that is, are interpreted as activities associated with these states. E. g., *a good owner of a Cadillac* may mean that the owner of the Cadillac treats it well, while *a skillful lover of Mozart* may be used for a musician who admires Mozart and hence skillfully performs his works.

good and *skillful* "involve properties of an agent", as has been discussed in Section 4.1. In contrast, manner adjectives like *lawful*, whose meaning does not involve properties of an agent, can modify nouns that are derived from verbs denoting individual-level states:[11]

(46) (a) John is a lawful owner of this Cadillac.
      (b) John is a hopeless lover of chocolate.

If manner modification implies repetitivity, it is not clear why manner adjectives like *lawful* can modify individual-level statives as in (46), which denote once-only predicates. Although an analysis of this fact is outside the scope of this paper, an explanation of it may possibly be given along the lines of Chierchia's (1995) account of individual-level predicates as being inherently generic. In particular, individual-level statives may be assumed to introduce a generic quantifier of a special type, which is not pluractional, i. e., does not presuppose repetitivity.

5   Conclusion and Outlook

This paper presented arguments for an analysis of manner adjectives, such as *skillful* and *good*, as predicates of events introduced either in the semantics of the modified nouns or contextually. Furthermore, the event argument that manner adjectives are predicated of has been argued to be bound by a generic quantifier, which accounts for the restrictions on the type of events that can be modified by manner adjectives. To conclude, I will briefly discuss how this analysis relates to some other accounts proposed in the literature and point out directions for future research.

In knowledge representation, it is common to formalize generic events of the sort discussed in this paper as a special ontological type of *roles* (Guarino 1992, Sowa 2000, Steimann 2000, Masolo et al. 2005, Loebe 2007), and the same strategy is occasionally employed in semantics (cf., e. g., Croft 1984). Thus, using the

---

[11] In some cases, manner adjectives that involve properties of an agent *are* able to modify nouns with underlying individual-level states, as, e. g., in *Bill is a passionate admirer of Picasso's art*. However, following Katz (2008), I assume that *passionate* in this example is not a manner modifier of a state. Rather, it is either a manner modifier of an activity associated with the state of admiration (the "event-related" reading), or a degree modifier that indicates *how much* Bill admires Picasso's art and not *how* he admires it. Note that the latter reading is therefore unavailable with non-gradable states, as, e. g., in *David is a passionate owner of a Stradivarius*.

semantic type of roles, Croft represents the ambiguity of *beautiful dancer* as in (47); cf. Larson's (1998) semantic representation of this phrase in (31).

(47)   Marya is a beautiful dancer.
    (a) **dancer(marya)** & ∃r [**beautiful(**r,**marya)**]
    (b) **dancer(marya)** & **beautiful(marya)**

This analysis may be seen as a formal implementation of an idea that goes back to Aristotle, who argued that an adjective like *good* modifies relative to the "function" of its argument, since someone can be a good man and a bad cobbler at the same time (*Sophistical Refutations*, 177b). Nouns can be then assumed to have an additional role argument that corresponds to Aristotelian functions. Accordingly, being good with respect to one role will not imply being good also with respect to some other role, which will account for substitution failure.

Roles seem to be indeed linguistically real, as they can be explicitly introduced by means of *as*-phrases, which can accompany manner adjectives, as in the examples below.

(48)   (a) Peter is a careful driver.
      (b) ∼ Peter is careful as a driver.

(49)   (a) David is a just king.
      (b) ∼ David is just as a king.

(50)   (a) John is a skillful violinist.
      (b) ∼ John is skillful as a violinist.

Moreover, the ability to take such *as*-phrases appears to distinguish manner adjectives from intersective adjectives, as well as from some types of non-intersective adjectives, as the following examples demonstrate:

(51)   (a) Peter is a married engineer.
      (b) ≁ *Peter is married as an engineer.

(52)   (a) Peter is an electrical engineer.
      (b) ≁ *Peter is electrical as an engineer.

(53)   (a) Peter is a former engineer.
      (b) ≁ *Peter is former as an engineer.

In fact, however, manner adjectives are not the only variety of adjectives that can take such *as*-phrases; for example, adjectives like *useful, necessary, famous,* and *respected*, which are not manner modifiers, are able to take them as well:

(54)   (a)   This paper is a useful background reading.
         (b)   ∼ This paper is useful as a background reading.

(55)   (a)   Knowledge of statistics is a necessary prerequisite for this course.
         (b)   ∼ Knowledge of statistics is necessary as a prerequisite for this course.

Hence, a role-based analysis is likely not to be fine-grained enough, as it does not distinguish between manner adjectives and such adjectives as *useful* and *necessary*, all of which intuitively seem to be predicated relative to roles. Moreover, a role-based analysis will need to provide an independent explanation for the restrictions on the type of eventualities that manner adjectives can modify, see Section 4.2. By contrast, the analysis presented in this paper straightforwardly accounts for these restrictions. Finally, a more general advantage of it compared to a role-based analysis is that it does not extend the ontology of basic semantic types by an additional type of roles, modeling roles as events in the scope of a generic quantifier.

On the other hand, manner adjectives differ from adjectives of other semantic classes insofar as they can take *in-/at*-gerunds of the following type:

(56)   (a)   Peter is a careful driver.
         (b)   ∼ Peter is careful in driving.

(57)   (a)   David is a just king.
         (b)   ∼ David is just in ruling.

(58)   (a)   John is a skillful violinist.
         (b)   ∼ John is skillful at playing the violin.

Thus, the analysis presented in this paper needs to be extended such that it accounts for the semantics of these prepositional gerunds. This is a direction for future research.

Acknowledgements

I would like to thank Peter Bosch, Yael Greenberg, Cornelia Ebert, and Carla Umbach for useful comments on earlier versions of this paper. I also wish to thank Nora Boneh, Olga Kagan, Malka Rappaport Hovav, as well as the audiences of the linguistic departmental seminar at the Hebrew University of Jerusalem and of the Second Conference on Concept Types and Frames for their helpful feedback. Special thanks go to Edit Doron for discussions on parts of this paper and her general support. I am also grateful to Vicky Lichtman for her help with English, as well as Katya Ovchinnikova and Konstantin Todorov for their assistance. This work was financially supported by the Graduiertenkolleg *Adaptivity in Hybrid Cognitive Systems* as part of my PhD studies at the Institute of Cognitive Science in Osnabrück, which is hereby gratefully acknowledged.

References

Beesley, K. 1982. Evaluative adjectives as one-place predicates in Montague Grammar. *Journal of Semantics* 1 (3). 195–249.

Bierwisch, M. 1989. The semantics of gradation. In M. Bierwisch & E. Lang (eds.), *Dimensional adjectives*, 71–262. Berlin: Springer.

Bolinger, D. 1967. Adjectives in English: Attribution and predication. *Lingua* 18. 1–34.

Boneh, N. & E. Doron. 2008. Habituality and the habitual aspect. In S. Rothstein (ed.), *Theoretical and Crosslinguistic Approaches to the Semantics of Aspect*, 321–347. Amsterdam: John Benjamins.

Bosch, P. 1995. Meanings and contextual concepts. In M. Bierwisch & P. Bosch (eds.), *Semantic and Conceptual Knowledge*, 79–99. Arbeitspapiere des Sonderforschungsbereichs 340, Vol. 71. Universität Tübingen.

Carlson, G. 1977. Reference to kinds in English. University of Massachusetts: Ph.D. dissertation.

Chierchia, G. 1995. Individual-level predicates as inherent generics. In G. Carlson & J. Pelletier (eds.), *The Generic Book*, 176–223. Chicago: The University of Chicago Press.

Cresswell, M. J. 1976. The semantics of degree. In B. Partee (ed.), *Montague Grammar*, 261–292. New York: Academic Press.

References

Croft, W. 1984. Representation of adverbs, adjectives and events in logical form. SRI International Technical Notes 344.

Davidson, D. 1967. The logical form of action sentences. In N. Rescher (ed.), *The Logic of Decision and Action*, 81–95. Pittsburgh, PA: University of Pittsburgh Press.

Dowty, D. R. 1979. *Word meaning and Montague grammar*. Dordrecht: Reidel.

Ernst, T. 2002. *The syntax of adjuncts*. Cambridge: Cambridge University Press.

Fradin, B. 2008. On the semantics of denominal adjectives. In G. Booij, A. Ralli & S. Scalise (eds.), *Online Proceedings of the 6th Mediterranean Morphology Meeting, 2007, Ithaca, Greece*, .

Guarino, N. 1992. Concepts, attributes and arbitrary relations: Some linguistic and ontological criteria for structuring knowledge bases. *Data and Knowledge Engineering* 8 (3). 249–261.

Hare, R. 1957. Geach: Good and evil. *Analysis* 17. 103–111.

Katz, G. 2008. Manner modification of state verbs. In L. McNally & C. Kennedy (eds.), *Adjectives and Adverbs: Syntax, Semantics and Discourse*, 220–248. Oxford: Oxford University Press.

Kennedy, C. 2007. Vagueness and grammar: The semantics of relative and absolute gradable adjectives. *Linguistics and Philosophy* 30 (1). 1–45.

Kennedy, C. & L. McNally. 2005. Scale structure, degree modification, and the semantics of gradable predicates. *Language* 81 (2). 345–381.

Klein, E. 1980. A semantics for positive and comparative adjectives. *Linguistics and Philosophy* 4. 1–45.

Krifka, M., F. Pelletier, G. Carlson, A. ter Meulen, G. Chierchia & G. Link. 1995. Genericity: An introduction. In G. Carlson & J. Pelletier (eds.), *The Generic Book*, 1–124. Chicago: The University of Chicago Press.

Lahav, R. 1989. Against compositionality: The case of adjectives. *Philosophical Studies* 57. 261–279.

Larson, R. 1998. Events and modification in nominals. In D. Strolovitch & A. Lawson (eds.), *Proceedings from Semantics and Linguistic Theory (SALT) VIII*, 145–168. Ithaca, NY: CLC Publications.

Lawler, J. 1973. Studies in English generics. University of Michigan, Ann Arbor: Ph.D. dissertation.

Leslie, S. J. 2008. Generics: Cognition and acquisition. *Philosophical Review* 117 (1). 1–47.

Loebe, F. 2007. Abstract vs. social roles – Towards a general theoretical account of roles. *Applied Ontology* 2. 127–158.

Masolo, C., G. Guizzardi, L. Vieu, E. Bottazzi & R. Ferrario. 2005. Relational roles and qua-individuals. In *AAAI 2005 Fall Symposium on Roles, an Interdisciplinary Perspective (Roles2005), AAAI Technical Report*, vol. FS-05-08, Menlo Park, CA: AAAI Press.

Mezhevich, I. 2002. English compounds and Russian relational adjectives. In G. S. Morrison & L. Zsoldos (eds.), *Proceedings of the North West Linguistics Conference, 2002, Burnaby, Canada*, 95–114.

Mittwoch, A. 2005. Do states have a Davidsonian argument? Some empirical considerations. In C. Maienborn & A. Wöllstein (eds.), *Event arguments: Foundations and Applications*, 69–88. Tübingen: Niemeyer.

Parsons, T. 1968. A semantics for English. Unpublished manuscript.

Parsons, T. 1990. *Events in the semantics of English: A study in subatomic semantics*. Cambridge, MA: MIT Press.

Partee, B. 1995. Lexical semantics and compositionality. In L. Gleitman & M. Liberman (eds.), *An Invitation to Cognitive Science*, vol. 1: Language, 311–360. Cambridge, MA: MIT Press 2nd edn.

Rimell, L. 2004. Habitual sentences and generic quantification. In V. Chand, A. Kelleher, A. J. Rodríguez & B. Schmeiser (eds.), *Proceedings of the 23rd West Coast Conference on Formal Linguistics*, 663–676. Somerville, MA: Cascadilla Press.

Sampson, G. 1970. Good. *Linguistic Inquiry* 1. 257–260.

Siegel, M. 1976. Capturing the adjective. University of Massachusetts: Ph.D. dissertation.

Sowa, J. 2000. *Knowledge representation: Logical, philosophical and computational foundations*. Pacific Grove, CA: Brooks/Cole.

von Stechow, A. 1984. Comparing semantic theories of comparison. *Journal of Semantics* 3 (1–2). 1–77.

Steimann, F. 2000. On the representation of roles in object-oriented and conceptual modelling. *Data and Knowledge Engineering* 35 (1). 83–106.

de Swart, H. 1991. Adverbs of quantification: A generalized quantifier approach. Rijksuniversiteit Groningen: Ph.D. dissertation.

Vendler, Z. 1968. *Adjectives and Nominalizations*. The Hague: Mouton.

References

Author

Sascha Alexeyenko
University of Osnabrück
Institute of Cognitive Science
olalyeks@uos.de

Converging Evidences on the Eventivity of Italian Nouns

Irene Russo & Tommaso Caselli

Abstract

This paper aims at shedding lights on the semantic concept of "event noun". Starting with the working hypothesis that linguistic context and corpus-based distributional information can be decisive, we propose a measure for eventivity that relies on syntagmatic cues. By means of a comparison between speakers' judgments and syntagmatic evidence obtained from a corpus study, we propose a measure of eventivity for nouns. The comparison with annotated data proves its soundness.

1 Introduction

Defining what is an event noun is not an easy task: this notion is widely based on deverbal nouns as morphologically marked items, but some deverbal nouns are not purely eventive and other event nouns are not morphologically derived, i. e. do not have a corresponding verb. Most previous research (Grimshaw 1990, Zucchi 1993, Alexadiou 2001, Alexadiou & Grimshaw 2008 among others) on the status of event nouns and methods for their identification has mainly concentrated on nominalizations (i. e. the morphological process of creating a noun from a verb), but providing this kind of definition for an event noun cannot assure a well balanced semantic description of this concept.

Following Firth's 1957 intuition that "[y]ou shall know a word by the company it keeps" (Firth 1957:11), the relevance of linguistic context and corpus-based distributional information for the definition of word semantic representations is widely acknowledged (Hovy 2010, Basili & Pennacchiotti 2010, McDonald & Schillcock 2001 among others). The idea that co-occurrence statistics of words extracted from text corpora can provide a basis for semantic representations has been investigated in Computational Linguistics (see the distributional semantic models proposed by Baroni & Lenci 2010) but it is useful also from a theoretical point of view (Lenci 2008).

In this work we support the hypothesis that the notion of event noun is a scalar concept which can be modulated along a *continuum* of eventivity (see also Simone 2008). The identification of event readings for nouns is accomplished in the linguistic context, i. e. by exploiting selectional preferences in terms of verbs and adjectives which co-occur with the noun. The focus of our work is on the factors that can potentially determine the emergence of a noun as eventive apart from morphological marking. We propose a measure for eventivity that relies on syntagmatic cues. The comparison between syntagmatic evidence and speakers' judgments will provide useful insights for event nouns that are not deverbal.

A measure of eventivity can be useful for practical implementations such as automatic event detection for information extraction and question-answering systems but it is also promising for theoretical linguistics because it is not sufficient to say that words display along a *continuum*, but it is necessary to find out how to represent this *continuum* and how to enrich it. Moreover, we believe that a measure for eventivity could be useful for detection of coercions as well.

In Section 2, we clarify the theoretical background of our analysis, without forgetting to highlight limitations and difficulties that arose in our work. Data gathered form corpora will support our assertions, paving the way for more detailed corpus analysis.

In Section 3, we describe the preliminary corpus analysis that has been useful to define our working hypothesis. First, we present the corpus-based measure of eventivity and, then, we evaluate its relationship with respect to other kind of information (speakers' judgements). Finally, we wrap up with conclusions and some suggestions for future research.

2 Decisive variables for the identification of event nouns

We started this analysis wondering what are the crucial factors which may help in identifying nouns that denote events. The first, most plausible variable pertains to morphological suffixation. In Italian, as well in other languages, nouns can be derived by verbs and different suffixes can apply to this derivation process. However, only a subset of them allows the derivation of eventive nouns.

Morphological derivation is only one of the factors which contribute to the individuation of an event noun because it is possible that a deverbal noun codifies more than one meaning and just one of these is eventive. As Bisetto & Melloni (2007) note, deverbal nominals, such as "*traduzione*" [translation], are semantically ambiguous since they can refer either to the action/event expressed by the base verb or to its result, i. e. the outcome of the action:

(1)   La *traduzione* di questo testo è lenta e faticosa. [EVENT]
      [The translation of this text is slow and difficult.]

(2)   Molte *traduzioni* sono piene di errori. [RESULT]
      [Many translations are full of mistakes.]

Moreover, according to the authors, nominals can also have a concrete result interpretation through metonymic transposition, for instance, when they denote the (physical) object which contains the translation:

(3)   La t*raduzione* è sul tavolo. [PHYS_OBJ]
      [The translation is on the table.]

The well-known polysemous alternation between an event and a result reading of a deverbal noun (Grimshaw 1990) poses a first, interesting constraint on the relationship between deverbal nouns and event nouns.

As a starting point to investigate this issue, we chose the first 12 most frequent deverbal nouns with suffixes – *mento, -aggio, -tura, -zione* in the corpus La Repubblica (Baroni et al. 2004). A detailed analysis of the senses of these nouns (Table 1) encoded in a lexicographic dictionary – the De Mauro-Paravia dictionary (De Mauro 2004) – has shown that among these deverbal nouns only 40 % encode only the eventive reading. On the other hand, in the vast majority of the cases, there is an eventive and a result reading or, even, idiosyncratic meanings that are not related to the meaning of the verb, i. e. which do not correspond to the classic pattern meaning of deverbal nouns "*the act/process of -V*".

A preliminary research question we address in this paper is: *if morphological suffixes will not be sufficient variables for event nouns identification, how to find these items in a corpus?*

Table 1: Number of morphologically derived nouns with a non-eventive sense

Suffix	nouns	non_eventive
-zione	12	9
-mento	12	10
-tura	12	8
-aggio	12	2
	48	29

Since Grimshaw's characterization of nominalizations, syntagmatic co-occurrences emerge as cues to disambiguate between an eventive and a non-eventive reading of the same noun. As Zucchi (1993) points out "[t]he *of*-phrase and the *by*-phrase occurring in event-denoting NPs are arguments of the nouns with which they combine." (Zucchi 1993:135).

(4) La *costruzione* (del palazzo) è durata due anni. [EVENT]
     [The building (of the house) took two years.]

(5) La *costruzione* (*del palazzo) è alta due piani. [RESULT]
     [The building (*of the house) is two floors high.]

Unfortunately, such information is not explicitly available in corpora. To overcome this shortcoming, we considered as relevant cues for the identification of event readings of deverbal nouns other syntagmatic cues. To accomplish this task, the following quote by Vendler (1967: 141) suggested a promising direction:

> "There are certain nouns that are not verb derivatives, yet behave like nominalised verbs; that is, they can enter container contexts without suggesting suppressed nominals. Fires and blizzards, unlike tables, crystals, or cows, can occur, begin, and end, can be sudden or prolonged, can be watched and observed – they are, in a word, events and not objects." (Vendler 1967:141).

If events are basically things that happen, event nouns denote things that happen, that occur, that begin, that can be prolonged. Such an approach is not innovative *per se*, because according to linguists co-occurrences with some verbs (e.g. *to attend*) can be used as a diagnostic for eventivity even when nouns are not morphologically derived:

(6) I rarely attend beer festivals. (BNC)[1]

---

[1] Examples (7) and (8) are extracted from the British National Corpus (BNC), available at http://www.natcorp.ox.ac.uk/

(7)   He wished to attend a workshop in Hawaii. (BNC)

Even among non-deverbal nouns, issues linked to polysemy and alternate readings between eventive and non-eventive readings are present and the role of the co-textual elements with which they co-occur is pivotal to disambiguate and identify the correct reading, as illustrated in examples (8) and (9) below:

(8)   L'assemblea ci sarà il 20 Marzo. [EVENT]
      The meeting will be on March, 20th

(9)   L'assemblea ha deliberato l'approvazione del bilancio. [HUMAN_GROUP]
      The board/assembly has approved the budget proposal.

In (8), the noun "*assemblea*" [meeting] acquires an eventive reading due to the presence both of the verb "to be" and of the temporal expression which locates the event on the time line, while in (9), the verb "*deliberare*" [to approve] has a semantic preference for the ontological type of "human/human group" in the subject position which is realized by the noun "*assemblea*" [assembly/board]. Notice that these two cases are not to be confused with cases of type coercion of the noun "*assemblea*", but they are due to the intrinsic polysemy of this noun[2].

Previous semantic analyses (Gross & Kiefer 1995) exploited a limited set of tests based on the occurrences with peculiar verbs, such as phasal or aspectual predicates like "*to begin*", "*to conclude*", adjectives (10a), modification by temporal adverbs (10b) or temporal prepositions (10c). However, we believe these tests are not fully satisfying because they don't asses the ultimate import of all these syntagmatic cues in determining to what extent a noun denote an event, i.e. its degree of eventivity.

(10) (a) The *frequent* trips were a nuisance.
      (b) The destruction of the city *in only two days* appalled every one.
      (c) *During* the party, John left.

One intuitive way to deal with this problem – the imperfect matching between deverbal nouns and event nouns – is to characterize contextually an event noun, discovering salient syntagmatic cues.

---

[2] Notice that the English translations of the Italian noun "assemblea" are two different nouns, namely "meeting" for the eventive sense and "assembly" for the human group

It is promising to operationalize classical diagnostic tests in corpus analysis by providing representations with prototypical and less prototypical elements that sound at least more objective than representations based only on intuitions. Distributed and contextually derived representations obtained by syntagmatic evidence are useful to make automatic identification of semantically similar words and categorical distinctions among semantic classes (Lin 1998, Boleda et al. 2004).

As a consequence, summing the frequencies in several syntagmatic contexts could potentially guarantee a better understanding of the concept of event noun. On the basis of an extended corpus analysis we have identified a preliminary list of verbal and adjectival cues of eventivity for Italian nouns (see Section 3 for a detailed description of the methodology used). Here, we report the data relative to nouns not morphologically derived that most frequently co-occur in the corpus La Repubblica with the verbs "*continuare*" [to continue], "*cominciare*" [to begin] and with the adjectives "*precedente*" [previous] and "*successivo*" [following] (see Table 2 below). They are – at least partially in several cases – nouns that denote events but are not morphologically derived by verbs, such as "*guerra*" [war], "*campionato*" [championship], "*crisi*" [crisis].

If we compare their co-occurrence frequencies divided by the overall corpus frequency with those of the most frequent deverbal nouns, it clearly emerges that not morphologically derived nouns frequently co-occuring with "*cominciare*" and "*successivo*" can be as eventive as deverbal nouns (see Table 3 and Table 4).

Table 2: Most frequent nouns that co-occur with relevant syntagmatic cues.

Noun	frequency	cominciare	continuare	precedente	successivo
guerra	133072	202	246	34	19
trattativa	51517	172	189	27	25
campagna	56937	166	62	40	11
partita	89172	145	15	88	51
campionato	36762	116	11	28	25
avventura	19428	101	35	14	11
attività	84840	62	112	49	16
riunione	52559	55	17	105	112
colloquio	28830	48	36	17	36
crisi	107664	60	33	56	39
battaglia	49687	125	194	4	7
offensiva	10215	21	60	0	5

Table 3: Normalized frequencies of nouns with the verb "*cominciare*" [to begin/to start].

Non – deverbal nouns	Normalized Frequency	Deverbal nouns	Normalized Frequency
avventura	.519	pestaggio	.410
trattativa	.333	montaggio	.170
campionato	.315	monitoraggio	.146
campagna	.291	operazione	.137
battaglia	.251	riciclaggio	.105
offensiva	.205	marcatura	.094
colloquio	.166	boicottaggio	.093
partita	.162	lettura	.092
guerra	.151	trasferimento	.091
riunione	.104	manifestazione	.070
attività	.073	risanamento	.059
crisi	.055	sabotaggio	.057

Table 4: Normalized frequencies of nouns with the adjective "*successivo*" [following].

Non – deverbal nouns	Normalized Frequency	Deverbal nouns	Normalized Frequency
riunione	.213	passaggio	.334
colloquio	.124	pestaggio	.082
campionato	.068	riapertura	.062
partita	.057	dichiarazione	.054
avventura	.056	monitoraggio	.048
offensiva	.048	montaggio	.048
trattativa	.048	elezione	.047
crisi	.036	pagamento	.026
campagna	.019	sondaggio	.019
attività	.018	movimento	.019
guerra	.014	fallimento	.018
battaglia	.014	fornitura	.016

2.1 A caveat on polysemy

The graded representation available for event nouns, i.e. the existence of a *continuum* of eventivity, is mainly due to polysemic alternations: a single word is less perceived as an event by a speaker and displays a lower eventivity value if it has also another sense – for instance a result reading – available.

The degree of eventivity for a deverbal noun could intuitively depend on the number of non-eventive senses codified. For instance, if we consider the senses encoded into a lexical resource like ItalWordNet (IWN), we could state that the lexeme "*sabotaggio*" [sabotage] is more eventive than "*formazione*" [training]: the former has 3 senses/readings encoded into the resource and all of them denote an event, while the latter has 6 senses/readings encoded and only 3 of them are eventive.

However, for polysemous nouns it is not so automatic to establish a ranking because a sense could be more salient than the others. Looking at the normalized frequencies of co-occurrences with relevant syntagmatic cues (from column "cominciare" to "sum" in Table 5 below) could be useful because they provide a graded representation in place of the static representation of the lexicographic resources (columns "# of senses", "eventive senses" Table 5 below).

Unsurprisingly, syntagmatic cues select as more eventive nouns that codify just eventive sense(s), such as "*pestaggio*" [beating], "*manifestazione*" [manifestation], "*risanamento*" [recovery]. On the other hand, the salience on the eventive reading for polysemous nouns is signalled by the frequent co-occurrences with "*continuare*" [to continue], "*cominciare*" [to begin/to start] and similar, even when the nouns have just one eventive sense while the others are not eventive, such as for "*dichiarazione*" [declaration] and "*lettura*" [reading].

Table 5: Eventive readings from IWN vs. occurrences with relevant syntagmatic cues ("*continuare*" [to continue], "*cominciare*" [to begin/to start], "*precedente*" [preceeding] and "*successivo*" [following])

noun	# of senses	eventive senses	comiciare	continuare	precedente	successivo	sum
pestaggio	1	1	.410	.493	.0	.082	.986
dichiarazione	3	1	.021	.029	.250	.054	.359
operazione	3	3	.137	.056	.101	.015	.311
sondaggio	1	1	.014	.009	.242	.019	.285
montaggio	2	2	.170	.0	.024	.048	.243
manifestazione	4	4	.070	.099	.041	.010	.223
amministrazione	3	1	.005	.001	.199	.001	.207
lettura	3	1	.092	.076	.025	.010	.204
risanamento	4	4	.059	.126	.0	.0	.185
produzione	3	2	.053	.051	.055	.016	.177
regolamento	3	2	.054	.006	.088	.013	.163
riciclaggio	1	1	.105	.052	.0	.0	.158
sabotaggio	3	3	.057	.057	.0	.0	.115

Converging Evidences on the Eventivity of Italian Nouns

Through syntagmatic co-occurrences, it is possible to find out common nouns occasionally coerced to an event reading. As stated in Pustejovsky (1995), type-coercion is a directional phenomenon. Although additional research is needed, it is the syntactic head which preserves its type in composition and determines the typing of the other element(s). If we consider the syntagmic cues previously reported (*"continuare", "cominciare", "precedente", "successivo"*) and we look at nouns that rarely co-occur with them, we find coercions as occasional usages of non-eventive nouns like for the noun *"bombe"* [bombs] and *"fumo"* [smoke] in example (11) and for the noun *"impegni"* [commitments] in (12):

(11) Rimanemmo quieti senza parlare, con raffiche di mitraglietta, ma a quel punto cominciarono le *bombe*, così forti che parte dell'edificio cadeva, e cominciò il *fumo*.
[We stood quietly without talking, with bursts of machine gun, but then the bombs began, so strong that part of building fell, and the smoke began.]

(12) Come è pensabile chiudere il contratto con un governo fortemente indebolito che assumerebbe *impegni* che poi dovrebbero essere realizzati da un esecutivo successivo.
[How is it thinkable to terminate the contract with a government weakened to make commitments which should then be made by a new government the following year.]

The notion of coercion has been widely investigated in linguistics (de Swart 1998, Michaelis 2004, among others) and, in general terms, can be described as a semantic-type shifting, that is an implicit contextual reinterpretation necessary to resolve semantic conflicts.

Verbs are not the only items which can cause the coercion of noun types; adjectives have a role as well, even if in the GL model adjectives show less coercive power (Pustejovsky & Bouillon 2004).

However, looking at real data, coercions caused by adjectives seem to be equally plausible with respect to coercions caused by verbs. For example, *"frequent"* is an adjective used as a diagnostic criterion for event-denoting nouns. As Meinschaefer (2005) notes, there are nouns not morphologically derived by verbs which are compatible with *"frequent"* (example (13)).

(13) (a) Jane's frequent illness lead to her dismissal.
(b) Video technology has made this a frequent topic of male sporting conversation. (BNC)
(c) Frequent trains run from London Victoria and Charing Cross. (BNC)

Frequency adjectives, such as "*frequent*", "*occasional*", and "*yearly*", can be interpreted in a formal semantics framework (Schäfer 2007) as quantification over realizations of kinds of events. As a consequence, they can highlight coercions from simple common nouns to complex event expressions (through the enrichment of nouns with an event-kind argument) as in (14):

(14) Agent Cooper likes an occasional cup of coffee.

The importance of adjectives in selecting event nouns – the relevance of syntagmatic cues as "*frequent*", "*future*", and "*sudden*" for coercion – is undeniable.

3 Methodology and Experiments

In this section, we will illustrate the methodology used in order to develop a set of experiments for the identification of a statistical measure of eventivity for nouns. The main motivation behind the idea of an eventivity measure for nouns is related to the hypothesis that the notion of event is a scalar one (Simone 2008 among others). Such a measure may provide empirical support to this statement.

The methodology is adapted from Rumshimky et al. (2007), Pustejovsky & Jezek (2008) and Pantel & Pennacchiotti (2006). For the identification of event triggers, we have not limited our choice to verbs but we have included adjectives as well.

3.1 Identifying relevant event triggers cues

The identification of syntagmatic cues that trigger the eventive reading has been conducted by means of an extensive corpus exploration on two sets of data.

The first set of data is composed by the most frequent nouns in the ISST (Italian Syntactic Semantic Treebank, Montemagni et al. 2003). We have used this reference corpus of Italian to extract the most frequent common nouns. Due to its small dimension (only 305 K tokens), we have set the threshold for "highly frequent" to all common nouns which occur in the corpus with a minimum frequency of 20 occurrences. In order to ease the identification of event nouns, we have connected this set of nouns, which for clarity reasons we will call Nouns_Treebank, to a Generative Lexicon-based Lexical Resource, namely SIMPLE/CLIPS (Ruimy et al. 2003).

In SIMPLE/CLIPS lexical units are structured in terms of a semantic type system and are characterized and interconnected by means of a rich set of semantic features and relations. The type system consists of 157 language- and domain-independent semantic types designed for the multilingual lexical encoding of concrete and abstract entities, events and properties. The Ontology is a multi-dimensional type system based on both hierarchical and non-hierarchical conceptual relations, which reflects the Generative Lexicon assumption that lexical items are multidimensional entities with different degrees of internal complexity and thus need lexical semantic descriptions able to account for different ranges of meaning components.

By means of a set of queries, we have extracted from the Noun_Treebank set only those nouns which have at least one semantic type belonging to the "*event*" node in the SIMPLE/CLIPS Ontology. This reduced set of nouns contains both purely eventive nouns and instances of dot types. We will call this list of nouns SIMPLE_nouns.

The identification of the event triggers, or syntagmatic cues, has been accomplished by means of a second corpus exploration and through a deep exploitation of the SIMPLE_nouns list. In this second experiment, we have used a larger corpus of Italian, namely the La Repubblica corpus which is composed by 308 million tokens. The large dimensions of this corpus allows the identification of a relevant and restricted set of event trigger cues on the basis of the co-occurrences with the SIMPLE_nouns list. In particular, we have queried the La Repubblica corpus with four patterns of occurrence, namely:

- noun – VERB;
- VERB – noun;
- ADJECTIVE – noun
- noun – ADJECTIVE

Due to the lack of access to a parsed version of the La Repubblica corpus, the position of the noun in the co-occurrences patterns with verbs try to mimick the syntactic / grammatical position of subject and object.

After having extracted the four patterns of occurrence for each noun in the SIMPLE_noun list, we have selected only those event trigger cues with a high frequency, namely at least 800 occurrences for verbs and 1,000 occurrences for adjectives. This reduced list of patterns of occurrence has been manually inspected in order to identify which semantic type of the nouns in the SIMPLE_nouns list was selected. Only those verbs and adjectives which selected the event reading of the nouns were retained and considered good syntagmatic cues for eventivity. In this way, we have selected 76 syntagmatic cues: 37 verbs and 39 adjectives. In Table 6 below we report a sample of the selected cues:

Table 6: Verbal and Adjectival syntagmatic cues.

Verbs for nouns in subject position	Verbs for nouns in object position	Pre- and postmodifier adjectives
avvenire	annullare	anticipato
continuare	auspicare	attuale
restare	cessare	imprevisto
risultare	evitare	odierno
	ostacolare	successivo

The exploration of the extracted data from the La Repubblica corpus has led to the identification of a further set of cues, namely three verbs which frequently co-occur in light verb constructions in Italian, i. e. "*mettere*" [to put], "*fare*" [to do] and "*dare*" [to give]. Though in these cases it is the whole construction (verb + noun in object position) which acquires an eventive reading, we choose to include these verbs both because the nouns co-occurring with them are assumed to have an eventive reading.

3.2 Normalized frequencies of nouns

The development of the eventivity measure relies on the idea that specific syntagmatic cues, if relevant, may determine the perception of the degree of eventivity for nouns. Under this perspective, the eventivity measure corresponds to the *normalized frequency* of a noun in a reference corpus, that the sum of the co-occurrence frequencies of the noun with the syntagmatic cues divided by its absolute frequency, according to the formula in (15):

(15) $$\frac{\text{frequency noun\_cue1} + \text{frequency noun\_cue2} + ... + \text{frequency noun\_cue76}}{\text{absolute frequency noun}}$$

To test the validity of this hypothesis and the relevance of the selected cues we choose a subset of 200 nouns from the ISST (ISST_test). The nouns which form the ISST_test list have been selected by taking into account two parameters:

- the opposition between morphologically marked (e. g. "*costruzione*" [building], "*occuppazione*" [occupation], "*pestaggio*" [beating],) and "*frenata*" [braking]) and morphologically unmarked nominalizations (e. g. "*accusa*" [prosecution], "*disegno*" [drawing], "*corsa*" [run]) from corresponding verbs; and
- non-derived nouns (e. g. "*guerra*" [war], "*assemblea*" [meeting], "*barone*" [baron]).

For the first set of nouns, we have taken into account the productivity of the morphological suffix as reported in Gaeta (2004), in order to balance our data set. The two groups are well balanced since we have 100 nouns for derived forms and 100 nouns for not derived ones.

For each noun in the ISST_test list, we have extracted from the La Repubblica corpus the frequencies of each noun with the set of syntagmatic cues, and have computed its normalized frequency on the basis of the formula described in (15) A sample of the results is reported in Table 7 below:

Table 7: A sample of the results from the first experiment.

Noun	Event measure
assemblea	.040
aumento	.032
relazione	.015
aborto	.010
partecipazione	.007
telegiornale	.004
biotecnologia	.001

A preliminary analysis of the normalized frequencies shows that the nouns in the ISST_test list cluster into three main groups along a *continuum* whose poles are represented by eventive nouns and non-eventive nouns. It is interesting to notice that the eventive pole of the *continuum* does not contain only purely eventive nouns such as "*pestaggio*" [beating], "*sconfitta*" [defeat] but also the vast majority of dot types of the kind "EVENT ○ NOT_EVENT" (45 out of 88, 51.13%) such as "*dichiarazione*" [declaration], "*incremento*" [increase]. This element provides support to the hypothesis that the types which compose a dot type are not always on the same level, but it can be the case that one type is more salient that the other.

3.3 Lexical resources, eventivity ans syntagmatic cues

A further experiment for the validation of the syntagmatic cues and the eventivity measure is the analysis of the correlation between the normalized frequencies of the nouns in the ISST_test list and two language resources, namely a lexical resource, ItalWordNet (IWN), and the De Mauro-Paravia Dictionary. Such an analysis is also useful to provide a preliminary evaluation of the two language resources in terms of quality and coverage of the lexical items.

In this case, we have considered the degree of eventivity of a noun as the ratio of the sum of the eventive readings of a noun in the two resources by the total number of senses encoded for that noun, as illustrated in the formula (16):

$$(16) \quad \frac{\text{event readings IWN\_noun1} + \text{event readings De Mauro\_noun1}}{total \text{ number of senses IWN\_noun1} + total \text{ number of senses DeMauro\_noun1}}$$

The two resources are very different in terms of their internal structure and this has called for the application of different strategies for the identification of the eventive readings. As for IWN, we have extensively exploited the internal hierarchical organization of the lexical resource and its corresponding ontology by looking for each sense of the nouns in the ISST_test list for the "*event*" node among its hypernyms. On the other hand, in the De Mauro dictionary, we have looked for key phases in the sense definitions such as the "*act of X*", or the "*process of X*" and similar. In Table 8 below we report a sample of the eventivity measures we have obtained in this experiment.

Similarly to that for speakers' judgements, to evaluate the soundness of the eventivity measure obtained by the formula in (16) we have computed the Spearman correlation between the values obtained from the lexical resources and the syntagmatic cue frequencies. The results are positive since we have obtained a ρ value of .516 for IWN and of .607 for the De Mauro. Though these values are statistically significant, they are somehow biased by the nature of the two language resources which contain information with potential errors. In particular, a detailed analysis of the entries showed that some largely used senses of some nouns are not present in IWN, and that some eventive readings in the De Mauro-

Table 8: Average of eventivity from the two language resources (IWN and De Mauro).

Noun	Event average from language resources (IWN & De Mauro)
assemblea	.125
aumento	.333
relazione	.625
aborto	.433
partecipazione	.751
telegiornale	.0
biotecnologia	.0

Paravia are quite obsolete and infrequent. For these reasons, we have decided not to include the contribution of the language resources in the development of the eventivity measure, without integrating the formula in (16) with that reported in (15).

3.4 Speakers' judgments on eventivity and correlation with the normalized frequencies

The normalized frequencies we have obtained from the corpus data are numbers: they are not very informative about the validity of the eventivity measure. The only reliable result is represented by the evidence that eventive nouns are more frequent with event triggers cues and non eventive ones are less frequent. Nevertheless, the most interesting results can be derived from the analysis of the "grey zone" of the *continuum*, that is the large cluster of nouns in the middle between the eventive and non eventive poles.

Since we support the idea that theoretical semantic concepts should be cognitively plausible (Pustejovsky 1995), we compare the results of the corpus analysis with speakers' judgements. When the focus is on semantic categorizations, human judgments are widely acknowledged as a useful source to establish a *gold standard* or, more generally, they represent the best benchmark, especially when the representation is fuzzy. In computational linguistics, human judgments are used for the evaluation of automatic approaches to linguistic tasks but they also help theoretical linguistics because they provide insights complementary to introspective analysis or evidences gathered from corpora.

Following Hoey's (2005) theoretical characterization of the psycholinguistic notion of priming, according to which every word is mentally primed for collocational use and our knowledge of it includes its co-occurrences features, the comparison between the speakers' representations and corpus information is essential to understand the regularity of the lexical structure. In particular, under this perspective a lexical item is primed for eventivity when its frequencies of co-occurrences with specific triggers are statistically relevant.

Even if the cognitive status of frequency is undeniable for linguistic phenomena, there is a lively debate on the correlation between salience and frequencies in corpora because mappings between structural properties of the mental lexicon and corpus descriptive operationalities in terms of semantic associations measures could not be straightforward (Lindsey et al. 2007).

To test the validity of the syntagmatic cues, we have performed an experiment with 7 Italian subjects, all of them BA students in Linguistics, in order to compare the speakers' judgements and the corpus observations.

The subjects were asked to classify each noun in the ISST_test list on an eventivity scale ranging from 1 to 5, where 1 states that the noun has no eventive reading, 5 states that the noun has only the eventive reading, while the other numbers in the scale correspond to mixed readings. The subjects did not receive a special training for this task, but they were provided with a brief description of the task and some examples. It is important to point out the fact that the definition of event which was provided corresponds to the most intuitive definition, i.e. "*the noun describes or denotes something which happen or occur in the world*". In Table 9 below, we report the average measures of eventivity provided by the speakers:

Table 9: Average of the speakers' judgments on eventivity

Noun	Event average from speakers' judgements
assemblea	2,86
aumento	3,86
relazione	2,86
aborto	5
partecipazione	3,86
telegiornale	1,71
biotecnologia	1

In order to identify a statistical threshold of eventivity, we have computed the correlation between the speakers' judgments and the normalized frequencies by means of the Spearman coefficient. The results of the correlation are very encouraging since we have a highly convergent ρ value (ρ = .731). This value, on the one hand, supports the validity of the syntagmatic cues we have identified and, on the other hand, it provides further support to the proposal of the notion of eventivity as a scalar concept in the noun domain. In addition to this, it is interesting to notice that the speakers' judgments correlate more with the syntagmatic cues for non morphologically derived nouns than with the morphologically marked ones.

4 A practical application: event annotation by means of the eventity measure

On the basis of the analyses described in the previous sections, and in particular on the basis of the high correlation between the normalized frequencies between the syntagmatic cues and speakers' judgments, we have decided to consider as a good threshold for eventivity a measure of the normalized frequencies equals or higher than 0.01 (it corresponds to the 4th quartile of the frequency distribution). We thus propose to use this measure as a statistical parameter to support the annotation of event nouns in corpora.

In order to evaluate our proposal, we have performed an annotation experiment on an Italian corpus. The corpus is composed by 149 newspaper articles, for a total of more than 63 thousand tokens, with 18,308 of them being labelled as nouns. Six human annotators have manually applied TimeML specifications (Pustejovsky et al. 2003) by distinguishing between temporal expressions, events and signals. 4,369 noun tokens have been tagged as event. The overall annotation accuracy is 77 %, a level which guarantees a good reliability. The set of nouns in the annotated corpus will represent the *gold standard* against which we will evaluate the validity of the eventity measure. Before applying the eventity measure, we have lemmatized the nouns and cleaned this list by means of two stop-word lists which have been created from SIMPLE/CLIPS. The first is a list of items which are always eventive. This list contains words such as "*causa*" [cause], "*occasione*" [occasion] and all the nouns belonging to type "*phenomenon*" which is a subtype of the "*event*" type, but excluding nouns like "*calore*" [heat] which are phenomena but may assume an eventive reading only in special contexts. The second list, on the contrary, is a list of words which are never events. This second list has been obtained by extracting all the nouns which belong to the types "*time*" and "*amount*".

After this operation the following data are available to be analyzed by means of the eventivity measure: (i) 811 lemmas which have never been annotated as eventive (non-eventive nouns); (ii) 485 lemmas which have been annotated as eventive and on which annotators agree (eventive nouns); (iii) 78 lemmas on which annotators disagree (disagreement). Once again, the measure has been computed by means of queries from the corpus La Repubblica. Each lemma in the three groups – non eventive nouns, eventive nouns and disagreement – has been automatically annotated either as eventive or as non-eventive on the basis of the threshold. The results are illustrated in Table 10.

Table 10: Percentages of eventive items retrieved by applying the eventivity measure to the three groups of nouns.

Noun subgroup	Eventive items
non-eventive	105 (13 %)
eventive	288 (60 %)
disagreement	22 (29 %)

The figures are impressive since following the measure more that 60 % of the lemmas which had been annotated as event by humans have been identified. This suggests that the eventive measure could be used either as a feature for automatic annotation of event nouns or to support the development of manual datasets for event nouns. Moreover, the very low number of false positives – i.e non-eventive noun types which are above the threshold – is encouraging since it supports the validity and consistency of the syntagmatic cues we have identified. Finally, the non-eventive nouns which are above the threshold can be considered as good candidates for identifying instances of qualia exploitation and coercion phenomena. As for the disagreement group, the eventivity measure suggests that some items could have an eventive reading, thus providing a statistical index for identifying challenging cases which require a more fine-grained analysis.

5 Conclusion and Future Work

The main contribution of this paper is the identification of a measure for the eventivity of nouns based on syntagmatic cues that is promising from a theoretical point of view (i. e. Generative Lexicon) and useful for practical applications.

In a lexical semantic theory the inclusion of a lexical item in wide semantic classes such as the event nouns class should be based on language usages. The *continuum* that emerges by the corpus based analyses proposed in this work indicates that the membership is a matter of degree.

From a practical point of view, the eventivity measure can be used as a statistical measure to automatically annotate event nouns in corpora. Moreover, the measure can be used as a strategy to implement robust annotation systems which integrate information from large lexical resources, like SIMPLE/CLIPS and IWN. A further advantage of the measure is the fact that it could be used to discover probable instances of dot types or coerced events. This can be achieved by lowering the threshold. For instance, nouns with an eventivity measure very near to the threshold, e. g. 0.008, could be good candidates.

It is interesting to point out that the eventivity measure can be used also to weight noun types. For instance, it could be the case that some dot types objects are perfectly balanced between the two types, but it could also be the contrary, that is, several dot type objects could be assembled with components that vary for their salience. Evidence to this hypothesis could be found among the disagreement nouns which are above the threshold.

References

Baroni, M., Bernardini S., Comastri F., Piccioni L., Volpi A., Aston G., & Mazzoleni M. 2004. Introducing the "la Repubblica" corpus: A large, annotated, TEI(XML)-compliant corpus of newspaper italian. *Proceedings of the Fourth International conference on Language Resources and Evaluation* (LREC-04).

Baroni, M. & A. Lenci. 2010. Distributional Memory: A general framework for corpus-based semantics, *Computational Linguistics*, 36 (4). 1–49.

Basili, R., & M. Pennacchiotti. 2010. Distributional Lexical Semantics: Toward uniform representation paradigms for advanced acquisition and processing tasks. *Natural Language Engeneeringing* 16 (4). 347–358.

Bertuccelli Papi, M., M. Cappelli, & S. Masi (eds.). 2007. *Lexical complexity: theoretical assessment and translational perspectives*. Pisa: Plus Pisa University Press.

Boleda, G., T. Badia, & E. Batlle. 2004. Acquisition of semantic classes for adjectives from distributional evidence. *Proceedings of Coling* 2004, 1119–1125.

De Mauro, T. 2004. *Il Dizionario di Italiano Paravia*. Paravia, Milano.

de Swart, H. 1998. Aspect shift and coercion. *Natural Language and Linguistic Theory* 16 (2). 347–385.

Lin, D. 1998. Automatic retrieval and clustering of similar words. *Proceedings of the 36th Annual Meeting of the Association for Computational Linguistics*, 768–774.

Gaeta, L. 2004. Nomi d' azione. In M. Grossmann & Rainer F., (eds.), *La formazione delle parole in italiano*, 314–351. Tübingen: Niemeyer.

Grimshaw, J. 1990. *Argument Structure*. Cambridge: MIT Press.

Gross, G. & F. Kiefer. 1995. La structure événementielle des substantifs. *Folia Linguistica* 29 (1–2). 45–65.

Hoey, M. 2005. *Lexical Priming: A new theory of words and language*. London: Routledge.

Hovy E. 2010. Distributional Semantics and the Lexicon. *Proceedings of the 2nd Workshop on Cognitive Aspects of the Lexicon* (CogALex 2010).

Lindsey, R., V. D. Veksler, A. Grintsvayg, & W. D. Gray. 2007. Be Wary of What Your Computer Reads: The Effects of Corpus Selection on Measuring Semantic Relatedness. *Proceedings of the 8th International Conference on Cognitive Modeling*.

Lenci, A. 2008. Distributional semantics in linguistic and cognitive research, in A. Lenci (ed.), *From context to meaning: distributional models of the lexicon in linguistics and cognitive science, Italian Journal of Linguistics* 20 (1). 1–31.

McDonald, M. A. & R. C. Schillcock. 2001. Rethinking the word frequency effect: the neglected role of distributional information in lexical processing. *Language and Speech* 44 (3). 295–323.

Meinschaefer, J. 2005. Event-oriented adjectives and the semantics of deverbal nouns in germanic and romance: The role of boundedness and the mass/count distinction. In A. M. Thornton & M. Grossmann (eds.), *La formazione delle parole in italiano*, 355–368. Roma: Bulzoni.

References

Montemagni, S., F. Barsotti, M. Battista, N. Calzolari, O. Corazzar, A. Lenci, V. Pirelli, A. Zampolli, F. Fanciulli, M. Massetani, R. Raffaelli, R. Basili, M. T. Pazienza, D. Saracino, F. Zanzotto, N. Mana, F. Pianesi, & R. Delmonte. 2003. The syntactic-semantic treebank of Italian. An overview. *Special Issue: Linguistica Computazionale, Computational Linguistics in Pisa*, XVIII–XIX, 461–493.

Pantel, P. & M. Pennacchiotti. 2006. Espresso: Leveraging generic patterns for automatically harvesting semantic relations. *Proceedings of the 21st International Conference on Computational Linguistics and 44th Annual Meeting of the Association for Computational Linguistics*, 113–120.

Pustejovsky, J. & P. Bouillon. 2004. On the proper role of coercion in semantic typing. *Proceedings of the 15th International Conference on Computational Linguistics (COLING-94)*, 706–711.

Pustejovsky, J. & E. Jezeck. 2008. Semantic coercion in language: Beyond distributional analysis. *Italian Journal of Linguistics – Special Issue: Distributional Models of the Lexicon in Linguistics and Cognitive Science*, 20(1).

Pustejovsky, J., J. Castao, R. Ingria, R. Saur'ı, R. Gaizauskas, A. Setzer, & G. Katz. 2003. TimeML: Robust specification of event and temporal expressions in text. *Fifth International Workshop on Computational Semantics (IWCS-5)*.

Pustejovsky. J. 1995. *The Generative Lexicon*. Cambridge: MIT Press.

Ruimy, N. M. Monachini, E. Gola, N. Calzolari, M.C. Del Fiorentino, M. Ulivieri, & S. Rossi. 2003. A computational semantic lexicon of Italian: SIMPLE. *Special Issue: Linguistica Computazionale, Computational Linguistics in Pisa*, XVIII–XIX, 821–864.

Rumshimsky, A., V. Grinberg, & J. Pustejovsky. 2007. Detecting selectional behaviour of complex types in text. *Proceedings of the 4th International Workshop on Generative Approaches to the Lexicon*.

Schäfer, R. 2007. On frequency adjectives. In E. Puig-Waldmüller (ed.), *Proceedings of Sinn und Bedeutung* 11, 555–567.

Simone, R. 2008. Coefficienti verbali nei nomi. In P.M. Bertinetto (ed.), *Il verbo. Atti del Congresso annuale della SIG – Società Italiana di Glottologia*.

Vendler, Z. 1967. *Linguistics in Philosophy*. Ithaca: Cornell University Press.

Zucchi, A. 1993. *The Language of Propositions and Events*. Dordrecht: Kluwer Academic Publishers.

Authors

Irene Russo
Istituto di Linguistica Computazionale
CNR
irene.russo@ilc.cnr.it

Tommaso Caselli
Trento RISE
t.caselli@gmail.com

Diachrony of Stative Dimensional Verbs in French[1]

Brigitte Schwarze & Hans Geisler

Abstract

In the present paper we will trace the evolution of French verbs like *peser* 'weigh' and *coûter* 'cost' which encode a dimension – WEIGHT and PRICE, respectively – and allow for the external specification of a value of this dimension as in *peser 2 kilos* 'weigh 2 kilos' and *coûter 5 euros* 'cost 5 euros.' We call these verbs stative dimensional verbs (SDVs). Our main focus will be on SDVs which evolve from verbs encoding sensorimotor concepts such as main body postures (e. g., STANDING) or elementary hand actions (e. g., GRASPING). We will try to delineate the semantic changes they undergo in the course of their development. Special attention will be paid to the correlation between source concepts and the emergence of specific dimensional readings.

1 Stative dimensional verbs, functional nouns and dimensional adjectives

Stative dimensional verbs (henceforth SDVs) include verbs such as *peser* 'weigh' and *coûter* 'cost' that encode a dimension (or attribute) – WEIGHT and PRICE, respectively – and allow for the external specification of a value of this dimension as in *peser 2 kilos* 'weigh 2 kilos' and *coûter 5 euros* 'cost 5 euros.' Constructions with SDVs can be described in terms of a mathematical function f(x)=y, where f is the dimension given by the verb meaning, x is the subject argument and y is

---

[1] The subject matters tackled in the present paper are part of two projects ("Dimensional Verbs" and "The development of functional concepts in French") funded by the German Research Foundation (DFG) within the Research Unit FOR 600 "Functional Concepts and Frames."

the predicatio
the dimension

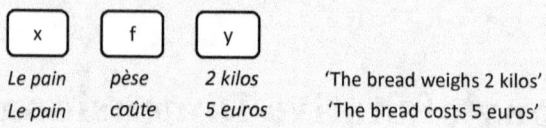

Table 1: SDV construction

SDVs c
or, for
serve t
a funct
French
therefo

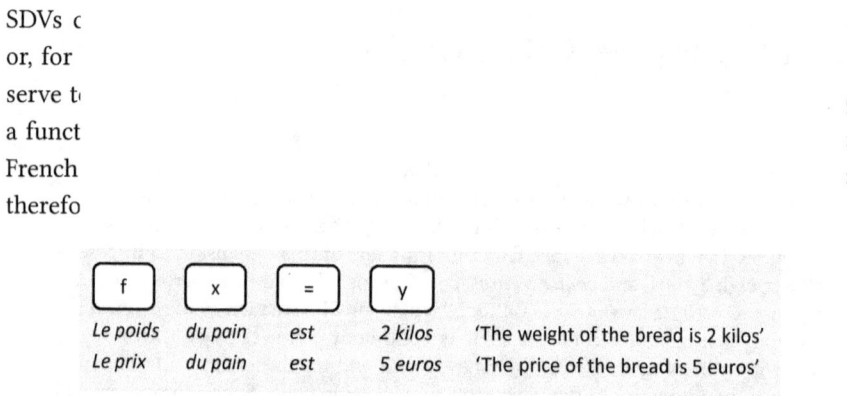

Table 2: Functional noun construction

The variants presented in Tables 1 and 2 both specify the value '2 kilos' for the dimension WEIGHT and '5 euros' for the dimension PRICE. However, in the nominal variant in 2, the dimension is explicitly referred to, whereas in the verbal variant in 1, the verb encodes the respective dimension without explicitly expressing it.

Moreover, there is a third means of expressing functional concepts, namely by dimensional adjectives such as Fr. *lourd* 'heavy' and *cher* 'expensive.' Dimensional adjectives only imply the dimension and, in contrast to SDVs and functional nouns, they are usually value-specific, i.e., they themselves denote a certain value. Thus, they are generally less flexible; in most cases, they cannot be combined with explicit value specifications, as demonstrated in Table 3.

However, some languages – like German, for example – allow for the use of the verbal, the nominal, and the adjectival variant at the same time. As shown

---

[2] For the notion of functional concept, the corresponding lexical noun type and the role of determination cf. Löbner (1979), (1985), (2011).

Diachrony of Stative D.

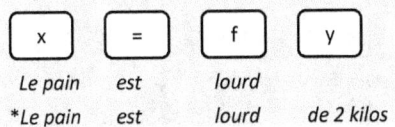

| Le pain | est | lourd | |
| *Le pain | est | lourd | de 2 kilos |

in Tables 4 to   a
noun

Das

| Das Brot | ist | 2 Kilo | schwer | lit.: 'The bread is 2 kilos heavy' |

Table 6: Dimensional adjective construction (German)

The lexical devices for expressing functional concepts vary considerably across languages. In modern Indo-European languages, the nominal variant seems to outweigh dimensional verbs and dimensional adjectives, both in number and frequency. Our cross-linguistic investigation of functional concepts clearly shows

---

[3] In French, the combination of dimensional adjectives and explicit value specifications is mainly restricted to a subset of spatial adjectives (e. g., *long* 'long,' *haut* 'high,' *large* 'large, wide,' *profond* 'deep,' etc.), whereas such a restriction does not exist in German. This does not mean that there are no restrictions at all in German; in many cases, the availability of the adjectival paraphrase is at least questionable (cf.: ?*Das Brot ist fünf Euro teuer*. Lit.: 'The bread is five euros expensive.'). Starting out from a large-scale analysis of German SDVs, Gamerschlag (2014) demonstrates that even in German only few SDVs can be paraphrased by adjectives.

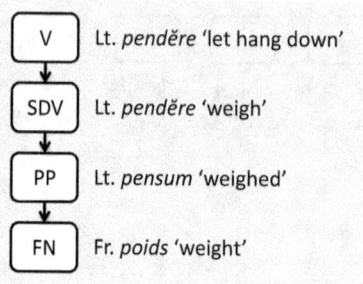

Figure 1: Lt. *penděre* > Fr. *poids*

that this class of nouns saw a significant upsurge in German and French in scientific discourse and all kinds of expository texts that try to impart depersonalized, objective knowledge during the last centuries. Nevertheless, there are many dimensions which are encoded alternatively by nouns or by SDVs. Furthermore, in many cases SDVs seem to have constituted a preliminary stage for the later nominal encoding of functional concepts. This is true, for example, of French *poids* 'weight.' It can ultimately be traced back to the Latin verb *penděre* which originally meant 'let hang down.' As it was used in the context of weighing ('let the scales of a balance hang down in order to weigh something'), it acquired the transitive reading 'weigh something' as well as the dimensional reading 'weigh'; the noun then derives from a nonfinite form of *penděre*, namely the past participle *pensum*.

A comparable development is attested in case of Fr. *coût* '(the) cost(s),' a near synonym of *prix* 'price.' *Coût* goes back to Lt. *constāre* which is composed of the prefix *con/com* (from the Old Latin comitative preposition *cum*) and the verb *stāre* 'stand.' Its original meaning is 'come to stand' or 'stand still.' In commercial discourse it developed the dimensional reading 'cost.' Here again it is a nonfinite form, the infinitive in this case, from which the noun is finally derived.

A third example is Fr. *contenu* 'content.' It stems from the Latin verb *continēre* 'hold (together).' Once more, an SDV reading, 'enclose'/'contain' in this case, had been acquired before the functional noun was coined on the basis of the nonfinite past participle form of the verb.

These examples also indicate that the dimensional reading of the verbs themselves can often be traced back to nondimensional usage. The verbs initially refer to intersubjectively stable bodily experience, to body posture or motion and hand

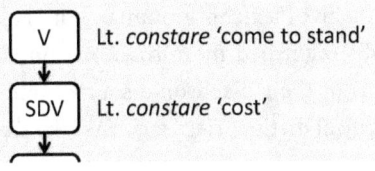

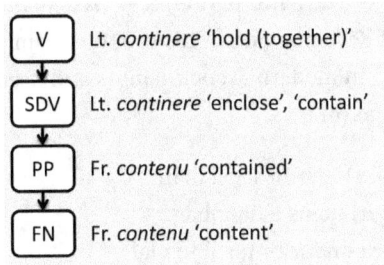

Figure 3: Lt. *continere* > Fr. *contenu*

action. In the following sections we will take a closer look at possible origins and lines of development of SDVs. We will try to outline how these anthropomorphic concepts are transformed into more abstract concepts by means of associative processes like metonymy and metaphor, and how this finally leads to the isolation of a single semantic property that allows us to assign a dimension to an object.

2 Diachrony of stative dimensional verbs in French

2.1 Data

Our inventory of French SDVs has mainly been developed by analyzing approximately 2500 entries in the verb dictionary compiled by Busse & Dubost (1977/²1983). The SDVs and SDV readings identified here were revised and extended by means of other synchronic dictionaries (e. g., Petit Robert and TLFi), the syntactic semantic thesaurus of French verbs by Dubois & Dubois-Charlier (1997), the data offered in the realm of lexicon-grammar,[4] and French text corpora (Frantext). We eventually distinguished more than one hundred items[5] which have been examined in terms of their diachronic sources and stages of development using different etymological dictionaries (e. g., EWFS, FEW, Robert Historique).[6]

2.2 Origins of SDVs

The analysis has shown that the majority of SDVs are transparent. Most of them do indeed go back to dynamic verbs or special groups of stative verbs, which originally encode sensorimotor concepts. In many cases, the source concepts which can be attested for the Latin period, e. g., basic hand actions like HOLDING reoccur in more recent developments. This can, for example, be illustrated by Fr. *tenir* < Lt. *tenēre* 'hold.' In modern French *tenir* is still used in the sense of 'hold' in sentences like (1a) and (b)

(1)   (a)   La petite fille tient un sac à main.
           'The little girl holds a handbag.'
    (b)   Tiens-moi ça un instant, s'il te plaît.
           'Hold this for me a moment, please.'

but it is also used as an SDV denoting CAPACITY, e. g., in (2):

(2)   La cuve tient mille litres.
     'The vat holds a thousand liters.'

---

[4] See particularly the material available on the website (http://infolingu.univ-mlv.fr/).

[5] Note that the number of SDV readings is actually higher than the number of items (verbs) in our inventory, since one verb generally displays several SDV readings (cf. infra).

[6] There are different types of SDVs which we cannot discuss in detail in this paper. Some SDVs like *peser* and *sentir* can take an absolute use without a value argument. In this case, they denote a fixed (positive or negative) high value (cf.: *Ce sac pèse*. 'This bag weighs (a lot).'/ *Ce poisson sent*. 'This fish smells (bad).'). Other verbs can adopt a dimensional reading in special contexts (cf. *vendre* 'sell' in *Cette voiture se vend bien*. 'This car sells well.'). Still others may be used to specify more than one dimension like, for instance, German *sitzen* 'sit' (POSTURE and LOCATION) or *kleben* 'stick' (CONTACT and LOCATION). As has already been pointed out in other contexts (cf. Talmy 1985, Schwarze 1993), these 'bidimensional' uses can be described as rare in Modern French as well as in other Romance Languages; French makes use of resultative constructions instead (cf. *être assis* 'be seated', *être collé* 'be stuck'). For an overview of the different types of SDVs cf. Schwarze (2008), for a more detailed account cf. Gamerschlag (2014).

Diachrony of Stative Dimensional Verbs in French

Not every speaker accepts this kind of construction, but it is attested.[7] So once again, it is the concept of HOLDING which gives rise to a CAPACITY reading.

Another example which is completely uncontroversial among native speakers of French is *composer*. It is derived from OFr. *poser* 'rest'/'put in a place' which goes back to Lt. *pausare* 'pause, halt, seize' and whose meaning was presumably influenced by Lt. *ponere* 'lay down'/'put down' and *componere* 'put together'/'compose'. Although the sense of Lt. *componere* is (still) vivid in Modern French, the middle construction as well as the resultative yield a dimensional reading and allow us to specify the dimension STRUCTURE or COMPOSITION:

(3) (a) Le groupe se compose/est composé de garçons et de filles.
'This group is composed of/consists of boys and girls'
(b) Cet ouvrage se compose/est composé de trois parties.
'This work is composed of/consists of three parts.'

Only minor groups of SDVs do not evolve from verbs but from adjectives – such as Lt. *durus* 'hard' which gives rise to Lt. *durare*, Fr. *durer* 'last'. Another (and apparently more frequent) source is nouns. Denominal derivation can be of two kinds: Derivation from sortal nouns which designate (classes of) objects with specific salient characteristics seems to be typical of particular semantic groups of SDVs, such as SDVs denoting light emission (cf.: *chatoyer* 'shimmer' < *chat* 'cat' (supposedly because of the cat's eyes), *étinceler* 'sparkle' < *étincelle* 'spark,' *flamboyer* 'blaze' < OFr. *flambe* 'flame'/'blaze' etc.). On the other hand, we assert that more concrete functional nouns, such as *bouche* 'mouth' or *bout* 'limit'/'endpoint,' constitute the basis for the derivation of verbs displaying an SDV reading. *Bouche* gives rise to *déboucher* (*dans/sur*) 'flow into'/'lead to,' *bout* yields *aboutir* (*à*) 'lead to (an end)'; both specify the dimension ENDPOINT, GOAL or OUTCOME:

(4) (a) La rue débouchait sur une place immense.
'The street led to an enormous square.'
(b) Une philosophie qui débouche sur l'action.
'A philosophy which leads to action.'

---

[7] The example is taken from Dubois & Dubois-Charlier (1997). Standard dictionaries of modern French do not unambiguously account for a CAPACITY reading. The judgements of native speakers on the acceptability of CAPACITY denoting uses vary considerably. According to Petit Robert one meaning of *tenir* is "occuper (un certain espace)" (Petit Robert s. *tenir* I, 8), TLFi is more explicit in this respect, since they add "avoir une certaine capacité" (TLFi s. *tenir* IV/A, 2).

(5) (a) Le chemin aboutit au village.
          'The path leads to the village.'
     (b) Ses recherches n'ont abouti à rien.
          'His research didn't lead to anything.'

However, we have to be considerate here because in some cases this kind of denominal derivation as well as the deadjectival derivation does not *immediately* lead to an SDV reading. As for Fr. *déboucher* (*dans/sur*) and Lt. *durare*, dynamic uses of the verbs in question might be older.[8] Taking this into account, we state that the SDV readings develop, once again, from a verb.[9] Nevertheless, these verbs usually do not pertain to the most prototypical group of source verbs, namely the one encoding sensorimotor concepts, which we will look at in the remainder of this paper.

2.3 From sensorimotor concepts to functional concepts

Some of the most frequent sensorimotor concepts originally expressed are 'drag,' 'put,' 'give,' 'hold,' 'take,' 'touch,' 'carry,' etc. These concepts give rise to a number of different dimensional readings. In (6) to (10) this is illustrated by French *porter* which also keeps the 'original' meaning, that is the meaning of the Latin verb *portare* 'carry.'[10]

(6) RANGE: Le canon porte (jusqu') à 10 km.
                 'The range of the cannon is 10 km.'
                 (Lit.: 'The cannon carries (up) to 10 km.')
(7) SUBJECT: Cette étude porte sur le chômage.
                 'This study deals with unemployment.'
                 (Lit.: 'This study carries on unemployment.')

---

[8] *Déboucher* is initially used in the sense of 'appear,' 'come out of,' *durare* first means 'make hard.' Less controversial for the second denominal type are German verbs like *abstammen* < *Stamm* 'trunk (of a tree)' and *beinhalten* < *Inhalt* 'content.'

[9] Moreover, the nominal base of the verb in question may ultimately go back to a dynamic verb (cf. *bout* 'limit'/'endpoint' which, according to most scholars, is derived from *bouter* < Old Low Franconian **bōtan* 'push'/'beat').

[10] Note that the following SDV uses are not meant to cover the full meaning range of French *porter*.

(8) LOCATION: L'accent porte sur la dernière syllabe.
'The accent lies on the last syllable.'
(Lit.: 'The accent carries on the last syllable.')

(9) POTENTIAL: Un argument qui porte.
'A convincing/valid argument.'
(Lit.: 'An argument that carries.')

(10) PREGNANCY TIME: La chatte porte soixante jours.
'Cats' pregnancy lasts sixty days.'
(Lit.: 'Cats carry sixty days.')

The development of deverbal SDVs from the above mentioned source concepts is propelled by associative processes such as metonymy and metaphor. These processes rely on gestalt principles of perception (like figure and ground, proximity or contiguity and similarity) and can be specified for every step in concept development.[11] In initial stages, metonymic profiling strategies in verbally encoded event frames appear to dominate. Metonymies serve to highlight specific meaning components and to profile noncanonical roles (like theme, path, source, goal, instrument etc.). Subsequently, metaphors enable domain mapping of functional concepts.

This development can be illustrated by means of Lt. *ducere* 'drag' (Figure 4). According to different syntactic as well as semantic parameters (such as animacy, control and volitionality on the side of the agent), Lt. *ducere* can be regarded as a prototypical transitive verb. The semantic changes motivated by metonymies involve a gradient loss of transitivity. In a first step, the meaning of *dūcere* shifts from the concept of DRAGGING to the concept of LEADING and ACCOMPANYING, and this is how Fr. *conduire* (< VLt. *conducere*) is first used. Apart from the agent and the experiencer, the underlying concept frame comprises elements such as instrument, path and goal. Since Old French, the orientation or goal component becomes central, while the comitative reading recedes.[12] This tendency seems to be a prerequisite for subsequent argument alternations and the emergence of

---

[11] There is a whole wealth of contemporary literature dealing with the different associative processes and their relevance in (synchronic) language variation and (diachronic) change. For comprehensive discussions which draw especially on French and other Romance Languages cf. Blank (1997), Waltereit (1998), Koch (2001) and Gévaudan (2007).

[12] "Dès l'ancien français, l'extension des sens s'est faite [...] par la valorisation de l'idée d'«orientation» aux dépens de celle d'«accompagnement»" (Robert Historique, s. *conduire*).

dimensional readings: The agent is finally shifted out of its canonical subject

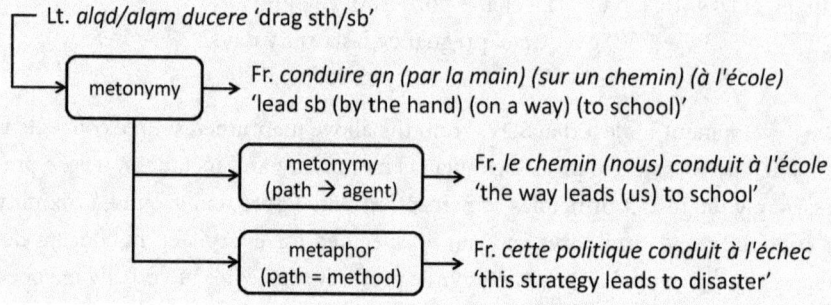

Figure 4: Lt. *ducere* > Fr. *conduire à*

Unergative and unaccusative verbs denoting elementary movements, such as *go, run, fall*, transform in a similar way. In accordance with transitive verbs, less prominent components of the original event frame become highlighted while all anthropomorphic and dynamic aspects are lost. Starting from a complex event verb, the associative processes even allow us to single out different attributes leading to different dimensional readings, as has already been illustrated for French *porter* above. In the following, we will go into more detail for the intransitive French verb *descendre* to demonstrate how this diversity may occur.

For French *descendre* (< Lt. *descandere* 'move down'/'go down' < *scandere* 'jump up'/'climb') at least three SDV readings can be distinguished:

(11)   ORIGIN: Elle descend d'une ancienne famille./L'homme descend du singe.
       'She descends from an ancient family.'/'Man descends from ape.'

(12)   GRADIENT: La rue descend à pic.
       'The street falls away/drops steeply.'

(13)   DEPTH: Le puits descend à 40 mètres.
       'The well is 40 meters deep.'

The original reading given in (11), which is first attested in the 12th century, is metaphorically motivated. The underlying conceptual metaphor is GENEALOGY IS A PATH. The relevant aspect of the DESCENDRE concept is that DESCENDRE is a movement that implies a change of location of the subject referent leading from a starting point, the high point A, down to a low point B (*descendre* = 'move/go down from A to B'). The starting point of the downward movement is overtly expressed when *descendre* is followed by a prepositional phrase introduced by *de* (e. g., *descendre du grenier* 'move/go down from the loft'). Transferred to the concept of genealogy, *descendre de* acquires a purely relational meaning. Since movement is lost, it serves to express the 'starting point,' i.e., ORIGIN of the subject referent.[13]

The SDV reading in (12) dates back to the 17th century and is based on a transitive use of *descendre* (e. g., *descendre une rue* 'move/go down a street'). The gradient reading arises out of a metonymical shift parallel to the one observed in the *ducere* example above. In the case of *descendre,* the coding of the path argument in the subject position leads to the isolation of the downward orientation (=GRADIENT); accordingly, the adverbial, which in the underlying event frame would serve to express the manner of the downward movement (cf. *descendre rapidement/en courant* 'go/move down fast/in a running manner'), turns out to express the value that the object acquires with reference to this dimension (i.e., measure of GRADIENT).

Finally, the depth reading given in (13) is best interpreted as the outcome of a metaphorical transfer. Due to its downward orientation *descendre* can be applied to (subterranean) vertical cavities such as wells and shafts. From the point of view of the observer, objects of this nature are essentially characterized by the directional dimension DOWN (or having DEPTH). Now, *descendre à* which originally serves to express the endpoint of the downward movement (e. g., *descendre à la cave* 'move/go down to the cellar') allows the specification of the value that the object acquires along the dimension of DEPTH.[14]

---

[13] In our opinion, the downward orientation of *descendre* does not play any crucial role for the metaphorical transfer. Nevertheless, *descendre* originally may have been preferred against other options due to its orientation, since family trees, for example, are usually arranged in a top-down manner.

[14] Note that the depth reading is neither recorded in etymological dictionaries nor in standard dictionaries of modern French. It is attested in Dubois & Dubois-Charlier (1997) and the online version of the Larousse encyclopedia (*Larousse Encyclopédie sur Internet,* cf.: http://www.larousse.fr/).

2.4 Correlation between source concepts and dimensional readings

Up to now, we have seen how different dimensional readings emerge from one and the same source concept – depending on which aspect or attribute of the underlying frame becomes isolated. However, if we take specific dimensional readings as a :
as ORIGIN and
particular sou:
guages. A ma
verbs of move

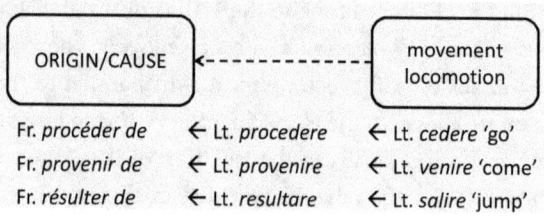

SDVs whi
tions like ¡

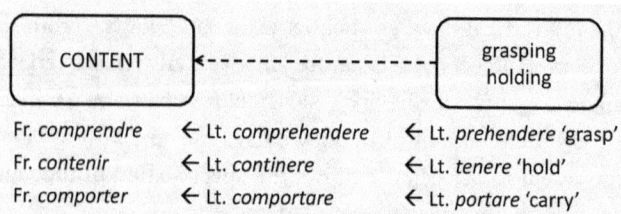

Figure 6: Correlation of source and dimension: CONTENT

The meaning changes leading to the SDV readings are usually motivated by common types of metonymies and metaphors which remain stable over time, e. g., starting point of movement → origin of state or entity → cause of state or entity, container → contained/content. Therefore they occur more than once within a

given language a
the German exa

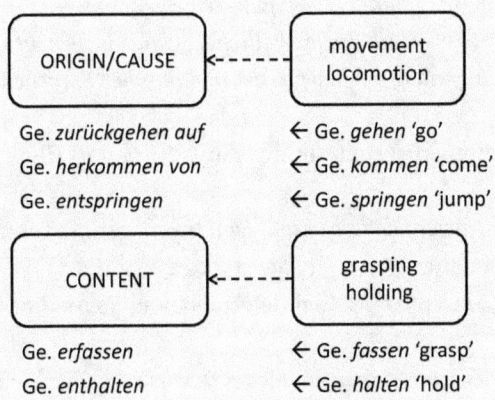

Figure 7: ORIGIN/CAUSE and CONTENT in German

3 Conclusion

Our analysis of the historical development of SDVs shows that even highly abstract functional concepts are rooted in sensorimotor experience. There are striking parallels to concept formation in general as put forth by the *embodied cognition theory* (cf. Ziemke 2003 for an overview). The idea that concepts are embodied assumes that we have a species-specific view of the world, due to the nature of our physical bodies. This is corroborated by our work on SDVs (and functional concepts in general), since we could demonstrate that a restricted set of action and posture verbs combined with a handful of locational and directional particles and prepositions seem to be a convenient remedy for all denotational needs.

References

Blank, A. 1997. *Prinzipien des lexikalischen Bedeutungswandels am Beispiel der romanischen Sprachen*. Tübingen: Niemeyer.

Gamerschlag, T. 2014. Stative Dimensional Verbs in German. *Studies in Language*, 38 (2). 275–344.

Geisler, H. 1988. Das Verhältnis von semantischer und syntaktischer Transitivität im Französischen. *Romanistisches Jahrbuch* 39. 22–35.

Gévaudan, P. 2007. *Typologie des lexikalischen Wandels. Bedeutungswandel, Wortbildung und Entlehnung am Beispiel der romanischen Sprachen.* Tübingen: Stauffenburg.

Koch, P. 2001. Metonymy: Unity in diversity. *Journal of Historical Pragmatics* 2 (2). 201–244.

Löbner, S. 1979. *Intensionale Verben und Funktionalbegriffe.* Tübingen: Narr.

Löbner, S. 1985. Definites. *Journal of Semantics* 4. 279–326.

Löbner, S. 2011. Concept types and determination. *Journal of Semantics* 28 (3). 279–333.

Schwarze, B. 2008. Verbos dimensionales estáticos en el diccionario. In D. Azorín Fernández et al. (eds.), *Actas del II Congreso Internacional de Lexicografía Hispánica*, 271–277. Alicante: Universidad de Alicante.

Schwarze, Chr. 1993. Primäre und sekundäre Lokalverben im Französischen. In F. Beckmann & G. Heyer (eds.), *Theorie und Praxis des Lexikons*, 103–122. Berlin: de Gruyter.

Talmy, L. 1985. Lexicalization Patterns: Semantic Structure in Lexical Forms. In Th. Shopen (ed.), *Language Typology and Syntactic Description. Vol. III: Grammatical Categories and the Lexicon*, 57–149. Cambridge: Cambridge University Press.

Waltereit, R. 1998. *Metonymie und Grammatik. Kontiguitätsphänomene in der französischen Satzsemantik.* Tübingen: Niemeyer.

Ziemke, T. 2003. What's that Thing Called Embodiment? In R. Alterman & D. Kirsh (eds.), *Proceedings of the 25th Annual Meeting of the Cognitive Science Society*, 1305–1310. Mahwah, NJ: Lawrence Erlbaum.

Dictionaries

Busse, W. & Dubost, J.-P. 1977/²1983. *Französisches Verblexikon.* Stuttgart: Klett-Cotta.

Dubois, J. & Dubois-Charlier, F. 1997. *Les verbes français.* http://rali.iro.umontreal.ca/Dubois/

References

EWFS = Gamillscheg, E. ²1969. *Etymologisches Wörterbuch der französischen Sprache.* Heidelberg: Winter.

FEW = Wartburg, W. v. 1922ss. *Französisches Etymologisches Wörterbuch. eine darstellung des galloromanischen sprachschatzes.* Bonn: Fritz Klopp Verlag.

Georges, K. E. ⁸1913/1918. *Ausführliches lateinisch-deutsches Handwörterbuch.* 2 Vol. Reprint: Darmstadt 1998.

Petit Robert = Rey-Debove, J. & Rey, A. 1993. *Le nouveau Petit Robert.* Dictionnaire alphabétique et analogique de la langue française, Paris.

Robert Historique = Rey, Alain et al. 1992. *Dictionnaire historique de la langue française*, Paris. TLFi = ATILF / CNRS / Université de Nancy 2: *Trésor de la langue française informatisé.* http://atilf.atilf.fr/tlf.htm

Authors

Brigitte Schwarze
Heinrich-Heine-Universität Düsseldorf
Department of Romance Languages
bs@phil.hhu.de

Hans Geisler
Heinrich-Heine-Universität Düsseldorf
Department of Romance Languages
geisler@phil.hhu.de

SEMANTIC FIELDS

Linguistic Realizations of the Concept of FEAR

Liane Ströbel

Abstract
There is something about fear... This paper is an attempt to look into patterns of use and variation concerning the conceptualization of 'fear.' Analyzing the semantic field and syntactic structure of fear expressions in French, the following questions will be tackled: Which of the parameters associated with fear play a role in the linguistic encoding? Are there conceptual differences between the different realizations of this complex concept? Is it possible that 'fear' only has one central core or source? And finally, can members of the semantic field of fear function as a conceptual source themselves?

1 Introduction[1]

'Fear' is an emotional response to threats and danger and one of our most important survival mechanisms. Fear can be conditioned, based on experience, gender specific, real or imaginary. Fear can be regarded as a characteristic of a person (trait anxiety) or a reaction to the loss of control in a specific situation (state anxiety). In the latter case, the experience of fear involves two cognitive processes and is followed by an adequate reaction to the situation. The first stage (Stage 1) is marked by a primary appraisal of a negative, dangerous or even life-threatening situation (involving physical or mental pain). This stage is followed by a secondary appraisal of the resources needed in order to react to the situation (Stage

---

[1] The research presented in this paper was supported by the Collaborative Research Center 991, funded by the German Research Foundation (DFG).

2). Finally, Stage 3 presents an adequate response to this danger (Faust 1986, Fries 2000, Boerner 2003, Bandelow 2003, 2004).

While the last two stages hardly help to enlighten the concept of fear, Stage 1 represents a productive analyzing ground in order to illustrate the complexity of the semantic field of 'fear' in French. In this stage, the sensation of fear and its dimensions (life-threatening, individual, etc.) must be defined. This cognitive process will have a great impact on the linguistic realizations (see Sections 2 to 4). In the following, an overview about the complexity of the concept of fear and the different resulting linguistic encodings will be displayed. The semantic core of fear will be redefined by analyzing the distinct semes of the nominal representations of fear (see Section 2) and certain salient conceptual sources of prototypical fear metaphors and metonymies (see Section 3).

Furthermore, in Section 4, a hypothesis for the predominance of analytic constructions (and support verb constructions in particular) will be presented. Finally, it will be demonstrated that the parameters at work, in order to classify the different degrees of the fear experience, and the semantic core inherent to all fear expressions, also have an impact on further linguistic developments and even lead to the fact that formerly negatively marked lexemes from this domain can turn – via their function as intensifiers – into positive markers (see Section 5).

2 The parameters of the fear experience

Fear is a primary universal emotion; therefore it comes as no surprise that the semantic field of 'fear' in French is very complex and broad. The single entities of this complex semantic field can be regarded as different stages of an emotional process (Shah 1993: 321 f.). At the same time, the entities themselves can be composed of various different sensations, ranging from excitement to nervousness. Therefore, from a semantic perspective, there does not seem to be a clear-cut delineation between the single members of this particular semantic field, but rather a spectrum of fixed parameters with potential contextual overlaps, variations and interpretations.

Before looking at the parameters, it is important to separate the semantic core of fear, which exists independently from its contextual readings. Wierzbicka (1972:59-63) defines emotions as 'shorthand abbreviations for complex expressions, i.e., descriptions of some kind'. The semantic primitives for 'fear' could therefore be subsumed as: 'bad, do, happen, know' (Wierzbicka 1972: 59–63). In other words, the semantic field of 'fear' consists of a conglomeration of short forms expressing – in different degrees and depending on the context – the belief that something bad and unavoidable is very likely to occur in the near future. Interestingly, the degree or intensity of this 'bad event coming towards somebody' does not seem to be anchored in the core meaning. In contrast to this definition, the current paper will illustrate that it is the intensity of the experience which plays a role in the rise of new (grammatical and lexical) linguistic functions of these fear expressions.

In the following, the continuum of the prototypical linguistic realizations of 'fear,' will be analyzed without including specific fears, such as French *trac* 'stage fright' or diatopic, diastratic or diaphasic varieties. The nominal fear examples cited in this section also have (causative or non-causative) adjectival counterparts (for a detailed analysis see Masseron 2008). Semantic changes of the adjectival counterparts will be illustrated in Section 5.

The existence of adverbial counterparts with the suffix *-ment* (indicating the state of the subject while fulfilling an action, e. g., *peureusement* 'fearfully'), and the preposition 'with' (focusing on the experience the subject is exposed to in a given situation, e. g., *avec angoisse* [lit. 'with anguish']) will be analyzed in terms of the coexistence of synthetic and analytic constructions (Section 4) and their semantic divergences, e. g., *avec horreur* 'with horror' vs. *horriblement* 'horribly/tremendously' (Section 5).

The different parameters, such as degree in relevance, intensity, duration, appearance, control level and extension, will be illustrated with the help of dichotomies such as: strong vs. weak, permanent vs. non-permanent, sudden vs. (more or less) expected, loss of control vs. control, real vs. imaginary, and individual vs. non-individual, whereby: STRONG, PERMANENT, SUDDEN, CONTROL, REAL, and INDIVIDUAL serve as indications.

The definitions in this Section are derived from examples from Frantext (FT), Dubois, Dubois-Charlier (DDC), Trésor de la langue française (TLF) and related analyses of the semantic field of fear (Cislaru 2009, Fersenmeier 2010) and international classification schemata (Dilling, Mombour, Schmidt, & Schulte-Markwort 2004, Krohne 2010, Rupprecht & Moeller 2004).

As already mentioned, fear can be regarded as a characteristic of a person (trait anxiety) or a reaction to the loss of control in a specific situation (state anxiety).

Certain fear terms can be associated with negative and permanent traits or characteristics of a person and are therefore regarded as 'fear disorders.' Others refer more to a specific situation without necessarily influencing the mental health of a person on a permanent basis.

The most general widespread term in order to express the feeling of fear in French is *peur* [+ STRONG, +/- PERMANENT+, +/- SUDDEN, +/- REAL, +/- INDIVIDUAL].

In contrast to Spanish *miedo* or Portuguese *medo* (both outer Romance Languages), which are derived from Latin *metus* 'fear', French *peur* and its Italian counterpart *paura* (both central Romance Languages) are both derived from Latin *pavor* 'fright.' Another nominal representation, the Latin term *timor*, which originally signified the fear of God and is only preserved in Spanish to express a fear based on an experience (Spanish *sin temor de exagerar* 'without fear of exaggeration'), did not survive in French. Nevertheless, traces of this concept can be found in French *timide*. In French the feeling of preoccupation, worry or concerns is expressed through *crainte* 'worry' or *craindre* 'to worry' (see Section 4), which are derived from Latin *tremere* (> *cremere*) 'to shiver.' In the construction *de/par crainte/peur que/de* 'worrying/fearing that,' in particular, both nouns, *crainte* and *peur*, appear synonymous (Fersenmeier 2010).

While the term *peur* is generally used to describe the reaction of avoiding or anticipating a certain dangerous situation, the alternative term *anxiété* can be regarded as a response to a higher stress level due to an accumulation of repetitive and unprocessed fears (Hock, Kohlmann 2009, Ohman 2000). The use of the term *anxiété* underlines an inability to adequately react [- CONTROL, + INDIVIDUAL] to a particular situation (state anxiety) or indicates a permanent and/or repetitive inability [+/- PERMANENT, -/+ SUDDEN] faced with a specific situation or problem (trait anxiety). In the latter case, it can already be regarded as a disorder and linked to the physiological state of a person.

The word *panique* (derived from the god Pan, who took pleasure in suddenly appearing and frightening wanderers) focuses on the individual loss of control in a given situation [- CONTROL, + INDIVIDUAL] and subsumes a sudden, frantic and often groundless or at least not (always) life threatening fear [+ STRONG, + SUDDEN, -/+ REAL].

The major difference to *phobie* is the appearance and duration of the suffering. *Phobie* originally expressed the fear of an immediate danger (state anxiety), but over time started expressing a trait anxiety [- SUDDEN, + PERMANENT] and can therefore be regarded as a chronic version of *panique* [- PERMANENT]. Besides the prototypical phobias such as acrophobia, there also exist a great number of peripheral phobias, such as bibliophobia (fear of books), cynosiophobia (fear of knowledge), and caligynophobia (fear of beautiful women). In general, this lexeme is associated with a disproportional reaction to a potential or only imaginary danger [- REAL].

State anxieties, such as those described by the French word *terreur*, can be regarded as a 'short term abbreviation' for an intense, sudden and overpowering fear [+ STRONG, + SUDDEN, - CONTROL], which can be either individual or also underline that this negative feeling is forced upon a community [+/- INDIVIDUAL]. The latter reading, is often linked to historic events [+ REAL], such as in the *la régime de la terreur* 'the reign of terror'. It shares its key features [+ STRONG, + SUDDEN, - CONTROL] with *horreur*, but differs from the latter in respect to its peripheral features [-/+ REAL, + INDIVIDUAL]. *Horreur* can therefore be described as a sudden combination of real or imaginary fear or aversion.

The feelings aroused by the first realization of a potential danger can be expressed in French through *frayeur* and *effroi*. Both denote a sudden change of something and refer to a strong, sudden, momentary and individual experience [+ STRONG, + SUDDEN, - PERMANENT, + INDIVIDUAL].

The term *appréhension* is associated with a negative feeling of not being prepared enough for a specific future event, e. g., exam or speaking in public [+ REAL, + STRONG, - PERMANENT, - SUDDEN, + CONTROL, + INDIVIDUAL].

The term *angoisse* can, like *anxiété*, be regarded as a vague unpleasant emotional state and can be used to underline an inability to adequately react to a given situation [- CONTROL]. In contrast to *anxiété*, the focus of *angoisse*, is more on a specific event or situation [- PERMANENT, - SUDDEN], and most of the time is accompanied by a feeling of restraint. Etymologically, both can be traced back to Proto-Indo-European *angh-* 'painful, tight, restraint' (Cf. Watkins 1985, Drosdowski & Grebe 1963 or Kluge 1975). Nevertheless, the original meaning of 'tenseness, tightness,' a symptom accompanying the fear experience, appears to be more transparent in the latter.

Alongside this abundance of possibilities for expressing the sensation of fear, it is very salient that explicit fear terms are often avoided. Jacqueline de Romilly (Membre de l'Académie française) illustrates this phenomenon in her book *Dans le jardin des mots* (2007:244–247, highlighted by the author of this paper) with the help of an anecdote describing a train ride:

> 'J'étais dans un compartiment de chemin de fer avec un homme inconnu et nous avons été mêlés à une sorte d'aventure policière, un troisième voyageur s'étant caché dans notre compartiment. Il fut repris par la police. Et, au matin, j'avouais à mon compagnon de voyage que j'avais eu vraiment peur, À quoi il me répondit, l'air très satisfait, « non, non, je n'ai pas eu peur: simplement, je n'étais pas rassuré ! »'

This tendency to shrink from using fear expressions might be due to the fact that they are considered too 'strong' and therefore appear inappropriate in certain situations.

To sum up, all of the fear expressions analyzed in this section share the attribute that regardless of whether the sensation of fear is real (due to a perceivable cause) or imaginary, short or permanent, individual or not, and independent of the degree of control [+/- REAL, +/- PERMANENT, +/- SUDDEN, +/- CONTROL, +/- INDIVIDUAL], this sensation is always experienced as a powerful feeling [+ STRONG]. Therefore the intensity [+ STRONG], the only parameter, that all fear expressions display can be regarded as the common semantic core of all fear expressions. The intensity inherent in all fear expression and its influence on the rise of new analytic constructions and as intensifier markers will be analyzed in detail in Sections 4 and 5.

Finally, it is also interesting that many fear expressions focus on the parameters REAL and INDIVIDUAL. This might be due to the fact that, at least *in situ*, for the one experiencing fear, the fear (whether real or imaginary) always appears true and real and primarily a threat to oneself and one's own body. This also explains why a majority of fear expressions can be traced back to bodily reactions or movements accompanying the fear experience, e. g., *anxiété* or *angoisse* [<'painful, tight, restraint'], *crainte* [<'to shiver'], etc. This close connection between fear expressions and embodiment will be analyzed in the following two sections.

3 FEAR and embodiment

Fear is not only expressed in a semantic primary form (as illustrated in Section 2) but – from a linguistic perspective – metonymic and metaphoric processes are at work to create new ways of expressing fear in language.

Linguistic realizations of the concept of FEAR

Metaphor and metonymy have long been regarded by cognitive linguists (Lakoff 1987, 1993, Niemeier 1997, Schwarz-Friesel 2007, Sharifan, Dirven & Niemeier 2008, Steen et al. 2010) as the result of conceptual mappings and as a productive source for meaning extension. In metaphor mappings – which take place between different semantic fields – the source domain is used to illicit the target domain. Metonymy mappings, in contrast, are hierarchically structured within one single domain (Koevecses & Radden 1998).

Fear as a bodily experience starts in the brain. The amygdala, the hippocampus and the prefrontal cortex can be regarded as the key to and source of our fear experience (Ledoux 1996 or Roth 1997). From there it spreads to the whole body. The typical symptoms of fear include the widening of the eyes, the raising of the eyebrows, an either widely opened or shut and dry mouth, a feeling of breathlessness, a motionless body, a change in heartbeat, muscles shivering, etc.

All these symptoms also play a role in the linguistic realizations of fear. Their function is not only to describe the physical and emotional state of a person in a certain situation, but also to reduce the subjectivity of this emotion by attributing it linguistically to specific bodily reactions or inabilities. By doing so, different domains can be distinguished which allow a better identification of different degrees of fear.

Davitz (1969) produced a model consisting of twelve clusters (out of a corpus of 556 statements referring to 50 different emotions) and four dimensions of emotional meaning, namely activation, relatedness, hedonic tone, and competence.

Table 1: Davitz (1969) twelve clusters (slightly changed)

DIMENSIONS	CLUSTERS		
Activation	activation	hypoactivation	hyperactivation
Relatedness	moving towards	moving away	moving against
Hedonic tone	comfort	discomfort	tension
Competence	enhancement	dissatisfaction and inadequacy (~incompetence)	

The twelve clusters consist of activation, hypoactivation, hyperactivation, moving towards, away and against, comfort, discomfort, tension, enhancement, dissatisfaction and incompetence. Taking this model as a base, it is possible to distinguish at least three clusters (highlighted in bold in Table 1), namely 'hyperactivation', 'tension' and 'incompetence,' which are closely related to the experience of fear.

Hyperactivation subsumes symptoms such as an increase in heart rate or lapses in heartbeat (*avoir le cœur qui bat très fort/la chamade/à grands coups*), physical agitation, as in *il tremblait de peur*, or sweating (*Il avait des mains moites*), etc. A drop in temperature, as in *des sueurs froides*, and different incompetences, such as the inability to move (*Il était pétrifié*) or to speak (*la gorge serrée*), can be regrouped as signs of dissatisfaction or inadequacy.

Given the fact that fear is a very complex emotion and furthermore closely linked to neighboring emotions such as worry and concern (Gustafsson, Kronqvist, & McEachrane 2009, see Section 3), its symptoms and therefore also its linguistic realizations can spread to other clusters (highlighted in gray in Table 1), such as 'hypoactivation' (*avoir la bouche sèche*), 'moving away' (*la peur les poussait à fuir* [Frantext, Jonquet 1993:208, 26]) and 'discomfort' (*je n'étais pas rassuré*, as illustrated, for example, in the anecdote in Section 2).

What the examples have in common is that they indicate fear without directly referring to it: the physiological effects and behavioral reactions of fear stand for the experienced fear and increase with the increase of this fear.

In addition to the metonymic expressions there are also a large number of metaphorical expressions used to express the feeling of fear. While in the metonymic representation the term fear is usually avoided or can be suppressed (e. g., *Il était petrifié [de peur]*), in the metaphoric representation fear can even be personified, e. g., *la peur grandissait, la peur s'en va*, etc.

In contrast to Koevecses (1990) detailed distinctions (e. g., fear as a fluid in a container, an intrusion, an opponent, a vicious enemy, a tormentor, a natural force, a superior, etc.), his classification will be simplified and divided into two categories in this paper: 'internal fear' and 'external fear.'

The advantage of this contrastive classification is, firstly, that possible overlaps between semantically neighboring subcategories such as FEAR AS AN OPPONENT, VICIOUS ENEMY, TORMENTOR or SUPERIOR, which can all be traced back to the same source domain attribute [somebody wants to harm the subject], can be neglected here. Secondly, that a higher categorization level of the underlying source domains of the fear metaphors becomes distinguishable.

As members of the first group, 'internal fear' can be regarded all metaphors based on the perception that fear is already a part of the body before even being confronted with a dangerous situation, such as FEAR IS A FLUID IN A CONTAINER (e. g., *Il était rempli de peurs*).

The second group, 'external fears,' subsumes all metaphors grounded in the assumption that fear is originally not a part of the body, but something forced upon it from the outside, such as an INTRUSION, e. g., *la peur s'empare de lui*.

In the latter case, there is no distinction made as to whether the cause of the fear is personified (human, animal or ghost) or perceived as an illness or a natural force (*être submerge par la peur*).

Both categories, internal and external fear, share the attribute that 'fear' can appear in form of a fluid in both of them, e. g., *il était rempli de peurs* (CONTAINER) vs. *être submerge par la peur* (NATURAL FORCE).

Interestingly, given the fact that the semantic field of fear shares many of the cited metonymies and metaphors with other emotions such as 'love' (*le cœur qui bat la chamade*), the only metonymy which can be considered as exclusive for the domain of fear, the simultaneous appearance of hot and cold temperatures (*avoir des sueurs froides*), a very intense sensation, can also be traced back to a fluid taking over the whole body of the experiencer (Dobrovol'skij & Piirainen, 2005).

The fact that all fear metaphors fit either one of these two categories shows that fear is closely linked to the body. Fear is a bodily experience and this fact is also expressed linguistically with the help of the body as an anchorage point. Due to this close connection to the body, it comes as no surprise that the contrastive analysis represents little variation. The metaphoric and metonymic realizations of 'fear' seem to be very similar in French, Spanish, German and English: e. g., Spanish *estar dominado/atenazado por el miedo/pánico, quedarse petrificado/clavado de miedo, ser invadido por el miedo, ser vencido por el miedo*, German *von Angst beherrscht sein, vor Angst wie versteinert sein* (Bresson & Dobrovol'skij 1995, Dobrovol'skij & Piirainen 2005, Gyoeri 1998) with only slight differences or specification, such as in example 2c:

(2) (a) French
  Elle tremblait comme une feuille.
 (b) Spanish
  Temblaba como una hoja.
  'She was trembling like a leaf.'

(c) German
Sie zitterte wie Espenlaub.
'She was trembling like an aspen leaf [lit. aspen leaves]'

Interestingly, the color spectrum differs slightly from language to language. While in English a person experiencing fear can be pale, white as a sheet, gray with fear or caught in a blue funk, or even green about the gills (similar to French *pâlir* or *blêmir* 'to become pale', *être blanc/bleu de peur* 'to be white/blue from fear', *être/rester bleu* 'to be/stay blue', *devenir vert de peur/verdir de peur* 'to go green with fear'), in Spanish and Italian a scared person can also turn yellow (Spanish *ponerse amarillo*, Italian *diventare giallo* 'to go yellow'). The reaction of the skin is expressed in all analyzed languages through a comparison with poultry: 'goose' in English and German (English *goose bumps, goose pimples*, German *Gänsehaut* [lit. goose skin]), 'hen' in French *avoir la chair de poule* and Spanish *ponérsele carne de gallina* [lit. to have/get hen flesh].

To sum it up, the aim of this section was not to single out as many features as possible but to show that fear is – even linguistically – a bodily experience.

As has been illustrated, the bodily reactions (including the hypothalamus and the vegetative system) activated after the first realization of a potential danger (fear as a physical emergency state), such as accelerated heartbeat, changes in blood pressure, breathing, muscle tension, sweating, constipation, faint, rubescence, etc. have all left linguistic traces.

Fear in language is either presented as a physical reaction or as a threat to the body. The metonymic processes describe the symptoms of experience of fear (direct or internal process). In other words: fear and body are one.

The metaphoric examples represent fear as something that is already a part of the body (internal fear) or added to the body (external fear): fear and body are connected.

Both strategies, metaphor and metonymy, are used to render an entity of the so-called 'invisible world,' namely 'fear,' which attacks the whole body without always being visible or detectable for an outsider or potential recipient, although more visible for the latter. A similar strategy, which has even led to lexical and grammatical changes, will be analyzed in the following section.

4 Fear and the discourse world

The concept of 'fear' can be expressed with the help of nouns (Section 2), metaphors and metonymies (Section 3). This section will focus on the verbal realization of fear. In dealing with the semantic field of fear, it is very salient that the verbal counterparts seem either restricted or are absent. For example, the French terms *peur* 'fear', *anxiété* 'anxiety' and *horreur* 'horror' do not display verbal counterparts (e. g., in the case of French *peur* or *horreur* there only exist causative counterparts: *apeurer* or *horrifier*).

The gap in French is filled with verbs derived from different stems such as *redouter* or *craindre*. The semantic range of *redouter* and *craindre* varies, depending on the context, between 'to worry' and 'to fear.' In certain contexts, the meaning of these two verbs can even be interpreted as 'to expect,' as in examples (3a) and (3b). In combination with a negation *craindre* can also mean 'to like,' as in example (3c).

(3) (a) French (Manchette 1973:224 [FT])
     Il a pris les choses beaucoup mieux que je ne craignais.
  (b) French (Jonquet 1993:387 [FT])
     Dès que j'ai appris que Kafin avait vécu ici, j'ai redouté le pire!
  (c) French (DDC)
     On ne craintpas un peu de cognac?

As the quote from Stendhal 'Je tremble toujours de n'avoir écrit qu'un soupir, quand je crois avoir noté une vérité' and the etymology of French *craindre* (<Latin *tremere* 'to shiver') illustrate, fear can be expressed, as already shown in Section 3, as a bodily experience:

(4) French (Jonquet 1993:81 [FT])
  (a) L'humidité le fit frissonner. (...)
  (b) L'homme resta encore quelques minutes posté derrière sa fenêtre (...) puis disparut. Nadia frissonna (...).

While in example (4a) the shivering is not caused by fear, in example (4b) fear is not only the source of the shivering but the experience of fear is also the intended interpretation of the verb. A similar interpretation of 'fear as the target' is intended in *Tremblez riches votre Paris est encerclé on le brûlera* (Manchette 1972:164 [FT]).

The semantic field of fear can also be combined with a number of verbs marking the aktionsart or in other words focusing on a specific phase of the experience of fear, such as the French *prendre peur* [lit. 'take fear'] (inchoative), *perdre peur* 'lose fear' (terminative) or *faire peur, inspirer de la peur* [lit. 'make/inspire fear'] (causative). Interestingly sentences such as *je ressens de la peur* 'I am feeling fear' are not used in order to express fear at the actual moment of experiencing it (Cislaru 2009).

The immediate experience of fear is not communicated synthetically but with the help of an analytic construction of a noun or adjective and a copula or empty verb (Stroebel 2010, 2011). The fear experience is expressed as 'possessing' a psychological state, e.g., *Marie a peur* [lit. 'Mary has fear'] 'Mary is scared' or as being in a psychological state as in French *Marie est angoissée, anxieuse, effrayée* 'Mary is afraid, scared.'

In English too, to fear seems to be restricted to expressing the fact that somebody is experiencing fear at the moment of speech and an analytic construction such as 'to be afraid' or 'to be scared' is preferred. One of the reasons for this might be that 'to fear' is transitive and therefore needs an object. In many fear situations, the source of the fear is not always clear; most of the time it is just a vague feeling. With an analytic construction, the reason for the experience of fear can be left open and does not have to be named. Another reason – if we compare this with other utterances lacking syntactic verbal counterparts such as 'I am hungry' – is that by using the copula or an empty verb construction the utterance not only appears more closely linked to the speaker but also the relevance of the utterance for the discourse world is explicitly underlined (Stroebel 2010).

In other words, an utterance with 'to be afraid' is not only more closely linked to the speaker, but also refers to a more immediate or tangible situation. 'To fear,' in contrast to 'I am afraid,' implies a lack of knowledge and underlines the uncertainty of a future event (e.g., *fear the worst* vs. **to be afraid of the worst*, Wierzbicka 1999:74). The meaning of to be afraid can also be disconnected from fear and simply be used as an intensifier, e.g., *I am afraid, I cannot help you* (I really cannot help you, see Section 5), while to be scared is still clearly associated with the sensation of fear.

Linguistic realizations of the concept of FEAR

The semantic field of fear shares the fact that stative constructions are used in order to express a physical sensation relevant to the actual speech act (e. g., 'have + abstract noun') with many other sensations connected to the discourse world (e. g., French *J'ai faim, soif, mal à la tête* [lit. 'I have hunger, thirst, (a) headache']). While the use of *avoir* is possible with a great number of nominal representations of fear, e. g., *avoir peur, crainte, effroi, frayeur, terreur, angoisse, appréhension, couardise, frousse, trouille, panique, trac*, etc., the use is restricted with other emotions such as **avoir (de la) jalousie, *avoir (du) colère*, etc. This might be due to the fact, that in these cases the focus is more on the fact that the speaker is in a state of jealousy or anger (*je suis jaloux, je suis en colère*), than on the relevance to the discourse world. The combination with *avoir* can therefore be regarded as an attempt to render an 'entity of the invisible world' such as 'fear' less abstract by presenting it as an object in the possession of the speaker at the moment of speech.

The relation between fear and the body of the speaker is strengthened and the importance of the utterance for the actual situation is underlined.

While the French copula construction *Il est peureux* marks the trait of a person, the combination with *avoir* in *Il a peur* (lit. 'He has fear') underlines the relevance to the 'here and now' of the speech act. In these constructions, or in other words in combination with an abstract noun, *avoir* has lost its (original) durative or trait character (e. g., *elle a des yeux bleus, une maison*, etc.). As a consequence, in order to express that *avoir* in these examples is not related to a specific moment or situation, another linguistic element, such as 'always' has to be added, e. g., *Il a toujours peur* [lit. 'He has always fear']. Or vice versa, a specification, such as 'in this (particular) situation' has to be added to the copula construction in order to get rid of the durative interpretation, e. g., *Il était trop peureux dans cette situation* 'He was too afraid in this situation.'

In other words, the analytic or empty verb construction expresses that an individual experiences fear in the discourse world. This close connection to the present can fade with a rise in frequency of this construction. Further semantic developments will be analyzed in the following section.

5 Fear as source

In Sections 2 to 4 the semantic field of 'fear' has been analyzed with a focus on the nominal, metaphoric, metonymic and predicative representations of fear. In all these cases, the aim of the linguistic encoding was to express the experience of 'fear.' 'Fear' can be seen as the target – even outside of a linguistic perspective.

This last section will focus on the opposite case: 'fear as the source.' More specifically: the source for intensity markers.

With time, the close connection between the physical reactions that result from being confronted with a potential danger can fade, but also the connection with the trigger, or, in other words, the relevance to the dangerous situation itself. As a consequence, fear expressions can also surface in utterances, such as French *J'ai peur qu'il ne revienne très tard* (Vian 1948:29, FT). In these examples, expressions originating in the semantic field of fear are used in order to underline an assumption or even a conviction.

In French, it is quite common to see members of the semantic field turn into intensity markers of subjective statements, e. g., *ça craint!* [lit. 'it fears'] 'It sucks!' or *formidable* (< Latin *formidare* 'to fear') 'great,' similar to awesome (< Old English *ege* 'fear' [EO]).

In noun-adjective combinations, e. g., *une peur panique, une peur terrible*, it becomes clear that the adjective in the semantic field of fear is being used in order to intensify the noun from the same semantic field. The association to 'fear' can also be preserved in combination with a noun out of a different semantic field, e.g., *une expérience horrible, une chaleur horrible, un effrayant genie* (similar Iñesta & Pamies 2002). In other words, even the negative meaning vanishes and the adjectives and adverbs from the semantic field of fear are used as simple intensifiers, such as *c'est horriblement cher, il faisait horriblement chaud, sa lettre m'a fait terriblement plaisir*, etc.

In all these examples, fear expressions are used as intensifiers. In other words, members of the semantic field of fear are used as a source in order to express 'intensity' [target]. In this particular use, fear expressions are – via semantic bleaching – deprived of their original negative connotations and even function as 'positive' markers.

6 Conclusion

The analysis of the semantic field of fear has shown, that 'fear' – an entity of the 'invisible world' – is particularly suitable for analyzing the interaction between semantic and conceptual properties or, in other words, between the source and the target domain (Lakoff 1987, 1993).

It has been illustrated that the imagery and the meaning are closely connected. Embodiment plays a predominant role in the synthetic (e. g., nominal, adjectival and verbal realizations) and analytic (e. g., metonymic, metaphoric expressions and complex predicates) representations of this particular field. Embodiment can be regarded as a universal source domain for fear with two different ways of perception. First, fear as a part of the body independent of whether somebody is exposed to a dangerous situation or not, or secondly, as something external forced upon the body. Furthermore, the range of the linguistic encoding of fear combines two broad categories of experience, namely sensory and subjective. While the first type is related to image schemas (as presented in Sections 3 and 4), the second operates along fixed parameters (Section 2). Finally, it has been shown that 'intensity' plays an important factor not only in the experience of fear, but also in its linguistic encoding. As a consequence, negative marked expressions can not only function as a productive source for intensifiers (or quantifiers), but can also allow a positive reading in certain contexts.

References

Bandelow, B. (ed.) 2003. *Angst und Panik, Ätiologie–Diagnostik–Therapie*. Bremen: Uni-Med.

Bandelow, B. 2004. *Das Angstbuch*. 3. Aufl. Reinbek: Rowohlt.

Bergenholtz, H. 1980. *Das Wortfeld „Angst". Eine lexikographische Untersuchung mit Vorschlägen für ein großes interdisziplinäres Wörterbuch der deutschen Sprache*. Stuttgart: Klett-Cotta.

Boerner, R.J. 2003. Panikattacken und Panikstörung. Checkliste für die Diagnose. In MMW. *Fortschritte der Medizin*, 2003, vol. 145, NS2, 9–12. München: Urban & Vogel.

Bresson, D. & Dobrovol'skij, D. 1995. Petite syntaxe de la "peur". Application au français et à l'allemand. *Langue française* 105. 107–119.

Cislaru, G. 2009. Expression de la peur et interprétations sémantiques en contexte. In *Mémoires de la Société Néophilologique*, 45–57. Helsinki: Modern Language Society.

Davitz, J.R. 1969. *The Language of Emotion.* New York: Academic Press.

Dilling, H., Mombour, W., Schmidt, M.H. & Schulte-Markwort, E. (eds.) 2004. *Internationale Klassifikation psychischer Störungen* (ICD 10 Kapitel V). Bern: Huber.

Dobrovol'skij, D. & Piirainen, E. 2005. *Figurative Language: Cross-cultural and Cross-linguistic Perspectives.* Amsterdam: Elsevier.

Faust, V. (ed.) 1986. *Angst, Furcht, Panik.* Stuttgart: Hippokrates-Verlag.

Fersenmeier, Ludwig 2010. Synonyme: Zur Semantik der Absenz. In Grutschus, A. & Krilles, P. (eds.), *Figuren der Absenz – Figures de l'absence*, 225–237. Berlin: Frank und Timme GmbH.

Fries, N. 2000. *Sprache und Emotionen.* Bergisch-Gladbach: BLT.

Gustafsson, Y., Kronqvist, C. & M. McEachrane (eds.) (2009). *Emotions and Understanding: Wittgensteinian Perspectives.* Palgrave Macmillan.

Gyoeri, G. 1998. Cultural variation in the conceptualisation of emotions. In A. Athanasiaduo & E. Tabakowska (eds.), *Speaking of Emotions: Conceptualisation and Expression*, 99–124. Berlin/New York: Mouton de Gruyter.

Hock, M. & Kohlmann, C.-W. 2009. Angst und Furcht. In V. Brandstätter & J. H. Otto (eds.), *Handbuch der Allgemeinen Psychologie: Motivation und Emotion*, 623–632. Göttingen: Hogrefe.

Iñesta, E.M. & Pamies, A. 2002. *Fraseología y metáfora: aspectos tipológicos y cognitivos.* Granada: Granada Lingvistica / Método.

Koevecses, Z. 1986. *Metaphors of anger, pride and love: A lexical approach to the structure of concepts.* Amsterdam: J. Benjamins.

Koevecses, Z. 1990. *Emotion Concepts.* New York: Springer.

Koevecses, Z. 1998. Are there any emotion-specific metaphors? In A. Athanasiaduo & E. Tabakowska (eds.), *Speaking of Emotions: Conceptualisation and Expression*, 127–151. Berlin/New York: Mouton de Gruyter.

Koevecses, Z. & Radden, G. 1998. Metonymy: developing a cognitive linguistic view. In *Cognitive Linguistics*, 9 (1). 37–77.

Krohne, H. W. 2010. *Psychologie der Angst. Ein Lehrbuch.* Stuttgart: Kohlhammer.

Lakoff, G. 1987. *Woman, Fire, and Dangerous Things.* Chicago: Chicago University Press.

References

Lakoff, G. 1993. The contemporary theory of metaphor. In Andrew Ortony (ed.), *Metaphor and Thought*, 202–251. Second edition. Cambridge: Cambridge University Press.

Ledoux, J. 1996. *The Emotional Brain. The Mysterious Underpinnings of Emotional Life*. New York: Simon & Schuster.

Masseron, C. 2008. Pour une topic de la peur : aspects psychologiques, sémiotiques, linguistiques. In Grossmann, F. & Plane, S. (eds.), *Les apprentissages lexicaux, Lexique et production verbale*, 161–190. Villeneuve d'Ascq : Presses Universitaires du Septentrion.

Niemeier, S. 1997. *The language of emotions: conceptualization, expression, and theoretical foundation*. Amsterdam: Benjamins.

Ohman, A. 2000. Fear and Anxiety: Evolutionary, cognitive, and clinical perspectives. In M. Lewis & J.M. Haviland-Jones (eds.). *Handbook of emotions*, 573–593. New York: The Guilford Press.

Romilly de, J. 2007. *Dans le jardin des mots*. Paris: Éditions de Fallois.

Roth, G. 1997. *Das Gehirn und seine Wirklichkeit. Kognitive Neurobiologie und ihre philosophischen Konsequenzen*. Frankfurt: Suhrkamp Verlag.

Rupprecht, R. & Moeller, H.J. 2004. Hohes Risiko für Suizid und Substanzmissbrauch: Erkennen Sie Angstpatienten auf den ersten Blick? Diagnosis and treatment of panic disorder. In *MMW. Fortschritte der Medizin*, 2004, vol. 146, 42, 45–48. Munich: Urban & Vogel.

Schwarz-Friesel, M. 2007. *Sprache und Emotion*. Tübingen: A. Francke.

Sharifan, F., Yu, N., Dirven, R., & Niemeier, R. 2008. *Culture, Body, and Language: Conceptualizations of Internal Body Organs across Cultures and Languages*. Berlin: Mouton de Gruyter.

Shah, E. 1993. *The Lucy ghosts*. London: Corgi Books.

Steen, G. J., Dorst, A. G., Herrmann, J. B., Kaal, A, Krennmayr, T, & Pasma, T. 2010. *A method for linguistic metaphor identification: From MIP to MIPVU*. Amsterdam/Philadelphia: John Benjamins.

Stroebel, L. 2010. *Die Entstehung einer neuen Kategorie - Leerverben als paralleler Kopulastrang*. Frankfurt/Main: Peter Lang.

Stroebel, L. 2011. Invisible, Visible, Grammaticalization. In Callies, M. Lohoefer, A. Keller, W. (eds.), *Bi-Directionality in the Cognitive Sciences: Avenues, challenges, and limitations*. 2011. viii, 211–234. Amsterdam/New York: John Benjamins.

Wierzbicka, A. 1972. *Semantic Primitives*. Frankfurt/Main: Athenäum (*Linguistische Forschungen* 22).
Wierzbicka, A. 1991. *Cross-Cultural Pragmatics. The Semantics of Human Interaction*. Berlin: Mouton de Gruyter.
Wierzbicka, A. 1996. *Semantics: Primes and Universals*. Oxford: Oxford University Press.
Wierzbicka, A. 1999. *Emotions across Languages and Cultures*. New York: Cambridge University Press.

Databases

DDC: Dubois/Dubois-Charlier (http://rali.iro.umontreal.ca/Dubois/)
EO: http://www.etymonline.com
FT: Frantext (www.frantext.fr/)
Ernaux, A. (2007). L'événement. Paris: Gallimard.
Izzo, J.-C., (1996/2002). Chourmo. Paris: Gallimard.
Jonquet, T. (1993/2001). Les Orpailleurs. Paris: Gallimard.
Manchette, J.-P. (1973). Morgue pleine. Paris: Gallimard.
Manchette, J.-P. (1972/1999). Nada. Paris: Gallimard.
Perec, G. (2003). Entretiens et conférences II [1979–1981]. Paris: Joseph K.
Vian, B. (1948/1999). Le Grand sommeil [trad.]. Paris: Gallimard.
TLF: Trésor de la langue française (http://atilf.atilf.fr/tlf.htm)

Author

Liane Ströbel
Heinrich-Heine-University Düsseldorf
stroebel@phil.hhu.de

Metonymic Euphemisms from a Cognitive Linguistic Point of View

Alexander Tokar

Abstract
This article presents a classification of metonymy-based euphemism-formation mechanisms from a cognitive linguistic point of view. It is argued that all metonymic euphemisms can be analyzed as products of three major euphemism-formation strategies: 1) violation of the principle IMPORTANT OVER LESS IMPORTANT; 2) violation of the principle SPECIFIC OVER GENERIC; and 3) violation of the principle MORE TRUE OVER LESS TRUE.

1 Introduction

It is a well-known fact that taboo-marked concepts are often expressed by metonymic euphemisms, i.e., expressions like *to sleep with somebody* and *boyfriend*, whose euphemistic senses "to copulate with somebody" / "a regular male sexual partner of almost any age over puberty in a non-marital sexual relationship" are contiguously related to their literal senses "to be in the state of sleep" / "a friend who is a boy." Thus, a person with whom a woman has a regular non-marital sexual relationship is often perceived as her friend in the literal meaning of this word, i.e., as any person whom she "know[s] well and regard[s] with affection and trust" (WordNet). Additionally, copulation is often followed by physical sleeping, i.e., lovers have sex and then fall asleep together in the same bed.

However, despite the recognition of the role of metonymy as an important euphemism-formation mechanism (e. g., Blank, 1999), there have been almost no studies on the typology of metonymic euphemisms, i.e., studies dealing with the question of whether metonymy-based euphemisms prefer a particular semantic pattern (e. g., part-for-whole metonymy) and, if so, why this is the case. Drawing upon the seminal work on metonymy by Kövecses & Radden (1998), this article attempts to fill in the research gap by classifying metonymic euphemisms into the following three categories: 1) metonymic euphemisms whose vehicle concepts violate the principle IMPORTANT OVER LESS IMPORTANT; 2) metonymic euphemisms whose vehicle concepts violate the principle SPECIFIC OVER GENERIC; and 3) metonymic euphemisms whose vehicle concepts violate the principle MORE TRUE OVER LESS TRUE.

The article utilizes the following structure. The next section discusses the defining characteristics of euphemistic expressions. That is, for example, how do we know that the aforementioned *to sleep with somebody* and *boyfriend* are indeed euphemisms? The following section provides a general classification of euphemism-formation mechanisms into semantic and non-semantic types: Among other things, it will be argued that all semantically motivated euphemisms can be analyzed as products of either metonymic or metaphoric semantic change. The final sections present a critical discussion of the distinction between default and non-default metonymies proposed by Kövecses & Radden (1998) and elaborate on the classification of metonymic euphemisms into the three categories named above.

2 Euphemism and related phenomena

A euphemism can be defined as an indirect means of expressing a taboo-marked (i.e., a distasteful, unpleasant) concept.[1] For example, the euphemistic phrase *to sleep with somebody* expresses the taboo-marked meaning "to copulate with somebody" without explicitly referring to the taboo subject SEX: *To sleep with somebody* literally means "to spend time together while being in the state of sleep," not "to have sex." Similarly, the compound *boyfriend* expresses the taboo-marked meaning "a regular male sexual partner in a non-marital sexual relationship"

---

[1] In this respect, a euphemism may not differ from a dysphemism. For example, just like the euphemism *to sleep with somebody*, the dysphemism *to bang somebody* can also be seen as an indirect means of expressing the taboo-marked meaning "to have sex with somebody": *To bang* does not literally mean "to copulate" but "to strike sharply" (Merriam-Webster Online). The difference between the two expressions is that the euphemism *to sleep with somebody* is a much more polite means of expressing the meaning "to have sex" than the dysphemism *to bang somebody*. According to Merriam-Webster Online, the latter is a vulgar expression.

without explicitly referring to the fact that a boyfriend is a sexual partner: If we consider only the literal meanings of the components *boy* and *friend*, we arrive at the taboo-free meaning "a friend who is a boy," not "a sexual partner."

According to Holder (2008:vii), "In speech or writing we use euphemism for dealing with taboo or sensitive subjects. It is therefore the language of evasion, hypocrisy, prudery, and deceit." A more recent study (Moskvin, 2010:75–99), however, insists on the separation of euphemism from related phenomena, such as, for example, lie. To illustrate this point, let us consider the following utterance: *Daddy's in Heaven* to explain that "Daddy is dead." Like sexuality, death is (in many cultures) a taboo-marked topic, which has given rise to numerous euphemistic expressions. Already in 1936, Louise Pound published an article entitled "American Euphemisms for Dying, Death, and Burial: An Anthology" (1936), in which she mentioned such death-related phrases and utterances as *he has left us, gone from us, sunk into his last sleep, called to the eternal sleep, laid to rest, rests in peace till we meet again, gone to his Heavenly Father, gone to meet his Savior, answered the final call, played his last card*, etc.

What is particularly interesting about these expressions is that most of them can be used as both euphemisms and non-euphemisms. With regard to the latter, consider the following situation: The speaker of *Daddy's in Heaven* is a religious person who firmly believes in the afterlife. Evidently, the utterance *Daddy's in Heaven* is, for that speaker, in no respect different from an utterance like *Daddy's in Berlin now* (uttered when the speaker knows that Daddy is indeed in Berlin now) and, accordingly, cannot be regarded as a euphemism (Moskvin, 2010:105). Consider the opposite situation: The speaker of *Daddy's in Heaven* does not believe in life after death. S/he knows that, in reality, Daddy is not in heaven, but is dead and buried in the ground. However, in order not to shock the dead Daddy's small child who wants to know where his/her father now is, the speaker does not tell the truth, *Daddy's dead*, but instead says *Daddy's in Heaven*. In this case, the utterance in question is also not a euphemism but a lie, just like the utterance *Daddy's in Berlin now* uttered when the speaker knows that Daddy is now not in Berlin but instead in, e. g., Kabul.

According to Moskvin (2010:93–94), euphemism is different from lie in that in the former case, the speaker does not intend to deceive or mislead the hearer. That is, for example, when a speaker of English utters a euphemistic utterance like *John sleeps with Sarah* and *John is Sarah's boyfriend*, s/he does not want to disguise the facts that John and Sarah do not merely sleep together in the same bed and that John is more than just a friend who is a boy. Instead, the speaker wants to communicate the taboo-marked meanings "John copulates with Sarah" and "John is Sarah's regular sexual partner to whom she is not officially married" without explicitly referring to the taboo subject SEX. Hence, a death-related utterance like *Daddy's in Heaven* can be regarded as a euphemism only in one case: When the speaker wants to indirectly communicate the taboo-marked meaning "Daddy is dead," but not when the speaker wants to conceal the fact of Daddy's death from the hearer. While the former is a euphemism, the latter is a lie. (We will return to this distinction in the final section of this article.)

3 Euphemism-formation mechanisms: a general classification

Having specified the definition of euphemism, we can now proceed to euphemism-formation mechanisms, i. e., the question of how euphemistic expressions like *to sleep with somebody, boyfriend, to be in Heaven, gone from us*, etc. come into existence. This issue has been extensively dealt with in a number of studies. For example, Moskvin (2010:163–227, 2001:64–67) discusses how euphemisms are formed in present-day Russian. Reutner (2009:119–154) addresses the same question with respect to French and Italian. Farghal (1995) deals with euphemism-formation mechanisms in Arabic. Adams (1981) is concerned with the formation of sexual euphemisms in Latin. As far as the English language is concerned, this question has been dwelled upon by Warren (1992) and, more recently, by Linfoot-Ham (2005), Crespo Fernández (2008, 2007, 2006a, 2006b), and Halmari (2011). (The latter article is concerned with one particular instance of euphemization: a recent replacement of premodified nouns like *disabled people* by postmodified nouns like *people with disabilities*.)

Traditionally, euphemism-formation mechanisms have been classified into semantic and non-semantic types (e. g., Warren, 1992:134). An instance of the latter is the famous infixed form with an expletive meaning *absoschmuckinglutely* (which, according to Adams (1999), can be better described as a euphemistic dysphemism). The euphemistic effect is achieved here by means of a consonant change in the original expletive infix *–fucking–*: [f] is replaced by the cluster [ʃm], as a result of which *absoschmuckinglutely* can express the same expletive meaning as *absofuckinglutely*, without, however, evoking the negative connotations inherent in *-fucking-*. Also, instead of changing [f] to [ʃm], *fuck* can be abbreviated to *f-* e. g., *I'm sorry I said the f-word* (Davies, 2008-).

Apart from consonant interchange, abbreviation, and other phonetic modifications, non-semantic strategies are sometimes said to include borrowing (e. g., Moskvin, 2001:67). However, as will be shown below, a loanword often functions as a euphemism not only because it is a loanword, but also because its source language literal meaning is not identical with the taboo-marked meaning that it expresses in the language of a borrowing community. For instance, a doctoral thesis defended at a German university can be graded with the Latin expression *cum laude*, which literally means "with praise" (Brockhaus, 2005-2006). However, despite its literal meaning in Latin, *cum laude* is a rather poor dissertation grade in Germany. Thus, a person whose doctoral degree was awarded *cum laude* is not eligible for most post-doctoral stipends or fellowships, and his thesis will most likely not be accepted for publication by a serious academic press (see, e. g., "Forschungsstipendien für promovierte Nachwuchswissenschaftler (Postdoc-Programm)," n. d.). Accordingly, the euphemistic use of *cum laude* is possible not only because of the non-German origin of the phrase under consideration (i. e., the fact that the majority of German speakers do not know what *cum laude* means in Latin), but also because of its literal meaning in Latin ("with praise"), which is a converse of what it actually stands for in German ("poor dissertation"). (The latter fact allows the grader to maximize praise[2] of his doctoral student who presented a poorly written dissertation.) A somewhat similar example is the French borrowing *à outrance* (literally "to the utmost"), which, in English, is sometimes used as a euphemism for extramarital copulation – e. g., *I think if anyone read carefully they would say it was an affair à outrance* (Holder, 2008:75). Again, as in the case of *cum laude* in German, it can be argued that *à outrance* functions as a euphemism in English not only because it was borrowed from French but also because its French literal meaning of "to the utmost" is not identical with the euphemistic sense "extramarital copulation." (As a matter of fact, *à outrance* can be used in English not only as a euphemism for "extramarital copulation" but also as a non-euphemistic adverb meaning "to the limit" (Merriam-Webster Online), i. e., what *à outrance* means in French.)

---

[2] In the sense of the maxim of praise of the Leechian politeness principle (see, e. g., Cruse, 2004:37).

As for purely semantic means, euphemistic expressions can be classified into instances of metonymic and metaphoric semantic change. Following Lakoff and Turner (1989:103), the difference between metonymy and metaphor can be described as within-domain mapping (metonymy) versus cross-domain mapping (metaphor). A conceptual domain is "a more generalized 'background' knowledge configuration against which conceptualization is achieved" (Taylor, 2002:195). For example, in order to understand the meaning of *cum laude* in German, we need the concept of dissertation grades in German universities, of which the concept of cum laude is a part. Accordingly, we can claim that the former is the domain against which the latter is conceptualized in German.

Like other metonymic expressions, metonymic euphemisms can be classified into whole-for-part, part-for-whole, and part-for-part metonymies. A part-for-part metonymy is a metonymy like *cum laude*, whose vehicle concept (i. e., its literal meaning) stands for another element within the same conceptual domain. Thus, both the literal meaning "with praise" and the euphemistic sense "poor quality" can be regarded as evaluative characteristics of a doctoral dissertation: i.e., a grader can come to the conclusion that a Ph.D. thesis either deserves praise or is of poor quality. However, when the latter is the case, the thesis is graded *cum laude*, even though the grader knows that the thesis is of poor quality and thus does not deserve to be praised. (When the grader comes to the conclusion that the thesis is of good quality and hence deserves praise, s/he grades it with either *magna cum laude* or *summa cum laude*, but never with *cum laude*.) Accordingly, the euphemistic use of *cum laude* as a dissertation grade in Germany is an instance of part-for-part metonymy: one element of the domain EVALUATIVE CHARACTERISTICS OF A DOCTORAL THESIS ("with praise") stands for another element of the same domain ("poor quality").

A part-for-whole metonymy is a metonymy like *boyfriend*, whose vehicle concept stands for an entire conceptual domain of which it is a part: As stated in the beginning of the article, boyfriends are often perceived by their girlfriends as friends in the literal meaning of this word (i. e., as any persons whom they know well and regard with affection and trust). Accordingly, the literal concept of friendship can be said to constitute part of the concept of boyfriend-ship, i. e., a boyfriend is not only a sexual partner in a non-marital sexual relationship but also a friend.

Finally, a whole-for-part metonymy is a metonymy like *adult* for "erotic / pornographic" – e. g., in the phrase *an adult Web site* – whose euphemistic sense "erotic / pornographic" is an instance (or a part) of the vehicle concept "adult." The adjective *adult* literally means "fully developed and mature" (Merriam-Webster Online). Accordingly, the phrase *an adult Web site* could have meant "any Web site suitable for fully developed and mature people." However, an adult Web site is a particular instance of a Web site appropriate for adults: a Web site that contains pornographic material.

Metaphoric euphemisms fall into those that realize conceptual metaphors and those that are based on one-shot or image metaphors. Conceptual metaphors are characterized by systematic correspondences between their source and target domains (e. g., Lakoff & Johnson, 1980:52–55). This means that more than one expression pertaining to one and the same source domain can be used in connection with one and the same target domain. For example, the collocation *to come to an orgasm* (as well as its elliptic version *to come*) realizes the conceptual metaphor PURPOSES ARE DESTINATIONS (cf. Crespo Fernández, 2008:101): Apart from *an orgasm*, we also *come to a conclusion, a solution, a decision, a verdict, a result*, etc. Also, in addition to *coming*, an orgasm can be *reached* (e. g., "Are you having trouble reaching orgasm? A guide for women," 2011, May 22) and *arrived at* (e. g., *A very distinctive feature with the female orgasm is that women find it quite hard to arrive at an orgasm from intercourse alone*, "How to Make Your Woman Reach an Orgasm Fast!", 2012, February 29). By contrast, one-shot metaphors involve less systematic correspondences between their source and target domains and are, therefore, perceived as more metaphoric and figurative than conceptual metaphors (Tokar, 2009:8–10). For example, *to ride* meaning "to copulate with a man in the woman-on-top position" seems to have a much higher degree of metaphoricity than *to come* meaning "to achieve an orgasm." This is because apart from the visual similarity between a person sitting on a horse / bicycle while riding it and a woman sitting on her sexual partner while copulating with him, no other element of the source domain RIDING A HORSE / BICYCLE takes part in the mapping onto the target domain COPULATING IN THE WOMAN-ON-TOP POSITION. Thus, a male sexual partner whom a woman *rides* is neither a *horse* nor a *bicycle*. We are justified in claiming this because neither *to ride a horse* nor *to ride a bicycle* occurs in the sense "to copulate with a man while being on top."

Since metonymic mappings involve no more than one conceptual domain while metaphoric mappings are cross-domain mappings, metonymic euphemisms can usually be relatively easily distinguished from metaphoric euphemisms: In the former case, we feel that there is a more or less real link between what the expression under analysis literally means and what it denotes as a euphemism. For example, there is a real link between the meanings "with praise" and "poor quality": Both are evaluative characteristics that can be given to a doctoral thesis. Similarly, there is a real link between the meanings "a friend" and "a sexual partner": Sexual partners are often perceived as friends. Finally, there is a real link between the meanings "adult" and "pornographic": Pornography is believed to be harmful to children and is, therefore, appropriate for adults only. By contrast, in the case of a metaphoric euphemism, no such link can be established. Thus, there is no real link between the meanings "to come" and "to achieve an orgasm": Because copulation typically does not involve motion (i.e., lovers do not move from one place to another while having sex), reaching an orgasm cannot be an instance of coming. Similarly, there is no real link between the meanings "to ride" and "to copulate with a man while being on top of him": Since a male lover whom a woman copulates with while being on top is neither a horse nor a bicycle, sexual riding cannot be an instance of physical riding.

In addition to metonymic and metaphoric euphemisms, Warren (1992:131–132) classifies semantically motivated euphemisms into instances of the following mechanisms:

- particularization; e.g., *satisfaction* for "orgasm." This euphemistic meaning of "orgasm" represents a subcategory of the literal meaning "satisfaction": an orgasm is a kind of satisfaction.
- implication; e.g., *to go to the toilet* for "to urinate and / or defecate." There is an antecedent–consequent relationship between the literal meaning of "to go to the toilet" and the euphemistic meaning of "to urinate / defecate": First of all, we physically move to the place TOILET, and only then do we urinate and / or defecate in it.
- reversal or irony; e.g., *enviable disease* for "syphilis." The euphemistic use of this expression creates an ironic effect, since syphilis is, of course, not an enviable disease.

- understatement or litotes; e. g., *drug habit* for "drug addiction." The undesirable feature DRUG ADDICTION is downgraded to DRUG HABIT, which can be any habit concerning drugs.
- overstatement or hyperbole; e. g., *sanitary engineer* for "garbage collector." The non-prestigious occupation of a garbage collector is upgraded to that of an engineer.

This article argues against this classification. The major problem with Warren's approach is the fact that it distinguishes between particularization, implication, and metonymy-based euphemisms. Let us begin with the category of particularization. As stated above, particularization euphemisms are expressions like *satisfaction* for "orgasm," whose euphemistic senses represent a subcategory of what they literally mean. To be more precise, there exists a hyponym–hypernym relationship between the former and the latter. For example, the meaning "orgasm" is a hyponym of the meaning "satisfaction," since, as already mentioned, an orgasm is a kind of satisfaction. Similarly, the euphemistic meaning of *the pill*, as in, for example, *she is on the pill*, which stands for "she uses contraceptive pills," is a hyponym of the literal meaning of "pill": A contraceptive pill is a kind of pill. In summary, in particularization euphemisms, such as *satisfaction* and *the pill*, the euphemistic effect results from the replacement of a taboo-marked hyponym (*orgasm, contraceptive pill*) by a taboo-free hypernym (*satisfaction, the pill*), the latter having a very broad meaning that subsumes a number of taboo-free hyponyms – e. g., apart from contraceptive pills, there are headache pills, sleeping pills, vitamin pills, etc.

Following Moskvin (2001:65, 2010:194–195), this euphemism-formation mechanism can perhaps be better referred to as hypernymization, rather than as particularization; regardless of our terminological choice, however, it must be stressed that all euphemisms of this type are metonymies. Indeed, as correctly analyzed by Kövecses (2006:104), just like the previously mentioned example *adult* for "pornographic," the euphemistic use of *the pill* represents a whole-for-part metonymy in which the conceptual domain PILL evokes one of its members: the category of contraceptive pills. In the same way, in the case of *satisfaction* for "orgasm," the conceptual domain SATISFACTION stands for one of its parts: sexual satisfaction / orgasm.

Now, let us proceed to the category of implication. That the distinction between metonymy-based and implication euphemisms is untenable can be illustrated with the example *bathroom* for "toilet." According to Warren, *bathroom* can be analyzed as a metonymic euphemism because of the locative relationship between the senses "a room with a bath" and "toilet": Toilets often contain a bathtub. (Or alternatively, a bathroom is a room that, apart from a bathtub, also often contains a lavatory pan.) At the same time, however, it can be argued that the euphemistic use of *bathroom* is motivated by the antecedent–consequent relationship between the events of USING A LAVATORY PAN and USING A BATH. That is, before taking a bath, people usually urinate / defecate in a lavatory pan. (The fact that one and the same room often contains both a bathtub and a lavatory pan corroborates the antecedent–consequent motivation of *bathroom*.)

A very similar example is the utterance *Where can I wash my hands?* which, as Kövecses & Radden (1998:72) point out, can stand for "Where is the nearest toilet?" On the one hand, the underlying motivation seems to be of a locative character: Toilets contain washbasins so that toilet visitors can wash their hands. At the same time, however, the euphemistic use of this utterance can be said to be motivated by the antecedent–consequent relationship between the events URINATION / DEFECATION and WASHING HANDS. In the prototypical case, the latter immediately follows the former: People urinate / defecate in a lavatory pan and then wash their hands in a washbasin. (This explains why toilets are places that contain washbasins.)

The fact that one and the same euphemism can be plausibly analyzed as an instance of both implication and metonymy clearly indicates that the distinction between these two categories cannot be sustained. Like particularization euphemisms, euphemisms involving an antecedent–consequent relationship between their literal and euphemistic senses are also metonymies. The only difference is that implication euphemisms – such as *to go to the toilet* and *Where can I wash my hands?* – are not whole-for-part, but rather, they are part-for-whole metonymies. That is, for example, the act of (literally) going to some toilet is part of the prototypical scenario of using toilets: In order to urinate / defecate, we, first of all, literally go to the place TOILET. The same can be said about washing hands. This concept is also part of the prototypical scenario of using toilets: After urination / defecation, we typically wash our hands.

With regard to the categories of litotes / understatement and hyperbole / overstatement, the following must be noted. As analyzed by Warren (1992), using *drug habit* for "drug addiction" is an instance of litotes because the negative feature DRUG ADDICTION is downgraded to DRUG HABIT (which can be any feature regarding drugs), whereas the use of *sanitary engineer* acts as an instance of hyperbole because the non-prestigious occupation GARBAGE COLLECTOR is upgraded to ENGINEER. The problem with this analysis is that it confuses semantic euphemism-formation mechanisms (metonymy and metaphor) with pragmatic effects achieved by them (under- and overstatement). What is meant by this is that, similar to *satisfaction* and *the pill*, *drug habit* can also be analyzed as a whole-for-part metonymy in which the conceptual domain DRUG HABIT stands for one of its members: the category of drug addiction. This semantic strategy underlies the euphemistic use of *drug habit* and results in the pragmatic downgrading of the negative feature DRUG ADDICTION. (This effect arises because drug addiction is perceived as a bad habit. In contrast, in the case of *satisfaction* and *the pill*, there is no pragmatic downgrading because neither an orgasm nor a contraceptive pill is perceived as a bad subcategory of the domains SATISFACTION and PILL: An orgasm is not a bad satisfaction, and a contraceptive pill is not a bad pill.) Similarly, in *sanitary engineer* the underlying semantic strategy is not overstatement but a part-for-part metonymy in which one member of the domain PROFESSION (engineer) stands for another member of the same domain (garbage collector). As in the case of drug addiction, the upgrading effect arises because the occupation of a garbage collector is perceived as less prestigious than that of an engineer.

In stark contrast to Warren (1992) and some more recent studies (Reutner, 2009:119–154; Moskvin, 2010:163–227), which propose even more refined classifications, the present article recognizes only two semantic euphemism-formation mechanisms: either a metonymic or a metaphoric extension of the euphemism's literal meaning. This view is in full accord with present-day diachronic semantics (e. g., Traugott & Dasher, 2002), which recognizes only two types of semantic change: metonymy and metaphor. On the contrary, authors like Warren and Moskvin, who distinguish between metonymy and particularization / hypernymization, seem to be influenced by the very old logico-rhetorical typology of semantic change, whose origins "go back to Aristotle's analysis of metaphor" (Ullmann, 1967:203). Thus, for Anttila (1972:148) the semantic development of *hound* ("any dog" in Old English > "a hunting dog of a particular breed" in Modern English) is not a whole-for-part metonymy (in which, like in the case of *satisfaction* and *the pill*, the name of the conceptual domain has begun to be used as a metonym for one of its members) but an instance of semantic narrowing. Whereas metonymy and metaphor involve a "transfer to another conceptual sphere," narrowing of meaning as exemplified by *hound* constitutes a "change within the same conceptual sphere," i. e., a change that did not affect the semantic range of the item under consideration: *Hound* has retained the semantic component [dog]. As stated above, this article rejects the logico-rhetorical approach and regards semantic narrowing as a whole-for-part metonymy. Correspondingly, cases of semantic widening, such as *to arrive* for "to arrive at sea" in Old English > "to arrive anywhere and by any means of locomotion" in Modern English (Ullmann, 1967:204) are regarded as part-for-whole metonymies.

4   Default and non-default metonymies

In their landmark article entitled "Metonymy: Developing a Cognitive Linguistic Point of View," Kövecses & Radden (1998) raise the question of why some metonymic expressions are hardly recognizable as expressions that do not mean what they literally stand for. For example, *Prime Minister of England* is an unrecognizable part-for-whole metonymy meaning "Prime Minister of the entire United Kingdom of Great Britain and Northern Ireland (of which England is a part)": England does not have its own Prime Minister. If *Prime Minister of England* were a recognizable metonymy, its use would most likely give rise to a semantic anomaly (cf. *Prime Minister of Wales*). Similarly, *black coffee* seems to be a hardly recognizable part-for-whole metonymy meaning "coffee without added milk or cream" (Mel'čuk, 1995:182): The vehicle meaning "black color" is a characteristic of the intended target meaning "coffee without milk or cream" (i. e., the absence of milk or cream in a cup of coffee usually results in its black color).

According to Kövecses & Radden (1998), the non-recognizability of metonymies like ENGLAND FOR THE UNITED KINGDOM OF GREAT BRITAIN AND NORTHERN IRELAND and BLACK COLOR FOR ABSENCE OF MILK OR CREAM stems from the fact that the choice of their vehicle concepts ENGLAND and BLACK COLOR fulfills at least some of the cognitive principles of relative salience. These include, for example,

Metonymic Euphemisms from a Cognitive Linguistic Point of View

- HUMAN OVER NON-HUMAN
- CONCRETE OVER ABSTRACT
- INTERACTIONAL OVER NON-INTERACTIONAL
- IMMEDIATE OVER NON-IMMEDIATE
- DOMINANT OVER LESS DOMINANT
- SPECIFIC OVER GENERIC
- GOOD GESTALT OVER POOR GESTALT
- CENTRAL OVER PERIPHERAL
- RELEVANT OVER LESS RELEVANT
- IMPORTANT OVER LESS IMPORTANT

These principles "relate to three general determinants of conceptual organization" (p. 63):

1. human experience; e. g., HUMAN OVER NON-HUMAN, CONCRETE OVER ABSTRACT, etc.
2. perceptual selectivity; e. g., IMMEDIATE OVER NON-IMMEDIATE, DOMINANT OVER LESS DOMINANT, etc.
3. cultural preference; e. g., CENTRAL OVER PERIPHERAL, IMPORTANT OVER LESS IMPORTANT, etc.

What is important here is that "the more of [these] principles apply to a particular metonymic expression, the greater the cognitive motivation. As a result, the metonymy will be regarded as natural or 'default'" (p. 71). Thus, the unrecognizable metonymy *Prime Minister of England* is a default metonymy because its vehicle concept ENGLAND fulfills the principle DOMINANT OVER LESS DOMINANT (relating to perceptual selectivity): England is the most dominant part of the United Kingdom of Great Britain and Northern Ireland and can, therefore, be easily understood as a metonym for the entire UK. Similarly, the hardly recognizable metonymy *black coffee* is a default metonymy because its vehicle concept BLACK COLOR fulfills the principle IMMEDIATE OVER NON-IMMEDIATE (also relating to perceptual selectivity): i. e., first of all, we see that a coffee is black, and only then do we conclude that it contains no milk and cream.

Default metonymies like *Prime Minister of England* and *black coffee* can be contrasted with non-default metonymies, i. e., metonymic expressions whose vehicles violate one or more of the above-named principles. For example, the euphemism *boyfriend* can be considered a non-default metonymy because its vehicle concept

FRIEND violates the principle IMPORTANT OVER LESS IMPORTANT (or, alternatively, the principles RELEVANT OVER LESS RELEVANT or CENTRAL OVER PERIPHERAL), relating to cultural preference. The most important characteristic of boyfriend-ship is not friendship, but, rather, the sexual / romantic relationship between a woman and her boyfriend. Friendship is, by contrast, a less important and / or less relevant, even peripheral, characteristic. Thus, a woman can have more than one literal friend, but only the one, who, in addition to being her friend, is also her sexual partner qualifies as her boyfriend. Similarly, the euphemism *bathroom* can be analyzed as a non-default metonymy because its vehicle concept ROOM WITH A BATH violates the same principles. The defining characteristic of a toilet is that its visitors urinate / defecate in a lavatory pan, not that they wash themselves in a bathtub.

Given what has been said above, a question arises as to whether all metonymic euphemisms can be regarded as non-default metonymies. (This question is left unanswered by Kövecses and Radden because the focus of their article is not on metonymic euphemisms but on all kinds of metonymic expressions and semantic patterns underlying them.) The answer to this question depends on whether the researcher equates default metonymies with unrecognizable metonymies, i. e., if a given metonymic euphemism is not consciously recognized as an expression that underwent metonymic reinterpretation, it can be considered a non-default metonymy. Consider again the copulation euphemism *to sleep with somebody*. As a first approximation, this euphemism is also analyzable as a non-default metonymy in which the choice of the vehicle concept violates the principle IMPORTANT OVER LESS IMPORTANT. Physical sleeping is a peripheral characteristic of the copulation scenario: Far more important than spending time together in the same bed at night or day time while being in the state of sleep is the fact that lovers engage in sexual intercourse. At the same time, however, it is not clear whether English speakers are consciously aware of this euphemism's metonymic nature. Thus, observe the euphemistic use of *to sleep with somebody* in contexts that do not involve physical sleeping; e. g., sex with a prostitute, after which the customer typically goes away without literally sleeping with her (e. g., *I recently learned that my husband has slept with many prostitutes in third world countries*, "Reckless Endangerment of Spouse – Legal Recourse?", 2010). If *to sleep with somebody* were a recognizable metonymy, than this euphemism would most likely occur in sleeping contexts only. That is, it would refer not only to sexual intercourse (euphemistic meaning) but also to physical sleeping (literal meaning), in other words, to a prototypical copulation scenario in which the former is immediately followed by the latter. That *to sleep with somebody* does, however, occur in non-sleeping contexts as well (and, what is more, this use does not give rise to a semantic anomaly) corroborates the suggestion that the euphemistic meaning "to copulate" does not activate the literal meaning "to sleep." In this respect, *to sleep with somebody* does not seem to be different from the default metonymy *Prime Minister of England*.

Alternatively, we can discard the recognizability criterion, i.e., regard a metonymic euphemism like *to sleep with somebody* as non-default if its vehicle concept violates at least some of the above-named principles. However, in this case, we will inevitably run into the problem of mixed metonymies, i.e., metonymic expressions whose vehicle concepts simultaneously fulfill and violate one or the other principle. A good example illustrating this point is *to go to the toilet*. On the one hand, this euphemism is a non-default metonymy violating the principle IMPORTANT OVER LESS IMPORTANT: The literal act of going to a toilet is undoubtedly a less important aspect of the using-a-toilet scenario than the act of urination / defecation in it. On the other hand, however, *to go to the toilet* can be considered a default metonymy because it is motivated by the antecedent–consequent relation between its literal and euphemistic meaning and, accordingly, fulfills the principle IMMEDIATE OVER NON-IMMEDIATE: First of all, we physically go to the place TOILET and only then urinate / defecate in it. What is, then, the status of *to go to the toilet*? Is it a default or a non-default metonymy?

5 Classifying metonymic euphemisms

Since it is not entirely clear in which case a metonymic expression qualifies as default, this article does not apply the default–non-default distinction to metonymic euphemisms. What it does instead, however, is classify metonymic euphemisms with respect to the violation of one particular principle, the one which underlies its euphemistic use. Thus, the fact that the vehicle concept of *to go to the toilet* fulfills the principle IMMEDIATE OVER NON-IMMEDIATE does not really explain why this expression can function as a euphemism for urination / defecation. (This does explain, however, why *to go to the toilet* can be understood as a metonym for urination / defecation: In order to urinate / defecate, we, first of all, need to literally go to some toilet.) What underlies the euphemistic function of *to go to the toilet* is that the literal act of going to a toilet is a less important and a taboo-free aspect of the using-a-toilet-scenario. Similarly, the literal act of sleeping is a less important and a taboo-free characteristic of the copulation scenario; literal friendship between a woman and her boyfriend is a less important and a taboo-free characteristic of the concept of boyfriend-ship; etc.

5.1 Euphemisms violating the principle
IMPORTANT OVER LESS IMPORTANT

Metonymic euphemisms belonging to this category are metonymies like the aforementioned examples *to sleep with somebody, boyfriend, to go to the toilet,* and *bathroom*. In all of them, the euphemistic effect results from the replacement of a taboo-marked concept by a less important but taboo-free characteristic associated with the same taboo subject.

Below are some other examples of metonymic euphemisms whose vehicle concepts violate the principle IMPORTANT OVER LESS IMPORTANT. All of these examples have been taken from Richard Holder's (2008) *Oxford Dictionary of Euphemisms*.

As has been mentioned in connection with *to sleep with somebody*, metonymic euphemisms belonging to this category can be used in contexts that are not compatible with their literal meanings. That is, we can say *John sleeps with Sarah* even if John and Sarah never fall asleep together in the same bed (e. g., McGlone & Batchelor, 2003:251). Similarly, as Holder (2008:90) points out, the euphemistic query *Where's the basement?* can be "made in a building manifestly devoid of a lower level." The reason for this is obvious: Metonymic euphemisms like *to sleep with somebody* and *basement* have vehicle concepts denoting peripheral characteristics of the taboo-marked concepts that they express. That is, lovers do not always fall asleep together after sex, and lavatories are not necessarily located in building basements.

Given these uses of *to sleep with somebody* and *basement*, one of the anonymous reviewers of this article raises the question of whether euphemisms like these can still be regarded as metonymic euphemisms. That is, if lovers who have sex do not always literally sleep with each other in the same bed, can we still claim that in the case of *to sleep with somebody*, there exists a real link between the literal

Table 1: Metonymic euphemisms violating the principle SPECIFIC OVER GENERIC

	Euphemism	Euphemistic meaning	Violation of the principle
1	African-American	"black"	Much more important than being a person whose ancestors came from Africa is the fact that an African-American is a person who has a black skin.
2	basement	"lavatory"	The fact that a lavatory is frequently located in the basement of a shopping mall, school, etc. is a rather peripheral characteristic of the concept LAVATORY.
3	evacuee	"a German citizen (usually a Jew) killed by the Nazis"	Much more important than being literally evacuated (i.e., removed from a military zone or a dangerous place) is the fact that evacuees were actually killed.
4	disturbed, as in, e.g., disturbed child	"naughty"	Much more important than being literally disturbed by somebody or something is the fact that a disturbed child is naughty, i.e., that he or she does not behave well.
5	massage parlor / sauna	"brothel"	Much more important than being a place where customers can get a massage / wash themselves in a sauna is the fact that both a massage parlor and a sauna are places for paid sex.
6	mature	"old"	Much more important than being literally mature (i.e., fully developed) is the fact that a mature person is relatively old.
7	non-industrial country	"poor and relatively uncivilized country"	Much more important than the absence of industry is the fact that a non-industrial country is a poor country.
8	oldest profession	"prostitution"	Being the oldest profession is a peripheral characteristic of the concept PROSTITUTION.
9	red lamp / red light, as in, e.g., red light district	"brothel"	Even though many brothels use red lamps as their sign, this is, nevertheless, a peripheral characteristic of the concept BROTHEL.
10	visible	"not white-skinned"	Much more important than being literally visible is the fact that a visible person does not have a white skin.

meaning "to sleep" and the euphemistic meaning "to copulate"? According to the reviewer, it can also be argued that "the two activities (sleeping with someone and having sex with someone) share the aspect of privacy / intimacy, so that one may be used as a metaphoric expression for the other."

In my view, the proposed analysis of *to sleep with somebody* as a metaphoric euphemism is not correct. Despite the fact that sex is not always followed by lovers' co-sleeping, the expression *to sleep with somebody* still remains a metonymically motivated euphemism. That is, when asked "Why can *to sleep with somebody* be used as a euphemism for 'to have sex'?", a speaker of English, who uses this expression in both sleeping and non-sleeping contexts, will still attribute the idiomatic meaning "to have sex" to the antecedent–consequent relationship between the events of HAVING SEX and SLEEPING: The latter is often immediately followed by the former.

It is true that the activities of having sex and sleeping with someone share the aspect of privacy / intimacy. However, this does not mean that *to sleep with somebody* can be analyzed as a metaphoric euphemism. Quite the contrary – this fact corroborates the metonymic analysis advocated in this article: We can claim that *to sleep with somebody* is a part-for-part metonymy in which one element of the domain PRIVACY / INTIMACY – the concept of sleeping with someone – maps onto another element within the same domain: the concept of having sex.

5.2 Euphemisms violating the principle SPECIFIC OVER GENERIC

Another euphemism-formation strategy involving metonymy is the violation of the principle SPECIFIC OVER GENERIC (which, according to Kövecses & Radden (1998:67–68), relates not to cultural preferences, but to perceptual selectivity). This strategy underlies all whole-for-part metonymies like the previously mentioned *adult Web site* for "pornographic Web site," *satisfaction* for "orgasm," and *the pill* for "contraceptive pill," which Warren (1992) and Moskvin (2001, 2010) analyze as instances of particularization / hypernymization. Euphemisms belonging to this category violate the principle SPECIFIC OVER GENERIC because they express rather specific concepts like PORNOGRAPHIC WEB SITE, ORGASM, and CONTRACEPTIVE PILL by means of rather generic concepts like ADULT WEB SITE, SATISFACTION, and THE PILL. Usually, the latter represents a hypernym of the former, but observe the euphemistic use of *do it* in sentences like *They did it*, meaning "they had sex with each other." It is clear that *do it* cannot be a hypernym of *copulate* because *it* is a deictic pronoun, which has no literal meaning of its own. As argued by Moskvin (2010:197–201), in the case of euphemistic utterances like *They did it*, we are dealing with pronominalization, another important euphemism-formation mechanism, which must be distinguished from hypernymization. In my view, however, this distinction is superfluous. In both pronominalization and hypernymization euphemisms, the euphemistic effect results from the violation of one and the same principle: SPECIFIC OVER GENERIC: As in the case of *adult Web site*, *satisfaction*, and *the pill*, DO IT represents a vehicle that has a very generic meaning, i.e., apart from the taboo-marked target concept COPULATION, it can refer to almost any activity.

Table 2 provides some further examples of euphemistic expression whose vehicle concepts violate the principle SPECIFIC OVER GENERIC. All of these examples have been taken from Holder (2008).

5.3 Euphemisms violating the principle MORE TRUE OVER LESS TRUE

Finally, there are metonymic euphemisms like the previously mentioned *cum laude* for "a bad dissertation grade defended in a German university" and *sanitary engineer* for "garbage collector," whose vehicle concepts provide rather inaccurate characteristics of what these expressions denote as euphemisms. Thus, as argued in the previous section, a dissertation awarded *cum laude* is, in reality, a rather poor dissertation that does not deserve any praise. Similarly, the profession of a garbage collector is considerably different from that of an engineer. (Kövecses & Radden (1998) do not mention the principle MORE TRUE OVER LESS TRUE in their article, but I believe that it is precisely the violation of this principle that accounts for the euphemistic use of all metonymic expressions discussed in this section of the article).

Euphemisms whose vehicle concepts violate the principle MORE TRUE OVER LESS TRUE can often be found among names of various insurances. For example, a health insurance, which covers medical expenses when the insured falls ill, can be better described as an *illness* (rather than as *health*) insurance: We need this insurance mainly when we are ill, not when we are healthy. Similarly, a life insurance, which "guarantees a specific sum of money to a designated beneficiary upon the death of the insured" (American Heritage Dictionary), can be better referred to as a *death* (rather than as *life*) insurance. According to Holder (2008:211), in the case of *health insurance* and *life insurance*, the taboo subjects ILLNESSES and DEATH are avoided by talking about their converses: HEALTH and LIFE.

Table 2: Metonymic euphemisms violating the principle IMPORTANT OVER LESS IMPORTANT

	Euphemism	Euphemistic meaning	Violation of the principle
1	abnormal	"homosexual"	One can be perceived as abnormal in a variety of ways, not only by being homosexual.
2	to adjust your dress	"to do up the fasteners on your trousers"	One can adjust his dress in a variety of ways, not necessarily by doing up the fasteners on his trousers.
3	to betray / to deceive	"to copulate with a third party while married"	One can betray / deceive in a variety of ways, not only by copulating with a third party while being married / having a regular sexual partner.
4	career change	"dismissal from employment"	Our careers can change in a variety of ways, not necessarily through dismissal from employment.
5	to cleanse	"to free from enemy occupation or sympathizers"	One can cleanse in a variety of ways, not only by freeing from enemy occupation or sympathizers.
6	to do the right thing	"to marry a woman you have impregnated"	One can do a right thing in a variety of ways, not only by marrying an impregnated woman.
7	to downsize	"to dismiss employees"	One can downsize in a variety of ways, not only by dismissing employees.
8	erection	"an enlargement of the penis due to sexual excitement"	*Erection* literally means "the condition of being upright" (Holder:169). There are many things that can be in that condition, not only the penis of a sexually excited male.
9	financial assistance	"state aid for the poor"	State aid for the poor is not the only kind of financial assistance.
10	good time	"a sexual experience with a stranger"	One can have a good time in a variety of ways, not only by having a sexual experience with a stranger.

Some other examples of metonymic euphemisms belonging to this category are given in Table 3.

Metonymic euphemisms of this type are often hardly distinguishable from metaphoric euphemisms (and can perhaps be regarded as a borderline case between metonymy and metaphor). Like the former, the latter can also be analyzed as violations of the principle MORE TRUE OVER LESS TRUE. For example, we can say that the vehicle concepts of the metaphoric expressions *to come* for "to achieve an orgasm" and *to ride* for "to copulate with a man in the woman-on-top position"

Metonymic Euphemisms from a Cognitive Linguistic Point of View

Table 3: Metonymic euphemisms violating the principle MORE TRUE OVER LESS TRUE

	Euphemism	Euphemistic meaning	Violation of the principle
1	academy	"brothel"	The institution of an academy is considerably different from that of a brothel.
2	actress	"prostitute"	The profession of an actress is considerably different from that of a prostitute.
3	to angle with a silver hook	"to pretend to have caught a fish that you have bought"	A person who behaves in such a way does not literally angle with a silver hook.
4	art	"pornographic"	Pornography is not an art.
5	as planned (used as "corporate-speak when managers wish to suggest that their failure is not due to their incompetence"; Holder:83)	"regrettably"	Failures like these are not really planned by managers.
6	aunt	"a promiscuous woman or an elderly prostitute"	A promiscuous woman or an elderly prostitute is not an aunt in relation to the person who refers to her as an aunt.
7	bamboozled	"drunk"	A drunk person has not literally been bamboozled, i.e., deceived by underhanded methods (Merriam-Webster Online)
8	beaver[3]	"the female genitals viewed sexually" ("from the slang meaning a beard, whence the pubic hair"; Holder:92)	The pubic hair is not a beard.
9	bikini wax	"a procedure for the removal of women's pubic hair"	It is the skin of a woman's body that is waxed, not the bikini.
10	bimbo	"a sexually complaisant female" ("from the Italian, meaning 'little (male) child'"; Holder:95)	A sexually complaisant female is not a little male child.

[3] Like to bang somebody, beaver is in present-day English a dysphemism (i.e., a rather vulgar expression for "the female genitalia viewed sexually"), rather than a euphemism. It is not entirely clear why Holder (2008) analyzes it as a euphemism.

257

provide very inaccurate descriptions of what happens when people come to an orgasm and copulate while being on top. The reason why *to come* and *to ride* can, nevertheless, be better analyzed as instances of metaphor, while the examples in Table 3 are products of a metonymic semantic change, is that in contrast to the former, the latter fulfill the aforementioned within-domain-mapping requirement of metonymy. Consider, for example, the noun *beaver* for "the female genitals viewed sexually." At first glance, there does not seem to exist a real link between the meanings "beaver" and "the female genitals": Beavers do not seem to have much in common with the female genitalia viewed sexually. However, as Holder argues, the sexual sense of *beaver* goes back not to the literal meaning "beaver," but to the slang meaning "a beard" (which is a product of metaphorization of the literal meaning "beaver": There is a visual similarity between a beaver and a beard). In this case, *beaver* can be analyzed a part-for-part metonymy whose vehicle concept BEARD maps onto the target concept THE FEMALE GENITALIA within the same domain HUMAN BODY. Similarly, we can analyze *bimbo* as a part-for-part metonymy, rather than as a cross-domain metaphor, because its literal meaning in Italian, "a little male child," and its euphemistic sense in English, "a sexually complaisant female," are both human characteristics: i.e., a human being can be a little male child and a sexually complaisant woman. Accordingly, *bimbo* is a part-for-part metonymy whose vehicle concept LITTLE MALE CHILD maps onto the target concept SEXUALLY COMPLAISANT WOMAN within the same domain of HUMAN CHARACTERISTICS.

In addition to metaphoric euphemisms, metonymic euphemisms whose vehicle concepts violate the principle MORE TRUE OVER LESS TRUE are also often not easily distinguishable from instances of lying. Consider, for example, the famous abbreviation *GDR* for "German Democratic Republic." Like the examples discussed above, *GDR* is a part-for-part metonymy in which one element of the conceptual domain POLITICAL SYSTEMS – democracy – stands for another element within the same domain: totalitarianism. Since democracy is radically different from totalitarianism and *GDR* was indeed a totalitarian state rather than a democracy, it can be concluded that, in this abbreviation, the choice of the vehicle concept DEMOCRATIC violates the principle MORE TRUE OVER LESS TRUE. (This is presumably the reason for the inclusion of *GDR* in Holder's dictionary of euphemisms.) However, recall that euphemism is different from lie in that, in the former case, the speaker does not intend to deceive or mislead the hearer. That is, a German professor who grades a doctoral dissertation with *cum laude* does not want to be understood literally (i.e., that he indeed thinks that the dissertation he has graded deserves praise). On the contrary, by using the grade *cum laude*, s/he wants to indirectly communicate the meaning "this is a rather poor dissertation that cannot be praised." By contrast, the coiners of the abbreviation *GDR* (as well as *GDR* rulers) wanted to be understood literally (i.e., that *GDR* was a genuinely democratic country and not a totalitarian state). The use of *German Democratic Republic* as the official name of the East German State was, thus, a lie because the leaders of the country knew that *GDR* was not a democracy but nevertheless used this abbreviation for political propaganda.

5.4 Mixed types

A number of metonymic euphemisms have vehicle concepts that simultaneously violate the principles IMPORTANT OVER LESS IMPORTANT and MORE TRUE OVER LESS TRUE. A good example is *industrializing country* for "a poor and relatively undeveloped country." On the one hand, its vehicle concept clearly violates the principle IMPORTANT OVER LESS IMPORTANT: The most important characteristic of an industrializing country is its poverty and underdevelopment, not that it has an ongoing industrialization, as the adjective *industrializing* suggests. In addition to this, however, there is also a violation of the principle MORE TRUE OVER LESS TRUE: As Holder (2008:226) points out, *industrializing country* is a "coinage based on aspiration rather than reality." What is meant by this is that an industrializing country is typically a poor and underdeveloped country that has very little or no industry at all. (There is no ongoing industrialization.) Similarly, the educational euphemism *differently-abled* for "crippled or of low intelligence" violates both the principles IMPORTANT OVER LESS IMPORTANT and MORE TRUE OVER LESS TRUE. With regard to the former, the defining characteristic of a differently-abled person is his crippleness or low intelligence, not the presence of other abilities. With regard to the latter, *differently-abled*, like *industrializing country*, also seems to be a coinage based on aspiration rather than reality: A differently-abled person does not really have any different abilities. Finally, recall that *to sleep with somebody* and *basement* can be used to refer to lovers who do not fall asleep together in the same bed after having sex and to lavatories that are not located in building basements. Given these facts, we can claim that the vehicle concepts of the euphemisms *to sleep with somebody* and *basement* simultaneously violate the principles IMPORTANT OVER LESS IMPORTANT and MORE TRUE OVER LESS TRUE: Physical sleeping with somebody is a peripheral characteristic of the prototypical copulation scenario, which, in a number of cases (e. g., during sex with prostitutes), does not immediately follow the more important characteristic SEXUAL INTERCOURSE. Additionally, the fact that lavatories are often located in building basements is a peripheral characteristic of a lavatory that is not true of all lavatories. (As the examples *to sleep with somebody* and *basement* demonstrate, euphemisms whose vehicle concepts violate the principle IMPORTANT OVER LESS IMPORTANT are particularly prone to develop into euphemisms violating the principle MORE TRUE OVER LESS TRUE.)

6 Concluding remarks

The central claim of this article is that there exists a relatively small number of metonymy-based euphemism-formation mechanisms. One is to express a taboo-marked target by means of a less important but taboo-free vehicle associated with the target (violation of the principle IMPORTANT OVER LESS IMPORTANT). In addition, a euphemism can be created by means of replacing a taboo-marked target by either a very generic taboo-free vehicle (violation of the principle SPECIFIC OVER GENERIC) or by a not entirely accurate or even untrue taboo-free vehicle (violation of the principle MORE TRUE OVER LESS TRUE). The major advantage of this classification is that it provides an explanation for why a particular euphemistic expression can function as a euphemism, i. e., be used for indirectly expressing taboo-marked concepts. For example, *boyfriend* can function as a euphemism for "a male sexual partner in a non-marital sexual relationship" because its vehicle concept FRIENDSHIP provides a peripheral characteristic of the target concept BOYFRIEND-SHIP; *adult Web site* can function as a euphemism for "a pornographic Web site" because its vehicle concept ADULT WEB site provides a very generic description of what an adult Web site is. Furthermore, *health insurance* can function as a euphemism for "illness insurance" because its vehicle concept HEALTH INSURANCE provides a rather inaccurate description of why we need a health insurance. Another major advantage is that this classification demonstrates a connection between metonymy- and metaphor-based euphemism-formation mechanisms. As we have seen, metaphoric euphemisms like *to come* and *to ride* also violate the principle MORE TRUE OVER LESS TRUE and are, therefore, sometimes not easily distinguishable from metonymies like *health insurance, sanitary engineer, beaver*, and the like.

7 Acknowledgements

I would like to thank two anonymous reviewers for their extremely helpful comments on an earlier version of this article. Special thanks go to my former colleague Wiebke Ostermann for her scrupulous proofreading of the final version of the manuscript. I, alone, am responsible for any remaining errors and shortcomings.

References

Adams, J. 1981. A type of sexual euphemism in Latin. *Phoenix*, 35 (2). 120–128.

Adams, M. 1999. Another effing euphemism. *American Speech*, 74 (1). 110–112.

Adult. 2013. *Merriam-Webster Online*. Retrieved March 29, 2014 from http://www.merriam-webster.com/dictionary/adult

Anttila, R. 1972. *An introduction to historical and comparative linguistics.* New York: The MacMillan Company.

À outrance. 2014. *Merriam-Webster Online*. Retrieved March 29, 2014 from http://www.merriam-webster.com/dictionary/à+outrance

Are you having trouble reaching orgasm? A guide for women. (2011, May 22). Retrieved March 29, 2014 from http://tinyurl.com/cjq35ce

Bamboozle. 2014. *Merriam-Webster Online*. Retrieved March 29, 2014 from http://www.merriam-webster.com/dictionary/bamboozled

Bang. 2014. *Merriam-Webster Online*. Retrieved March 29, 2014 from http://www.merriam-webster.com/dictionary/bang

Blank, A. 1999. Why do new meanings occur? A cognitive typology of the motivations for lexical semantic change. In A. Blank, & P. Koch (eds.), *Historical semantics and cognition*, 61–91. Berlin/New York: Mouton de Gruyter.

Crespo Fernández, E. 2006a. Metaphor in the euphemistic manipulation of the taboo of sex. *Babel: Aspectos de Filoloxía Inglesa e Alemá*, 15, 27–42.

Crespo Fernández, E. 2006b. The language of death: Euphemism and conceptual metaphorization in Victorian obituaries. *SKY Journal of Linguistics* 19. 101–

130.

Crespo Fernández, E. 2007. *El eufemismo y el disfemismo: Procesos de manipulación del tabú en el lenguaje literario ingles*. Alicante: University of Alicante Press.

Crespo Fernández, E. 2008. Sex-related euphemism and dysphemism: An analysis in terms of Conceptual Metaphor Theory. *Journal of the Spanish Association of Anglo-American Studies* 30 (2). 95–110.

Cruse, A. 2004. *Meaning in language: An introduction to semantics and pragmatics* (2nd ed.). Oxford: Oxford University Press.

Cum laude. 2005–2007. In *Brockhaus – die Enzyklopädie in 30 Bänden* (21st fully revised ed.). Mannheim: F. A. Brockhaus.

Davies, M. 2008–. *The corpus of contemporary American English (COCA)*. Retrieved March 29, 2014 from http://corpus.byu.edu/coca/

Farghal, M. 1995. Euphemism in Arabic: A Gricean interpretation. *Anthropological Linguistics* 37 (3). 366–378.

Forschungsstipendien für promovierte Nachwuchswissenschaftler (Postdoc-Programm). (n. d.). *Deutscher Akademischer Austausch Dienst*. Retrieved March 29, 2014 from http://tinyurl.com/cdkgtan

Friend. 2014. *WordNet: A lexical database for English*. Princeton: Cognitive Science Laboratory of Princeton University. Retrieved March 29, 2014 from http://wordnetweb.princeton.edu/perl/webwn?s=friend&sub=Search+WordNet&o2=&o0=1&o8=1&o1=1&o7=&o5=&o9=&o6=&o3=&o4=&h=

Halmari, H. 2011. Political correctness, euphemism, and language change: The case of 'people first.' *Journal of Pragmatic* 43. 828–840.

Holder, R. W. 2008. *Oxford dictionary of euphemisms: How not to say what you mean* (4th ed.). Oxford: Oxford University Press.

How to make your woman reach an orgasm fast! 2012, February 29. Retrieved March 29, 2014 from http://www.articletrader.com/society/sexuality/how-to-make-your-woman-reach-an-orgasm-fast.html

Kövecses, Z. 2006. *Language, mind, and culture: A practical introduction*. Oxford: Oxford University Press.

Kövecses, Z., & Radden, G. 1998. Metonymy: developing a cognitive linguistic view. *Cognitive Linguistics* 9 (1). 37–77.

Lakoff, G., & Johnson, M. 1980. *Metaphors we live by*. Chicago: The University of Chicago Press.

References

Lakoff, G., & Turner, M. 1989. *More than cool reason: A field guide to poetic metaphor.* Chicago: The University of Chicago Press.

Life insurance. Fourth Edition 2000. Updated in 2009. *The American Heritage Dictionary of the English Language.* Published by Houghton Mifflin Company. Retrieved March 29, 2014 from http://www.thefreedictionary.com/Life-insurance

Linfoot-Ham, K. 2005. The linguistics of euphemism: A diachronic study of euphemism formation. *Journal of Language and Linguistics* 4 (2). 227–263.

McGlone, M., & Batchelor, J. 2003. Looking out for number one: Euphemism and face. *Journal of Communication* 53 (2). 251–264.

Mel'čuk, I. 1995. Phrasemes in language and phraseology in linguistics. In M. Everaert, E.-J. van der Linden, A. Schenk, & R. Schreuder (eds.), *Idioms: structural and psychological perspectives,* 167–223. Hilsdale: Lawrence Erlbaum Associates.

Moskvin, V. P. 2001. Èvfemizmy: Sistemnye svjazi, funkcii i sposoby obrazovanija [Euphemisms: Systemic relations, functions and formation mechanisms]. *Voprosy Jazykoznanija* 3. 58–70.

Moskvin, V. P. 2010. *Èvfemizmy v leksičeskoj sisteme sovremennogo russkogo jazyka* [*Euphemisms in the lexical system of modern Russian*] (4th ed.). Moscow: Lenand.

Pound, L. 1936. American euphemisms for dying, death, and burial: An anthology. *American Speech* 11 (3). 195–202.

Reutner, U. 2009. *Sprache und Tabu: Interpretationen zu Französischen und Italienischen Euphemismen.* Tübingen: Max Niemeyer.

Taylor, J. 2002. *Cognitive grammar.* Oxford: Oxford University Press.

Tokar, A. 2009. *Metaphors of the Web 2.0: With special emphasis on social networks and folksonomies.* Frankfurt am Main: Peter Lang.

Traugott, E. C., & Dasher, R. B. 2002. *Regularity in semantic change.* Cambridge: Cambridge University Press.

Ullmann, S. 1967. *The principles of semantics* (2nd ed.). Oxford: Basil Blackwell.

Warren, B. 1992. What euphemisms tell us about the interpretation of words. *Studia Linguistica* 46 (2). 128–172.

Author

Alexander Tokar
Department of Linguistics
University of California at Berkeley
alexandertokar1980@gmail.com

Concepts in Philosophy and Psychiatry

Philosophical Conceptual Analysis as an Experimental Method

Michael T. Stuart

Abstract

Philosophical conceptual analysis is an experimental method. Focusing on this helps to justify it from the skepticism of experimental philosophers who follow Weinberg, Nichols & Stich (2001). To explore the experimental aspect of philosophical conceptual analysis, I consider a simpler instance of the same activity: everyday linguistic interpretation. I argue that this, too, is experimental in nature. And in both conceptual analysis and linguistic interpretation, the intuitions considered problematic by experimental philosophers are necessary but epistemically irrelevant. They are like variables introduced into mathematical proofs which drop out before the solution. Or better, they are like the hypotheses that drive science, which do not themselves need to be true. In other words, it does not matter whether or not intuitions are accurate as descriptions of the natural kinds that undergird philosophical concepts; the aims of conceptual analysis can still be met.

Experimental philosophers have called into question the use of intuitions in philosophical conceptual analysis, which is claimed to be a cornerstone of traditional philosophical methodology. They argue that intuitions about philosophical concepts are unreliable because we cannot calibrate them against the world. What this or that group of people think of justice, is not necessarily what justice is. We need a way for conceptual analysis to make contact with the object of study—and bringing our culturally-indoctrinated and unstable intuitions into reflective equilibrium is not the way. Philosophy, it is claimed, is most reliable when it operates like science: collecting empirical data, testing hypotheses, and formalizing empirical generalities into mathematical relationships. Perhaps conceptual analysis should be left behind.

One reason this conclusion is mistaken is that conceptual analysis is already quite scientific. Science is a refinement of our normal thinking patterns with its roots going all the way back to child's play (see for example, Cook, Goodman & Schulz 2011). Why think that conceptual analysis, a refined version of other linguistic practices, is divorced from those same proud origins? Imre Lakatos argued that all of mathematics is nothing more than a series of conceptual reformations, which produces better and better definitions of mathematical concepts by a never-ending onslaught of counterexamples (1976). For Lakatos, this process is at once a mental, linguistic, and community activity and it achieves some epistemic good. Mathematics is thought to yield certainty, and plays an indispensable role in physical science. Perhaps philosophical conceptual analysis can be legitimated in a similar way, if philosophy plays an indispensable role in science as well. Yet this is not the argument I want to make. Rather, I argue that conceptual analysis in philosophy is a dynamic process which can be defended epistemologically because of important features it shares not with mathematics, but with the scientific method.

Conceptual analysis can be defined functionally. One of its goals is to specify the extension of a concept. For example, what does *justice* refer to? Part of this is finding properties common to all or most instances of a concept, or outlining relationships between the extensions or intensions of concepts. For example, are all the instances of *water* instances of H_2O? Are electrons only to be found in the context of an atom? Another goal that is somewhat independent of the last few is specifying the "normative profile" (or normative characteristics) of a concept. This goal asks what *should* be the extension of a concept, or its relation to other concepts. A successful conceptual analysis of *knowledge* should therefore reveal which things count as known, what it is about them that makes them known (for example, as opposed to only believed), how known things relate to true things, and so on. But also, such an analysis must tell us what *should* count as known, what *should* be the relation between the known and the true, and so on. The difference between conceptual analysis in philosophy on the one hand, and science on the other, is that the normative profiles of scientific concepts (for example, *quark*) can be quite thin. Determining their extensions and conceptual relations are often more important than sketching their normative profiles. Asking what *quark* should refer to is a sensible question, but in practice it is less central to scientific research than finding the properties common to quarks and the relations between quarks and other physical-theoretical entities. A different emphasis is often found in philosophical conceptual analysis, wherein normative considerations predominate. However, the difference is only one of degree.

One important motivation of *Meaning, Frames, and Conceptual Representation* is to push interdisciplinary boundaries, and considering conceptual analysis as an experimental method takes this motivation seriously because it brings together evidence from the study of language, cognitive science and philosophy of science. I argue that in both conceptual analysis and scientific inquiry we form hypotheses and then "test" them. The literature on scientific experiment is massive (for example, Ackermann 1985, Batens & Van Bendegem 1988, Bogen & Woodward 1988, Cartwright 1983, Collins & Pinch 1993, Franklin 1986, 1990, 2002, Galison 1987, 1997, Gooding 1990, Gooding et al. 1989, Hacking 1983, Latour & Woolgar 1986, Pickering 1985, Pinch 1986). Yet aside from a few German Idealists, very few have written about experimenting with concepts as linguistic entities (see Fehige & Stuart 2014). After presenting the problem from experimental philosophy in more detail, I look at conceptual experimentation from two sides. First, I examine some relevant literature from cognitive science as an attempt to describe the mechanisms at work in conceptual experimentation. Second, I propose a preliminary account that attempts to defend the epistemological status of conceptual analysis conceived as a type of experimental linguistic interpretation.

1 Experimental philosophy and skepticism about conceptual analysis

Weinberg, Nichols, and Stich helped found a sub-discipline in philosophy with their 2001 paper, "Normativity and Epistemic Intuitions." In it, they identified a type of philosophical strategy they called "Epistemic Romanticism." Accounts that employ this strategy, like Plato's, rely on the premise that conceptual knowledge, for example, knowledge of the Forms, is already implanted in us, and we may extract it in dialogue. Weinberg, Nichols and Stich call the family of theories that work this way "Intuition Driven Romanticism," since they consider shared intuitions as evidence for a kind of innate, *a priori* knowledge.

For these authors and many of those who followed them (for example, Alexander et al. 2010, Knobe & Nichols 2008, Machery et al. 2004, Mallon et al. 2009, Swain et al. 2008, Weinberg et al. 2006), an intuition is simply a spontaneous judgment about the properties of some case for which the agent may not be able to offer any plausible justification. Intuition Driven Romanticism takes intuitions as data, and then produces normative epistemic claims that are dependent on the intuitions used, at least in part. That is, if the input were different, the output would also be different (in proportion to the change in the input). Two examples they give of Intuition Driven Romanticism are reflective equilibrium (see Goodman 1955) and Alvin Goldman's "justificatory rules" (see Goldman 1986:60).

Thus, some group of cognitive agents might have intuitions and belief-formation processes that are different from those of western philosophers, and when they run their intuitions through their chosen method (for example, reflective equilibrium) they will emerge with different epistemic norms. The question is: how can we decide which set of norms to follow? There is no answer that is not also subject to objections about relativity, so the whole process is misguided. Epistemic norms will be relative to different cultures, socio-economic classes, and even the number of philosophy courses taken. And it is argued that such intuition-relativity does in fact exist. Here is a famous example of the type of evidence presented.

A scenario called "the Trutemp Case" is presented to survey volunteers. The case consists of the following report: A child on a deserted island gets hit on the head by a coconut, and as a result knows the exact temperature all the time, but does not know that he has this power. The survey volunteers are asked: when the child says, "It is 30 degrees Celsius," does he *know* this, or does he only believe it? Apparently, East Asian people are more likely than Westerners to say that a person so affected *only believes* their temperature guess. However, if you say instead that a team of scientists secretly tinkered with the boy's brain to cause this ability, the situation reverses and East Asian people become more likely than Westerners to report that the boy knows what he says. And finally, if you also say that many other people in the boy's community were secretly given the ability to tell the temperature, and then ask the knowledge question about a single member's belief about the temperature, East Asians are even more likely to attribute knowledge. The Westerners keep their judgments essentially constant over all these changes. The conclusion drawn is that the relation between a person and their community affects the epistemological status of their beliefs, but only if you are East Asian.

In another well-known example, a Gettier case is presented to different cultural groups with each group providing consistently different responses. A standard case is about my friend who thinks George has an American car. In fact, just yesterday George traded in his Buick for a Pontiac (which is still American), so my friend says something true, and justified, when she says "George has an American car." Now, when asked if my friend *knows* the above statement, more East Asians than Westerners respond in the affirmative.

Weinberg, Nichols and Stich conclude that intuition-based analyses only provide information about the people who participate in them, and not any mind-independent truths about the referents of philosophical concepts. Unfortunately, mind-independent truths are precisely what "epistemically romantic" philosophers seek.

If the above analysis of intuition-relativity is correct, I want to argue that this *still* would not affect the possibility of successful conceptual analysis, since the epistemic status of those intuitions is irrelevant to the outcome of conceptual analysis. They are epistemically irrelevant in exactly the same way that hypotheses in science are epistemically irrelevant to the status of the output of the experimental method: namely, good science can be done with false hypotheses. If successful, this argument would not make that output infallible: there are well known issues concerning the epistemic status of the scientific experimental method. Someone might object that it is not meaningful to talk about "the" experimental method as though it were one thing. Yet I will assume that there are interesting commonalities shared by different instances of experimental methods in science which we may focus on in a general way; that there *is* something we can call the experimental method of science, and it is among the best epistemic methods we have at our disposal, will be a shared assumption given the experimental nature of "experimental" philosophy.

Now that we know the criticism, let us look more closely at the role of intuition in conceptual analysis.

2 Conceptual analysis and linguistic interpretation

Conceptual analysis can be understood as an instance of linguistic interpretation (Cohnitz & Häggqvist 2009:9). When philosophers try to discover the content of say, *knowledge* or *justice*, they often begin by outlining how the concept is used (in philosophy, or in some other context of discourse) in order to discover the purpose it serves. Using this knowledge, we attempt to extrapolate or create meaning. We do the same thing when we consider the meaning of a linguistic entity. Conceiving of conceptual analysis as an act of interpretation helps to clarify the connection to experimentalism and avoid the problems of intuition skepticism, since the intuitions involved in linguistic interpretation need not be epistemically justified to serve their purpose. In cases of linguistic interpretation, we need to start *somewhere* to figure out the meaning of an utterance. If we begin with intuitions based on previous experience with a speaker, or a perceived *type* of speaker, or other contextual features, this will usually speed things up. But we need not begin with accurate information or accurate intuitions. Given the script of a conversation not meant specifically to deceive us, we can discover a great deal about the meaning of unfamiliar terms. This sort of activity is what Quine and Davidson discussed using models of Radical Translation and Radical Interpretation. The intuitions we begin with need not be true or accurate or innate or epistemically privileged because interpretation is a special kind of iterated process, one that can begin with false premises and proceed to true conclusions by repeated application of the same method. Perhaps beginning the process of interpretation with very bad intuitions will drag it out, because we have to throw out the unhelpful intuitions and begin again with others until we find the truth, but it will always be possible to complete, at least in principle. It is one of the very few methods that enjoy this status, the scientific method being another.

Here is a quick example. If my friend gestures towards a nearby harbour and remarks, "What an aggressive chine," I may guess that a chine is a type of boat, an in-harbour manoeuvring technique, a person, or almost anything else. What I know about my friend and human linguistic behaviour generally will constrain my guesses significantly. The resulting conversation will disqualify many possible interpretations and if we continue to discuss chines, I can adjust my questions and guesses without needing to ask what a chine is, until I arrive at the conclusion that it refers to the angle of a boat's hull. From there I can come to learn the differences between hard and soft chines and the advantages of each. This a common experience, especially for those who learn a new language. Is something similar going on when we perform conceptual analysis?

When we set out to analyze a concept in philosophy, we are immediately faced with several different aspects of that concept out of which we identify one (or some) to be more interesting than the rest. For example, concerning *knowledge* we have knowledge *that* and knowledge *how*. We could ask whether such a division is a *natural* division in the concept, for example, by comparing similar ones embodied by the French *savoir* and *connaître* and the Spanish *saber* and *conocer*. What we decide to analyze depends on what we want to know. This tells us that some complex concepts must be divided into sub-concepts for easier study, but it also informs us of the different norms that may lie hidden in the concept. Concepts can take the form of exemplars, prototypes, atoms, theories, family resemblances, necessary and sufficient conditions, and all kinds of hybrids (see Margolis & Laurence 1999, DePaul & Ramsey 1998). Instead of arguing which of these *really* captures what we desire from a theory of concepts (*pace* Prinz 2002), we should ask what these different characterizations of concepts are good for; what kinds of concept use they capture and which concepts types are better for characterizing specific concepts.

Despite being more complex, philosophical conceptual analysis appears essentially similar to the above example with the chine. We provisionally propose some definition for a concept. Then we imagine different cases in which the actual use (or proper use) of a term conflicts with the proposed definition. If by this process we do not reach an acceptable definition, we begin to look for ways of splitting up the concept, or ways of softening the requirement of necessary and sufficient conditions by seeking only exemplars, prototypes, or family resemblances. Supposing that there are correct answers to questions like, "What does S mean when she says x?" and, "What should S mean when she says x?", then likewise there will be answers to questions like, "What do we mean when we use concept x?" and, "What *should* we mean when we use concept x?"

Assuming that conceptual analysis is indeed an instance of linguistic interpretation, what evidence is there that the mechanisms which underlie these actions are experimental? Consider what Francis Jacob, a Nobel Prize winning biologist, recently had to say about the practice of science:

> In art as in science, the essential thing is to try out. On the one hand, to try out oppositions of colour or harmonizing themes or combinations of words, then to reject what you don't like. On the other hand, to try things; to try ideas, each idea that comes into our heads; each possibility one by one, systematically; then to toss out what doesn't work experimentally and accept what does work, even if that goes against our tastes and biases. Most of the time such attempts lead nowhere. But sometimes the most outlandish experiment happens to open up

a new rail. The beginning of any research is always a leap into the unknown. It's always after the event that we form judgements on the level of interest of the initial hypothesis. Wrong ideas and outlandish theories abound in science. They are as abundant as bad works of art. (Jacob 2001:118)

Science, for Jacob, is clearly continuous with everyday thinking. When faced with something we want to understand, we begin by "trying out" ideas, combinations of words, and so on, and many of these avenues become closed. What makes science special is the thoroughness with which the new ideas are tested. But, as he says, "The beginning of any research is always a leap into the unknown." Could the same be true of linguistic interpretation and conceptual analysis?

Recent research seems to indicate that it is. Reiner & Gilbert (2004) asked students to analyze a physical mechanism that behaves in an unexpected way (thanks to some hidden magnets). Given a list of the materials out of which the mechanism was built, different sets of students all followed a common natural method of inquiry: first they constructed various models that could capture what they observed in the mechanism. Then they created what the authors called a "representational space" or in other words, a series of abstract concepts and relations between them, often using pen and paper, that would capture the behaviour of the mechanism as represented in their models. Finally, they tested their abstract models in imaginary worlds using thought experiments.

Reiner and Gilbert argue that all of this is done spontaneously. Physical experiments and thought experiments intertwine seamlessly in the learning process. They claim that "the process of alternating between these two modes—empirically experimenting and experimenting in thought—leads towards a convergence on scientifically acceptable concepts" (p. 1819). According to Reiner and Gilbert, "Conceptual construction starts by negotiating meaning, with self and with others, through 'what-if' questions that turn into imaginary experiments in thought, ultimately being applied to the original physical situation (p. 1821). This sentiment is echoed in Reiner & Burko (2003), which argues that "as in the physics community, through social discussions of thought experiments, conclusions and thought processes are negotiated, leading to conceptual refinement" (2003:380) (see also Gilbert & Reiner 2000, Stuart forthcoming, Velentzas & Halkia 2013).

I highlight these passages which focus on thought experiments because of their use of the imagination. In the process of conceptual refinement, both students and experts have been documented using imaginary worlds to invent and refine hypotheses, in many different problem solving scenarios (see for example, Stephens & Clement 2006, Clement 2009, Kosem & Özdemir 2014).

Perhaps it is not far-fetched to claim that everyone, not just students of science, learn to build and evaluate models to invent, evaluate and refine new concepts in a way that draws on general knowledge about the world and individual experience, using the imagination. And this is precisely what we should expect if linguistic interpretation is in some sense an experimental method.

If this is true, we should discuss how conceptual analysis works by discussing the mechanisms that underlie it. We could begin with the input from the imagination, since hypotheses in science and proposed definitions in conceptual analysis both depend on it. Hypotheses are not beliefs; they are imaginings of ways the world could be. What makes a belief good or bad is whether it is true or false. This is not the case with an imagining. For example, my imagining an empty soda can on the dark side of the moon is not better (*qua* imagining) if there is in fact an empty soda can there.

What does make one imagining better than another? The answer to this depends on what we want to do with the imagining. Perhaps we want to devise an imagining that shows us an example of pure altruism. In this case, reading *A Tale of Two Cities* might be better than watching a children's cartoon. A more common and general aim is to provide a counterexample to a modal claim, and examples of these abound in science and philosophy (see Cohintz 2003, Häggqvist 1996, Sorensen 1992). Better imaginings will serve their purpose faster and more efficiently, or they will have wonderful consequences. But they need not be true. Christopher Columbus had a hypothesis about a route to India, and it was mistaken. But it was still eminently useful when tested (Lakatos 1976:14). The same considerations hold for scientific hypotheses. Atomism, for example, was important as a metaphysical hypothesis in Ancient Greece, but it was not a good scientific hypothesis until much later. And the phlogiston-theory was a good hypothesis although it was false, because it was fruitful, testable and had a certain degree of explanatory power. (For an argument against the use of the imagination in philosophy, see Thagard 2014. For a defence, see Stuart 2014).

In the case of science, conceptual analysis, and linguistic interpretation, we propose judgments which are then in some sense, tested. In science, these judgments are called hypotheses, and in conceptual analysis and linguistic interpretation they may be called intuitions. In all cases, they rely heavily on the imagination, and they appear at many stages of inquiry, even in testing. Furthermore, they need not be true or even formed reliably. No one is surprised or distraught that many or even most scientific hypotheses are incorrect as descriptions of the world, because science has a method for screening these out. Likewise, we should not be concerned that many or most of our intuitions concerning the referents of philosophical concepts are incorrect. Nevertheless, to justify the use of intuitions which are spontaneous and stem in the imagination in conceptual analysis, a philosophical account is necessary.

3 Epistemological considerations

Intuitions are involved as part of the guessing process we adopt on the way to understanding linguistic actions and events. Your friend asks if you would like to go to the restaurant across the street. But you know the street well and there is no restaurant there. You immediately have an intuition that she means the jazz bar, which does not serve food. Perhaps you have this intuition because your friend loves jazz, and the music has just now become audible. This intuition becomes your working assumption concerning the meaning of the term "restaurant" in this context, until it is confirmed or denied.

I propose to relate the epistemology of intuitions like these and the roles they play in linguistic interpretation to hypotheses and their roles in science. As Jacob said above, hypotheses are leaps into the unknown, and can be bad or even outlandish. In science they are found in all levels, from experimental, for example, in planning an experiment, to the most theoretical, for example, in dealing with anomalies or developing new formalisms. Leaving aside the exact sciences, hypotheses are never ultimately proven or disproven: they remain open to contradiction or vindication by future experience. The two things most important for my purposes is that they are not used as proof or evidence, and while they are being tested they are not true or false. We should oppose them to ideas, beliefs and commitments which are in this analogy like theories—put forth as candidates for knowledge. Extending this analogy, the goal of interpretation is the meaning of a term, including its intension, extension, relation to other terms and normative profile. The end goal of scientific investigation is something like accuracy or truth, but the more common achievement, which is taken to be a sign of a successful investigation, is what Francis Bacon called "power over nature." If I

Philosophical Conceptual Analysis as an Experimental Method

introduce a new term in discourse, I will be satisfied that you have understood it at least partially when you can use the new term in conversation to achieve your ends. Likewise, we understand a phenomenon in science at least partially when we can use it to achieve our ends. These practical abilities are signs of success, and are therefore epistemologically significant. In science, the iterated process of hypothesis, test and theoretical revision is well-known (see for example, Lauden 1973, Peirce 1898). Hasok Chang has coined the term "epistemic iteration" to refer to the scientific process in which "we start by adopting an existing system of knowledge, with some respect for it but without any firm assurance that it is correct; on the basis of that initially affirmed system we launch inquiries that result in the refinement and even correction of the original system. It is this self-correcting progress that justifies (retrospectively) successful courses of development in science, not any assurance by reference to some indubitable foundation" (2004:6). In science, we always have multiple hypotheses being developed at once, if for no other reason than underdetermination of theory by evidence. "Accepting plurality means accepting imprecision, which we can actually afford to do in quite a few cases, with a promise of later tightening" (Chang 2004:158). This "later tightening" consists in empirical testing, calibration of measurement devices, and refinements of cogency and applicability (p. 234). If the analogy to linguistic interpretation is to hold, there must be a tightening process analogous to the one in science.

I would like to argue that Donald Davidson's "principle of charity" could be seen as one such tightening mechanism. Davidson was not the first to propose a principle of charity, but his is perhaps the most influential account (see his 2001a, 2001b, 2005). For Davidson, the principle of charity is not *one* thing; it is an umbrella term that covers many different and complementary constraints. This group of constraints makes possible successful communication within reasonable time periods. By successful we do not mean flawless: we make mistakes and will be wrong about many of the beliefs and meanings we attribute. Here is Davidson's account.

We must know both the meaning of someone's utterance *and* their relevant underlying beliefs *and* their propositional attitudes (believing, doubting, fearing, etc.) if we want to understand their utterance. However, we can guess some of these elements if we know the others. For example if I say "The World Cup is my favourite sporting event" and you know what this sentence means and that

I believe it, then you will be able to surmise some of my beliefs about soccer. Likewise, if you know my beliefs about soccer and tournaments, you can garner an idea of what the sentence "The World Cup is my favourite Sporting Event" means when I point to the match schedule and I jump up and down clapping my hands, even if I utter the sentence in a language with which you are unfamiliar. But how can you understand my meaning if you do not know either my relevant beliefs, attitudes, or the meaning of my words? This is Davidson's famous case of Radical Interpretation. Here, the key is the propositional attitude of assertion. Davidson thinks we can easily discern this without help from either meaning or belief. If you can tell what someone holds true (or seems to hold true) you can make and test hypotheses for what they mean, and since these attributions will be constrained by certain factors, you can tighten your guesses until you find the correct theory of meaning. The principle of charity explains the way we do this guesswork. It tells us that we superimpose our logic on the speaker, posit events and objects as the ontology of our shared realities (known to both speaker and interpreter) and assume that the speaker's beliefs are mostly true. And we do not just assume them to hold mostly true beliefs; we try to *maximize* the truth of their beliefs, whenever possible. If I hear you say, "I saw the Grand Canyon flying to California" there are at least two ways to understand this, and you can bet I will not select the option which attributes to you the belief that canyons can fly. While it is not necessary that any specific belief of our speaker be true, his or her beliefs must be true on the whole, because you could not interpret someone who was in systematic error (that is, in error about everything). You could not even disagree with them. Given the way a speaker uses their words and this principle, we can create a theory of meaning for a speaker that could provide in advance the meaning of every possible utterance they might make, by recursion and composition.

However, using a principle of charity that maximizes the truth of your speaker to provide an account of meaning is not without its critics. Analysing some criticism is a good way to explore and update Davidson's principle of charity as an epistemological tool analogous to the method of scientific experimentation. I will focus on the influential criticism of Timothy Williamson.

Williamson argues that any principle of charity that "crudely maximizes true belief" (2004:139) will often recommend incorrect attributions. If I believe many things that are false about X but true about Y, it would seem that such a principle would recommend that my interpreter ascribe Y as the object of my X-utterances and beliefs so as to maximize the number of true beliefs that I hold, regardless of my intention that they be about X. We would like to think that some causal history between X and myself is what makes my thoughts have X-content, but why? Williamson says it is because causal history often implies past perceptual experience, which is a "channel" for knowledge (p. 140).

I bring up this worry because a similar objection is levelled at conceptual analysis from experimental philosophers, mentioned at the start. Namely, without an objective perspective on *knowledge* or *justice* themselves, we do not know whether we are analysing the same thing when different groups of people analyse their versions of these concepts. That is, our tightening procedure does not tighten enough.

Here is an example from Williamson. A psychic makes a prediction about the life history and personality of Santiago. It turns out that this life story and personality more accurately describe a third person, say, Nico. According to Williamson, Davidson's principle recommends that we attribute all of the psychic's beliefs about Santiago's character traits and history to Nico and not Santiago, since this will make more of our psychic's beliefs and utterances true. Since we know that the physic actually *intends* to have their utterances be about Santiago, and Davidson's principle forces us to attribute them to Nico, we have a *reductio* against Davidson's account. It is because of the causal (in this case visual) connection between the psychic and Santiago that we *still* take his or her beliefs and utterances to be about Santiago, even though they are truer of Nico.

And the same could be true about conceptual analysis. Making our own beliefs come out true and consistent would not guarantee that they refer to the right things, or even that such things exist and we can refer to them.

Another example concerns ascribing knowledge of quantum physical laws to people from the Stone Age, since this will help maximize the truth of their beliefs. These ascriptions do not occur on Williamson's account since we need to have a knowledge-channel (or causal connection) between the speaker and his or her objects of speech in order to ascribe something as the source of their belief. For these reasons, Williamson suggests a knowledge (instead of truth) maximizing principle of charity, which relies on being in the relevant *position to know* something.

According to Williamson, you cannot be in a position to know something unless that something is actually happening (that is, you cannot know that it is raining unless it true that it is). You also need the *right kind* of causal contact with the object of your utterance or thought. Finally, we also will not ascribe knowledge to people if that ascription would rely on inferences that are not sound.

My reply to this worry is that truth is a simpler concept than knowledge. It is easier to understand and less presumptuous to assume. Davidson calls it "beautifully transparent" (2001b:139). It seems natural to think that "snow is white is true" is equivalent to "snow is white." On the other hand, saying "snow is white is known" makes little sense without a subject that knows, and a context in which that something is known. If we provide a subject for whom "snow is white" is known, then several things might still be meant by such an ascription. To counter on behalf of Williamson, we could argue that "snow is white is true" can also be relativized to a person and context. However, to do so would be to ignore the adage: *ex contradictione sequitur quodlibet*—from a contradiction everything follows. If we allow truth to be relative to a speaker, then we must admit that, from a higher level, the same sentence can be both true and false. If this is granted, it makes possible the derivation of anything, even absurdities, from a set of beliefs we thought were conservative and rational (for more on this principle, see Priest et al. 1989). So it is unlikely that any account that allows this kind of simple truth relativization will be used by an opponent of Williamson.

Another point for the simplicity of truth is that in philosophical logic it is a much more basic concept than knowledge. Knowledge is usually introduced as an operator, and doing so creates intensional or opaque contexts. If we assume our speakers and audiences share a basic level of rationality, and we also assume that philosophical logic is a reasonably good model of that rationality, then truth is the simpler concept since logic tells us that an understanding of truth is necessary and antecedent to argumentative reasoning, unlike knowledge which creates situations where substitution of co-referential expressions does not necessarily preserve truth. Further, unlike knowledge, truth does not suffer from Gettier cases or the cultural variation effects found by experimental philosophers like Weinberg, Stich, and Nichols. What is simpler is also perhaps more likely to fit into an evolutionary picture of the development of language and interpretive strategies.

This focus on simplicity might seem strange; after all, Williamson might be providing a more complicated albeit more accurate account, and surely that would be relevant. And in some cases we do seem to attribute knowledge (and not just truth) when we interpret someone. Williamson argues that causal history is the connection between subject and object which opens the channel to knowledge. Whether something is true or false does not matter—what matters is whether there is a causal connection between the subject and some scenario that justifies their knowledge claims. This is appealing, but although he is not credited, Davidson also knew such causal history would be necessary. In fact, it is part of what his charity demands. He says, "[W]e interpret so as to make an agent as intelligible as possible ... finding him right means identifying the causes with the objects of his beliefs, giving special weight to the simplest cases, and countenancing error where it can be best explained" (2001b:152). It is a subtler principle than Williamson gives him credit for, as the causal history requirement falls right out of the rationality constraints. You would not ascribe an object as the source of someone's belief if they had never had any contact with it. And you wouldn't ascribe quantum physical knowledge to people in the Stone Age, either. For much the same reasons as Williamson, then, Davidson's principle explains why we ascribe what we do as the cause or content of people's beliefs or utterances, only if they have had relevant causal contact with them.

Finally, for Williamson, ascribing knowledge to a person means that such a person must have been in the requisite position to know. This means that the proposition known refers to a state of affairs that was actually happening, existing, or was in whatever sense, *actual* at the time of utterance. In other words, the proposition known is also *true*, since it matches the world. This means that whenever we ascribe knowledge we are also ascribing truth. So again, Williamson was right to focus on the causal connection, but not about truth being less desirable for charity than knowledge.

Williamson has a second and independent worry: should we agree with Davidson in thinking that the principle of charity is a *maximizing* process? Since our belief set is infinite (that is, all the beliefs that can be ascribed to any one of us at any time is infinite, because of recursion), and if we think of maximization as a simple, linear process, Williamson is surely right when he objects that *maximizing* truth is impossible. How do you maximize the amount of anything in an infinite set? An answer is given by Henry Jackman (2003). He argues that charity should be seen as applying only to the *weighted sum* of a speaker's *commitments*. You can think of the weighing function as analogous to the way we place different values on questions when devising a test. It need not be esoteric. And those beliefs to which we are committed form a set that is not infinite, because it contains only the beliefs to which we would be disposed to assent if queried. (It also contains our implicit presuppositions and assumptions, but these are included insofar as they can be clearly inferred from our actions, so the set remains finite). The heaviest (or core) commitments are those we would fight the hardest to retain in cases of conflict.

To understand the charity we confer to others, Jackman examines the way we interpret ourselves in cases where core commitments conflict. If, in Quinean fashion, we always save those beliefs we treasure the most, then in cases where some core commitments conflict, we will eliminate beliefs on a case-by-case basis by *maximization*. We do this depending on the level of importance we assign to our commitments. Jackman argues that such a process would naturally go hand in hand with the way we interpret others. Consider a situation in which you take a sip of what you believe is a mug of hot chocolate, and find that it tastes exactly like tea. Now you have a conflict between your belief that your cup contains hot chocolate, your belief that it contains tea, and your belief that the same cup cannot contain tea and hot chocolate at the same time. This conflict may be dealt with in various ways, but it is much more likely that you will give up the belief, for example, that your drink is hot chocolate, than your belief in the law of non-contradiction, or your belief that hot chocolate does not turn into tea without some serious chemical tampering. This is a simple example where maximization is used, to show that such a process is uncontentious as far as the maximization component is concerned.

If the application of Jackman's idea to this context is correct, this adds to the above defense of Davidson's principle of charity. Namely, if the object of our maximization is the weighted sum of commitments held by the speaker, then having a causal history with the cause of the belief or utterance will certainly make some beliefs *heavier* than others in meaning ascriptions. This helps to show that being in a position to know will be important for the way that we maximize truth, without showing that knowledge is what should be maximized. Being in a position to know is important for the practice of interpretation; it figures into the way we do it.

If the process of maximizing truth applies to the weighted sum of a speaker's commitments, and if we are also trying to minimize the amount of unexplained error, then we will usually be maximizing knowledge as well. Especially if Jackman is correct that "Capturing the interpretee's perspective on the world ... involves trying to understand the interpretee as she would, ideally, understand herself" (2003:161), because figuring out which beliefs the interpretee weighs the heaviest, will likely yield the beliefs that the interpretee feels she *knows*. This account is consistent with the results of psychological studies in empathy, which show that those who attempt to think like others really do understand them better (see Ickes 2003, Stueber 2006), and it also coheres with studies that show sociopaths have difficulty communicating because their ability to see things as others do is reduced (see Baron-Cohen 2011, Meffert et al. 2013, Skeem et al. 2011).

I do not deny that knowledge maximization is part of linguistic interpretation. But the simplicity and fundamentality of truth for interpretation suggests at least a logical and temporal order to the way we apply the principle of charity. First, we ascribe rationality, then truth, and *then* knowledge. These three levels will be separated in time because the psychological constraints that apply to each are different in terms of their respective strengths, and because there are more or less ways to complete each operation. There are very few ways to satisfy the rationality constraint, but there are more options in satisfying the truth constraint, and even more in maximizing knowledge. Since more and more conscious thought will be necessary to complete the latter requirements, they should take longer to complete, hence the chronological nature of the principle of charity. This demands empirical testing. For now, however, I will merely add a few more theoretical considerations.

Let us consider again the urgency of each type of constraint, beginning with rationality. Davidson says, "We have no choice ... but to read our own logic into the thoughts of a speaker" (2001b:149). If I had to determine consciously whether a speaker was following rules of logic that were relevantly similar to my own, I would never be able to communicate with anyone. If this were the case, it seems unlikely that language would have developed in the first place. Turning to truth, Jackman says that when we interpret ourselves we must assume the general truth of our weighed set of commitments. To see this, notice that we generally see little difference between our beliefs about the world and the beliefs that we hold true.

We could not interpret ourselves if we needed to determine the overall truth of our beliefs first. Instead, we merely assume they are true. However, if pressed we admit the unlikelihood that all of our beliefs are true, and we do expect to find some contradiction between them (2003:160). To extend this to our interpretation of others, not only will we generally assume the truth of most of our own beliefs, but we must assume the general truthfulness of someone else's beliefs, because again, if they were in massive error (if most of what they believed was false) they would not make any sense to us. It is easy to imagine *talking* to someone who thought up was down and alive was dead and real was fake and trees were lampshades, but it is very difficult to imagine *understanding* them. In this way, we must attribute truth and rationality to a speaker to understand them.

However, do we *need* to attribute knowledge to a speaker? Imagine someone who had mostly true but unjustified beliefs because they were raised by parents who were experts in creating Gettier cases. We would still easily understand the meaning of his or her words, since they would be talking about the same objects, events and relations with which we are familiar. However, we should not attribute to them knowledge of what they say. And this is the point. Williamson is right that we should take casual histories into account when we interpret others, he is wrong when he says that we should reject truth maximization in favour of knowledge maximization. Let me finish by presenting a case where ascribing knowledge leads to undesirable results.

Imagine you are certain that a mobster has committed murder. He told you he was going to kill Rocco, and shortly after the time specified, the police find Rocco murdered in the manner antecedently specified to you by the mobster. The mobster gloats and reveals that he knows specifics of the crime scene to which no one besides the police and the killer had access. You call the police and he is arrested. The police agree that he is guilty. Yet, there is not enough evidence to put him away (it is your word against his, he has a good lawyer and his alibi is carefully worked out). Suppose you say something true when you say, "That man is guilty." This, however, is not something that you can provide complete justification for, either to a jury of your peers in a court of law, or with absolute certainty to yourself. And this is the problem with knowledge maximization as a part of applying charity: knowledge is intimately linked to justification, which is not something we can *maximize*.

In fact, maximizing justification would be dangerous. It might invite overconfidence in ourselves, and lead us to expect radicalism or fanaticism in others. Most of our everyday beliefs, even the true ones, simply are not justified in any robust, skepticism-defeating sense. Williamson could reply that justification is not linked to knowledge this intimately, but I think his use of "positions to know" shows that it is. These positions are meant to justify knowledge ascriptions to a third party, but if we can interpret ourselves, and if knowledge is recursive, then you may only know that you know when you know you are in the requisite position to know, that is, when you know you have enjoyed the right kind of causal connection with the object of your knowledge. That is, when you are justified.

When we interpret a speaker, we apply the principle of charity and maximize the truth of their beliefs, and perhaps their knowledge as well. But without educated guesses concerning what our speaker means, we have nothing on which to work. Such guesses are a necessary first step, although this is not something Davidson focused on. These "guesses" fit the description of "intuition" given by experimental philosophers. That is, they are not themselves justified by anything, and we do not feel any need to justify them; they are not quite beliefs, and they appear seemingly out of nowhere. Finally, the outcomes of interpretation are counterfactually dependent on them. And yet, as we have seen, it is not important if these guesses are good or bad, since the constraints involved in applying the principle of charity are so strong that we are quickly forced from our starting point to converge on a better interpretation.

But we do not always stop when we have interpreted our speaker. Occasionally we ask if that speaker is using his or her terms according to the norms that he or she upholds. This is far more difficult than simply understanding someone's words, and there is evidence that this skill only appears later in life. According to Gilbert & Reiner (2000:276), students around 9 years of age attribute the same meaning to the phrases "theories which explain phenomena" and "the behaviour of phenomena." At ages of 12-16 years, students can see the difference between true and false explanations, but not until they are about 16 do they fully appreciate that knowledge claims are mostly conjectural. The ability to distinguish between what someone says and what they should say, is hard won. How do students decide what a concept should mean? As we saw above, students often invent imaginary scenarios to test their concepts and inter-conceptual relations. So again, guesses (or intuitions) are a necessary first step in the act of determining what a person *should* mean as opposed to what they do mean. And those intuitions are the material on which to run the method; they do not bear all of the epistemological weight of the method's output.

Let us now turn back to conceptual analysis and see how the principle of charity can be used to defend the charge from experimental philosophy.

Remember there are several aims of philosophical conceptual analysis: specifying and exploring the intension and extension of a concept, its relation to other concepts, and its normative profile. Just as in linguistic interpretation, which has similar goals, charity and intuition are called for in all cases. To determine the extension of a concept we often begin by considering its explicit or implicit definition in the hands of certain individuals (for example, *knowledge* for Plato or Descartes). We try to adopt these definitions ourselves, and assuming our own standards of rationality, try to maximize the truth of our beliefs. We invent imaginary scenarios in which to test the consistency of those beliefs. Once we have a handle on the problems and possible relations between this concept and others, we try to *improve* the concept. The point is that in many of the stages of this process, intuitions are involved as raw materials, which do not need to be accurate or true or justified. In this sense, intuitions in conceptual analysis function like scientific hypotheses. And so, only if the scientific method is a bad one, is philosophical conceptual analysis unreliable in principle.

One reply to this line of reasoning is the following. My argument attempts to justify *one* use of intuition in conceptual analysis. But there are others that are used as evidence, and it is *those* which are the focus of the Weinberg, Nichols and Stich school of experimental philosophy. For example, if you give me a counterexample to my proposed definition for *justice*, I might have an intuition that your counterexample is a good one, that indeed it disproves my definition. This sort of intuition is not a preliminary guess used to begin the process of conceptual analysis. Rather, it is the *source of justification* for this or that conceptual revision.

However, this type of intuition can also be treated as a provisional hypothesis that should be tested. It is nothing but another hypothesis, although it is accompanied with a strong emotional response. But it is not the response that justifies the eventual outcome of the test. Of course, some provisional hypotheses are more attractive, and upon hearing them we think "Yes! That must be the case!" however they later prove false. The reason they seem so attractive is perhaps because they highlight a new perceived coherence between what we have, and what we want (see Thagard & Stewart 2011).

Another objection is that by portraying conceptual analysis as linguistic interpretation, I have likened it once again to reflective equilibrium, since the focus here has been on making others and ourselves rational, consistent, true, and so on. However, applying the principle of charity calls for both coherence *and* correspondence. Our words have no meaning without interaction with the world and with others, which is why causal connection is one of the constraints in the principle of charity.

There is another important difference between interpretation, conceptual analysis and the scientific method on the one hand, and reflective equilibrium on the other. Reflective equilibrium is a method that has as its goal a very specific end state, and there are rules which we use to proceed to that state given the current state. Namely, proceed in a stepwise manner evaluating the system and its consequences with our intuitions until we achieve coherence. This is not the case with the scientific method or, in my view, conceptual analysis or linguistic interpretation. In general, science progresses from vague to specific, from less precise to more precise, from less mathematical to more mathematical. But these general trends are violated all the time, especially during scientific revolutions. And while many philosophers talk meaningfully about the "end of science", it is not such an end point that drives today's scientific investigations. It is local goals. And the same goes for conceptual analysis. We would like, we suppose, a perfectly clear definition of all human concepts, but that is not what motivates us in our quest to understand *knowledge* and *justice*. We have subsidiary aims which are more important. And even concerning individual concepts, we care more about finding a workable definition that is enlightening and useful than we do about the one true definition. I think this is because we recognize that concepts will and should change over time. And the same is true of linguistic interpretation. We would like to have a complete theory of meaning for a speaker, but we never actually try to find one. We use whatever methods we have until we reach a satisfactory understanding of our speaker's utterances. Perhaps we do not try to gain a complete theory of meaning because we know that what a speaker means will change over time, and so a complete theory of meaning is not a realistic end point for us. In each of science, conceptual analysis and linguistic interpretation, we do not contextualize our actions with reference to an end point, and we do not follow a simple strategy to get there. So with respect to these important points, conceptual analysis has not been reduced to reflective equilibrium.

The natural question to ask at this point is: well then, what *are* the sources of evidence for conceptual analysis? There is probably no simple answer to this, because a reliable method does not guarantee knowledge. A valid argument is not necessarily a sound one. Cognitive scientists who study conceptual change focus on the development of categorization schemas in children, undergraduates, scientists, and so on, mapping out complex webs of conceptual connections and simulating them in computers. But the exact way in which experience plays a role in learning and (re)evaluating concepts is not yet known, and this collection is a testament to how complex the problem is. What is necessary is some middle ground between the grand philosophical pictures (rationalism, empiricism, naturalism) of the relation between experience and knowledge, and the work of cognitive scientists and linguists.

To conclude: what I have tried to achieve in this paper is not a direct epistemological justification of the output of conceptual analysis, but merely to provide reasons to believe that the method of conceptual analysis is reliable. If we accept the practices of experimental science and everyday linguistic interpretation, we should also accept the method of conceptual analysis.

References

Ackermann, R. 1985. *Data, Instruments and Theory.* Princeton, N.J.: Princeton University Press.

Alexander, J., Mallon, R. & Weinberg, J. 2010. Accentuate the Negative. *Review of Philosophy and Psychology* 1: 297–314.

Baron-Cohen, S. 2011. *Zero Degrees of Empathy: A New Theory of Human Cruelty.* London: Penguin.

Batens, D. & Van Bendegem, J.P. (eds.) 1988. *Theory and Experiment.* Dordrecht: Reidel.

Bogen, J. & Woodward, J. 1988. Saving the Phenomena. *The Philosophical Review* 97: 303–352.

Cartwright, N. 1983. *How the Laws of Physics Lie.* Oxford: Oxford University Press.

Chang, H. 2004. *Inventing Temperature: Measurement and Scientific Progress.* Oxford: Oxford University Press.

References

Clement, J. 2009. Analogy Reasoning via Imagery: The Role of Transformations and Simulations. In B. Kokinov, K. Holyoak, & D. Gentner (eds.). *New Frontiers in Analogy Research*. New Bulgarian University Press.

Cohnitz, D. 2003. Modal Skepticism. Philosophical Thought Experiments and Modal Epistemology. In F. Stadler (ed.). *The Vienna Circle and Logical Empiricism: Re-Evaluation and Future Perspectives*. Dordrecht: Kluwer.

Cohnitz, D. & Häggqvist, S. 2009. The Role of Intuitions in Philosophy. *Studia Philosophica Estonia* 2.2: 1–14.

Collins, H. & Pinch, T. 1993. *The Golem: What Everyone Should Know About Science*. Cambridge: Cambridge University Press.

Cook, C., Goodman, N. D., & Schulz, L. E. 2011. Where Science Starts: Spontaneous Experiments in Preschoolers' Exploratory Play. *Cognition* 120: 341–349.

Davidson, D. 2001a. *Inquiries into Truth and Interpretation*. Oxford: Clarendon Press.

Davidson, D. 2001b. *Subjective, Intersubjective, Objective*. Oxford: Clarendon Press.

Davidson, D. 2005. *Truth, Language and History*. Oxford: Clarendon Press.

DePaul, M. & Ramsey, W. (eds.) 1998. *Rethinking Intuition: The Psychology of Intuition and its Role in Philosophical Inquiry*. New York: Rowman & Littlefield.

Fehige, Y. & Stuart, M. 2014. On the Origins of the Philosophy of Thought Experiments: The Forerun. *Perspectives on Science* 22: 179–220.

Franklin, A. 1986. *The Neglect of Experiment*. Cambridge: Cambridge University Press.

Franklin, A. 1990. *Experiment, Right or Wrong*. Cambridge: Cambridge University Press.

Franklin, A. 2002. *Selectivity and Discord: Two Problems of Experiment*. Pittsburgh: University of Pittsburgh Press.

Galison, P. 1987. *How Experiments End*. Chicago: University of Chicago Press.

Galison, P. 1997. *Image and Logic*. Chicago: University of Chicago Press.

Gilbert, J. & Reiner, M. 2000. Thought Experiments in Science Education: Potential and Current Realization. *International Journal of Science Education* 22: 265–283.

Goldman, A. 1986. *Epistemology and Cognition*. Cambridge: Harvard University Press.

Gooding, D. 1990. *Experiment and the Making of Meaning*. Dordrecht: Kluwer Academic Publishers.

Gooding, D., Pinch, T. & Schaffer, S. (eds.) 1989. *The Uses of Experiment.* Cambridge: Cambridge University Press.

Goodman, N. 1955. *Fact, Fiction, and Forecast,* Cambridge, MA: Harvard University Press.

Hacking, I. 1983. *Representing and Intervening.* Cambridge: Cambridge University Press.

Häggqvist, S. 1996. *Thought Experiments in Philosophy,* Stockholm: Almqvist & Wiksell International.

Ickes, W. 2003. *Everyday Mindreading.* New York. Prometheus Books.

Jacob, F. 2001. Imagination in Art and Science. *The Kenyon Review* 23: 113–121.

Jackman, H. 2003. Charity, Self Interpretation, and Belief. *Journal of Philosophical Research.* 28: 145–170.

Kosem, S.D., & Özdemir, Ö. F. 2014. The Nature and Function of Thought Experiments in Solving Conceptual Problems. *Science and Education* 23: 865–895.

Knobe, J. & Nichols, S. 2008. An Experimental Philosophy Manifesto. In J. Knobe & S. Nichols (eds.). *Experimental Philosophy.* New York: Oxford University Press.

Lakatos, I. 1976. *Proofs and Refutations.* Cambridge: Cambridge University Press.

Latour, B. & Woolgar, S. 1986. *Laboratory Life: The Construction of Scientific Facts.* Princeton: Princeton University Press.

Lauden, L. 1973. Peirce and the Trivialization of the Self-Correcting Thesis. In R. N Giere & R. Westfall (eds.). *Foundations of Scientific Method: The Nineteenth Century.* Bloomington: Indiana Press.

Machery, E., Mallon, R., Nichols, S., & Stich, S. 2004. Semantics, Cross-Cultural Style. *Cognition* 92: B1–B12.

Mallon, R., Machery, E., Nichols, S. & Stich, S. 2009. Against Arguments from Reference. *Philosophy and Phenomenological Research* 79: 332–356.

Margolis, E. & Lawrence, S. 1999. *Concepts: Core Readings.* London: MIT Press.

Meffert, H. Gazzola, V., den Boer, J. A., Bartels, A. A. J. & Keysers, C. 2013. Reduced Spontaneous but Relatively Normal Deliberate Vicarious Representations in Psychopathy. *Brain* 136: 2550–2562.

Peirce, C. S. 1898/1934. The First Rule of Logic. In C. Hartshorne & P. Weiss (eds.). *Collected Papers of Charles Sanders Peirce* vol. 5. Cambridge: Harvard University Press.

Pickering, A. 1995. *The Mangle of Practice.* Chicago: University of Chicago Press.

References

Pinch, T. 1986. *Confronting Nature*. Dordrecht: Reidel.

Priest, G., Routley, R., & Norman, J. (eds.) 1989. *Paraconsistent Logic: Essays on the Inconsistent*, München: Philosophia Verlag.

Prinz, J. 2002. *Furnishing the Mind: Concepts and their Perceptual Basis*. Cambridge: MIT Press.

Reiner, M. & Burko, L. 2003. On the Limitations of Thought Experiments in Physics and the Consequences for Physics Education. *Science and Education* 13: 365–385.

Reiner, M. & Gilbert, J. 2004. The Symbiotic Roles of Empirical Experimentation and Thought Experimentation in the Learning of Physics. *International Journal of Science Education* 26: 1819–1834.

Skeem, J. L., Polaschek, D. L. L., Patrick, C. J. & Lilienfeld, S. O. 2011. Psychopathic Personality: Bridging the Gap Between Scientific Evidence and Public Policy. *Psychological Science in the Public Interest* 12: 92–162.

Sorensen, R. 1992. *Thought Experiments*. Oxford: Oxford University Press.

Stephens, L. A., & Clement, J. 2006. Designing Classroom Thought Experiments: What we Can Learn from Imagery Indicators and Expert Protocols. *Proceedings of the 2006 Annual Meeting of the National Association for Research in Science Teaching*, San Francisco.

Stuart, M. 2014. Cognitive Science and Thought Experiments: A Refutation of Paul Thagard's Skepticism. *Perspectives on Science* 22: 264–287.

Stuart, M. (forthcoming). Imagination: A *Sine Qua Non* of Science. *Croatian Journal of Philosophy*.

Stueber, K. 2006. *Rediscovering Empathy: Agency, Folk Psychology, and the Human Sciences*. Cambridge: MIT Press.

Swain, S., Alexander, J. & Weinberg, J. 2008. The Instability of Philosophical Intuitions: Running Hot and Cold on Truetemp. *Philosophy and Phenomenological Research* 76: 138–155.

Thagard, P. 2014. Thought Experiments Considered Harmful. *Perspectives on Science* 22: 288–305.

Thagard, P. & Stewart, T. 2011. The Aha! Experience: Creativity Through Emergent Binding in Neural Networks. *Cognitive Science* 35: 1–33.

Velentzas, A. & Halkia, K. 2013. From Earth to Heaven: Using 'Newton's Cannon' Thought Experiment for Teaching Satellite Physics. *Science and Education* 22: 2621–2640.

Weinberg, J., Nichols, S. & Stich, S. 2001. Normativity and Epistemic Intuitions. *Philosophical Topics.* 29: 429–460.

Weinberg, J., Crowley, J., Gonnerman, C., Swain, S., & Vandewalke, I. 2006. Intuition & Calibration. *Essays in Philosophy* 13: 256–283.

Williamson, T. 2004. Philosophical Intuitions and Scepticism about Judgment. *Dialectica* 58: 109–153.

Author

Michael T. Stuart
Institute for the History and Philosophy of Science and Technology
University of Toronto

Analyzing Concepts in Action-Frames

Gottfried Vosgerau, Tim Seuchter & Wiebke Petersen

Abstract

In this paper, we want to argue for a frame-based analysis of action-related concepts as a means for understanding the thesis of grounded cognition, i. e. the thesis that concepts are grounded in sensorimotor processes. We will give an overview of frame analysis and specify frames for action-related concepts. We will then argue for the employment of the frame-based analysis-method and show why this method of analysis has clear advantages over other methods of analysis. The advantages of frames especially become apparent in the capability to specify sensorimotor parts of a concept, as well as in highlighting abstraction mechanisms within concepts. The representation of modal attributes without introducing modal operators is another specific advantage of frames over other formats of representation.

1 Introduction

The research concerning the problem of grounding language in action so far is mostly empirical. The field is dominated by cognitive psychology and neuroscience, where behavioral and neurological measures are used to relate the possession and processing of conceptual knowledge to sensorimotor processes. The work of Pulvermüller (2005) or Glenberg & Kaschak (2002), just to name two, clearly showed that there is a connection between concept processing and motor-processes. However, the theoretical framework of grounded cognition is not yet spelled out in detail, so it remains still an open question of what it exactly means for concepts to be grounded in action.

In this paper we will present and discuss a tool for adequately analyzing concepts. This special kind of concept analysis will then provide a better understanding of what it means for a concept to be grounded in sensorimotor processes. The idea is, in short, to analyze action-related concepts within frames. The frame theory in question was originally developed by Barsalou (1992) as a theory of a general format of concept representation; the frame theory underlying this paper is a specified and refined modification of Barsalou's proposal. According to this modification, frames are understood as recursive attribute-value structures. Frames have a lot of advantages over other forms of representing concepts, but due to brevity, we will focus on one special feature of frames concerning action-related concepts: The decomposition of action-related concepts via frame-analysis is able to specify motor-values within these concepts. If motor-values can be analyzed as very basic values in the frame of a certain concept, the conclusion clearly is that this concept is grounded in motor processes. Concepts that do not have motor values as very basic values can hardly be grounded in the relevant sense.

In the following, we will give examples of frames and the idea of special motor values, and we will then show why frames have clear advantages over other formats of representation e. g. first-order predicate logics. First of all, however, we will introduce the strategy of frame analysis.

2 Concepts and frames

Barsalou (1992) proposes that the content of concepts (understood as mental entities as opposed to linguistic entities) can be naturally accounted for in terms of frames. Frames as recursive attribute-value structures have been widely used as a general format for knowledge representation, e. g. for capturing linguistic knowledge (Fillmore 1970) or situational knowledge (Minsky 1974). Minsky (1974:1) regards a frame as a "data-structure for representing a stereotyped situation [...]. Once a frame is proposed to represent a situation, a matching process tries to assign values to each frame's terminals, consistent with the markers [restricting the admissible values] at each place." Minsky's aim is to simulate this cognitive process in applications of artificial intelligence. Like Minsky, most approaches consider a frame as a fixed flat set of attributes or slots the values of which get filled by the situation, the linguistic context or whatsoever. By sticking to a fixed set of attributes, those frames essentially reduce to feature lists and categorization to value pattern recognition (1992:23). In contrast, Barsalou (1992:21) argues in favor of frames as "dynamic relational structures whose form is flexible and context dependent". He presents psychological evidence for attribute-value structures de-

Analyzing Concepts

rived from behavioral animal studies. These studies indicate that animals encode stimulus information as attribute values and not as independent features. Furthermore, he gives empirical evidence for the importance of conceptual relations in human cognition. Here we will briefly sketch our frame account which builds on Barsalou's flexible cognitive approach, but provides it with a rigid formal foundation.

The attributes in a concept frame are the general properties or aspects by which the respective concept is described (e.g. SHAPE, LOCATION).[1] Their values are concrete or underspecified specifications (e. g., [SHAPE: *round*], [LOCATION: *forest*]). The attribute values can themselves be complex frames and thus described by additional attributes. For example the value *forest* of the attribute LOCATION can be further specified by attributes like SIZE or TREE SPECIES. Due to their recursivity, frames are flexible enough to represent information of any desired grade of detail. We assume that attributes in frames assign unique values to objects and thus describe functional relations. Formally, frames can be represented by connected directed graphs where the arcs correspond to attributes. As attributes are functions, no node may have two equally labeled outgoing arcs. The nodes may be labeled by types which restrict the attribute domains and ranges, i. e. the set of objects for which an attribute is adequate and the set of values an attribute can take. Figure 1 shows a simplified frame of the concept 'round shelter in an oak forest'.

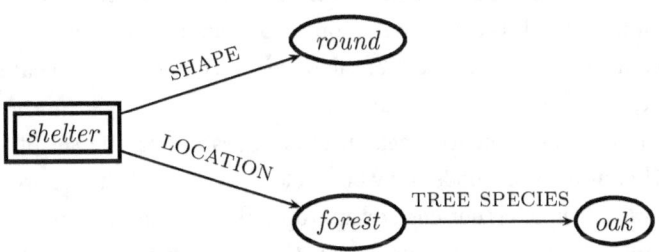

Figure 1: Frame of the concept 'round shelter in an oak forest'

Figure 1 shows two additional notational devices which we use in our graph representations of frames: First, the double border at the *shelter* node marks it as the central node of the frame; it indicates that the graph represents a frame

---

[1] Throughout this paper attributes are typeset in capitals and their values in italics.

about shelters. Second, by using a rectangular node for the central *shelter* node, we identify the whole frame as a concept or category frame which corresponds to a 1-place predicate the argument of which is represented by the shelter node. A round central node would indicate instead that it is a frame of a not further specified category member of the category 'round shelter in an oak forest'. As types correspond to 1-place predicates and attributes to functions, the information modeled in the frame can be expressed in the logical formula:

$$\lambda x.shelter(x) \wedge round(\text{SHAPE}(x)) \wedge forest(\text{LOCATION}(x))$$
$$\wedge\, oak(\text{TREE SPECIES}(\text{LOCATION}(x)))$$

In contrast to other frame theories, our frames are capable of representing not only sortal concepts like 'shelter', which denote classical categories, but also relational ones like 'sibling'or 'mother' (Petersen 2007/2015); the referents of the latter concepts are given by a relation to a possessor ('sibling of', 'mother of'). Frames of relational concepts differ from frames of sortal concepts in that they have an additional rectangular node for the possessor argument. Figure 2 shows the frame for the sibling concept. It consists of three nodes, one for the sibling itself (rectangular, double border), one for the person it is the sibling of (rectangular, single border) and one for the mother of both (round). The relation between the two persons is constituted by the fact that they both have the same mother.[2] This is modeled by the single node to which the two MOTHER-arcs point. Note that in contrast to classical frame accounts our approach does not presuppose that the central node of a frame, i. e. the node which determines what is denoted by a frame, is a root node of the frame graph.[3]

An adequate frame theory needs means of restricting the set of admissible frames. Therefore, frame nodes may be labeled by types. The types are ordered in a type hierarchy which is enriched by appropriateness conditions which constrain the domain and range of attributes. Thus the type signature tells which type of entities can have a certain attribute and of which type the values of each attribute are. Thus we can infer the type of a nodes from the connecting attribute, unless it

---

[2] Note that all frames in this paper are severely simplified. For example, the frame in figure 2 models the sibling concept as being purely determined by the mother relation, leaving aside fathers or socially established family relations.

[3] A root of a directed graph is a node from which all other nodes can be reached via paths of directed arcs.

Analyzing Concepts

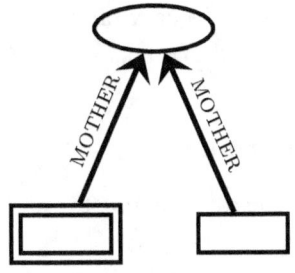

Figure 2: Frame for the concept 'sibling'

is further restricted by other constraints in a particular frame. For example, if a type signature specifies that the domain of the attribute MOTHER is *person* and that its range is *woman*, then the information modeled by the frame in figure 2 can be expressed by

$$\lambda y \lambda x. \text{MOTHER}(x) = \text{MOTHER}(y) \land person(x)$$
$$\land\, person(y) \land woman(\text{MOTHER}(x))$$

In contrast to figure 2, figure 1 shows an example of a frame in which the type labels at the nodes effectively restrict the attribute domains and ranges. For instance LOCATION is a very general attribute which applies to all kind of physical objects (not only to shelters) and which takes all kinds of locations as values (not only forests). The formal details of our frame account can be found in Petersen (2007/2015) and Petersen & Osswald (2014).

Although the informational content of a frame can be expressed in classical logical formulas, it is more natural to assume that concepts are mentally stored in terms of frames than in terms of formulas. As Barsalou (1992) points out, there is empirical evidence for attribute-value sets and relations in cognition. In frames, concepts remain units although they may be highly structured. This unity is concealed in logical formulas by multiple occurring variables. Within frame theory we are not forced to stipulate a fixed arity for each predicate as in predicate logic where predicates are constants. Finally, due to the non-linear structure of frames, one is not required to stipulate an order on the arguments. Rather, substructures can be addressed via labeled symbols instead of ordered argument positions which is cognitively more adequate. By using oscillatory neural networks as a biologically motivated model, Petersen & Werning (2007) give evidence for the cognitive adequacy of our frame model and shows how frames might be implemented in the cortex.

3 Motor processes in frames

This framework can now be used to address the question of how the nature of grounded concepts can be specified.

We will introduce some examples of concepts which explicitly involve action and show how action-involvement as a property of a concept can be defined in frames. Because these concepts have a quite simple structure, they serve as an ideal starting point. In the next step, the framework will be generalized to cover other types of (and especially linguistically expressible) concepts.

As we have seen above, frames are characterized by recursive attribute-value structures. Attributes are taken to assign unique values to objects. The values of our interest here are motor-values. They are understood as explicitly representing a movement or a set of movements within a frame. So, the values in these action frames are really parameters that are used in movement control, and not mere numbers or other kinds of abstract values.

Let us start with a simple example: Ants are dynamically representing the location of their nest in terms of the angle to the sun in which the ant has to walk and the number of steps it has to make (Gallistel 1993, Wittlinger et al. 2006). A frame for the ant's representation of the location of the nest is shown in figure 3.

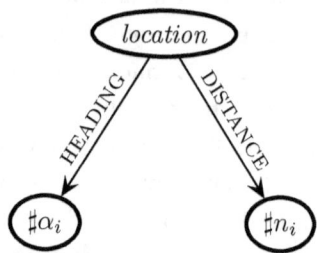

Figure 3: Frame for an ant's representation of the location of the nest

What is crucial here is the meaning of the two values in the lower nodes. Although the graphic shows number variables, the values in the nodes represent

Analyzing Concepts

specific motor-parameters, in this case the angle the ant has to turn and the number of steps it has to make.[4] As ants are generally held to be unable to count, for ants have no concept of numbers as numbers, those values are simply movements the ant can make. Of course, the ant "knows" how many steps it takes to return to the nest, but it does not "know" it in terms of numbers (Franks et al. 2006). One would be inclined to say that a specific motor-program is running that determines how long and in which direction the ant has to travel to reach the nest. But the ant is not just unable to count, it is also unable to represent these movements as a property of the nest, so we would not want to speak of the ant representing various properties of the nest, namely the heading and the distance (Vosgerau 2007). Rather, it is a good example of a movement representation.

As our interest is in grounded concepts, we need to give an example of a conceptual representation which implies action in the above sense. To stick with the example, a frame thus characterized is shown in figure 4.

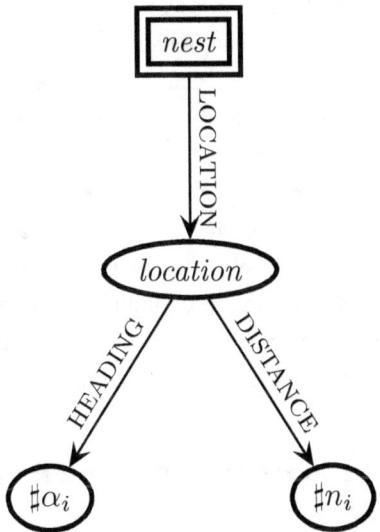

Figure 4: Frame for a conceptual representation of the location of the nest

---

[4] In the current paper, the dynamic changes of the motor values which occur while actual moving are not in focus. These changes could be modeled as dynamic updates of event frames in a multi-layered architecture as proposed by Naumann (2012).

Here, the location of the nest is represented as a property of an object, namely the nest. Thus, the representation can in principle be used to represent very different locations of different objects. Technically, this is done by exchanging the specific value of the central node to denote another object. In this sense, this representation can be said to be conceptual: One and the same property can be ascribed to different objects (Newen & Bartels 2007), and we can clearly analyze one part of the frame to stand for an object (the central node) and another part to stand for a property (the rest of the frame standing for the property of being located at this-and-that point) (Vosgerau 2008).

What we have here is a tool for describing the internal structure of concepts. A concept is constituted by a central node to which properties are assigned by different attributes which assign values. These values, as we have shown, can be motor-processes, in that they represent movements.

The next question obviously has to address the motor-values. What are the constraints to represent motor processes?

Every concept can be analyzed and decomposed. This process of analysis will at one point or another come to a basal level. Basal-level properties are reflected in the end nodes of a concept-frame. One way of dealing with motor processes in concepts is to define them as basal-level-values and to put them in the end nodes of a frame. A concept which contains motor values as basal-level-values can then be said to be grounded in motor abilities. However, if a concept does not contain basal-level-values (i. e. it only contains values that can be further analyzed) or if it contains basal-level-values that are not motoric, then it cannot be characterized as being grounded in motor abilities. (It might still be the case that a concept is grounded in sensory processes if its basal-level-values are sensory values; however, this is not the focus of this paper.)

4 Significance of frames over other methods of analyzing concepts

The crucial point so far is that end-values in frames can be motor-parameters. This means that the same values can figure in motor-control mechanisms. This can be displayed most easily when motor processes are represented in frames as well. The possibility of analyzing motor processes (and the specific representations involved in them) in frames directly follows from the claim that frames

Analyzing Concepts

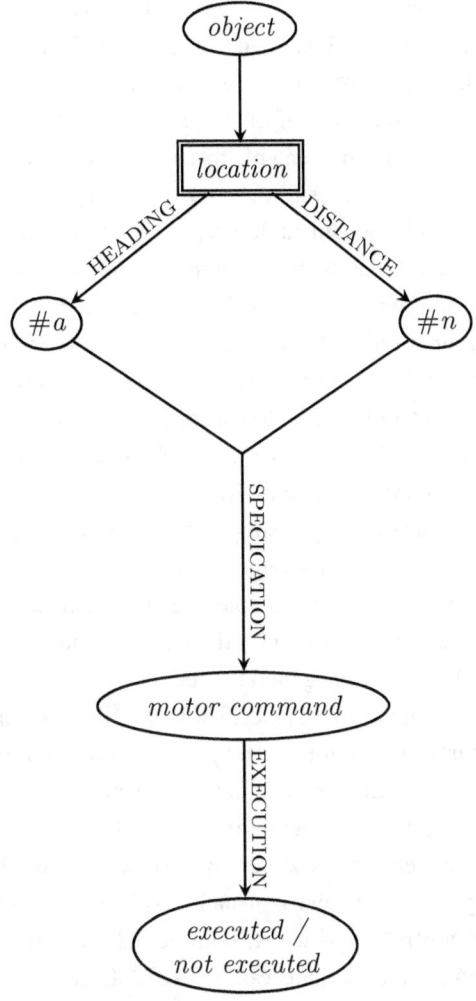

Figure 5: Frame for a specific reaching movement

constitute a general format of representation. In this sense, the frame of a specific reaching movement can be displayed like shown in figure 5.

According to this (simplified) analysis, the movement is specified by parameters which are in turn further specified and transformed into a specific motor command (cf. diagrams of motor control in Synofzik et al., 2008). This motor command can now be executed (i. e. be sent to the muscles) or not. In the latter case, the movement is merely "imagined" or "simulated" (although not necessarily consciously). The important point here is that the upper part of figure 5 has to be understood as a representation of the location of an object whereas the lower part is a representation of a movement; these parts in combination represent a location of an object as a movement (or in terms of a movement).

Usually, motor control mechanisms are depicted in flow-charts (e. g. in Synofzik et al., 2008). The general idea is that each movement (except for reflexes) starts with a "motor intention", which is a usually unconscious and non-conceptual part of motor control (as opposed to the "primary" intention; see Vosgerau & Synofzik, 2010). For example, if you are going to chop up an onion, your primary intention is to chop up the onion (completely). In contrast, for every cutting of a slice there is a separate motor intention to move the knife in a specific way. This motor intention is usually unconscious and is already in a motor format (something like to move the knife forward while pressing it down). However, the motor intention does not suffice for executing a movement, since several background conditions have to be taken into account. For example, the movement will depend on the actual posture (e. g. where your hand with the knife is) and the surroundings (e. g. where the onion is). Moreover, general facts about the kinematics of the own body have to be taken into account (specified in the "body schema"; see e. g. Vosgerau, 2009). The part of the motor control process, in which the exact parameters of the movement are specified, is often called "specification of movement". The output of the specification is then a motor command which can be sent to the effectors to elicit the movement. However, this last step is not obligatory—indeed, our ability to imagine movements is usually explained by the capacity to run through the motor control sequence without actually executing the movement. Thus, the motor control mechanisms can be used "off-line" to represent a movement rather than to elicit a movement. This aspect of frame analysis provides two main advantages over other formats of description (e. g. logical notations):

First, motor processes can be described as processes in which certain parameters play a role (e. g. motor intentions, posture). Therefore, the specific features of motor control mechanisms can be displayed as shown in figure 6, as opposed to logical notations in which there is no difference (explicitly) displayed between motor-attributes and conceptual attributes (they are, in logical terms, all predicates).

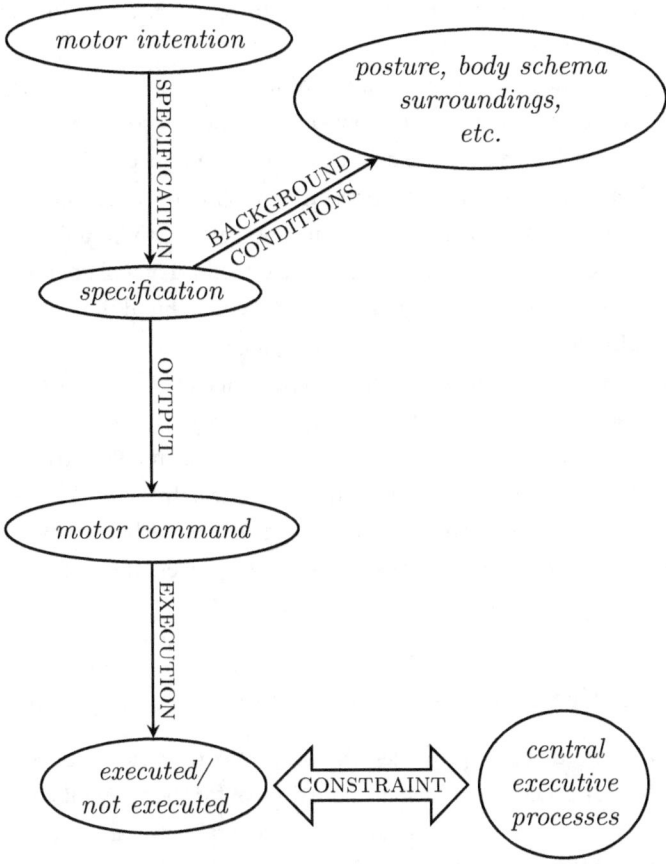

Figure 6: Frame description of motor control

This allows for a reformulation of the question of how grounded abstract concepts are in terms of frames: Are the values of the end-nodes of frames of concepts values that we can also find in sensorimotor processes? In other words: Concept-frames can be combined with motor-control-frames if and only if there is a certain overlap, i. e. if motor-values occur in the concept frame. This formulation of the thesis of grounded cognition directly shows the explanatory advantage of the thesis: It would explain why and how concepts can have a direct impact on our behavior. For example, the motor intentions in the example above (onion chopping) could be values that also occur in the concept frame for 'knife', since cutting is an affordance of knifes.

Second, the conceptual categorization of an object does, of course, not automatically lead to a behavior. The movement which is specified by the motor-values needs not be executed. Thus, entertaining a concept like 'knife' can involve the "activation" of a motor-representation without triggering the according movement (this is what Barsalou Barsalou, 1999 calls "simulation"). In this sense, frames can represent possibilities without introducing a modal operator: The possible movement is represented by motor values which build the basis for a motor command although the motor command is not executed. This fact makes the representation modal in the sense that it represents a merely possible movement and not an actual movement. The specific advantage of frames over other formats of representation is twofold: 1) we can represent modal attributes without introducing modal operators, and 2) there is a straightforward sense in which attribute values can be motor-parameters and not just arbitrary symbols which do not stand in any meaningful relation to motor processing (as it is the case for constants in predicate logic, for example).

5 Implications for the thesis of grounded cognition

According to the thesis of grounded cognition, the content of concepts is based on sensorimotor processes, which are constitutive for the relevant concept. What is to be analyzed to understand cognition in general is not mechanisms of computation and abstract symbol manipulation, but rather the relation between conceptualization and basal motor-processes. These motor processes therefore have to be somehow encoded in the concept, they have to be a part or a property of the concept. This view conforms with the fact that these encoded motor processes are not (necessarily) reflected in the verbal structure of the concept. However that holds as well for other functional and physical properties of a concept, which are not reflected in the word form in most cases: The word for the concept 'dog' does not reflect dog-properties nor does it refer to physical or functional properties of dogs (Glenberg & Kaschak 2002).

Decomposition of concepts via frame analysis is a way to get to a cognitively adequate account of the concept-structure, i. e. the properties assigned to objects by this concept. The most important point, however, is that frame analysis of concepts allows us to specifically define what being grounded in action means: If and only if the frame of a concept contains motor-values as base-level-values, it is grounded on motor abilities. Concepts that do not contain such values cannot be said to be grounded in action. Thus, frame analysis goes beyond the rather vague and unspecific claim that concepts are based on modal representations as opposed to abstract symbols (Barsalou 2008). It gives us a clear notion of being grounded which can be applied not only to concepts *tout court*, but also to parts of concepts. In this way, the "internal" structure of a concept can be taken into account, which leads to a more specific notion of groundedness that can come in well-defined degrees: The transition between grounded and abstract concepts is not a matter of on and off; rather, it is possible that a mid-level concept contains some grounded parts and at the same time already involves other non-grounded, abstract parts.

Weber & Vosgerau (2012) discuss different ways in which the (unspecific) thesis of grounded action cognition can be interpreted. They argue that three versions can be distinguished: The strong thesis basically collapses into the thesis that thoughts (and a fortiori concepts) are a kind of motor ability. The moderate thesis states that some concepts are constituted by motor processes but others not. The weak thesis amounts to the claim that some motor abilities are necessary to acquire certain concepts but can be lost after acquisition without damage to the concept (i.e. motor abilities are among the acquisition conditions for some concepts but they do not constitute them). In their paper they argue on theoretical and empirical grounds, that the moderate thesis is the most plausible one.

The problem with the strong thesis is present already at a theoretical level, since this thesis faces a serious threat of infinite regress (for details see Vosgerau & Newen, 2007). Moreover, the thesis is somewhat self-refuting: If it is true that all concepts are a kind of motor ability, then it cannot be said anymore that they are grounded in motor abilities.[5] Thus, the strong thesis has to be refuted. The weak thesis, on the other hand, can be rejected on the basis of results from empirical studies (see Weber & Vosgerau, 2012 for details).

Having rejected both the strong and the weak version, there still is evidence that at least some concepts are grounded in motor processes, and this exactly can

---

[5] This is, of course, not a counter-argument against the thesis that thoughts are motor processes. However, this thesis cannot be understood as a thesis of grounded cognition, and this is the important point here.

be shown in frames. Obviously, not every part of a frame for a concept is based on or related to motor-processes, but at least some parts of it should be interpreted as values for motor-processes. So it is empirical evidence on the one hand that advises for the rejection of both the strong versions of grounded cognition, but on the other hand, conceptual frame-analysis offers good reason to defend and even further refine the moderate version. As reasons for dismissal of a version of a thesis are not sufficient reasons for accepting another version, the contribution of frame-analysis can be seen in the light of giving independent motivations to support the moderate version as described above.

6 Development of concepts

The analysis of concepts in terms of frames yields a cognitively adequate representation of concepts. In particular, the sensorimotor grounding of concepts is represented in frames by introducing sensorimotor values. However, concepts apparently differ in degree of groundedness: There are a lot of concepts that are very unlikely to contain motor values (e.g. concepts like 'state', 'freedom', or 'kinship'). Thus, the question of how abstract concepts can develop on the basis of sensorimotor-grounded concepts has to be answered by theories of grounded cognition.

Again, frame analysis turns out to be a useful tool for this task. As shown above, frame analysis is apt to analyze simple representations as they occur in ants. These representations are grounded in the full sense and are not yet abstract enough to be called "concepts". Starting with such simple frames, we have shown that more and more abstract frames of concepts can be developed. First of all, other nodes are added in order to represent a certain property (e.g. the location) of an object as the property of the object. This concept is more abstract since it now allows the representation of one and the same property in different objects and the representation of different properties of the same object (Newen & Bartels 2007).

One possible next step is to abstract from the concrete values specifying a movement to more abstract forms of motor-representations specifying general schemata of movements. For example, the frame in figure 5 may be appropriate to display my representation of the location of a discussion partner in terms of the head movement I have to execute in order to look at him/her. At the same

Analyzing Concepts

time, it is very plausible that I am able to represent the location of a discussion partner in a more general format that comprises not only head movements but also arm movements (how to reach him/her). Even more abstract are representations in terms of allocentric coordinates that occur both later in the ontogenesis of humans and later in the evolutionary development of species (Vosgerau 2007).

In this way, frame analysis provides a powerful tool to detect abstraction mechanisms that lead from very basic representations that only presuppose sensorimotor abilities to more abstract concepts that get more independent of sensorimotor grounding. Thus, both phylogenetic and ontogenetic development of conceptual abilities is analyzable within frames in terms of different abstraction mechanisms. Of course, it remains an open question how many different abstraction mechanisms there are at work and how far up such mechanisms can get us in terms of abstractness.

7 Conclusion

To sum up, we have laid out the foundations of our frame-theory and argued for its advantages over other formats of representing concepts. The frames specified here are capable of representing concepts and information of any desired grade of detail. The frames are not restricted to sortal concepts but can easily represent relational concepts as well. Although it is in principle possible to express the content of the frames in logical formulas, the representation in frames has clear advantages over e. g. predicates of first order logics: no fixed arities have to be stipulated for the predicates, as well as no order of the arguments have to be stipulated, due to the non-linear structure of frames. These advantages concern the formal aspects of frame-representation, so it is worth pointing to one of the psychological incitements for adopting the frame theory: There clearly is evidence that cognitive processes can be understood in terms of attribute-value sets and relations, so the explanatory role of frames within cognitive science is quite clear.

With the frame-theory as a foundation of cognitive representation and processing of concepts, the idea of grounding concepts in action can thus be formulated in a cognitively adequate way and be embedded in a formalizable model of concept-representation. We have shown what it can mean for a concept to be grounded in sensorimotor processes, i. e. to rely on sensorimotor values in frames at a very basal level. This notion of groundedness suits well the idea of high-level and low-level processing, where sensorimotor processes are thought to be low-level processes which are at play at a very early stage in concept development but do not cease to be a part of higher-level concept processing. Frames reflect this hierarchical understanding of concept development in an appropriate way, as higher-level concepts come along with higher degrees of abstraction within concepts. These degrees and the responsible mechanisms of abstraction can be made visible via frame analysis. The capability of frames to highlight abstraction combined with the possibility to implement modality within representations of motor-based concepts marks frames as a perfect tool for analyzing action-related concepts.

Some further questions remain: As already mentioned above, it is far from clear how concepts exhibiting a very high degree of abstractness could be sensibly understood as grounded on sensorimotor processes. If one adopts our account of analyzing concepts via frames, at least a promising strategy for detecting mechanisms of abstraction is at hand, worth to be persecuted. Another question concerns the scope of the idea of grounded concepts: do literally all concepts have to be grounded in the above sense, or would it already be sufficient for the thesis of grounded cognition that some concepts are straightforwardly grounded, allowing for the possibility of non-grounded concepts? To answer these questions, a lot more empirical and conceptual research on abstract concept grounding has to be done. Our method of analyzing can thus be understood as just a starting point, but a very promising one.

References

Barsalou, L. W. 1992. Frames, Concepts and Conceptual Fields. In A. Lehrer & E. F. Kittay (eds.), *Frames, Fields and Contrasts*, chap. 1, 21–74. Hillsdale, Hove and London: Erlbaum.

Barsalou, L. W. 1999. Perceptual symbol systems. *Behavioral and Brain Sciences* 22. 577–609. http://journals.cambridge.org/action/displayIssue?jid=BBS&volumeId=22&issueId=04#.

Barsalou, L. W. 2008. Grounded Cognition. *Annual Review of Psychology* 59. 617–645.

Fillmore, C. J. 1970. The Case for Case. In E. Bach & R. T. Harms (eds.), *Universals in Linguistic Theory*, 1–88. London, New York, Sydney, Toronto: Holt, Rinehart

References

and Winston, Inc.

Franks, N. R., A. Dornhaus, B. G. Metherell, T. R. Nelson, S. A. J. Lanfear & W. S. Symes. 2006. Not everything that counts can be counted: ants use multiple metrics for a single nest trait. In *Proceedings of The Royal Society B*, vol. 273, 165–169.

Gallistel, C. 1993. *The Organization of Learning*. Cambridge MA: The MIT Press.

Glenberg, A. M. & M. P. Kaschak. 2002. Grounding language in action. *Psychonomic Bulletin & Review* 9. 558–565.

Minsky, M. 1974. A framework for representing knowledge. *MIT-AI Laboratory Memo 306*.

Naumann, R. 2012. Relating ERP-effects to theories of belief update and combining systems. In M. Aloni, V. Kimmelman, F. Roelofsen, G. Sassoon, K. Schulz & M. Westera (eds.), *Logic, Language and Meaning*, vol. 7218 Lecture Notes in Computer Science, 160–169. Berlin, Heidelberg: Springer. 10.1007/978-3-642-31482-7_17. http://dx.doi.org/10.1007/978-3-642-31482-7_17.

Newen, A. & A. Bartels. 2007. Animal Minds and the Possession of Concepts. *Philosophical Psychology* 20. 283–308.

Petersen, W. & M. Werning. 2007. Conceptual Fingerprints: Lexical Decomposition by Means of Frames. In U. Priss, S. Polovina & R. Hill (eds.), *Proceedings of the ICCS 2007, LNAI 4604*, 415–428. Berlin: Springer.

Petersen, W. & T. Osswald. 2014. Concept Composition in Frames: Focusing on Genitive Constructions. In T. Gamerschlag, D. Gerland, R. Osswald & W. Petersen (eds.), *Frames and Concept Types. Applications in Language, Cognition, and Philosophy*, vol. 94 Studies in Linguistics and Philosophy, 243–266. Heidelberg, New York, Dordrecht, London: Springer.

Petersen, W. 2015. Representation of Concepts as Frames. In Gamerschlag T., D. Gerland, R. Osswald & W. Petersen (eds.) *Meaning, Frames, and Conceptual Representation*, 39-63. Studies in Language and Cognition 2. Düsseldorf: Düsseldorf University Press. (Reprinted from J. Skilters; Toccafondi, F. & Stemberger, G. (eds.): Complex Cognition and Qualitative Science. Volume 2 of *The Baltic International Yearbook of Cognition, Logic and Communication*, 151–170, University of Latvia, Riga, 2007.)

Pulvermüller, F. 2005. Brain mechanisms linking language and action. *Nature Reviews Neuroscience* 6. 576–582.

Synofzik, M., G. Vosgerau & A. Newen. 2008. Beyond the comparator model: A multifactorial two-step account of agency. *Consciousness and Cognition* 17. 219–239.

Synofzik, M., G. Vosgerau & A. Newen. 2008. I move, therefore I am: A new theoretical framework to investigate agency and ownership. *Consciousness and Cognition* 17. 411–424.

Vosgerau, G. & A. Newen. 2007. Thoughts, Motor Actions, and the Self. *Mind & Language* 22 (1). 22–43.

Vosgerau, G. 2007. Conceptuality in Spatial Representation. *Philosophical Psychology* 20. 349–365.

Vosgerau, G. 2008. Adäquatheit und Arten mentaler Repräsentationen. *Facta Philosophica* 10. 67–82.

Vosgerau, G. 2009. *Mental Representation and Self-Consciousness. From Basic Self-Representation to Self-Related Cognition.* Paderborn: mentis.

Vosgerau, G. & M. Synofzik. 2010. A Cognitive Theory of Thoughts. *American Philosophical Quarterly* 47. 205–222.

Weber, A. & G. Vosgerau. 2012. Grounding Action Representations. *Review of Philosophy and Psychology* 3. 53–69.

Wittlinger, M., R. Wehner & H. Wolf. 2006. The ant Odometer: Stepping on Stilts and Stumps. *Science* 312. 1965–1967.

Authors

Gottfried Vosgerau, Tim Seuchter
Department of Philosophy
Heinrich-Heine-University Düsseldorf
Düsseldorf, Germany
{seuchter,vosgerau}@phil.hhu.de

Wiebke Petersen
Departement of Linguistics and Information Science
Heinrich-Heine-University Düsseldorf
Düsseldorf, Germany
petersew@phil.hhu.de

Applying Frame Theory to Psychiatric Classification

Jürgen Zielasek, Gottfried Vosgerau, Wolfgang Gaebel, Karin Fauerbach, Irem Girgin, Sarah Jungbluth, Julia Weiland & Sebastian Löbner

Abstract
We applied Barsalou's Frame Theory to analyze the structure of operationalized classificatory texts used in psychiatry, such as the International Classification of Disorders, Chapter V (ICD-10), and the Diagnostic and Statistical Manual (DSM-IV), which provide the basic terminology for today's psychiatric classification system. We studied the classificatory principles of "schizophrenia" and "specific phobias" as examples of mental disorders. In addition, we studied Parkinson's disease as an example of a disorder on the border between neurology and psychiatry. Initial results suggest that although the texts of modern classification systems are highly operationalized and appear straightforward and simple, their internal structure is highly complex with subframe structures of divergent types emerging. Also, the comparison of both modern systems of classification shows that the differences are greater than just time-course differences or terminological differences. We show that by applying Barsalou's frame theory, internal structures of standard classificatory texts in psychiatry may become discernible, and that focusing on well-defined concepts of brain functions like the sense of agency promises to yield useful insights into the pathophysiology, symptomatology and classifications of major mental disorders.

1 Introduction

Barsalou developed a theory of frames as the general format of the representation of concepts in human cognition (Barsalou 1992a, 1992b). The theory was further developed, and integrated into Barsalou's theory of conceptual symbol systems (Barsalou 1999). Barsalou frames represent their referents by means of a recursive structure in terms of attributes and the values they take. Following the conventions developed in Petersen (2007/2015), Barsalou frames can be represented by directed graphs.[1] In a frame for an arbitrary category of objects, a central node represents the object itself; it is marked with a double line. The node is "central" in that all arrows originate directly from it or from nodes connected to it. Labeled arrows connect a node to other nodes. The arrows represent attributes, the labels name them. The nodes to which the arrows lead represent the values that the attributes take. The number of attributes is not limited, nor is the depth of embedding.

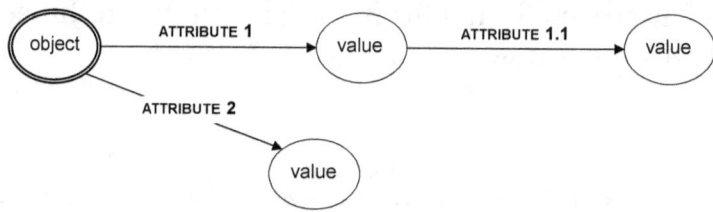

Figure 1: General structure of a Barsalou frame

Crucially, the attributes are functional relations: for any object they assign exactly one value and for any object the same attribute can only be applied once. In frame graphs it is not permissible to have more than one arrow with the same label originate from one and the same node. Different nodes may, however, have the same attribute. Think, for example, of a frame-format physical description of a person. Possible attributes can include HEIGHT, WEIGHT, and AGE.[2] Any person, at a given time, has the descriptive dimensions of height, weight or age only once and each of these take just one value. For a simple notation for the fact that for an object x the attribute a takes the value y, one can use the usual mathematical notation for a function taking a value for a given argument: "a(x)=y". One can write "HEIGHT(Jones) = 1.76 m" for the fact that the attribute HEIGHT for the person Jones takes the value 1.76 m. A nonfunctional attribute would be a characteristic such as a 'disease': namely, a person can have several, just one or no

---

[1] Barsalou (1992a, 1992b) uses directed labeled graphs, too. However, his representations have a more complex, although essentially equivalent, structure. See Petersen (2007/2015) for a discussion of the alternative graph representations of frames.

[2] We use small capitals for attribute terms.

diseases at all. Consequently, the attribute "disease" would not necessarily take a unique value. It would be inappropriate to notate the fact that Jones suffers from diabetes as "DISEASE(Jones) = diabetes"; if Jones suffered from a bronchitis at the same time, one would have to put this as "DISEASE(Jones) = bronchitis". However, if DISEASE really were to be a function(al attribute), its value for a given person at a given time cannot be both diabetes and bronchitis because these are different diseases. In constructing frames for the representation of concepts, attributes have therefore to be chosen very carefully to use only attributes that are really functions. Representing the fact that a person suffers from diabetes would require a frame with attributes such as INSULIN PRODUCTION or INSULIN RESISTANCE.

Frame-format descriptions are thus descriptions in terms of functional attributes and the values they take. Such descriptions are very frequently used in practice in one form or the other. For example, a lab report with values for various substances in the blood such as Fe, Mg, or cholesterol, represents a frame in terms of concentrations of these substances in the blood sample analyzed. A reference to a publication represents a frame-format description in terms of author(s), year of publication, title, publisher, etc. Another instance of frame-format description is passports; they contain a frame description of the bearer.

Barsalou frames may also contain various types of constraints that relate to the values of attributes. For example, a constraint might delimit the range of possible values for an attribute, or it might correlate the values of two attributes.

Frames for diseases or disorders would start from a frame for the person with attributes added for those parts or functions of the organism which are affected. A disease can be described at different levels. A description of diabetes at the level of diagnostics would refer to attributes such as blood sugar level, while a description at the organic level might relate to the function of the pancreas. Capturing the causes of the disease would require attributes relating to lifestyle or to the genetics of the person. The description of a disease would then essentially involve the choice of relevant attributes and the values they take. Such a frame may be restricted to a certain level of description or it may combine more than one level. Including both the organic and the symptomatic level would enable one to represent causal relations between elements of the frames, for example between insulin production and blood sugar.

Using frames for the analysis of mental disorders is demanding, but offers the opportunity for a more precise and explicit conceptual analysis. The available descriptions of disorders do not come in terms of functional attributes (see Tables 1 and 2 below). To begin with, in most cases of particular mental disorders it is not made explicit what the respective disorder is a disorder of. What exactly is disturbed in schizophrenia? Is there a uniform disorder underlying all those cases currently classified as a particular disorder? The usual descriptions of mental disorders describe symptoms and diagnostics, such has "hearing voices" in the case of schizophrenia. The description of a disorder may refer to behavioral characteristics or to other levels such as bodily symptoms or genetics. It may be in terms of phenomena or in terms of malfunctioning. It will include temporal characteristics such as the frequency and duration of symptoms, the age of the patient, the chronological progression of the disorder. It may also include causal components such as lifestyle, social environment, infections, intoxication, etc. It must provide for a weighting of symptoms, for exclusion criteria, and for provisions such that a certain number out of all possible symptoms must be present. A frame approach should first make a decision about the level(s) of description which it aims at and will then have to try to determine the appropriate set of attributes for capturing the characteristics of the disorder. In this article, we will represent initial exploratory heuristic frame descriptions of three disorders: schizophrenia, specific phobias, and Parkinson's disease. The last section represents considerations towards a more principled approach to the frame analysis of mental disorders in terms of faculties of the mind.

2 Classification of mental disorders

Two major classification systems for mental disorders have been developed and are in use globally: the World Health Organization (WHO) publishes the "International Classification of Disorders," which is currently in its 10th revision (hence "ICD-10") (World Health Organization, 1990) and the American Psychiatric Association (APA) publishes the "Diagnostic and Statistical Manual," which is currently available in its fourth edition (hence "DSM-IV") (American Psychiatric Association, 2000). Both systems are currently being revised by international working groups with a view to publish the newly revised versions ICD-11 and DSM-V in 2013/2014. Both classification systems share a number of features:

- They are operationalized: they explicitly specify rules on how to arrive at a certain diagnosis

- They are anosological: they do not make assumptions about the nosological entities that may underlie a certain diagnosis. This implies that they do not make assumptions about the pathophysiology of any of the mental disorders classified in the respective diagnostic system.

Both systems have been tested for inter-rater reliability in the early 1990's, and one of their strengths and advantages is clearly that they have reduced the ambiguities previously associated with psychiatric diagnostics. After appropriate training, the inter-rater reliability is around 80 %. These systems have become widely accepted internationally. The majority of international psychiatric scientific literature uses either ICD-10 or DSM-IV. A survey of the use of ICD or DSM in psychiatric journals showed that some country-specific preferences are still observable between both systems, i. e., US-psychiatrists prefer DSM-IV, whereas German psychiatrists prefer ICD-10 (Lopez-Munoz et al., 2008).

As a rule, the constitutive features of mental disorder specified in these classifications include *i)* a syndrome of clinical symptoms, *ii)* some disease course characteristics and *iii)* the results of laboratory tests or neuroimaging methods. The latter, however, are mainly used for detecting brain tumors, inflammatory or metabolic disorders as causes of mental disorders.

In Germany, the use of the ICD-10 has been mandatory since 2000 for in- and out-patient services. For example, reimbursement by health insurance companies in the somatic disorders is based on diagnosis-related groups, which are founded in ICD-10 diagnoses. The official version is published by the German Institute of Medical Documentation and Statistics (DIMDI), with annual updates of the German modification (ICD-10-GM), so that the actual 2010 version of the ICD-10-GM features some minor differences compared to the original WHO ICD-10 version (www.dimdi.de). The German-language version issued by DIMDI is a trinational version which is also valid in Austria and Switzerland.

ICD-10 contains all somatic and all mental disorders, the latter are listed in Chapter F and contain the following major diagnostic groups (Table 1).

While the somatic disorders are only listed in ICD-10 and no specification for their diagnosis is given, the mental disorders are explicitly defined considering characteristic symptoms, time-course criteria, and exclusion criteria. In contrast to ICD-10, DSM-IV only deals with mental disorders, but also contains explicit rules for arriving at certain diagnoses similar to chapter F of ICD-10. A number of differences still exist between the diagnostic rules for some – but not all –

Table 1: Mental Disorders in ICD-10 (Chapter F) (WHO, 1992)

Chapter F class	Designation
F0	Organic, including symptomatic mental disorders
F1	Mental and behavioral disorders due to psychoactive substance use
F2	Schizophrenia, schizotypal and delusional disorders
F3	Mood [affective] disorders
F4	Neurotic, stress-related and somatoform disorders
F5	Behavioral syndromes associated with physiological disturbances and physical factors
F6	Disorders of adult personality and behavior
F7	Mental retardation
F8	Disorders of psychological development
F9	Behavioral and emotional disorders with onset usually in childhood and adolescence

mental disorders between both classification systems, and those pertaining to the mental disorders discussed in this chapter will be delineated in the ensuing text. It should be mentioned at this point that there are also a number of regional variations of classification systems still in use for mental disorders, e.g., in China or Latin America, but in international research and for the purposes of international scientific projects, such regional codes have not gained any importance.

Besides the advantages of providing highly reliable, standardized and internationally widely accepted rules for diagnosing mental disorders, these classification systems have also been criticized for the aforementioned differences in operational details, for not including pathophysiological processes, and for agglomerating a range of putatively different nosological entities into single disease groups. These issues are currently being debated intensively in the APA and WHO workgroups in charge of revising DSM-IV and ICD-10. However, even considering the tremendous progress in elucidating pathophysiological processes involved in a range of mental disorders, it currently appears rather unlikely that these advances have already been made far enough to warrant the inclusion of pathophysiology criteria in DSM-V or ICD-11.

3 Applying frame theory to texts of psychiatric classification

The main purpose of this initial stage of a joint research project between the Department of Psychiatry and Psychotherapy and the Department of Linguistics and Information Science of the Heinrich-Heine-University Düsseldorf was to demonstrate the feasibility of using Barsalou's Frame Theory to analyze texts of psychiatric classification with a view to systematically assessing the structure underlying the classification of mental disorders. The selection of mental disorders to be studied in the first phase of the research project was guided by the idea that one of the more frequent mental disorders was to be included. It should be diagnosed on the basis of clinical symptoms and it should provide some variations of time-course. We chose schizophrenia for this purpose, as it provides a large number of cases and fulfills these criteria. It has a range of time-course variants, and it is characterized by a set of hierarchical clinical diagnostic criteria. A second mental disorder was studied because in the course of analyzing schizophrenia, we realized that the analysis was hampered by a lack of information about the neurobiological foundations of schizophrenia, and the frame structure turned out to indicate a high degree of complexity. We therefore chose the group of specific phobias, since the neurobiology of fear disorders is comparatively better known, and the clinical courses and characteristics are not as complicated as in schizophrenia. We decided to round up this initial set of investigations with a neurological disorder featuring a clearly defined neurobiological foundation and associated symptoms of a mental disorder: Parkinson's disease is characterized by the degeneration of a set of neurons in the midbrain and ensuing degeneration of the fiber tracts that connect these specific areas of the midbrain with other brain areas. This results in the typical shaking palsy of patients with Parkinson's disease. In addition, approximately 30 % of all patients with Parkinson's disease also suffer from affective or cognitive symptoms, which may lead to mental disorders such as depression and dementia.

3.1 Frame analysis of schizophrenia

Both DSM-IV-TR (DSM-IV Text Revision) and ICD-10 feature a range of schizophrenia-like symptoms of importance for diagnosing schizophrenia and schizophrenia-related disorders like persistent delusional syndromes or schizoaffective disorder, which constitutes an overlap of both mood symptoms and schizophrenia-like symptoms. For the purpose of the initial analysis of these criteria, our project focused on the major groups of "schizophrenia" (F20 in ICD-10; 295.10-90 in DSM-IV). The diagnosis of schizophrenia according to DSM-IV or ICD-10 is a multi-step process. First, it is important for the clinician to ascertain that a number of symptoms are present for a sufficiently prolonged period of time. While the types of symptoms are compatible – but not identical – between both diagnostic systems, the time course criterion varies significantly (four weeks in ICD-10 and six months in DSM-IV). The symptoms comprise so-called "positive" symptoms like hallucinations and delusions and "negative" symptoms like loss of interest, lack of initiative and social withdrawal. Table 2 gives an overview of the diagnostic criteria comparing DSM-IV (text revision edition of 2000, hence "DSM-IV-TR") and ICD-10:

It is important to realize that two partly divergent sets of diagnostic categories exist. However, the principal components are comparable. We chose to use the ICD-10 criteria for a first analysis, since it is the type of criteria set relevant for Germany, and since it is widely used in Europe as compared to the DSM-IV criteria. Figure 2 shows some aspects that a frame for the ICD-10 definition of schizophrenia may contain.

This frame shows that one of the major challenges will be to determine which functions underlie the pathophysiology of the major symptoms like hallucinations and delusions. We have added place holders, because much more work is needed to demonstrate whether functional systems such as a "reality check" system exist in the human brain, and whether they become dysfunctional in schizophrenia. We are currently performing such investigations by deriving information from the scientific literature on the set of such systems as identified by neuroimaging or other assessment techniques. It is likely that such systems, or "modules" as they are called in systems analyses of the central nervous system, are at the root of the pathophysiology of the functional impairments observed in mental disorders (Zielasek & Gaebel, 2008; Seitz et al., 2011). Also, this initial analysis shows that the structure of the schizophrenia frame will be very complicated, probably leading to a substantial number of subframes. As there are associations between the positive symptoms as a group of symptoms, this may lead to a formal constraint (for example between the various types of delusions differentiated in the ICD-10 criteria). In the course of developing DSM-V, the

Table 2: Operationalized diagnostic criteria of schizophrenia compared between ICD-10 (WHO, 1992) and DSM-IV-TR (American Psychiatric Association, 2000).

ICD-10	DSM-IV-TR
Clinical criteria	Criterion A
A) Thought echo, thought insertion or withdrawal, and thought broadcasting	
B) Delusions of control, influence of passivity; delusional perception	1) Delusions
C) Hallucinatory voices giving running commentary on the patient's behavior, or discussing the patient among themselves, or other types of hallucinatory voices coming from some part of the body	2) Hallucinations
	3) Disorganized speech
D) Persistent delusions of other kinds that are culturally inappropriate and completely impossible	
E) Persistent hallucinations in any modality when accompanied either by fleeting of half-formed delusions without clear affective content, or by persistent over-valued ideas, or when occurring every day for weeks or months on end	
F) Breaks or interpolations in the trains of thought, resulting in incoherence or irrelevant speech, or neologisms	
G) Catatonic behavior	4) Grossly disorganized or catatonic behavior
H) Negative symptoms	5) Negative symptoms
A significant and consistent change in the overall quality of some aspects of personal behavior	
Evaluation criterion	**Evaluation criteria for criterion A:**
A minimum of one very clear symptom (and usually two or more if less clear-cut) belonging to any one of the symptoms in groups (A) to (D) above, or symptoms from at least two of the groups referred to as (E) to (H)	Two or more symptoms Only one Criterion A required if delusions are bizarre or hallucinations consist of a voice keeping up a running commentary on the person's behavior or thoughts, or two or more voices conversing with each other
	Criterion B
	Social/occupational dysfunction
Time criterion	**Time criterion**
	Criterion C
One month or more	Duration: continuous signs of the disturbance persist for at least 6 months. This 6 month period must include at least one month of symptoms that meet Criterion A
Exclusion criteria	**Exclusion criteria**
Extensive depressive or manic symptoms unless it is clear that schizophrenic symptoms antedated the affective disturbance	Criterion D
	Schizoaffective and mood disorder exclusion
	Criterion E
Presence of overt brain disease	Substance/general medical condition exclusion
States of drug intoxication or withdrawal	
	Criterion F
	Relationship to a pervasive developmental disorder

search for such "clusters" of symptoms became very important. Nevertheless, the associations are merely statistical, since every positive symptom may occur independently of others. The same holds for the association between symptoms and course characteristics. Even the association between certain symptoms and prognosis is not a strict association, but rather a statistical association. This leads to the question as to how the different course specifiers may be incorporated into a frame analysis. Schizophrenia has different course types which are specified in DSM-IV as shown in Table 3.

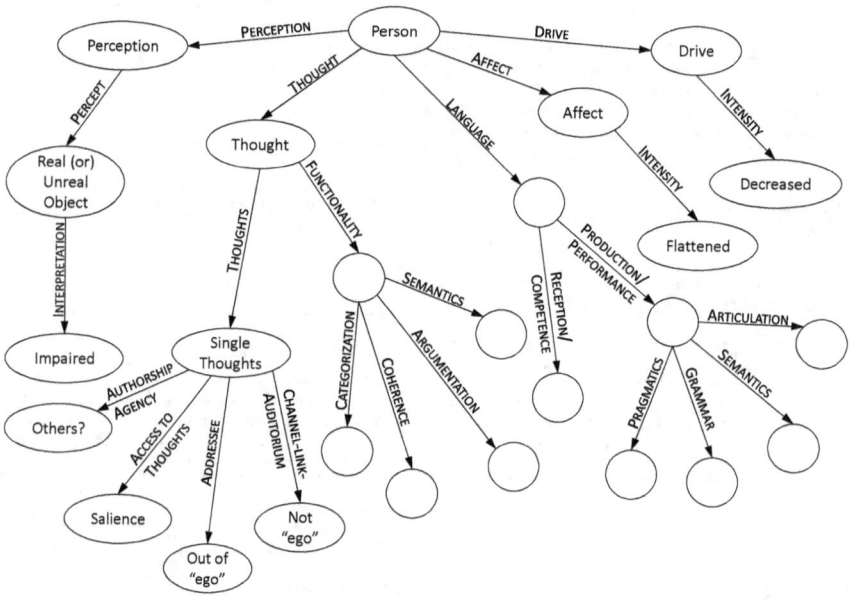

Figure 2: Some aspects of a schizophrenia frame analysis

It will be a major issue to devise methods of representing such temporal aspects of mental disorders in the usual notation of frames. This initial analysis is at best very preliminary and subject to change as research into the pathophysiology advances. However, schizophrenia does not lend itself easily to frame analysis, and may even indicate necessary extensions of frame theory once temporal and causal aspects come into play. Another challenge arises when sets of criteria with not yet clarified relations to functional systems of the brain are used. Although the latter is not necessary for establishing diagnostic categories with prognostic validity

Applying Frame Theory to Psychiatric Classification

Table 3: Course specifiers of schizophrenia in DSM-IV-TR (American Psychiatric Association, 2000)

	Description
1.	Episodic with inter-episode residual symptoms
2.	Episodic with no inter-episode residual symptoms
3.	Continuous
4.	Single episode in partial remission
5.	Single episode in full remission
6.	Other or unspecified pattern

and for indicating the necessity of therapy, it would become a necessity if functional subsystems and their relationship to symptoms needed to be defined for frame analysis. With the current knowledge, frame analysis could still be useful for analyzing historic shifts in the definition and understanding of "schizophrenia" as a diagnostic construct in psychiatry – not relying on the identification of the "true" modules disturbed in schizophrenia, but rather on terminological descriptions. This will be the focus of the ongoing analysis besides the definition of the dysfunctional modules. Central texts for such an analysis would be the conception of "dementia praecox" by Kraepelin (1899), the initial definition of the schizophrenias as a group of mental disorders by Bleuler (1911), and the introduction of a hierarchy of schizophrenia-defining symptoms by Schneider (1971).

3.2 Frame analysis of specific phobias

While fear is a normal and physiological element of human existence serving to protect an individual in dangerous situations, its diagnostic value relates to inappropriate fears occurring in harmless situations, or with negative consequences for the individual in excess of any useful warning function of fear. Both ICD-10 and DSM-IV define a variety of fear disorders ranging from stimulus-specific anxiety disorders like the so-called "specific phobias" (including fear of narrow rooms, fear of spiders etc.) to generalized anxiety disorders. ICD-10 (http://www.who.int) defines specific phobias as "phobias restricted to highly specific situations such as proximity to particular animals, heights, thunder, darkness, flying, closed spaces, urinating or defecating in public toilets, eating certain foods, dentistry, or the sight of blood or injury." For the purpose of frame analysis, we chose specific phobias because in contrast to schizophrenia they are characterized by a rather narrow spectrum of symptoms, clearly defined fear-inducing stimuli, and a rather well-known neurocircuitry. Thus, it could be hoped that frame analysis would lead to rather simple frame structures. However, neuroimaging frequently shows that phobic stimuli activate a range of neurocircuits (Pull, 2008; Damsa et al., 2008) including the amygdala and other structures of the brain like the anterior cingulate cortex and the insular cortex. Such "fear circuitries" are necessary conditions for bringing about fear, but it is still not completely known what exactly goes wrong with this circuitry in phobias. An intriguing question also arises as to the role of variations in genes involved in the metabolism of the neurotransmitter serotonin (Munafo et al., 2008), as these seem to increase the likelihood of the development of fear disorders. Also, learning experiences seem to play an important role. Thus, while it is quite well known which brain regions are involved and which normal functions are usually served by such regions, it is still a considerable step to fully explain the psychopathology, i.e., the set of signs and symptoms so characteristic of specific phobias. There are still missing links in the chain of events from genetic predisposition via learning experiences and initial fear reactions to the full clinical picture of a specific phobia. All of these steps would ideally be modeled in frame analyses of the future. A peculiar challenge lies in the delineation from "healthy" fear reactions. Similar to the dimensional assessment of hallucinations and delusions in schizophrenia, there appears to be a substantial overlap between fear reactions in the healthy control population and in those individuals who develop anxiety disorders. In addition, there is not only an emotional reaction to fear stimuli, but also a vegetative reaction with a diverse range of somatic signs like sweating and increased heart rates. Thus, a frame for specific phobias will need to include a range of functional circuits. An initial proposal is made in Figure 3.

3.3 Frame analysis of Parkinson's disease

Parkinson's disease used to be characterized as a neurodegenerative disorder with relatively specific degeneration of a set of neurons in the substantia nigra of the midbrain. The neurotransmitter produced by these neurons is dopamine, and consequently there is a loss of dopaminergic neurotransmission in the target projection area of these neurons in the striate corpus of the basal ganglia. This leads to the main symptoms of Parkinson's disease, i.e., resting tremor, akinesia,

Applying Frame Theory to Psychiatric Classification

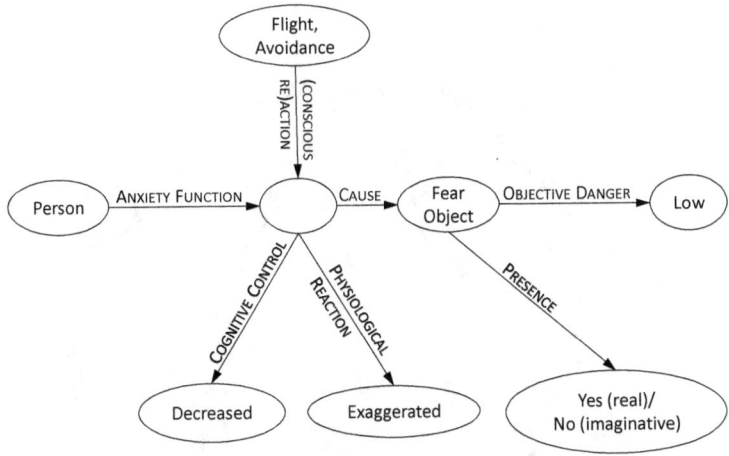

Figure 3: Aspects of a frame analysis of specific phobias

and rigor (Lees et al., 2009). However, other neurotransmitter systems are also involved in the neurodegenerative process. An intricate neurocircuitry of motor control underlies these pathophysiological processes.

A simple first approach towards a frame analysis of the impairment of the motor system in Parkinson's disease would result in a frame as depicted in Figure 4. This frame does not yet take into account the fact that a significant proportion of patients with Parkinson's disease not only suffer from motor symptoms, but also from affective and cognitive impairments. It is not completely understood how these are related to the primary nigrostriatal degenerative process, but may involve a spread of the initially locally confined neurodegenerative process to serotonergic and noradrenergic brain systems in depressive symptoms (Storch et al., 2008) and a more widespread involvement of cholinergic neurotransmission and frontostriatal circuits in patients with cognitive symptoms (Zgaljardic et al., 2004). A unifying hypothesis for the relationship between the loss of dopaminergic neurons and the ensuing neurocircuitry alterations leading to affective and cognitive symptoms has been proposed by Calabresi and colleagues (2006). Thus, similar to schizophrenia and specific phobias, the pathophysiology of mental disorders even in the framework of well-defined neurodegenerative processes involves a large number of brain areas and neurocircuits, making frame analysis

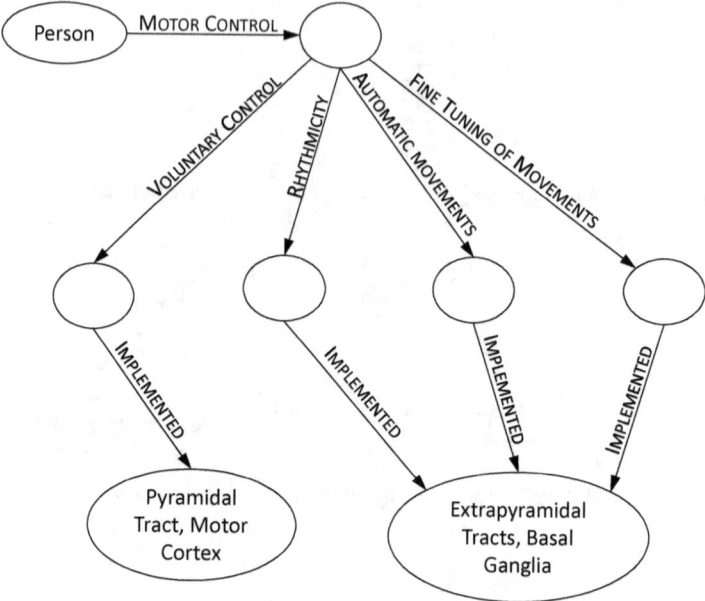

Figure 4: Frame of neuronal elements involved in motor symptoms in Parkinson's disease

difficult especially when higher brain functions involved in mood and cognition are affected.

4 Frame analysis of the pathophysiology of mental disorders

In order to gain a foothold in this complex area, we began an analysis of the concept of "agency," which is central to understanding many core features of mental disorders. We assume that the sense of agency is based on an integration process (weighting) of different agency cues which are provided by different processes (or "modules"), including motor control, perception, proprioception, thinking (background beliefs). Therefore, delusions of control cannot be explained by a breakdown in motor processes only – in contrast, we need a multifactorial account of agency that integrates the different agency cues mentioned above (Synofzik, Vosgerau & Newen 2008). This account can thus serve as an example of the analysis of symptoms in terms of faculties of the mind.

Applying Frame Theory to Psychiatric Classification

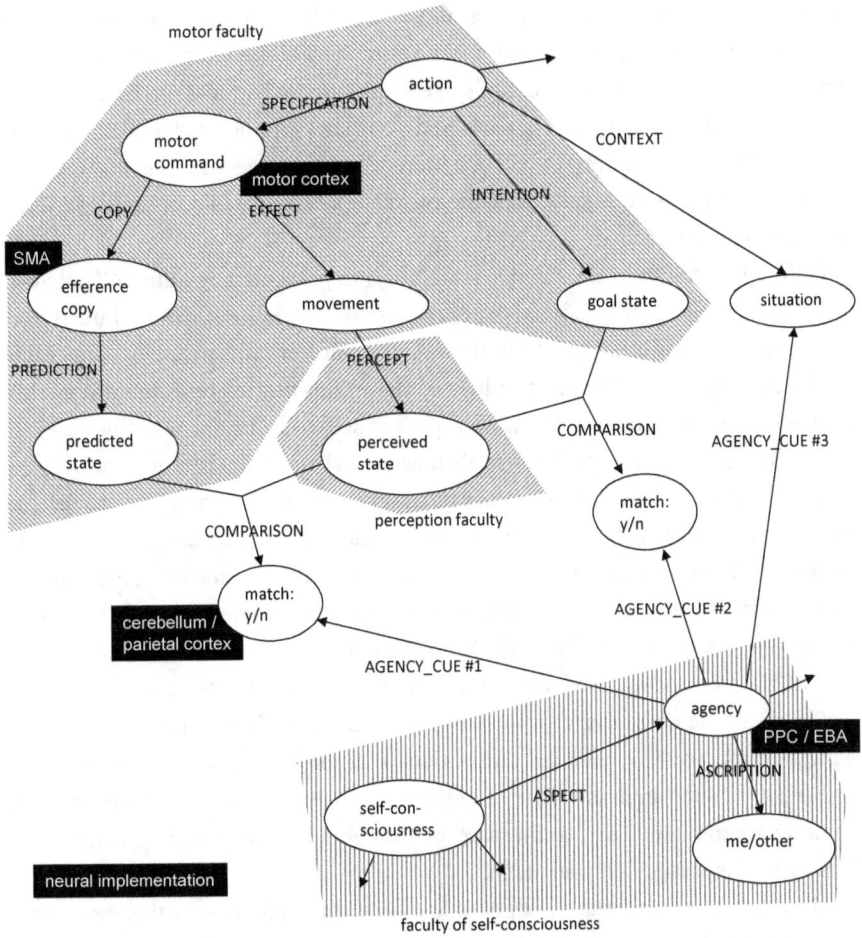

Figure 5: A multifactorial account of agency in frames. Different faculties of the mind are presented by shaded areas. Possible neural implementations are attached to the according nodes as black rectangulars (SMA: supplementary motor area, PPC: posterior parietal cortex, EBA: extrastriate body area).

In Figure 5, a frame is shown that (partly and exemplarily) describes the multifactorial account of agency. For example, a mismatch at the comparator comparing perceived state and goal state serves as one agency cue indicating that I am not the agent of the action (this is the case, for instance, when someone nudges your arm during an arm movement such that you do not reach your goal).

However, in other situations such a mismatch might not lead you to think that you are not the agent of the action: e.g., perceived state and goal state will not match when you fail to hit the bull's eye as planned when playing darts. Nevertheless, the situation of playing darts and your background knowledge that your skills in darts are not perfect will function as another cue which is, in this situation, weighted more highly than the mismatch. This results in your ascribing the agency to yourself.

Different faculties of the mind (exemplarily) re presented by differently shaded areas since the two-dimensional paper makes an adequate depiction of the different faculties as attributes of a central "person" node very inconvenient. The frame analysis shows how different faculties of the mind interrelate in the production of specific phenomena (agency as an aspect of self-consciousness in this case).

Delusions of control can be described as disturbances in specific values in the frame, for example by unusual values of the comparison outcomes due to deficits in the comparison process or by unusual values of agency ascriptions due to deficits in the weighting process of different cues. At the same time, the frame is able to display the complex effects that disturbances in single nodes can have; e.g., a disturbed value of a COMPARISON node might lead to disturbed values in the ASCRIPTION node in cases where it is not outweighed by other agency-nodes.

This example of analyzing specific phenomena and their pathological disturbances is, moreover, embedded into a general theory of self-consciousness (Vosgerau 2009), such that the general pattern of analysis can be fruitfully applied to other phenomena (e.g., authorship of thoughts or ownership of body parts; Synofzik, Vosgerau & Newen 2008).

Moreover, the frame makes it possible to integrate data concerning neural circuits. Just to give a few examples: some brain areas are attached to some nodes in the frame; there is some evidence that renders these brain areas plausible candidates for being the neural correlate of the according values in the frame. The motor cortex is likely to be involved in forming and issuing the motor command (Beurze et al. 2010); there is considerable evidence that the supplementary motor area (SMA) plays a crucial role in the generation of a copy of the motor command ("efference copy") that is further used in prediction (Haggard & Whitford 2004). It has been suggested that the comparison process between predicted state and perceived state may involve the cerebellum and the parietal cortex (Blakemore, Wolpert & Frith 1999); in addition, it has also been suggested that the posterior parietal cortex (PPC) and the extrastriate body area (EBA) may participate in the network of areas correlating with the sense of agency (Yomogida et al. 2010). These examples show how experimental data on the neural correlates of the different faculties of the mind can be straightforwardly integrated into the frame analysis, such that a comprehensive picture of the complex interrelations between different faculties of the mind, different disruptions of specific processes, and different brain regions involved in these processes emerges.

5 Discussion

Frame theory can be applied to modern operationalized diagnostic criteria of mental disorders, but its use is limited in two ways: *i)* the mental processes underlying the pathophysiology of mental disorders are not yet sufficiently clarified and *ii)* frame theory cannot yet render temporal and causal dimensions of mental disorders. Also, the diagnostic structure of some mental disorders is complicated, since such disorders involve a number of functional brain modules, leading to intricate frame structures. During our initial analyses, frequently the question arose as to which functions of the human brain are impaired and how this results in a clinical symptom. As exemplified even by the relatively simple case of phobias, there is an intricate network of interacting brain modules and the pathophysiology of the psychopathologic phenomena proves to be of a very intricate nature. Identifying constraints between attributes in frames for mental disorders will prove to be difficult because in clinical reality there is hardly ever a strict correlation, but rather a certain predisposition or statistical association. Another aspect which needs to be addressed is the question of a continuum between symptoms of mental disorders and "diluted" or less intense similar symptoms in healthy people. This has been analyzed for some major symptoms of mental disorders like delusions and hallucinations, and could indicate that there may be no absolute boundaries between "health" and "disease." This issue is referred to as the "dimensional" nature of mental disorders and one of the central topics of the current revision process of DSM-IV (Brown & Barlow, 2005). It will be necessary to include such aspects in the Frame Analysis of mental disorders.

With such limitations and challenges at hand, it seems attractive to postpone any further frame analysis of mental disorders until the pathophysiology of the mental disorders to be analyzed is known. However, as the example of Parkinson's disease shows, it seems unlikely that "simple" pathophysiologies will be discovered. Thus, we decided to focus on core features of the pathophysiology and symptomatology of psychotic disorders, in this case the disturbance of the concept of self-agency, to limit the scope of phenomena to be explained by more detailed frame analyses of mental disorders. Two features speak in favor of using frame theory: *i)* it provides a systematic and well-defined approach which provides general rules usable for all mental disorders as regards their pathophysiology, symptomatology and classification, and *ii)* it may also be useful for analyzing the historic changes of diagnostic conceptions of mental disorders. Thus, the approach to progress in this area – as exemplified by schizophrenia – needs to be twofold: firstly, it is well worth the effort to analyze historic texts of the early times of the conceptualization of schizophrenia as an example, because these definitions were made without any knowledge about the pathophysiology of the disorder and have developed over time. Secondly, it is necessary to analyze the neurobiological underpinnings of core concepts of mental disorders using frame analyses including time-variability and individual precipitating factors for their disturbances in mental disorders.

Acknowledgement

This project was supported by a grant from the "Human Sciences Research Center" (Humanwissenschaftlich-Medizinisches Forschungszentrum) of the Heinrich-Heine-University Düsseldorf.

References

American Psychiatric Association. 2000. *Diagnostic and Statistical Manual of Mental Disorders*, Fourth Edition, Text Revision. Washington: American Psychiatric Association.

Barsalou, L. W. 1992a. *Cognitive Psychology*. Hillsdale, NJ: Lawrence Erlbaum Associates.

Barsalou, L. W. 1992b. Frames, Concepts, and Conceptual Fields. In A. Lehrer & E. F. Kittay (eds.), *Frames, fields, and contrasts*, 21–74. Hillsdale, NJ: Lawrence Erlbaum Associates.

Barsalou, L. W. 1999. Perceptual Symbol Systems. *Behavioral and Brain Sciences* 22. 577–660.

References

Beurze, S. M., I. Toni, L. Pisella & W. P. Medendorp 2010. Reference Frames for Reach Planning in Human Parietofrontal Cortex. *Journal of Neurophysiology* 104. 1736–1745. 10.1152/jn.01044.2009.

Blakemore, S.-J., D. M. Wolpert & C. D. Frith 1999. The Cerebellum Contributes to Somatosensory Cortical Activity during Self-Produced Tactile Stimulation. *NeuroImage* 10. 448–459.

Bleuler, E. 1911. *Dementia praecox oder die Gruppe der Schizophrenien.* Leipzig und Berlin: Verlag Franz Deuticke.

Brown, T. A., & D. H. Barlow 2005. Dimensional versus categorical classification of mental disorders in the fifth edition of the Diagnostic and Statistical Manual of Mental Disorders and beyond: comment on the special section. *Journal of Abnormal Psychology* 114. 551–556.

Calabresi, P., B. Picconi, L. Parnetti & M. Di Filippo 2006. A convergent model for cognitive dysfunctions in Parkinson's disease: the critical dopamine-acetylcholine synaptic balance. *Lancet Neurology* 5. 974–983.

Damsa, C., M. Kosel & J. Moussally 2008. Current status of brain imaging in anxiety disorders. *Current Opinion in Psychiatry* 22. 96–110.

Haggard, P., Whitford, B. 2004. Supplementary motor area provides an efferent signal for sensory suppression. *Cognitive Brain Research* 19. 52–58.

Kraepelin, E. 1899. *Psychiatrie. Ein Lehrbuch für Studierende und Ärzte.* 5th Edition. Leipzig: Barth.

Lees, A. J., J. Hardy & T. Revesz 2009. Parkinson´s disease. *Lancet*, 373. 2055–2066.

López-Muñoz, F., P. García-García, J. Sáiz-Ruiz, J. E. Mezzich, G. Rubio, E. Vieta & C. Alamo 2008. A bibliometric study of the use of the classification and diagnostic systems in psychiatry over the last 25 years. *Psychopathology* 41. 214–225.

Munafo, M. R., S. M. Brown & A. R. Hariri 2008. Serotonin transporter (5-HTTLPR) genotype and amygdala activation: a meta-analysis. *Biological Psychiatry* 63. 852–857.

Petersen, W. 2015. Representation of Concepts as Frames. In Gamerschlag T., D. Gerland, R. Osswald & W. Petersen (eds.) *Meaning, Frames, and Conceptual Representation*, 39-63. Studies in Language and Cognition 2. Düsseldorf: Düsseldorf University Press. (Reprinted from J.; Toccafondi, F. & Stemberger, G. (eds.): Complex Cognition and Qualitative Science. Volume 2 of *The Baltic International Yearbook of Cognition, Logic and Communication*, 151–170, University of Latvia, Riga, 2007.)

Pull, C. B. 2008. Recent trends in the study of specific phobias. *Current Opinion in Psychiatry* 21. 43–50.

Schneider, K. 1971. *Klinische Psychopathologie*. 9th Edition. Stuttgart: Thieme Verlag.

Seitz, R. J., Gaebel W., Zielasek J. 2011. Modular networks involving the medial frontal cortex: towards the development of neuropsychiatry. *World Journal of Biological Psychiatry*. 12 (4). 249–59.

Storch, A., G. Ebersbach, G. Fuchs, W. H. Jost, P. Odin, G. Reifschneider & M. Bauer 2008. Depression beim idiopathischen Parkinson-Syndrom. Teil 1: Epidemiologie, Pathophysiologie, Klinik und Diagnostik. *Fortschritte der Neurologie und Psychiatrie* 76. 715–724.

Synofzik, M., G. Vosgerau & A. Newen 2008. 'I move, therefore I am: A new theoretical framework to investigate agency and ownership'. *Consciousness and Cognition* 17: 411–424.

Vosgerau, G. 2009. 'Die Stufentheorie des Selbstbewusstseins und ihre Implikationen für das Verständnis psychiatrischer Störungen'. *Journal für Philosophie und Psychiatrie* 2, 16 pages, http://www.jfpp.org/jfpp-2-2009-02.html.

World Health Organization 1992. *The ICD-10 classification of mental and behavioural disorders*. Geneva: World Health Organization.

Yomogida, Y., M. Sugiura, Y. Sassa, K. Wakusawa, A. Sekiguchi, A. Fukushima, H. Takeuchi, K. Horie, S. Sato & R. Kawashima 2010. The neural basis of agency: An fMRI study. *NeuroImage* 50. 198–207.

Zgaljardic, D. J., N. S. Foldi & J. C. Borod 2004. Cognitive and behavioral dysfunction in Parkinson's disease: neurochemical and clinicopathological considerations. *Journal of Neural Transmission* 111. 1287–1301.

Authors

Jürgen Zielasek
Heinrich-Heine-University Düsseldorf
Dept. of Psychiatry and Psychotherapy
juergen.zielasek@lvr.de

Gottfried Vosgerau
Heinrich-Heine-University Düsseldorf

References

Dept. of Philosophy
vosgerau@phil.hhu.de

Wolfgang Gaebel
Heinrich-Heine-University Düsseldorf
Dept. of Psychiatry and Psychotherapy
wolfgang.gaebel@hhu.de

Karin Fauerbach
Heinrich-Heine-University Düsseldorf
Dept. of Psychiatry and Psychotherapy
karin.fauerbach@lvr.de

Irem Girgin
Heinrich-Heine-University Düsseldorf
Dept. of Psychiatry and Psychotherapy
irem.girgin@lvr.de

Sarah Jungbluth
Heinrich-Heine-University Düsseldorf
Dept. of Psychiatry and Psychotherapy
sarah.jungbluth@lvr.de

Julia Weiland
Heinrich-Heine-University Düsseldorf
Dept. of Psychiatry and Psychotherapy
julia.weiland@lvr.de

Sebastian Löbner
Heinrich-Heine-University Düsseldorf
Departement of Linguistics and Information Science
loebner@phil.hhu.de

www.ingramcontent.com/pod-product-compliance
Lightning Source LLC
Chambersburg PA
CBHW071154300426
44113CB00009B/1204